Cisco Storage Networking Cookbook

For NX-OS release 5.2

MDS and Nexus Families

Seth Mason and Venkat Kirishnamurthyi

Comments: mds-cookbook@cisco.com

5 Logical Interfaces

6 VSANs

■

9   Fibre Channel Over Ethernet (FCoE)

10   Top of Rack (ToR) Switches

11   FCIP

Dedication

As the Grateful Dead once said, "What a long strange trip its been…" Well here we are as "The Cookbook" enters it's third major revision since 2005 coming from humble beginnings covering SAN-OS 1.x aimed at engineers building their very first MDS based fabrics and exploring new concepts such VSANs and Port Channels, to SAN-OS 2.x with IVR and SAN Extension, to the architects leveraging the 3.x version in building multi-site, multi-protocol fabrics. Now with this version we increase the coverage even further into areas such as FICON and FCoE. It's not just about SAN = Fibre Channel = MDS, but covering any platform that moves storage packets from one place to another.

So why do we, who are not professional authors, hunch over our keyboards, wear out our mice and toil away for this book?

For those that carry a pager.

For those that get up at 2am to answer it.

For those that drive into the datacenter or log on to the SAN without waking their family.

For those that have made more zones than a city planner.

For those that know that Fibre Channel has nothing to do with whole wheat products.

For those that Storage isn't related to closet space.

For those that once migrated a roomful of disks to a single array.

For those that realize that storage is the end of the line for any operation.

For those that know the difference between VSANs, VLANs, pecans and toucans.

For those that keep the disks spinning, the tape running, the data intact and there when we need it again.

And last but certainly not least, for our families, wives, and children for whom without their support and patience, none of this would be possible. We couldn't have done it without you.

Seth and Venkat

Preface

This document addresses the configuration and implementation of fabrics using the Cisco MDS 9000 and Nexus Family of Switch and Director Class products. The configuration procedures and components provided have been tested and validated by Cisco's Solution-Interoperability Engineering department.

This cookbook provides simplified, concise recipes (procedures) for tasks that might be required to configure either a Cisco MDS 9000 Family switch or a Nexus switch for use in Storage Area Networks. This guide does not replace the MDS 9000 or Nexus Configuration Guides, but complements them with concise procedures for specific tasks.

Within this book, some sections include "tips" that look like this:

Best Practice

These tips are best practices for implementing the features of the Cisco MDS and Nexus platforms. They are a result of in-depth knowledge of the platform, as well as extensive experience implementing Storage Area Networks.

Audience

This document is designed for use by those that install, design, architect, support, sell, manage, troubleshoot and others responsible for the design and deployment of multi-protocol MDS and Nexus SANs in the data center environment.

This is a field-driven book, meaning that the intended audience (storage administrators, technical support engineers, SEs, and CEs) is also the source of information for these procedures. Their requirements for a procedure determine the content.

If there are procedures that should be covered in this book, or if you have any other comments or questions, please notify us through e-mail at mds-cookbook@cisco.com. Please state the document name, page number, and details of the request.

About the Authors

Seth Mason, CCIE #20847, is a Technical Leader with Advanced Services' Data Center team at Cisco Systems. His areas of expertise are data center migration, disaster recovery, FCoE, and large scale storage architectures. He graduated from Auburn University in 1998 with a Bachelor of Computer Engineering and has focused on SANs ever since, including roles as a Product Engineer with IBM's Storage Subsystems Group, Silicon Valley Operations team lead with StorageNetworks, and Network Consulting Engineer with Andiamo Systems. Seth has continued to further his expertise in storage by authoring both the *MDS-9000 Family Cookbook for SAN-OS 1.x* and *MDS-9000 Family Cookbook for SAN-OS 2.x,* as well as the *MDS-9000 Switch to Switch Interoperability Configuration Guide.* He is a member of the team that authored the CCIE exam in Storage Networking, and has been presenting at Cisco Live since 2006.

Venkat Kirishnamurthyi, CCIE #16016, is a Technical Leader with Advanced Services' Data Center team at Cisco Systems. His areas of expertise are SAN design, migration, and storage replication for disaster recovery. He graduated from Bangalore University in 1992 with a Bachelor of Electronics and Communications Engineering. Since then he has worked as a Systems Administrator at Hughes Software Systems, India and as a Senior Systems Administrator and Senior Storage Administrator at Cisco Systems. Venkat has continued his storage expertise by authoring SAN migration guides for HPUX and Solaris hosts, both the *MDS-9000 Family Cookbook for SAN-OS 1.x* and *MDS-9000 Family Cookbook for SAN-OS 2.x.* He is a member of the team that authored the CCIE exam for Storage Networking.

Document Conventions

Command descriptions use these conventions:

Convention	Indication
boldface font	Commands and keywords are in boldface.
italic font	Arguments for which you supply values are in italics.
[ ]	Elements in square brackets are optional.
{x | y | z}	Required alternative keywords are grouped in braces and separated by vertical bars.
[x | y | z]	Optional alternative keywords are grouped in brackets and separated by vertical bars.
string	A nonquoted set of characters. Do not use quotation marks around the string or the string will include the quotation marks.

Screen examples use these conventions:

Convention	Indication
`screen` font	Terminal sessions and information the switch displays are in screen font.
`boldface screen` font	Information you must enter is in **`boldface screen`** font.
`italic screen` font	Arguments for which you supply values are in *`italic screen`* font.
< >	Nonprinting characters, such as passwords are in angle brackets.
[ ]	Default responses to system prompts are in square brackets.
!, #	An exclamation point (!) or a pound sign (#) at the beginning of a line of code indicates a comment line.

This document uses the following conventions:

Note   Means reader *take note*. Notes contain helpful suggestions or references to material not covered in the manual.

Best Practice   Means *the following information will help you solve a problem*. These tips are suggested as best practices and are based on in-depth knowledge of the Cisco MDS and Nexus families and experience implementing SANs.

Caution   Means *reader be careful*. In this situation, you might do something that could result in equipment damage or loss of data.

CHAPTER 1

Managing Cisco MDS Switches

In addition to recipes covering areas that enable devices to communicate with each other, one topic that must be addressed prior to the deployment of MDS and Nexus switches into production is managing the MDS itself. The topics in this section provide common recipes for those areas in which the SAN administrator would need when they are initially setting up the switch or are looking for ways to streamline their administration duties. These non datapath topics include access control, accounting, event resolution, and monitoring.

Questions such as, "What do I want to monitor? How do I want to monitor it? and What do I want to do once I've received a notification?" should be considered during the design phases of the deployment.

Event Notification

Event notification is the process by which the MDS or a Nexus device itself provides notification to another device about an event. For example an e-mail notification or SNMP trap that a fan or power supply has failed. This notification is received by some system which processes the event and takes some sort of action, such as paging out the appropriate resource to replace the failed component. In this section, three types of event notification mechanisms will be examined: SNMP, call-home (e-mail-based) and syslog.

Using SNMP to Monitor MDS Switches

Cisco MDS and Nexus switches support a large number of MIBs and events to notify administrators and support personnel. The monitoring solution should provide them with the relevant traps or notifications. To address this need, a standard list of events and thresholds have been identified for a SAN administrator to monitor.

Table 1-1 lists a subset of the full set of events that the Cisco MDS and Nexus switches support. Table 1-5 lists standard thresholds to monitor. Customers have the flexibility to customize the monitoring solution to meet their specific needs. The MIBs listed in this chapter are a baseline to begin implementing your specific monitoring framework.

Events

The Cisco MDS and Nexus NX-OS software supports over 100 MIBs and supports Simple Network Management Protocol (SNMP) versions v1, v2, and v3. In this section, SNMP events are covered, events are triggered when a specific condition is met that does not require exceeding a threshold. Such events could be a power supply or fan failure.

Cisco MDS and Nexus NX-OS provide the ability to configure traps that are sent out. To enable the SNMP traps, for which a recommended set is provided below, the MDS must be configured to send out the traps themselves.

Table 1-1   Switch Status Traps

Trap	MIB	Event Name
VSAN Segmentation	CISCO-DM-MIB	dmDomainIdNotAssignedNotify
VSAN Status	CISCO-VSAN-MIB	vsanStatusChange
Topology Changes	CISCO-FCS-MIB	dmNewPrincipalSwitchNotify
Build Fabric	CISCO-DM-MIB	dmFabricChangeNotify
Domain ID Mgmt	CISCO-DM-MIB	dmNewPrincipalSwitchNotify
Reconfigure Fabric	CISCO-DM-MIB	dmFabricChangeNotify
Zoneset Merge Failure	CISCO-ZS-MIB	zoneMergeFailureNotify
CFS Merge Failure	CISCO-CFS-MIB	ciscoCFSMergeFailNotify
Linecard Failure	CISCO-ENTITY-FRU-CONTROL-MIB	cefcModuleStatusChange
Linecard Reset	CISCO-ENTITY-FRU-CONTROL-MIB	cefcModuleStatusChange
Linecard Insertion	CISCO-ENTITY-FRU-CONTROL-MIB	cefcFRUInserted
Linecard Removal	CISCO-ENTITY-FRU-CONTROL-MIB	cefcFRURemoved
Supervisor Switchover	CISCO-ENTITY-FRU-CONTROL-MIB	ciscoRFSwactNotify
Supervisor Failure	CISCO-ENTITY-FRU-CONTROL-MIB	ciscoRFSwactNotify
NTP Monitoring	CISCO-NTP-MIB	ciscoNtpGeneralConnFailure

Table 1-2   **Environmental Status Traps**

Trap	MIB	Event Name
Temperature alarm	CISCO-ENTITY-FRU-CONTROL-MIB	entSensorThresholdNotification
Power supply failure	CISCO-ENTITY-FRU-CONTROL-MIB	cefcPowerStatusChange
Fan failure	CISCO-ENTITY-FRU-CONTROL-MIB	cefcFanTrayStatusChange

Table 1-3   **ISL Status Traps**

Trap	MIB	Event Name
(E)ISL Up	CISCO-FC-FE-MIB	fcTrunkIfUpNotify
(E)ISL Down	CISCO-FC-FE-MIB	fcTrunkIfDownNotify
GigE Port Up	IF-MIB	ciscoFcipMgmtExtMIB
GigE Port Down	IF-MIB	ciscoFcipMgmtExtMIB

Table 1-4   **F-Port Status Traps**

Trap	MIB	Event Name
Link Up	CISCO-IF-EXTENSION-MIB	cieLinkUp
Link Down	CISCO-IF-EXTENSION-MIB	cieLinkDown

Note   For more information on SNMP MIBs, such as how to download them and their programmable syntax, see the *Cisco MDS 9000 Family MIB Quick Reference*, Cisco Nexus 7000 Series NX-0S MIB Quick Reference and Cisco Nexus 5000 Series and Cisco Nexus 2000 Series MIB Quick Reference documents on http://www.cisco.com.

To enable the MDS/Nexus switches to send traps to a monitoring station perform the following procedure via the CLI:

In this example, the following assumptions are made:

- SNMP Server or Management Application: 192.168.1.55, using snmp version 2c
- SNMP Community string required by Management Application: l3tme1n
- SNMP Community string used by the Management Application to access the MDS: l3tme1n
- Contact: SAN_Team
- Location: SJC_J_3_ROW_6

Step 1   Compile into your Network Management Software the appropriate SNMP MIBs as per your application's instructions. Detailed instructions for downloading the MIBs are located in the *Cisco MDS 9000 Family MIB Quick Reference* document on Cisco.com.

Step 2   Configure the snmp trap destination, which is the IP address of the Management Application

```
MDS-9513-1# config t
MDS-9513-1#(config) snmp-server host 192.168.1.55 version 2c l3tme1n
```

Step 3   Configure the traps to be sent

```
MDS-9513-1#(config) snmp-server enable traps cfs
MDS-9513-1#(config) snmp-server enable traps zone
MDS-9513-1#(config) snmp-server enable traps license
MDS-9513-1#(config) snmp-server enable traps fcdomain
MDS-9513-1#(config) snmp-server enable traps entity fru
MDS-9513-1#(config) snmp-server enable traps link
MDS-9513-1#(config) snmp-server enable traps vsan
```

Step 4   Configure the contact and location for the device and the device location should be customized for each device.

```
MDS-9513-1#(config) snmp-server contact SAN_Team
MDS-9513-1#(config) snmp-server location SJC_J_3_ROW_6
```

Step 5   Configure the SNMP read-only community string on the MDS to enable the Management Application to query for additional information

```
MDS-9513-1#(config)snmp-server community l3tme1n group network-operator
```

Configuring Thresholds with Port-Manager

In NX-OS, the MDS platform has the ability to monitor specific counters to determine if they have exceeded a specific condition and then notify appropriately. Port-Manager provides this ability building upon the RMON framework. In many environments, interfaces are required to be monitored to determine if they have problems such as a link flap, or are about to have problems such as an increasing number of CRC errors.

Port-Manager monitors a management information base (MIB) object for a specified interval, triggers an alarm at a rising threshold value, and then resets the alarm at another, lower value (falling threshold). Similar to the SNMP traps, Port-Manager leverages the SNMP infrastructure to notify the Network Management Software as part of the alerting and notification process. Multiple Port-Manager profiles can be created to apply different policies to monitor ports of either access (hosts/storage devices) or trunks (ISLs). You can also apply different severity levels to the different values within the profile depending on the type of switch (core, access) or the type of port profile.

Note   For more information on SNMP MIBs, such as how to download them and their programmable syntax, see the *Cisco MDS 9000 Family MIB Quick Reference* document on Cisco.com.

Table 1-5 lists some of the recommended MDS thresholds. To read the table using the first row as an example, if during a 900 second Interval, the Link Loss counter, becomes equal to or greater than the Rising Threshold,5, an Event Level 4 SNMP notification will be sent. The alarm will not be reset until the Threshold Variable falls below the Falling Value, 1, during another 900 second Interval.

Table 1-5   *SNMP Thresholds*

Threshold Variable	MIB	Object	Interval (sec.)	Rising Value	Falling Value	Event Level
Link Loss	CISCO-FC-FE-MIB	fcIfLinkFailures	900	5	1	4
Sync Loss	CISCO-FC-FE-MIB	fcIfSyncLosses	900	5	1	4
Signal Loss	CISCO-FC-FE-MIB	fcIfSigLosses	900	5	1	4
Invalid Words	CISCO-FC-FE-MIB	fcIfInvalidTxWords	900	2	0	4
Invalid CRCs	CISCO-FC-FE-MIB	fcInvalidCrcs	900	5	1	4
Protocol Errors	CISCO-FC-FE-MIB	fcIfPrimSeqProtoErrors	900	1	0	4
Credit Loss Recovery	CISCO-FC-FE-MIB	fcIfCreditLoss	1	1	0	4
Timeouts and Discards	CISCO-FC-FE-MIB	fcIfTimeOutDiscards	900	5	1	4

Note   The values contained within Table 1-5, are examples only. These values should be evaluated in a proper lab environment prior to being put into production.

The user also has the ability to manually define the severity levels that the Port-Manager feature will use. Some recommendations are listed in Table 1-6 which are in-line with the definitions for syslog severity levels.

Table 1-6   *Notification Descriptions*

Event Number	Description	Owner/contact
1	FATAL(1)	santeam@acme.com
2	CRITICAL(2)	santeam@acme.com
3	ERROR(3)	santeam@acme.com
4	WARNING(4)	santeam@acme.com
5	INFORMATION(5)	santeam@acme.com

To configure Port-Manager as per the values in Table 1-5 and Table 1-6 the following procedure should be followed with the below assumptions:

- SNMP v1 community string: l3tm31n
- Port-Manager policy type: access (only monitors host ports)
- Port-Manager policy name: end_device_policy

Step 1   Configure the SNMP destination

```
MDS-9513-1# config t
MDS-9513-1#(config) snmp-server host 192.168.1.55 version 2c l3tme1n
```

Step 2   Configure the RMON notification descriptions.

```
MDS-9513-1# conf t
MDS-9513-1#(config)
MDS-9513-1#(config) rmon event 1 log trap l3tm31n description FATAL(1) owner
santeam@acme.com
MDS-9513-1#(config) rmon event 2 log trap l3tm31n description CRITICAL(2) owner
santeam@acme.com
MDS-9513-1#(config) rmon event 3 log trap l3tm31n description ERROR(3) owner
santeam@acme.com
MDS-9513-1#(config) rmon event 4 log trap l3tm31n description WARNING(4) owner
santeam@acme.com
MDS-9513-1#(config) rmon event 5 log trap l3tm31n description INFORMATION(5) owner
santeam@acme.com
```

Step 3   Enable Port-Monitor

```
MDS-9513-1#(config) port-monitor enable
```

Step 4   Disable default slow-drain policy as this is covered by existing counters, timeout-discards and
credit-loss-recovery

```
MDS-9513-1#(config) no port-monitor activate slowdrain
```

Note   When configuring a new port-monitor policy, any counters not removed or changed will still be in the new
port-monitor policy using the defaults.

Step 5   Create the Port-Monitor policy and specify the policy type

```
MDS-9513-1#(config) port-monitor name end_device_policy
MDS-9513-1#(config-port-monitor) port-type access-port
```

Step 6   Configure the appropriate counters

```
MDS-9513-1#(config-port-monitor) counter link-loss poll-interval 900 delta
rising-threshold 5 event 4 falling-threshold 1 event 4
MDS-9513-1#(config-port-monitor) counter sync-loss poll-interval 900 delta
rising-threshold 5 event 4 falling-threshold 1 event 4
MDS-9513-1#(config-port-monitor) counter signal-loss poll-interval 900 delta
rising-threshold 5 event 4 falling-threshold 1 event 4
MDS-9513-1#(config-port-monitor) counter invalid-words poll-interval 900 delta
rising-threshold 1 event 4 falling-threshold 0 event 4
MDS-9513-1#(config-port-monitor) counter invalid-crc poll-interval 900 delta
rising-threshold 5 event 4 falling-threshold 1 event 4
MDS-9513-1#(config-port-monitor) counter timeout-discards poll-interval 900 delta
rising-threshold 5 event 4 falling-threshold 1 event 4
```

Step 7   Activate the policy

```
MDS-9513-1#(config-port-monitor) port-monitor activate end_device_policy
```

Configuring Call Home

The next type of event notification is Call Home. With Call Home, the MDS switch sends an e-mail-based notification based on the type of event. The e-mail message can either be tailored for a pager, e-mail program, or Cisco TAC if a Cisco SmartNet subscription is covering support for the MDS.

Defining Alert Groups

Alert groups determine which events are sent to specific destinations by using profiles. For example, a profile may be configured to include the facilities team. When an environmental alert is triggered, all members of the facilities team would then receive the notification. Table 1-7 provides a listing of the Alert groups available.

Table 1-7   Alert Group Descriptions

Alert Group	Description	Executed Commands
System	Events generated by failure of a software system critical to unit operation.	show tech-support show system redundancy status
Environmental	Events related to power, fan, and temperature.	show module show environment
Line Card Hardware	Events related to standard or intelligent line cards.	show tech-support
Supervisor Hardware	Events related to supervisor or fabric cards.	show tech-support
License	Events related to unlicensed use of licensed features.	show license all show running-config
Inventory	Inventory is a noncritical event. Status should be provided whenever a unit is cold booted or when FRUs are inserted or removed.	show version
RMON	Events related to RMON, triggered by Threshold Manager to set alerts.	
Syslog-group-port	Events related to syslog messages filed by Port Manager when a port goes up or down.	
Test	User-generated test messages.	show version
Cisco-TAC	Events intended for only Cisco TAC.	

Configuring Call Home to Send All Notifications to a Single E-Mail Address

The simplest MDS notification strategy is to send an e-mail for all events. E-mail is a better choice than a pager notification because e-mail is not space-limited and can contain full details of the event.

In this recipe, CFS will not be enabled for Call Home.

Note   If all the switches use the same Call Home configuration, then CFS should be enabled.

In this example, these assumptions are made:

- Contact: Storage Admins
- Phone number: 123-456-7890
- Mail address: storageadmins@acme.com
- Street address: 123 Main Street
- Switch's e-mail address: mds-callhome@acme.com
- Destination e-mail address (who to mail the error to): NOC@acme.com
- SMTP server: 192.168.1.2

To Configure Call Home to Send All Notifications to a Single E-Mail Address, follow these steps:

Step 1   In Device Manager, from the Admin pull-down menu, choose **Events**.

Step 2   Choose **Call Home...** You see the screen in Figure 1-1.

Figure 1-1   *Call Home General Tab*

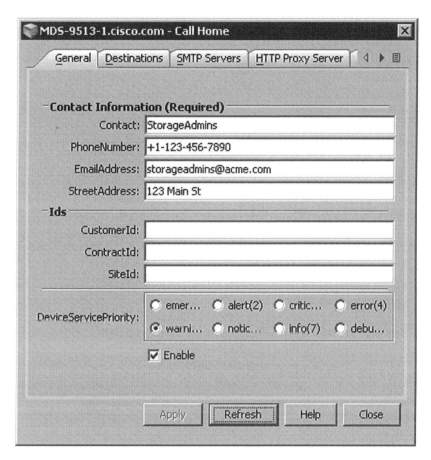

Step 3   Complete the appropriate fields (see Figure 1-1). The Device Service Priority you select will be included in e-mail notifications.

Step 4   Check the **Enable** check box (see Figure 1-1).

Step 5   Click **Apply** (see Figure 1-1).

Step 6   Click the **Email Setup** tab (see Figure 1-2).

Step 7   Complete the **From** and **SMTP** fields (see Figure 1-2).

Step 8   Click **Apply** (see Figure 1-2).

■ Configuring Call Home

Figure 1-2   *Call Home E-mail Setup*

Step 9 Choose the **Profiles** tab (see Figure 1-3). A profile determines what types of notifications are sent.

Step 10 Click **Create...** (see Figure 1-3)

Step 11 Enter a name for the profile (see Figure 1-3).

Step 12 Select the message level **debug** (see Figure 1-3)

Step 13 Select MaxMessageSize **0** (zero limit to message size) See Figure 1-3.

Step 14 Check all of the Alert Groups. (See Defining Alert Groups, page 1-7 for more information on Alert Groups). See Figure 1-3.

Note If you do not want to receive a Call Home message every time a port goes up or down, un check **syslogGroupPort**.

Figure 1-3   *Call Home Profile*

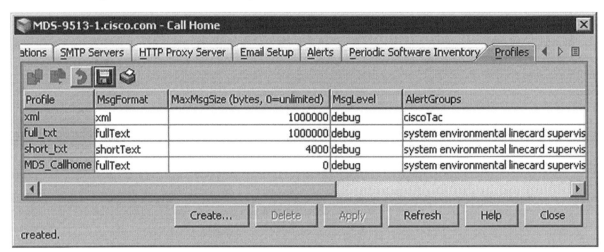

Step 15 Click **Create...** (see Figure 1-3)

Step 16 Choose the **Destinations** tab (see Figure 1-4).

Step 17   Click **Create...**

Step 18   Change the profile to the one you just created in the Profiles tab.

Note   •   Use **XML** if the Call Home message's destination is Cisco TAC.

       •   Use **full_txt** if the Call Home message will be read as an e-mail.

       •   Use **short_txt** if the Call Home message is destined for a pager or similar device.

Step 19   Enter the e-mail address for the Call Home message.

Step 20   Click **Create...**

Step 21   Click **Close** (see Figure 1-4).

Figure 1-4   *Call Home Destinations*

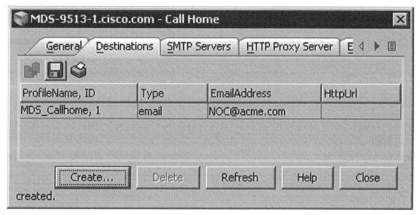

Step 22   To test the configuration choose the **Alerts** tab, the **Test** action, then click **Apply**. If errors occur, they are displayed in the Failure Cause text box.

Implementing Syslog

The syslog facility allows the MDS 9000 Family of switches to send a copy of the message log to a server running the syslog process for more permanent storage and automated parsing. This can be useful if the logs need to be examined over a long period of time or if the MDS switch is not accessible.

This example configures an MDS switch to use the syslog facility on a Solaris platform. Although a Solaris host is being used, syslog configuration on all UNIX and Linux systems is very similar.

Syslog can discriminate between messages of different severity and handle them differently. For example, messages can be logged to different files or sent by e-mail to a particular person. Specifying a level of severity determines that all messages of that severity level and greater (lower numbers are higher severity) are acted upon.

╷╷│╷╷│╷╷

Best Practice   MDS messages should be logged to a different file than the standard syslog file so they are not confused with non MDS syslog messages. The log file should not be located on the / file system to prevent log messages from filling up the / file system.

In this example, the following resources are used:

- Syslog client: MDS-9513-1
- Syslog server: 192.168.1.1 (Solaris)
- Syslog facility: local1
- Syslog severity: notifications (level 5, the default)
- File to log MDS messages to: /var/adm/MDS_logs

To configure an MDS switch to use the syslog facility on a Solaris platform, follow these steps:

Step 1   Enter configuration mode and configure the MDS switch.

```
MDS-9513-1# config terminal
Enter configuration commands, one per line.  End with CNTL/Z.
MDS-9513-1(config)# logging server 192.168.1.1 5 facility local1
```

Step 2   Display the switch configuration with the **show logging server** command

```
MDS 9513-1# show logging server
Logging server:              enabled
{192.168.1.1}
         server severity:    notifications
         server facility:    local1
```

Step 3   Configure the Syslog server.

    a. Modify /etc/syslog.conf to handle local messages. For Solaris, there must be at least one tab between the facility.severity and the action (/var/adm/MDS_logs)

```
#Below is for the MDS 9000 logging
local1.notice                   /var/adm/MDS_logs
```

    b. Create the log file.

```
#touch /var/adm/MDS_logs
```

    c. Restart the syslogd with the commands **syslog stop** and **syslog start**.

```
# /etc/init.d/syslog stop
# /etc/init.d/syslog start
syslog service starting.
```

    d. Verify that the syslog started.

```
# ps -ef | grep syslogd
    root 23508   1 0 11:01:41 ?      0:00 /usr/sbin/syslogd
```

Step 4   Test the syslog server by creating an event on the MDS switch. In this example, port fc1/2 is reset and the information is listed on the syslog server. Notice that the IP address of the switch (192.168.1.2) is listed in brackets.

```
# tail -f /var/adm/MDS_logs
Sep 17 11:07:41 [192.168.1.2.2.2] : 2011 Sep 17 11:17:29 pacific:
%PORT-5-IF_DOWN_INITIALIZING: %$VSAN 1%$ Interface fc1/2 is down (Initializing)
```

```
Sep 17 11:07:49 [192.168.1.2.2.2] : 2011 Sep 17 11:17:36 pacific: %PORT-5-IF_UP: %$VSAN
1%$ Interface fc1/2 is up in mode TE
Sep 17 11:07:51 [192.168.1.2.2.2] : 2011 Sep 17 11:17:39 pacific:
%VSHD-5-VSHD_SYSLOG_CONFIG_I: Configuring console from pts/0
(dhcp-171-71-49-125.cisco.com)
```

Cisco Fabric Services

Starting with Cisco SAN-OS Release 2.0, Cisco MDS 9000 switches can propagate and synchronize the configuration of an application on multiple switches across the fabric. This infrastructure, Cisco Fabric Services (CFS), provides the underlying transport for applications such as NTP, device aliases, and IVR to distribute configurations to other switches in the fabric. This feature provides a central point of management for any of the supported applications.

Before Cisco SAN-OS 2.0, on each switch in the fabric, the administrator either had to configure an application manually, using host-based scripting, or using DCNM-SAN. With CFS, the administrator executes commands from one switch and they are distributed to the rest of the switches in the fabric. In addition, the CFS protocol provides application locking so that two administrators cannot simultaneously perform configuration changes to the same application.

CFS uses common terminology across its supported applications:

- **Pending Database:** When configuration changes are made to a CFS application, they are first made to the pending database and then distributed to all switches in the fabric. To activate these changes into the switch's running configuration, execute an explicit **commit** command. Alternatively, you can clear the application's pending database by entering an explicit **abort** command.

  a. **Locking:** Before modifying the pending database, the application uses the CFS transport to obtain a lock, preventing other users and switches from modifying the pending database. Applications outside the scope of the lock can still be modified.

  – When initializing the configuration, the application first attempts to obtain a lock. The CFS infrastructure knows which switch and user has obtained the lock.

- **Scope:** The scope of an application can be either physical or logical. This scope determines whether multiple users can simultaneously modify the same application.

  – A physical scope encompasses all the switches in the physical fabric such as NTP. While an NTP lock is active, no other user can modify NTP within the physical fabric. There are two types of physical scope:

  Physical-fc: This scope encompasses all MDS switches connected through Fibre Channel, FCoE or FCIP.

  Physical-fc-ip: This scope encompasses all MDS switches connected through Fibre Channel, FCoE or native IP. (In SAN-OS 3.x and NX-OS, CFS can be configured to traverse IP.)

  – A logical scope encompasses only the VSAN being configured. For example, port security could be locked in a VSAN. While that port security lock is active, no other user can modify port security for that particular VSAN. However, port security could be modified for another VSAN since it is outside of the scope of the lock.

- **Merge Control:** If two fabrics are merged, each application is responsible for merging its configuration with that of the same application in the other physical fabric. The basic rule for merging is that a union of the two configurations is produced. However, conflicting entries are not merged. Conflicting entries must be manually created in the merged configuration.

Note   Failure to fully merge a CFS application when merging two fabrics, will *not* isolate the ISL.

- **Regions**: CFS regions provide the ability for CFS to isolate an application from the same application elsewhere in the fabric. CFS regions are configured on a per application basis and an application on a single switch can not participate in multiple CFS regions. This enables the fabric to have multiple instances of the application which are configured, distributed, and synchronized independently from each other.

    - One example is with CFS distribution of NTP with a single fabric that spans multiple data centers across multiple time zones. The switch should be accessing a local NTP server, however, without regions configured, all the switches would be accessing NTP servers in both data centers. If the MDS switch's CFS region for NTP in datacenter one are configured for CFS region 1, and MDS switch's CFS region for NTP in datacenter two are configured for CFS region 2, then the two CFS configurations will not merge and local switches will access local NTP servers.

Best Practice   If CFS is used with an application, all the switches in the fabric should be configured to use CFS for that application. For example, if there are five switches in a fabric, and Network Time Protocol (NTP) will be configured leveraging CFS, all five switches should have NTP leveraging CFS.

As Figure 1-5 shows, a CFS application flow is executed:

1. Before the first configuration, CFS enables distribution for the application, then enters the configuration mode for the specified application.

2. The local switch requests an application lock from the other switches in the fabric according to the scope of the application (VSAN or physical). If available, other switches grant the lock to the local switch. If the lock is not available, access to the application's pending database is denied.

3. Changes are made to the pending database. The changes are then either explicitly committed or aborted.

4. The local switch informs the other switches in the scope to commit the changes then the lock is released. Until the lock is released, users on other switches cannot make changes to the locked application. However, other applications can still be modified.

Figure 1-5   *CFS Application Flow*

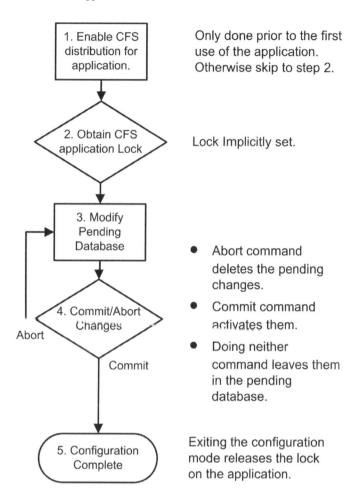

DCNM-SAN has the ability to leverage the underlying transport of CFS. The proposed changes still need to be committed, because committing is an explicit activity.

Best Practice   If an application is configured to use CFS in the fabric, CFS should be enabled for that application on all switches in the fabric. DCNM-SAN can use either CFS or a method of configuring each switch individually. It is recommended to use CFS so that configurations are in sync whether done via CLI or DCNM-SAN.

How Does CFS Work?

If DCNM-SAN uses CFS to distribute a configuration, one switch performs the locking and distribution. This switch is referred to as the master switch (see Figure 1-6). In the case of DCNM-SAN, the master switch is determined by its WWN: the switch with the lowest WWN becomes the master switch. In the case of CLI access, the local switch when the lock is obtained, is the CFS master.

Figure 1-6   *CFS Master in DCNM-SAN*

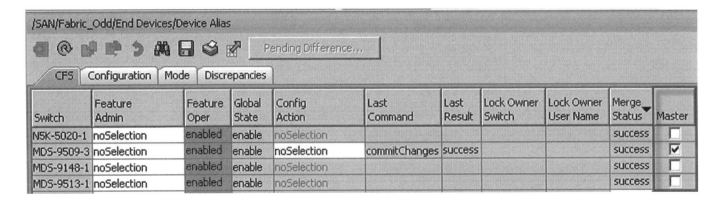

/SAN/Fabric_Odd/End Devices/Device Alias

Switch	Feature Admin	Feature Oper	Global State	Config Action	Last Command	Last Result	Lock Owner Switch	Lock Owner User Name	Merge Status	Master
N5K-5020-1	noSelection	enabled	enable	noSelection					success	☐
MDS-9509-3	noSelection	enabled	enable	noSelection	commitChanges	success			success	☑
MDS-9148-1	noSelection	enabled	enable	noSelection					success	☐
MDS-9513-1	noSelection	enabled	enable	noSelection					success	☐

CFS CLI Commands

CFS is not directly interacted with because it is an underlying infrastructure. Instead, we use applications that leverage CFS, for example NTP, device-alias or IVR. It is more important to know the status of an NTP merge or commit than to know how CFS is set up. However, there are some situations when only CFS can provide the required information. In the case of selecting a CFS master, the switch that initiates the lock, or begins the configuration, is the CFS master.

Which Switches are CFS Capable?

The **show cfs peers** command lists switches that can use CFS.

```
MDS-9513-1# show cfs peers

Physical Fabric
-------------------------------------------------
Switch WWN               IP Address
-------------------------------------------------
20:00:00:05:30:00:86:9e  192.168.1.9    [Local]
20:00:00:05:30:00:68:5e  192.168.1.10
20:00:00:0d:ec:02:1d:40  192.168.1.11
20:00:00:0c:85:e9:d2:c0  192.168.1.12

Total number of entries = 4
```

Note   The CFS protocol is enabled by default. However, most applications are not enabled by default to leverage CFS. You can later enable an application to use CFS for application locking, configuration propagation and synchronization.

Which CFS Applications Do I Have and What Is Their Scope?

The **show cfs application** commands show the Cisco applications using CFS. However, some applications will not show up here unless the feature is enabled.

A physical scope spans all switches physically connected together over FC, FCIP, or via CFS over IP, regardless of VSAN configuration. While a Logical scope applies only to the VSAN for a configuration.

```
MDS-9513-1# show cfs application

-----------------------------------------------
Application    Enabled    Scope
-----------------------------------------------
ntp            No         Physical-fc-ip
fscm           Yes        Physical-fc
role           No         Physical-fc-ip
rscn           No         Logical
radius         No         Physical-fc-ip
fctimer        No         Physical-fc
syslogd        No         Physical-fc-ip
callhome       No         Physical-fc-ip
fcdomain       No         Logical
fc-redirect    Yes        Physical-fc
device-alias   Yes        Physical-fc

Total number of entries = 11
```

Why has CFS Locked Me Out of an Application?

CFS provides locking (physical or logical). If the lock is already in use, you see the error **Failed to acquire lock**.

```
MDS-9513-1(config)# ntp peer 192.168.10.10
Failed to acquire Lock
```

To find out which user (on which switch) has the lock, enter the **show cfs lock** command.

```
MDS-9513-1# show cfs lock
Application: ntp
Scope      : Physical

-----------------------------------------------------------------
Switch WWN              IP Address      User Name    User Type
-----------------------------------------------------------------
 20:00:00:0c:85:e9:d2:c0  192.168.1.142    admin       CLI/SNMP v3
Total number of entries = 1
```

A CFS lock is released only when the CFS session is either committed or aborted. However, in abnormal situations, the lock may need to be forcefully removed or cleared. The **clear ntp session** command clears the pending database and all pending changes for the specified application are lost.

```
MDS-9513-1# clear ntp session
```

Command Line Enhancements

To aid the use of Command Line usage, NX-OS supports the many new additions to the basic command line syntax above those that were available in SAN-OS. These enhancements can aid in the automation of both repetitive and mundane tasks.

How do I use Variables and Aliases?

Variables and Aliases are two concepts introduced in NX-OS that allow the user to perform CLI substitution. Variables are replaced during execution and represent a single word or phrase, while aliases can represent an entire command.

By default, two variables are defined, $(TIMESTAMP) and $(SWITCHNAME). To use these you put the variable name into the command and during execution of the command the variable is replaced with a timestamp or the switch's name. Variables can either be permanently created using the command **cli variable name** *variable_name* (if created in config mode) or session-based if created in exec mode.

To display the currently defined variables, execute the following:

```
MDS-9513-1# show cli variables
VSH Variable List (* = session vars)
----------------
SWITCHNAME="MDS-9513-1"
TIMESTAMP="2011-10-07-21.24.34"
```

Variables are illustrated further in the "Command Scheduler" section on page 1-20

Aliases enable the user to provide substitutions for entire commands. For example, there is predefined alias called "alias" which translates to the command **show cli alias**.

To create and use an alias perform the following:

The following assumptions are made:

- Alias name: save
- Command: copy running-config startup-config

Step 1   Create the alias using the **cli alias** command.

```
MDS-9513-1# conf t
Enter configuration commands, one per line.  End with CNTL/Z.
MDS-9513-1(config)# cli alias name save copy running-config startup-config
```

Step 2   Display the aliases

```
MDS-9513-1(config)# show cli alias
CLI alias commands
==================
alias   :show cli alias
cls     :clear screen
save    :copy running-config startup-config
```

Step 3   Test the alias

```
MDS-9513-1(config)# save
[#######################################] 100%
Copy complete, now saving to disk (please wait)...
```

What other CLI tricks are available?

In addition to variables and aliases, and building upon the basic CLI parsing available in SAN-OS, namely the ability to include or exclude lines based on a pattern, NX-OS also provides the following options commands that can be used after the 'pipe' ("|") symbol:

```
cut        Print selected parts of lines.
diff       Show difference between current and previous invocation (creates
           temp files: remove them with 'diff-clean' command and dont use it
           on commands with big outputs, like 'show tech'!)
egrep      Egrep - print lines matching a pattern
grep       Grep - print lines matching a pattern
head       Display first lines
last       Display last lines
less       Filter for paging
no-more    Turn-off pagination for command output
section    Show lines that include the pattern as well as the subsequent lines
           that are more indented than matching line
sed        Stream Editor
sort       Stream Sorter
sscp       Stream SCP (secure copy)
tr         Translate, squeeze, and/or delete characters
uniq       Discard all but one of successive identical lines
vsh        The shell that understands cli command
wc         Count words, lines, characters
begin      Begin with the line that matches
count      Count number of lines
end        End with the line that matches
exclude    Exclude lines that match
include    Include lines that match
```

While the above commands are derived from Linux and are commonly used in UNIX environments, the vsh command is unique to NX-OS.

How do I use the VSH command?

The vsh command takes any text sent to it and executes it at the command line with the privilege of the logged in user.

In this example, the problem needed to be solved is to clear all of the counters on all of the port-channels attached to the local MDS. You could manually specify all of the port-channel interfaces in a comma delineated list, the following also works using multiple NX-OS CLI enhancements:

Step 1   Create the alias, **cpcc** which in this case is short for clear port-channel counters.

```
MDS-9513-1# config t
MDS-9513-1(config)# cli alias name tester show port-channel database |include port-channel
| sed 's/port-channel/clear counters interface port-channel/g' | vsh
```

Step 2   Display the created alias, the alias called "alias" is a system default alias.

```
MDS-9513-1# show cli alias
CLI alias commands
==================
alias  :show cli alias
cpcc   :show port-channel database |include port-channel | sed 's/port-channel/clear
counters interface port-channel/g' | vsh
```

Step 3   Execute the alias

```
MDS-9513-1# cpcc
MDS-9513-1#
```

The advancements in the CLI between SAN-OS and NX-OS truly enable the administrator to perform complex tasks that normally would have required an external server to perform the operation.

Command Scheduler

This section provides recipes for using the switch command scheduler.

Automated Switch Configuration Backup

Before SAN-OS 2.0, the only method for automated backup of a switch configuration was to set up a management station to periodically log into the switch and issue appropriate scripting commands to copy the configuration to a TFTP server. The drawback of that method is that, if the management station goes down, the configuration is not backed up. By enabling the MDS switch to "back itself up," its' configuration is pushed to a TFTP server. Additionally, in SAN-OS 3.0, the ability to timestamp a filename was provided so that new iterations of the script do not overwrite the previous backups.

Best Practice   Backing up the startup-configuration to a server should be done on a daily basis and before any changes. A short script can be written to be run on the switch to save, then back up, the configuration. The script needs to contain only two commands: **copy running-configuration startup-configuration** and **copy startup-configuration tftp://**tftp_server/*$(SWITCHNAME)_*$(TIMESTAMP)**. To execute the script use the **run-script** *filename* command.

Command Scheduler can now be used to regularly backup switch configuration to a TFTP server.

In this example, the following resources are used:

- Switch: MDS-9513-1
- TFTP Server: 192.168.100.1
- Schedule: "nightly_10pm" Every night at 10 PM.

To back up a switch configuration to a TFTP server, follow these steps:

Step 1   Enable the command scheduler with the **scheduler enable** command.

```
MDS-9513-1# config terminal
Enter configuration commands, one per line. End with CNTL/Z.
MDS-9513-1(config)# feature scheduler
```

Step 2   Define the job to be run. Do this by saving the running configuration and then copying it to a TFTP server. The (config-job) prompt works the same as the switch exec-mode prompt. Therefore, any command on the switch can also be executed.

```
MDS-9513-1(config)# scheduler job name backup_config
MDS-9513-1(config-job)# copy running-config startup-config
MDS-9513-1(config-job)# copy startup-config
tftp://192.168.100.1/$SWITCHNAME/$(SWITCHNAME)_config_($TIMESTAMP)
MDS-9509-2(config-job)# end
```

··|··|··|··

Best Practice   Leveraging **variables** such as $(TIMESTAMP) and $(SWITCHNAME) one can execute a single command on any NX-OS switch without having to create unique commands. The variables $(SWITCHNAME) and $(TIMESTAMP) would embed both the switch name and date automatically in the filename. For example, the file could read MDS-9513-1_config_2007-11-07-10.40.18 if the script was executed on November 7, 2011 at 10:40:18.

Step 3   Display the defined job with the **show scheduler** command.

```
MDS-9513-1# show scheduler job name backup_config
Job Name: backup_config
----------------------
copy running-config startup-config
copy startup-config tftp://192.168.100.1/$(SWITCHNAME)/$(SWITCHNAME)_config_$(TIMESTAMP)
==========================================================================
```

Step 4   Create the schedule. Assign the time (20:00) and the job that will be assigned to it (backup_config).

```
MDS-9513-1# conf terminal
Enter configuration commands, one per line.  End with CNTL/Z.
MDS-9513-1(config)# scheduler schedule name nightly_10pm
MDS-9513-1(config-schedule)# time daily 20:00
MDS-9513-1(config-schedule)# job name backup_config
```

Step 5   Display the schedule with the **show scheduler** command.

```
MDS-9513-1# show scheduler schedule name nightly_10pm
Schedule Name       : nightly_10pm
---------------------------------
User Name           : admin
Schedule Type       : Run every day at 20 Hrs 0 Mins
Last Execution Time : Yet to be executed
-----------------------------------------------
    Job Name            Last Execution Status
-----------------------------------------------
    backup_config                   -NA-
==========================================================================
```

Step 6   After the job runs, examine the status of the job and the details of the execution with the **show scheduler** command.

```
MDS-9513-1# show scheduler schedule name nightly_10pm
Schedule Name        : nightly_10pm
-----------------------------------
User Name            : admin
Schedule Type        : Run every 0 Days 0 Hrs 1 Mins
Start Time           : Fri Aug 22 20:00:00 2011
Last Execution Time  : Fri Aug 22 20:00:00 2011
Last Completion Time : Fri Aug 22 20:00:15 2011
Execution count      : 1
-----------------------------------------------
    Job Name            Last Execution Status
-----------------------------------------------
backup_config                   Success (0)
===============================================================================
```

Detailed log:

```
MDS-9513-1# show scheduler logfile
===============================================================================
Job Name       : backup_config              Job Status: Success (0)
Schedule Name  : nightly_10pm               User Name : admin
Completion time: Fri Aug 22 20:00:15 2011
------------------------------ Job Output ------------------------------

`copy running-config startup-config `
[####                                   ]    7%
[#######                                ]   14%
[##########                             ]   23%
[#############                          ]   30%
[################                       ]   37%
[###################                    ]   46%
[######################                 ]   53%
[#########################              ]   60%
[############################           ]   69%
[###############################        ]   76%
[##################################     ]   84%
[####################################   ]   92%
[#######################################] 100%

`copy startup-config tftp://192.168.100.1/MDS-9513-1_config_2011-08-22-20.00.00
Trying to connect to tftp server......

TFTP put operation was successful
===============================================================================
```

Copying Files to and from a Switch

You can move files to and from an MDS switch. These files can be log, configuration, or firmware files. There are two methods for copying files to and from the switch: using the command-line interface (CLI) and using DCNM-SAN.

Copying Files Using the CLI

The CLI offers four protocols for copying files to or from the switch, FTP, SCP, SFTP, and TFTP. Because the switch always acts as a client, a session originates at the switch. The switch either pushes files to an external system or pulls files from an external system.

In this example, the following resources are used:

- File server: **192.168.100.1**

- File to be copied to the switch: **/etc/hosts**

The switch's **copy** command supports four transfer protocols and twelve different sources for files.

```
MDS-9513-1# copy ?
  bootflash:       Select source filesystem
  core:            Select source filesystem
  debug:           Select source filesystem
  ftp:             Select source filesystem
  licenses         Backup license files
  log:             Select source filesystem
  modflash:        Select source filesystem
  nvram:           Select source filesystem
  running-config   Copy running configuration to destination
  scp:             Select source filesystem
  sftp:            Select source filesystem
  slot0:           Select source filesystem
  startup-config   Copy startup configuration to destination
  system:          Select source filesystem
  tftp:            Select source filesystem
  volatile:        Select source filesystem
```

Secure Copy Protocol

Secure copy protocol (SCP) transfers use this syntax:

scp:[//[username@]server][/path]

To copy the file /etc/hosts from the server 192.168.100.1 to the switch destination file hosts.txt (using user id user1) enter:

```
MDS-9513-1# copy scp://user1@192.168.100.1/etc/hosts bootflash:hosts.txt
user1@192.168.100.1's password:
hosts                    100% |*****************************|  2035    00:00
```

How to Securely copy a file from the MDS

To copy a file from the MDS, such as the startup configuration to a Secure File Transfer Protocol (SFTP) server, enter:

```
MDS-9513-1# copy startup-config sftp://user1@172.22.36.10/MDS/startup-configuration.bak1
Connecting to 172.22.36.10...
User1@172.22.36.10's password:
MDS-9513-1#
```

Managing Files on the Standby Supervisor

These recipes are often used when a firmware upgrade fails because there is not enough free bootflash capacity on the standby supervisor for the new firmware images, or logs need to be copied from the standby supervisor to the active supervisor.

How to Delete a File from the Standby Supervisor

To delete a file from the standby supervisor, follow these steps:

Step 1   Determine which supervisor is the standby with the **show module** command. In this example, the standby is module 6.

```
MDS-9513-1# show module
Mod  Ports  Module-Type                         Model                Status
---  -----  ----------------------------------  -------------------  ----------
1    48     1/2/4/8 Gbps FC Module              DS-X9248-96K9        ok
4    48     1/2/4/8 Gbps FC Module              DS-X9248-96K9        ok
5    0      Supervisor/Fabric-2                 DS-X9530-SF2-K9      active *
6    0      Supervisor/Fabric-2                 DS-X9530-SF2-K9      ha-standby
7    22     4x1GE IPS, 18x1/2/4Gbps FC Module   DS-X9304-18K9        ok
```

Step 2   Connect to the standby supervisor using the **attach module** command. The prompt now displays the word "standby."

```
MDS-9513-1# attach module 6
Attaching to module 6 ...
To exit type 'exit', to abort type '$.'
Cisco Nexus Operating System (NX-OS) Software
TAC support: http://www.cisco.com/tac
Copyright (c) 2002-2011, Cisco Systems, Inc. All rights reserved.
The copyrights to certain works contained in this software are
owned by other third parties and used and distributed under
license. Certain components of this software are licensed under
the GNU General Public License (GPL) version 2.0 or the GNU
Lesser General Public License (LGPL) Version 2.1. A copy of each
such license is available at
http://www.opensource.org/licenses/gpl-2.0.php and
http://www.opensource.org/licenses/lgpl-2.1.php
MDS-9513-1(standby)#
```

Step 3   List the files on the boot flash with the **dir** command.

```
MDS-9513-1(standby)# dir bootflash:
      26179     Oct 11 23:12:00 2010   anatest
      44551     Mar 25 10:00:07 2009   dcn-config.cfg
      44551     Mar 25 10:00:38 2009   dcn-j.cfg
    1876628     Jun 07 00:26:21 2010   dp413a
      28388     Oct 12 00:19:51 2010   fc-cap
     311235     Jun 07 00:25:01 2010   libficoncli.so
      49152     Jul 21 17:24:26 2010   lost+found/
   17265757     Nov 18 22:13:01 2009   m9000-ek9-ssi-mz.4.1.3i.bin
    1876628     Jun 07 00:26:10 2010   m9500-sf2ek9-dplug-mzg.4.1.3a.bin.S16
   22582784     Apr 08 10:49:24 2009   m9500-sf2ek9-kickstart-mz.4.1.3a.bin
   23097856     Jul 21 17:24:06 2010   m9500-sf2ek9-kickstart-mz.4.2.5.bin
   21764608     Aug 27 13:58:32 2010   m9500-sf2ek9-kickstart-mz.4.2.7a.bin
   98205692     Apr 08 10:50:09 2009   m9500-sf2ek9-mz.4.1.3a.bin
  103404167     Jul 21 17:23:40 2010   m9500-sf2ek9-mz.4.2.5.bin
  103575233     Aug 27 13:58:09 2010   m9500-sf2ek9-mz.4.2.7a.bin
       5284     Sep 07 14:11:59 2011   mts.log

Usage for bootflash://sup-local
  457052160 bytes used
  441036800 bytes free
  898088960 bytes total
```

Step 4   Delete the file with the **delete** command.

```
MDS-9513-1(standby)# delete bootflash:fc-cap
```

Step 5   Enter the **exit** command, and the prompt returns to the active supervisor prompt:

```
MDS-9513-1(standby)# exit
rlogin: connection closed.
MDS-9513-1#
```

Deleting a File using Device Manager

To delete a file using Device Manager, follow these steps:

Step 1   Select the **Admin** menu.

Step 2   Select **Flash Files**.

Step 3   Select the supervisor that you want to delete the file from. It can be either sup-local or sup-standby. See Figure 1-7.

Figure 1-7   Deleting a File with Device Manager

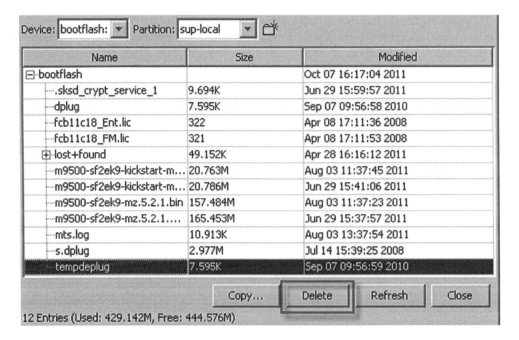

Step 4   Select the file to be deleted.

Step 5   Click **Delete**.

Firmware Upgrades and Downgrades

Upgrading has not changed since SAN-OS 1.x and the process remains the same in NX-OS. However, downgrading between firmware versions does require special attention.

Upgrading Firmware with the CLI

NX-OS can be upgraded using either the **install all** command or the Firmware Upgrade wizard in DCNM-SAN.

Best Practice   Always carefully read the output of the compatibility check of the **install all** command. This tells you exactly what needs to be upgraded (BIOS, loader, firmware) and what modules are not hitless)non-disruptive). If there are any questions or concerns about the results of the output, select **n** to stop the installation and contact the next level of support.

Verify before starting the download that there is sufficient space on the bootflash of both supervisors

Verify that an Ethernet cable is plugged into the standby supervisor, as that will become the new active supervisor after the upgrade is complete.

The following example below demonstrates upgrading to NX-OS 5.2(1) using the **install all** command with the source images located on a SCP server:

Step 1   Upgrade firmware using the **install all** command.

```
MDS-9513-1# install all system scp://testuser@192.168.1.1/m9500-sf2ek9-mz.5.2.1.bin
kickstart scp://192.168.1.1/m9500-sf2ek9-kickstart-mz.5.2.1.bin
For scp://testuser@192.168.1.1, please enter password:
For scp://testuser@192.168.1.1, please enter password:

Copying image from scp://testuser@192.168.1.1/m9500-sf2ek9-kickstart-mz.5.2.1.bin to
bootflash:///m9500-sf2ek9-kickstart-mz.5.2.1.bin.
[####################] 100% -- SUCCESS

Copying image from scp://testuser@192.168.1.1/m9500-sf2ek9-mz.5.2.1.bin to
bootflash:///m9500-sf2ek9-mz.5.2.1.bin
[####################] 100% -- SUCCESS

Verifying image bootflash:/m9500-sf2ek9-kickstart-mz.5.2.1.bin for boot variable
"kickstart".
 -- SUCCESS

Verifying image bootflash:/m9500-sf2ek9-mz.5.2.1.bin for boot variable "system".
 -- SUCCESS

Verifying image type.
 -- SUCCESS

Extracting "slc2" version from image bootflash:/m9500-sf2ek9-mz.5.2.1.bin.
 -- SUCCESS

Extracting "bios" version from image bootflash:/m9500-sf2ek9-mz.5.2.1.bin.
 -- SUCCESS

Extracting "slc2" version from image bootflash:/m9500-sf2ek9-mz.5.2.1.bin.
 -- SUCCESS

Extracting "system" version from image bootflash:/m9500-sf2ek9-mz.5.2.1.bin.
 -- SUCCESS

Extracting "kickstart" version from image bootflash:/m9500-sf2ek9-kickstart-mz.5.2.1.bin.
 -- SUCCESS

Extracting "slc2" version from image bootflash:/m9500-sf2ek9-mz.5.2.1.bin.
 -- SUCCESS

Extracting "18_4" version from image bootflash:/m9500-sf2ek9-mz.5.2.1.bin.
 -- SUCCESS

Extracting "ssi" version from image bootflash:/m9500-sf2ek9-mz.5.2.1.bin.
 -- SUCCESS

Performing Compact Flash and TCAM sanity test.
 -- SUCCESS

Performing module support checks.
 -- SUCCESS

Notifying services about system upgrade.
 -- SUCCESS
```

```
Compatibility check is done:
Module  bootable         Impact  Install-type  Reason
------  --------  --------------  ------------  ------
     1       yes  non-disruptive          none
     4       yes  non-disruptive          none
     5       yes  non-disruptive          none
     6       yes  non-disruptive          none
     7       yes  non-disruptive     copy-only


Other miscellaneous information for installation:
Module  info
------  ----------------------------------
     7  FC ports 1-18 are hitless, GigE 1-4 are hitful, and Intelligent Applications
running are hitful


Images will be upgraded according to following table:
Module       Image            Running-Version(pri:alt)  New-Version  Upg-Required
------  ----------  ---------------------------------------  --------------------  --
     1        slc2                                  5.2(1)                5.2(1) no
     1        bios  v1.0.19(02/01/10): v1.0.19(02/01/10)     v1.0.19(02/01/10) no
     4        slc2                                  5.2(1)                5.2(1) no
     4        bios  v1.0.19(02/01/10): v1.0.19(02/01/10)     v1.0.19(02/01/10) no
     5      system                                  5.2(1)                5.2(1) no
     5    kickstart                                 5.2(1)                5.2(1) no
     5        bios  v1.0.10(01/08/09): v1.0.10(01/08/09)     v1.0.10(01/08/09) no
     6      system                                  5.2(1)                5.2(1) no
     6    kickstart                                 5.2(1)                5.2(1) no
     6        bios  v1.0.10(01/08/09): v1.0.10(01/08/09)     v1.0.10(01/08/09) no
     7        slc2                                  5.2(1)                5.2(1) no
     7        18_4                                  5.2(1)                5.2(1) no
     7         ssi                                  5.2(1)                5.2(1) no
     7        bios  v1.0.16(10/23/08): v1.0.16(10/23/08)     v1.0.19(02/01/10) yes

Do you want to continue with the installation (y/n)?  [n] y

Install is in progress, please wait.

Performing runtime checks.
 -- SUCCESS

Syncing image bootflash:/m9500-sf2ek9-kickstart-mz.5.2.1.bin to standby.
 -- SUCCESS

Syncing image bootflash:/m9500-sf2ek9-mz.5.2.1.bin to standby.
 -- SUCCESS

Setting boot variables.
 -- SUCCESS

Performing configuration copy.
 -- SUCCESS

Module 1: Refreshing compact flash and upgrading bios/loader/bootrom.
Warning: please do not remove or power off the module at this time.
 -- SUCCESS

Module 4: Refreshing compact flash and upgrading bios/loader/bootrom.
Warning: please do not remove or power off the module at this time.
 -- SUCCESS

Module 5: Refreshing compact flash and upgrading bios/loader/bootrom.
Warning: please do not remove or power off the module at this time.
```

```
-- SUCCESS

Module 6: Refreshing compact flash and upgrading bios/loader/bootrom.
Warning: please do not remove or power off the module at this time.
 -- SUCCESS

Module 7: Refreshing compact flash and upgrading bios/loader/bootrom.
Warning: please do not remove or power off the module at this time.
 -- SUCCESS

Module 6: Waiting for module online.
 -- SUCCESS

Notifying services about the switchover.
 -- SUCCESS

"Switching over onto standby".
```

Step 2 To watch the progress of the installation from the new active supervisor, reconnect to the switch and use the **show install all status** command.

```
MDS-9513-1# show install all status
There is an on-going installation...
Enter Ctrl-C to go back to the prompt.

Continue on installation process, please wait.
The login will be disabled until the installation is completed.
Trying to start the installer...

Module 5: Waiting for module online.
 -- SUCCESS

Module 1: Non-disruptive upgrading.
 -- SUCCESS
```

Note The installation continues first with the new standby, and then with the modules. If any module fails to upgrade, the entire process stops. You should then contact your next level of support.

Downgrading Firmware with the CLI

Before downgrading firmware, you must turn off or disable any features that are not supported by the older version (see Steps 1-3). Failure to do so can disrupt the downgrade.

To downgrade firmware on the switch from the CLI, follow these steps:

Step 1 Verify there are no features enabled that are not supported in the lower level firmware using the **show incompatibility** command. Always run this command before a downgrade, even if no incompatible features were explicitly enabled.

Caution Failure to disable the features listed in the incompatibility check, can result in a disruptive firmware downgrade.

For example, when downgrading from NX-OS 5.2(1) to 5.0(7), you see the following exception because FCoE is not supported in NX-OS 5.0(7):

```
MDS-9513-1# show incompatibility system bootflash:m9500-sf2ek9-mz.5.0.7.bin
The following configurations on active are incompatible with  the system image
1) Service : feature-mgr , Capability : CAP_FEATURE_SET_FCOE_NEW
Description : feature-set fcoe is installed or enabled in the system
Capability requirement : STRICT

Disable command : All FCoE cards must be powered down with "poweroff module <n>"
 and then use "no feature-set fcoe" to disable and  "no install feature-set fcoe" to
uninstall the feature-set
```

Step 2   Disable unsupported features using the configuration commands:

```
MDS-9513-1# conf t
Enter configuration commands, one per line.  End with CNTL/Z.
MDS-9513-1(config)# poweroff module 13
```

Step 3   Rerun the incompatibility check to verify that all unsupported features are gone:

```
MDS-9513-1# show incompatibility system bootflash:m9500-sf2ek9-mz.5.0.7.bin
No incompatible configurations
```

Step 4   Proceed with the downgrade using the **install all** command as described in Upgrading Firmware with the CLI, page 1-26.

Upgrading Firmware with DCNM-SAN

To upgrade the firmware of one or more MDS switches with DCNM-SAN, follow these steps:

Step 1   Click the **Software Install Wizard** from the tool bar in DCNM-SAN.

Figure 1-8   *DCNM-SAN Software Wizard*

Step 2   Select the switches to upgrade and click **Next** (see Figure 1-9).

Figure 1-9   *Select Switches to Upgrade*

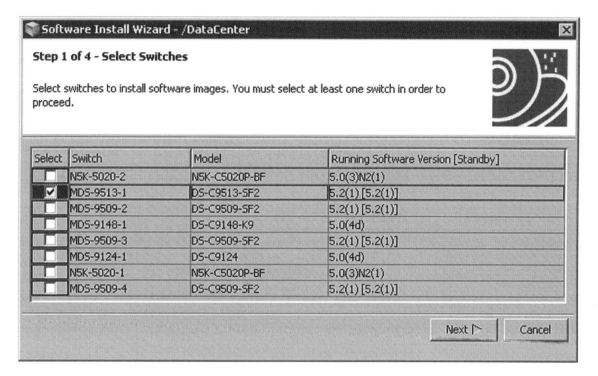

Step 3   Specify the location of the firmware images (see Figure 1-10).

   a.   Provide the file information to transfer the file from the server to the switch. If the files are to be downloaded during the install, provide the path and filename of the images as well.

   a.   Select **Skip Image Download** to upgrade using images already located on the supervisor's boot flash.

Figure 1-10   *Specify Firmware Images*

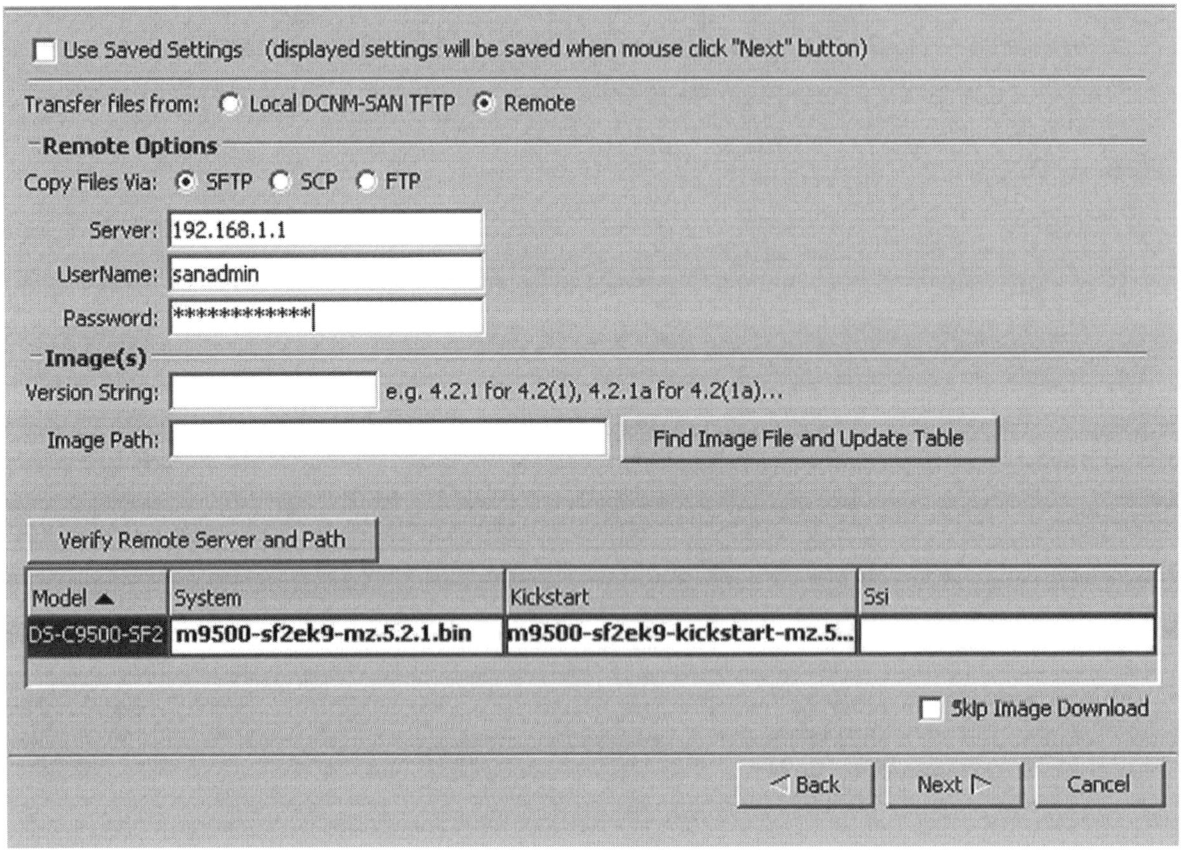

Step 4   Click **Next**.

Depending on the installation method (already downloaded to bootflash, or download during the install), the wizard may ask for additional file locations. The fourth and final screen provides a summary and lets you start the actual installation.

During installation, a compatibility screen popup displays the same version compatibility information that was displayed during the CLI upgrade. Click **Yes** to continue with the upgrade.

Note   Unlike a CLI upgrade, DCNM-SAN maintains a connection to the switch and provides detailed upgrade information. You do not have to manually reestablish connectivity to the switch during the supervisor switchover. If there is a failure, the last screen displays the reasons for a failed upgrade.

Password Recovery

If an admin password is lost and there are no other accounts on the switch with either network-admin or user account creation privileges, you need to recover the password for the admin account.

Caution   This procedure requires console access to the switch and requires a reboot of the switch.

Best Practice   Another CLI user with network-admin privileges can change the password of the admin user without reloading the switch.

To recover the admin password on the switch, follow these steps:

Step 1   Connect a console cable to the active supervisor of the MDS switch:

Figure 1-11   *Console Connection on 9500 and 9200 Series MDS switches*

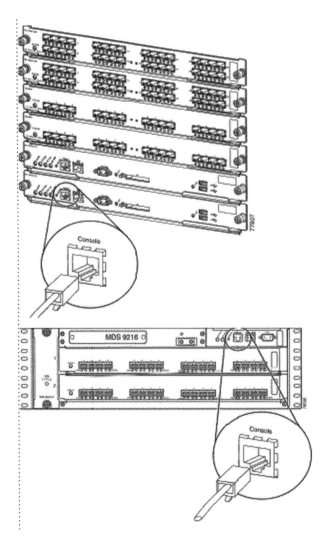

Step 2   Attach the RS-232 end of the console cable to a PC.

Step 3   Configure HyperTerm, putty or similar terminal emulation software for 9600 baud, 8 data bits, no parity, 1 stop bit, and no flow control.

Step 4   Establish a connection to the switch so a login prompt is displayed to verify console and terminal settings.

Step 5   For a multi-supervisor switch, MDS-9509 switch, or MDS-9513 switch, physically remove the standby supervisor. It is not necessary to remove it from the chassis, just loosen it until it does not make contact with the backplane.

Step 6   Reboot the switch either by cycling the power or entering the **reload** command from the PC hyper terminal.

Step 7   Press the **Ctrl**-] key sequence (when the switch begins its NX-OS software boot sequence) to switch to the switch(boot)# prompt.

Step 8   Enter configuration mode.

```
switch(boot)# config terminal
```

Step 9   Issue the **admin-password** *new password* command.

```
switch(boot-config)# admin-password temppassword
```

```
switch(boot-config)# exit
```

Step 10   Load the system image to finish the boot sequence.

```
switch(boot)# load bootflash: m9500-sf2ek9-mz.5.2.1.bin
```

Step 11   Log on to the switch using the admin account and the temporary password.

```
login as: admin
Password:
Cisco Nexus Operating System (NX-OS) Software
TAC support: http://www.cisco.com/tac
Copyright (c) 2002-2011, Cisco Systems, Inc. All rights reserved.
The copyrights to certain works contained in this software are
owned by other third parties and used and distributed under
license. Certain components of this software are licensed under
the GNU General Public License (GPL) version 2.0 or the GNU
Lesser General Public License (LGPL) Version 2.1. A copy of each
such license is available at
http://www.opensource.org/licenses/gpl-2.0.php and
http://www.opensource.org/licenses/lgpl-2.1.php

MDS-9513-1#
```

Step 12   Change the admin password to a new permanent password.

```
MDS-9513-1# config terminal
Enter configuration commands, one per line.  End with CNTL/Z.
MDS-9513-1(config)# username admin password g05ox
```

Step 13   Save the configuration that includes the new password.

```
MDS-9513-1# copy running-config startup-config
[#########################################] 100%
```

Installing a License

To run certain licensable features on an MDS 9000 Family switch, a license key is required after 120 days. The 120-day grace period allows you to try out new features or resume operation if a replacement chassis needs a license key installed.

Caution   If a license grace period expires, all features that depend on that license are disabled even if they are currently running or in production.

You can install a license key using one of two methods, either from the CLI or using DCNM-SAN's License Installation Wizard. These examples use the scp server 192.168.1.1.

Using the CLI to Install a License

To install a license from the CLI, follow these steps:

Step 1   Copy the license file to the boot flash of the supervisor.

```
MDS-9513-1# copy scp://user1@192.168.1.1/tmp/FM_Server.lic bootflash:FM_Server.lic
user1@172.22.36.10's password:
FM_Server.lic    100% |*****************************|  2035     00:00
```

Step 2 Verify the license file with the **show license file** command.

```
MDS-9513-1 show file bootflash:FM_Server.lic
FM_Server.lic:
SERVER this_host ANY
VENDOR cisco
INCREMENT FM_SERVER_PKG cisco 1.0 permanent uncounted \
       VENDOR_STRING=MDS HOSTID=VDH=FOX0313532X \
       NOTICE="<LicFileID>lic_template</LicFileID><LicLineID>0</LicLineID> \
        <PAK>dummyPak</PAK>" SIGN=D8EF17EA26D2
```

Step 3 Cross-reference the switch's host ID (VDH=FOX0713037X) with the one listed in the license file.

```
MDS-9513-1# show license host-id
License hostid: VDH=FOX0313532X
```

Step 4 Install the license file.

```
MDS-9513-1# install license bootflash:FM_Server.lic
Installing license ..done
```

Step 5 Verify that the license has been installed with the **show license** command.

```
MDS-9513-1# show license
FM_Server.lic:
SERVER this_host ANY
VENDOR cisco
INCREMENT FM_SERVER_PKG cisco 1.0 permanent uncounted \
       VENDOR_STRING=MDS HOSTID=VDH=FOX0713037X \
       NOTICE="<LicFileID>lic_template</LicFileID><LicLineID>0</LicLineID> \
        <PAK>dummyPak</PAK>" SIGN=D8CF07EA26C2
```

To display a summary of the installed licenses, use the **show license usage** command:

```
MDS-9513-1# show license usage
Feature                        Ins  Lic   Status Expiry Date Comments
                                    Count
--------------------------------------------------------------------------------
IOA_184                        No    0    Unused              -
XRC_ACCL                       No    -    Unused              -
IOA_SSN16                      No    0    Unused              -
DMM_184_PKG                    No    0    Unused              -
FM_SERVER_PKG                  Yes   -    Unused never        -
MAINFRAME_PKG                  Yes   -    Unused never        -
ENTERPRISE_PKG                 Yes   -    In use never        -
DMM_FOR_SSM_PKG                Yes   1    Unused never        -
SAN_EXTN_OVER_IP               Yes   1    Unused never        -
SME_FOR_SSN16_PKG              No    0    Unused              -
PORT_ACTIVATION_PKG            No    0    Unused              -
SME_FOR_IPS_184_PKG            No    0    Unused              -
STORAGE_SERVICES_184           No    0    Unused              -
SAN_EXTN_OVER_IP_18_4          No    0    Unused              -
SAN_EXTN_OVER_IP_IPS2          Yes   4    Unused never        -
SAN_EXTN_OVER_IP_IPS4          Yes   4    Unused never        -
SAN_EXTN_OVER_IP_SSN16         No    0    Unused              -
STORAGE_SERVICES_SSN16         No    0    Unused              -
10G_PORT_ACTIVATION_PKG        No    0    Unused              -
STORAGE_SERVICES_ENABLER_PKG   Yes   4    Unused never        -
--------------------------------------------------------------------------------
```

To determine which features within a license package are being used, specify the package name. In this case, QoS is using the Enterprise package:

```
MDS-9513-1# show license usage ENTERPRISE_PKG
Application
-----------
Qos Manager
-----------
```

Using DCNM-SAN to Install a License

To install the licenses with the DCNM-SAN License Wizard, follow these steps:

Step 1   Click the **License Install** icon shown in Figure 1-12 to launch the License Installation Wizard.

Figure 1-12   Launching the License Installation Wizard

Step 2   Indicate whether you already have license key files or if you have only a Product Authorization Key (PAK) at this time. If you already have the files, you will be asked to indicate their location. If you have a PAK, then the license files will be downloaded and installed from Cisco's website. Click **Next**.

Figure 1-13   Choose License Installation Method

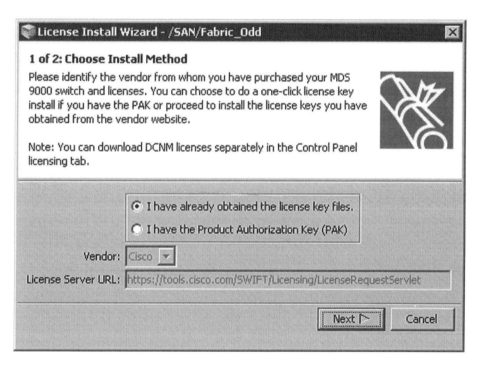

a.   If you indicated that you have the license key files, then you are asked to specify the name and location of the license key files, in Figure 1-14.

Figure 1-14   License File Location

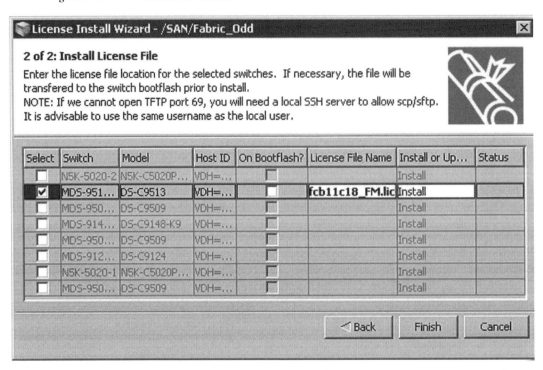

b. If you indicated that you have only the PAK numbers, DCNM-SAN will obtain the license files directly
    from Cisco.com. When you see the screen shown in Figure 1-15, provide your PAK.

Figure 1-15   Install License Using PAK

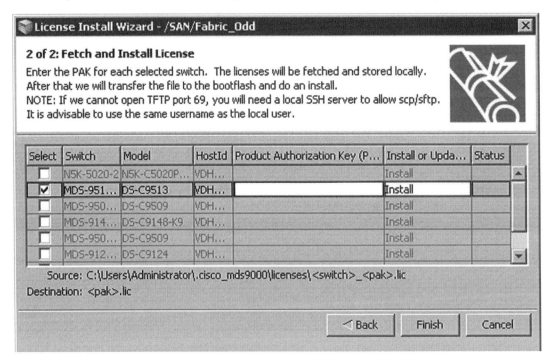

Step 3   Click **Finish** to complete license installation.

Which Feature Enables the License Grace Period?

When you enable a feature that is licensed but not covered by your current license, you receive a syslog message, an e-mail or other warnings that the feature, such as DCNM-SAN Server, has entered its grace period. To determine what features have enabled a specific license, use either the CLI or DCNM-SAN.

Check License Usage With DCNM-SAN

In the Physical Attributes Pane, click **Switches** then **Licenses** to see which feature triggered the warning. In the resulting middle pane, click the **Usage** tab. See Figure 1-16.

Figure 1-16   License Usage

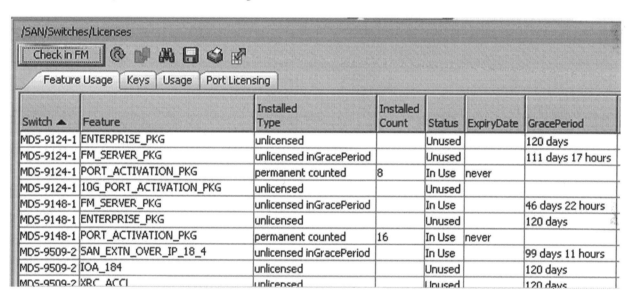

Switch ▲	Feature	Installed Type	Installed Count	Status	ExpiryDate	GracePeriod
MDS-9124-1	ENTERPRISE_PKG	unlicensed		Unused		120 days
MDS-9124-1	FM_SERVER_PKG	unlicensed inGracePeriod		Unused		111 days 17 hours
MDS-9124-1	PORT_ACTIVATION_PKG	permanent counted	8	In Use	never	
MDS-9124-1	10G_PORT_ACTIVATION_PKG	unlicensed		Unused		
MDS-9148-1	FM_SERVER_PKG	unlicensed inGracePeriod		In Use		46 days 22 hours
MDS-9148-1	ENTERPRISE_PKG	unlicensed		Unused		120 days
MDS-9148-1	PORT_ACTIVATION_PKG	permanent counted	16	In Use	never	
MDS-9509-2	SAN_EXTN_OVER_IP_18_4	unlicensed inGracePeriod		In Use		99 days 11 hours
MDS-9509-2	IOA_184	unlicensed		Unused		120 days
MDS-9509-2	XRC_ACCL	unlicensed		Unused		120 days

How to Check License Usage with the CLI

With the CLI, use the **show license usage** *license name* command to see which feature triggered the warning.

```
switch1# show license usage ENTERPRISE_PKG
Application
-----------
IP Security
-----------
```

Once the feature that is in grace period has been identified, either disable it or install a new license.

Copying Core Files from the Switch

If a switch process crashes, it may create a core file to send to Cisco TAC for further troubleshooting. This procedure explains how to retrieve this core file from the MDS switch.

The resource used in this procedure is FTP server: 192.168.1.1

Note   Use any of the possible methods to copy, including FTP, TFTP, SFTP, and SCP.

To copy a core file from an MDS switch, follow these steps:

Step 1   Before copying a core file to another server, identify the PID of the core file with the **show cores** command.

```
MDS-9513-1 show cores
Module-num Process-name PID Core-create-time
---------- ------------ --- ----------------
5          fspf         1524    Sep 27 03:11
```

Step 2   Copy the core file (this example uses FTP) with the **copy core** command.

core://<module-number>/<process-id>

```
MDS-9513-1# copy core://5/1524 ftp://192.168.1.1/tmp/fspfcore
```

Step 3   Send the file to the support engineer as per their instructions

Restoring a Fixed Switch Configuration

This procedure describes backing up and restoring a switch configuration for one of the MDS 9000 Family fixed configuration switches, such as a 9100 or 9200 series switch.

Caution   Parts of this procedure are disruptive and should only be done during an emergency, such as the chassis or fixed supervisor needing replacement.

This procedure uses the following resources:

- Old switch: MDS-9148-1
- File server: 192.168.1.1

Note   Restore a switch configuration only to a switch with the same firmware version used to create the switch configuration. If an upgrade is required, first restore the configuration then upgrade the firmware.

To restore a switch configuration, follow these steps:

Step 1   Save the running configuration with the **copy running-config** command.

```
MDS-9148-1# copy running-config startup-config
[#####################################] 100%
```

Step 2 Copy the start up-configuration to the file server using any of the available methods on the switch (FTP, TFTP, SFTP, SCP).

```
MDS-9148-1# copy startup-config scp://user@192.168.1.1/MDS-9148-1_old.config
user@192.168.1.1's password:
sysmgr_system.cfg    100% |*****************************| 10938        00:00
MDS-9148-1#
```

Step 3 Capture the port assignments using the FLOGI database. This will be used to verify that all the cables are placed in their correct locations.

```
MDS-9148-1# show flogi database
--------------------------------------------------------------------------
INTERFACE  VSAN   FCID        PORT NAME               NODE NAME
--------------------------------------------------------------------------
fc1/8      600    0x7c0007    50:05:07:63:00:ce:a2:27  50:05:07:63:00:c0:a2:27
fc1/13     1001   0xef0001    50:06:0e:80:03:4e:95:13  50:06:0e:80:03:4e:95:13
fc1/15     600    0x7c0004    50:06:0b:00:00:13:37:ae  50:06:0b:00:00:13:37:af
```

Note At this point the old switch is no longer needed, so you can disconnect its mgmt0 port from the LAN.

Step 4 Log on to the new switch using the console connection and clear the switch configuration. Do not run the setup script, if prompted. The **write erase** command erases the switch's configuration.

```
MDS-9148-1 write erase
Warning: This command will erase the startup-configuration.
Do you wish to proceed anyway? (y/n)  [n] y
```

Step 5 Reload the switch.

```
MDS-9148-1 reload
This command will reboot the system. (y/n)?  [n] y
```

Step 6 The switch comes up in factory default mode and prompts for basic system configuration. You can ignore the prompt by pressing CRL+Z, because all the configuration options are contained in the old switch's start up configuration. Manually configure the IP address.

```
switch# config terminal
Enter configuration commands, one per line.  End with CNTL/Z.
switch(config)# int mgmt 0
switch(config-if)# ip address 172.22.36.8 255.255.254.0
switch(config-if)# no shut
```

Step 7 If interface (fc X/Y)-based zoning was done, obtain the WWN of the new switch with the **show wwn switch** command. Otherwise, skip this step.

```
switch# show wwn switch
Switch WWN is 20:00:00:0d:ec:02:1d:40
```

Step 8 On the file server, make a copy of the configuration file, then open the copy in a text editor such as vi (or emacs). Make these changes:

a. Remove the lines that contain the SNMP user accounts, as the encrypted passwords are tied to the MAC address of the chassis.:

```
$ cp switch1.config switch1.config.orig
$ vi switch1.config
```

The user accounts are all grouped together and begin with **snmp-server user** command.

```
snmp-server user admin network-admin auth md5 0x46694cac2585d39d3bc00c8a4c7d48a6
 localizedkey
snmp-server user guestadmin network-admin auth md5 0xcae40d254218747bc57ee1df348
```

26b51 localizedkey

b. If interface (fc X/Y)-based zoning was done, replace the WWN of the old switch in the zone member commands with the WWN of the new switch. Otherwise, skip this step.

zone name Z_1 vsan 9
  member interface fc1/9 swwn **20:00:00:0d:ec:02:1d:40**

c. If IVR was configured on this switch, the IVR topology will need to be modified as that is based upon the sWWN and the old sWWN should be replaced with the new sWWN.

ivr vsan-topology database
  autonomous-fabric-id   1 switch-wwn **20:00:00:0d:ec:02:1d:40** vsan-ranges 500,3002
  autonomous-fabric-id   1 switch-wwn 20:00:00:0c:85:e9:d2:c0 vsan-ranges 500,3000

Note   If there are multiple IVR-enabled switches in the fabric, the sWWN from the old switch should be removed from ALL of the IVR topologies in the fabric and replaced with the new sWWN. This step should be done before bringing the new switch online. These modifications can be done on the other switches using either the CLI or DCNM-SAN.

d. Save and exit the configuration file.

Step 9   From the new switch, copy the modified config file from the file server to the running configuration of the new switch. As the file is copied, it is executed and the configuration is applied. The commands being applied are displayed in single quotes. Any errors resulting from the commands are displayed immediately after the command that caused it. When finished, the prompt changes to reflect the new switch name.

```
switch# copy scp://user@192.168.1.1/MDS-9148-1_old.config running-config
user@192.168.1.1's password:
switch1.config   100% |*****************************| 10938          00:00
MDS-9148-1#
```

Step 10   Save the configuration by copying the startup configuration to the running configuration.

```
MDS-9148-1# copy running-config startup-config
[#######################################] 100%:
```

Step 11   The switch can now be accessed with the CLI. Complete the configuration restoration:

a. Recreate SNMP user accounts.

b. If the switch is accessed with SSH, remove the MDS switch entry from the host's known_hosts file because the switch's public key has changed.

c. Install any required license keys.

Step 12   Move the cables from the old switch to the new switch, using the **show flogi database** command output on the old switch as a reference to verify that each cable is in the correct location.

Step 13   Verify that all devices have logged in and all features are running is as they are supposed to be and save the running configuration to the start up configuration with the **copy running-config startup-config** command.

Step 14   Reload the switch to verify that it boots correctly with the configuration.

Configuring an NTP Server

Network Time Protocol (NTP) is a protocol used by devices to synchronize their internal clocks with other devices. The switch can only be used as an NTP client and can talk to other NTP systems with a higher stratum (or authority). NTP is hierarchical in nature, so that lower stratum numbers are closer to the source of the time authority. Devices that are at the same stratum can be configured as peers so that they work together to determine the correct time by making minute adjustments. Normally, MDS switches are configured as peers, while a router or other dedicated machine is configured as an NTP server.

Configuring NTP with CFS

CFS (see "Cisco Fabric Services, page 1-13") lets you perform a single configuration for NTP and have it propagated to other switches. Also, if a new switch comes online it can be set to inherit the NTP configuration from the existing switches. The new switch merges its configuration (no configuration) with the existing NTP CFS configuration and the result is that the new switch has an NTP configuration.

NTP does not set the time zone (or offset from UTC) for the switch; it must be set manually, as follows. This example uses Eastern Standard Time and Eastern Daylight-Savings Time:

```
switch(config)# clock timezone EST -5.0
switch(config)# clock summer-time EDT 2 Sunday Mar 02:00 1 Sunday Nov 02:00 60
```

ıılııılıı

Best Practice   If your fabric spans multiple sites, each with their own NTP server, use CFS regions to provide isolation between the sites otherwise all the MDS switches will end up using the same NTP servers.

For this example, these resources are used:

- MDS-9513-1's IP address: 192.168.1.1
- MDS-9509-2's IP address: 192.168.1.2
- NTP server: 192.168.100.1

To configure NTP for switch 1, follow these steps:

Step 1   Enter configuration mode and enable CFS distribution for NTP for switches 1 and 2.

    a. For MDS-9513-1:

```
MDS-9513-1# conf t
Enter configuration commands, one per line.  End with CNTL/Z.
MDS-9513-1(config)# ntp distribute
```

    b. For MDS-9509-2

```
MDS-9509-2# conf t
Enter configuration commands, one per line.  End with CNTL/Z.
MDS-9509-2(config)# ntp distribute
```

Note   Steps 2 through 5 can be done from configuration mode of either switch.

Step 2 Change to configuration mode with the **config t** command, and then add the NTP server to the configuration.

```
MDS-9513-1# conf t
MDS-9513-1(config)# ntp server 192.168.100.1
```

Step 3 Add the NTP peer switches to the configuration.

```
MDS-9513-1(config)# ntp peer 192.168.1.1
MDS-9513-1(config)# ntp peer 192.168.1.2
```

Step 4 Commit the NTP configuration and end configuration mode.

```
MDS-9513-1(config)# ntp commit
MDS-9513-1(config)# end
```

At this point, NTP is configured and the switch will slowly adjust to the new time.

To view the NTP configuration on the local switch, use the **show ntp peers** command.

```
switch1# show ntp peers
-------------------------------------------------
  192.168.100.1                Server (configured)
  192.168.1.1                  Peer
  192.168.1.2                  Peer
```

To view the NTP configuration on the remote switch, log onto the remote switch and use the **show ntp peers** command.:

Step 5 Save the configuration on both switches. CFS can be used to instruct both switches to save their configuration by running the **copy running-config startup-config** command. See Saving the Configuration Across the Fabric, page 1-47.

```
MDS-9513-1# copy running-config startup-config fabric
[########################################] 100%
```

Configure NTP without CFS

To configure NTP without CFS, log on to each switch in the fabric and configure NTP. This is the same procedure used in a SAN-OS environments.

Note NTP does not set the time zone (or offset from UTC) for the switch. You must set it manually. This example uses Eastern Standard Time and Eastern Daylight-Savings Time:

```
switch(config)# clock timezone EST -5.0
switch(config)# clock summer-time EDT 2 Sunday Mar 02:00 1 Sunday Nov 02:00 60
```

For this example, these resources are used:

- MDS-9513-1 IP address: 192.168.1.1
- Switch #2 IP address: 192.168.1.2
- NTP server: 192.168.100.1

To configure NTP for switch 1, follow these steps:

Step 1   Change to configuration mode with the **config t** command, and then add the NTP server.

```
MDS-9513-1# conf t
Enter configuration commands, one per line.  End with CNTL/Z.
MDS-9513-1(config)# ntp server 192.168.100.1
```

Step 2   Add the NTP peer switch, and then end configuration mode.

```
MDS-9513-1(config)# ntp peer 192.168.1.2
MDS-9513-1(config)# end
```

At this point, NTP is configured and the switch will slowly adjust to the new time.

To view the NTP configuration, use the **show ntp peers** command:

```
MDS-9513-1# show ntp peers
--------------------------------------------------
  192.168.100.1                Server (configured)
  192.168.1.2                  Peer
```

At this point NTP will slowly adjust the clock as per the NTP server. This process can be viewed with the **show ntp peer-status command**.

```
MDS-9513-1# show ntp peer-status
Total peers : 1
* - selected for sync, + -  peer mode(active),
- - peer mode(passive), = - polled in client mode
    remote              local              st   poll   reach delay
--------------------------------------------------------------------
*192.168.100.1          0.0.0.0             2    64     377   0.00145
+192.168.1.2            0.0.0.0             3    16       6   0.00029
```

What to Do Before Calling TAC

When you need to contact the Cisco TAC or an OSM for additional assistance, follow these steps: This will reduce the amount of time needed to resolve the issue.

Caution   **Do not reload the line card or switch until at least** Step 1. Some logs and counters are kept in volatile storage and will not survive a reload.

Step 1   Collect switch information and the switch configuration both before and after the issue has been resolved. These three collection methods have the same result:

- CLI method:

    - Configure the Telnet/SSH application to log the screen output to a text file and enter the **show tech-support details** command.

    - Alternatively, there are feature-specific versions of the **show tech-support details** command in the syntax, such as the **show tech-support** *feature*.

- Enter the **tac-pac** *filename* command, for example, **tac-pac bootflash://showtech.$(SWITCHNAME)**. The **tac-pac** command redirects the output of a **show tech-support details** command to a file which is gzipped. If no filename is specified, the file created is **volatile:show_tech_out.gz**.

- Copy the file from the switch using the procedure Copying Files to and from a Switch, page 1-22.

- DCNM-SAN method:

  - Choose **Tools > Health > Show tech support**. DCNM-SAN can capture switch configuration information from multiple switches simultaneously. This dialog box also provides an option to run any command on the switch, such as a feature specific version of show tech support. The file can be saved on a local PC.

- For issues with DCNM-SAN, capture the fmserver.log log file.

Step 2 Capture the exact error codes:

a. The error occurs in DCNM-SAN, take a screen shot of the error. In Windows, use **ALT+PrintScreen** to capture the active window and for the entire desktop press **PrintScreen**. Then paste this screen shot into a new **MSpaint.exe** (or similar program) session and save the file.

b. Copy the error from the message log. Display it using either the **show logging log** command, or to view the last X lines of the log, use the **show logging last #** command.

Step 3 Ensure that you have answers to the following questions before calling TAC:

1. Which switch, HBA, or storage port is having the problem? List the switch firmware, driver versions, operating systems versions, and storage device firmware.

2. What is the network topology? (From DCNM-SAN, select **Tools ->show tech** and save the map.)

3. Were you making any changes to the environment (zoning, adding line cards, upgrades) before or at the time of this event?

4. Are there other similarly configured devices that could have this problem but do not?

5. To what is the problem device connected (MDS switch Z, interface x/y)?

6. When did this problem first occur?

7. When did this problem last occur?

8. How often does this problem occur?

9. How many devices have this problem?

10. Have you examined the syslog (from the **show logging log** command) and accounting log (from the **show accounting log** command) to see if there are any relevant errors or actions that may have caused this condition?

11. Were any traces or debug outputs captured using tools such as:

    a. Fcanalyzer, PAA-2, Wireshark/Ethereal, local or remote SPAN

    b. CLI debug commands

    c. FC traceroute, FC ping

    d. DCNM-SAN/Device Manager SNMP trace

12. What troubleshooting steps have already been done?

Saving the Configuration Across the Fabric

Rather than logging on to every switch using a script or relaunching DCNM-SAN each time, save the configuration on switches in a fabric with CFS.

```
MDS-9513-1# copy running-config startup-config fabric
[########################################] 100%
```

This command takes slightly longer than a single **copy running-config startup-config** command takes.When it finishes, all the switches have saved configurations.

Device Aliases

Device aliases provide a plain text name to port world-wide name (pWWN) mapping. This one-to-one mapping technique was developed to identify devices within the switch environment by labels rather than pWWNs. The device alias can be used in areas such as zoning, QoS, IVR, and throughout DCNM-SAN java client and web client utilities. This CFS aware mapping extends to CLI output, where device aliases are used where appropriate.

Some rules for devices aliases are as follows:

- Mapping is one-to-one of pWWN to a plain text name.

- The CFS scope is physical, however it can be limited via CFS Regions.

- A device alias database is not tied to a particular VSAN so if you move an end device, such as an HBA, from one VSAN to another, the device alias still applies.

- The merging of two device alias databases produces a union of the two databases. Conflicts are not imported into the resulting database and must be manually resolved. This will not keep the non conflicting entries from being merged into the new database. The merge failure will not isolate an ISL.

- The CLI manages device aliases in a central database while DCNM-SAN manages them under their respective types (hosts and storage).

- There are two types of device aliases. Regular and enhanced device aliases.

Best Practice   Use the device alias to describe both the host name and HBA instance of the device. For example, host123_lpfc0 or SYMM7890_FA14ab are better names than just host123 or SYMM7890.Additionally, the device alias can become the basis for a DCNM-SAN Enclosure. Device aliases SYMM7890_FA14ab and SYMM7890_FA14ba would be part of the enclosure SYMM7890.

Standard Device Aliases

With standard device aliases, introduced in SAN-OS 2.0, the switch performs a world-wide name (WWN) substitution for the device alias, and then passes the WWN to the service or application that is being configured. As a result, changes to the device alias do not reflect changes in the application or service. For services that leverage device aliasing (zoning, IVR, QOS, etc.), updating the device alias with a new pWWN does not automatically propagate the new information to the services. To update those services, remove the device, update the device alias, and then add the device alias again to the service.

Enhanced Device Aliases

With Enhanced device aliases, introduced in SAN-OS 3.0, the device alias, not the WWN it represents, is passed to the application or service being configured. Therefore, changes to the device alias mapping, such as changing the WWN represented by the device alias, is immediately reflected in the application. This advantage is reflected when performing operations that would change the WWN, such as replacing server host bus adapters (HBAs). After changing the WWN that the enhanced device alias represents, you do not need to modify every application that was configured with this enhanced device alias.

Enabling enhanced mode device aliases on a SAN that already has standard device aliases configured, converts the entire device alias database. However, the fabric services or applications, since they contain pWWNs, will not be converted to using device alias as their members.

Caution   Deleting an enhanced mode device alias will remove it from the applications or services that use it. If you need to rename the device alias or replace the WWN it maps to, do not delete it.

To enable Enhanced mode device aliases, follow these steps:

Step 1   Enter configuration mode.

```
MDS-9513-1# config terminal
Enter configuration commands, one per line.  End with CNTL/Z.
```

Step 2   Enable enhanced mode device alias.

```
MDS-9513-1(config)# device-alias mode enhanced
```

Step 3   If using CFS (highly recommended), commit the change.

```
MDS-9513-1(config)# device-alias commit
```

Zone Set Output with Enhanced Device Aliases

With Enhanced mode device aliases, the device alias itself, and not the WWN it represents is stored in the zone server. For example:

```
MDS-9513-1# show zoneset active vsan 1000
zoneset name ZS_DNA vsan 1000
zone name ca-aix2_fcs1 vsan 1000
* fcid 0x7f0006 [device-alias ca-aix2_fcs1]
* fcid 0x670005 [device-alias HDS10208-CL5G]
```

Contrast this with the output from a standard device alias:

```
zone name Z_test2 vsan 1000
* fcid 0xef0005 [pwwn 50:06:0e:80:04:27:e0:46] [HDS10208-CL6G]
* fcid 0xec0100 [pwwn 50:06:0b:00:00:13:37:ae] [ca-hpux2_td1]
```

Note   It is important to notice that the zone members are a different type. With Enhanced mode device aliases, the members are of type device alias, while in the standard device alias example, the members are pWWN.

Manipulating Device Aliases with the CLI

Device aliases can be manipulated with the CLI. These recipes demonstrate the integration of the device aliases in the CLI. These procedures apply to standard device aliases or enhanced device aliases.

Displaying Device Aliases with the CLI

The CLI can display device aliases in **show** commands such as the following:

1. Display the name server

    ```
    MDS-9513-1# show fcns database vsan 1

    VSAN 1:
    --------------------------------------------------------------------------------
    FCID        TYPE  PWWN                      (VENDOR)      FC4-TYPE:FEATURE
    --------------------------------------------------------------------------------
    0x620000    N     10:00:00:00:c9:32:8b:a8   (Emulex)      scsi-fcp:init
                      [ca-sun1_lpfc0]
    0x65000a    N     10:00:00:00:c9:34:a6:3e   (Emulex)
                      [ca-aix1_fcs0]
    ```

2. Display the active zone set containing IVR and regular zones (Standard device aliases):

    ```
    MDS-9513-1# show zoneset
    zoneset name nozoneset vsan 501
      zone name IVRZ_IvrZone1 vsan 501
        pwwn 50:06:0e:80:03:4e:95:23 [HDS20117-c20-9]
        pwwn 10:00:00:00:c9:32:8b:a8 [ca-sun1_lpfc0]

      zone name ca_aix2_HDS vsan 600
        pwwn 10:00:00:00:c9:34:a5:94 [ca-aix2_fcs1]
        pwwn 50:06:0e:80:03:4e:95:23 [HDS20117-c20-8]
    ```

3. Display the flogi database:

    ```
    MDS-9513-1# show flogi database
    ---------------------------------------------------------------------------------
    INTERFACE  VSAN   FCID       PORT NAME               NODE NAME
    ---------------------------------------------------------------------------------
    fc2/5      1000   0xef0008   50:06:0e:80:03:4e:95:23  50:06:0e:80:03:4e:95:23
                                 [HDS20117-c20-9]
    ```

Creating Device Aliases with the CLI

In the following examples, the following resources are used:

*   Host: ca-aix1
*   HBA Instance: fcs0
*   PWWN: 10:00:00:00:c9:34:a6:3e

To create a device alias using the CLI, follow these steps.

Step 1 The device alias is enabled by default, so enter configuration mode, and then enter the **device-alias database** command.

```
MDS-9513-1# conf terminal
Enter configuration commands, one per line.   End with CNTL/Z.
MDS-9513-1(config)# device-alias database
MDS-9513-1(config-device-alias-db)#
```

Step 2 Create an entry for the device alias using the **device-alias name** command.

```
MDS-9513-1(config-device-alias-db)# device-alias name ca-aix1_fcs0 pwwn 10:00:00:00
c9:34:a6:3e
```

Step 3 Display the pending changes with the **show device-alias** command. The plus sign (+) means that the entry is being added to the database, while the minus sign (-) means that it will be removed from the database during CFS commit as in Step 4.

```
MDS-9513-1(config-device-alias-db)# show device-alias database pending-diff
 + device-alias name ca-aix1_fcs0 pwwn 10:00:00:00:c9:34:a6:3e
```

Step 4 Commit the changes with the **device-alias commit** command.

```
MDS-9513-1(config-device-alias-db)# device-alias commit
MDS-9513-1(config)#
```

How to Convert Fibre Channel Aliases into Device Aliases

Fibre Channel aliases in an existing MDS environment can be duplicated to device aliases by importing the FC aliases using the CLI. Only those FC aliases that are also valid device aliases will be imported. An FC alias is eligible to be imported or converted if the following conditions are true:

- The FC alias represents a pWWN.
- The FC alias represents exactly one device and not a group of devices.
- A device alias with the same name does not already exist.
- A device alias with the same pWWN does not already exist.

Note
- While the device alias database is maintained on all switches, it has a physical scope. FC aliases have a VSAN scope and may not be present or replicated to all switches if Full Zoneset Distribution is not enabled. You may have to log on to multiple switches to import all of the FC aliases.

- Importing FC aliases does not automatically update any zones based on FC aliases. The zones must be manually converted to zones based on device aliases.

- Importing FC aliases does not delete the FC aliases. The FC aliases need to be manually deleted.

In this example the following Fibre Channel aliases are imported and converted into device aliases:

```
fcalias name alias123 vsan 1

fcalias name temphost vsan 1
    pwwn 11:11:11:11:11:11:11:11

fcalias name temphost vsan 2
    pwwn 11:11:11:11:11:11:99:99
```

```
fcalias name temphost2 vsan 2
  pwwn 11:11:11:11:11:22:22:22
```

Ineligible Fibre Channel aliases are listed in VSAN 1 and 2; these Fibre Channel aliases failed to be imported.

To import and convert Fibre Channel aliases to device aliases, follow these steps:

Step 1   Enter configuration mode.

```
MDS-9513-1# conf terminal
Enter configuration commands, one per line.  End with CNTL/Z.
MDS-9513-1(config)#
```

Step 2   Import the FC aliases with the **device-alias import** command.

```
MDS-9513-1(config)# device-alias import fcalias vsan 1-2
WARNING: Some fc aliases from the specified VSAN range could not be imported due to
conflicts.
```

   a.   If a warning is displayed, check the logs to determine which FC aliases did not import:

```
MDS-9513-1(config)# show device-alias internal errors
1) Event:E_DEBUG, length:111, at 608209 usecs after Wed Sep 14 16:25:13 2005
     [109] ddas_import_fcalias(703): CONFLICT: fcalias temphost on vsan 2 has same
name as fcalias temphost on vsan 1

2) Event:E_DEBUG, length:127, at 607826 usecs after Wed Sep 14 16:25:13 2005
     [109] ddas_import_getnext_alias_resp_handler(1119): not importing alias
alias123 from vsan 1 as the number of members are not 1.
```

The error message explains that the FC alias **temphost** which is located in VSAN 2 was not imported because the name temphost already exists on VSAN 1. Also, **alias123** was not imported. Examining FC alias **alias123** determines that it is not a valid device alias because it either has no members or has multiple members. Examining the fcalias definition confirms that it has no members.

   b.   These conflicts should be resolved by deleting the FC alias **alias123** and renaming the conflicting alias **temphost**.

Note   FC aliases might be part of an existing zone, so the appropriate zone(s) should be updated accordingly.

Step 3   Display the pending device alias database to see the newly imported device aliases.

```
MDS-9513-1(config)# show device-alias database pending-diff
 + device-alias name temphost2 pwwn 11:11:11:11:11:22:22:22
```

Step 4   CFS commit the pending changes.

```
MDS-9513-1(config)# device-alias commit
```

How to Rename a Device Alias

There may come a time when the device-alias needs to be renamed from one plain text name to another. This can be easily accomplished via the CLI using the following recipe:

Old Device Alias: dcn-o-w2k3-1-even

New Device Alias: dcn-o-wn2k3-1-even2

CFS for Device Aliases: enabled

Step 1 Enter the Device Alias database

```
MDS-9513-1# conf t
Enter configuration commands, one per line.  End with CNTL/Z.
MDS-9513-1(config)# device-alias database
MDS-9513-1(config-device-alias-db)#
```

Step 2 Using the **rename** command, rename the device alias

```
MDS-9513-1(config-device-alias-db)# device-alias rename dcn-o-w2k3-1-even
dcn-o-w2k3-1-even2
```

Step 3 Display the device alias pending-diff output, to verify that it will perform the action requested. "+" means it will be added to the configuration and "-" means it will be removed from the configuration.

```
MDS-9513-1(config-device-alias-db)# show device-alias pending-diff
 - device-alias name dcn-o-w2k3-1-even pwwn 21:00:00:e0:8b:05:48:e9
 + device-alias name dcn-o-w2k3-1-even2 pwwn 21:00:00:e0:8b:05:48:e9
```

Step 4 Commit the changes

```
MDS-9513-1(config-device-alias-db)# device-alias commit
```

How to Change the PWWN mapping of a Device Alias

In some cases the pwwn that the device alias is mapped to will need to be changed. For example, if an HBA needs to be replaced. While the device alias won't need to be altered, the pwwn mapped to it will need to be. This recipe covers that procedure.

- Device Alias: dcn-o-w2k3-1-even
- Old PWWN: 21:00:00:e0:8b:05:48:e9
- New PWWN: 21:00:00:e0:8b:05:48:aa
- CFS for Device Aliases: enabled

Step 1 Enter the Device Alias database

```
MDS-9513-1# conf t
Enter configuration commands, one per line.  End with CNTL/Z.
MDS-9513-1(config)# device-alias database
MDS-9513-1(config-device-alias-db)#
```

Step 2 Using the force operator, change the pwwn mapping

```
MDS-9513-1(config-device-alias-db)# device-alias name  dcn-o-w2k3-1-even pwwn
21:00:00:e0:8b:05:48:aa force
```

Step 3 Display the device alias pending-diff database to verify that the new pwwn will be added

```
MDS-9513-1(config-device-alias-db)# show device-alias pending-diff
 < device-alias name dcn-o-w2k3-1-even pwwn 21:00:00:e0:8b:05:48:e9
 > device-alias name dcn-o-w2k3-1-even pwwn 21:00:00:e0:8b:05:48:aa
```

Step 4 CFS commit the changes

```
MDS-9513-1(config-device-alias-db)# device-alias commit
```

Device Aliases with DCNM-SAN

DCNM-SAN can leverage device aliases to provide plain text names in many locations including the map, zoning, and QoS. However, to do this, DCNM-SAN needs to be configured to use device aliases instead of FC aliases. Device aliases can be enabled either during installation or afterward. See Enabling DCNM-SAN to use Device Aliases, page 1-53. DCNM-SAN can leverage either standard or enhanced device aliases.

Best Practice   It is recommended not mix both modes of device aliases within the same fabric.

In Figure 1-17, DPVM is using device aliases to represent the pWWNs in its configuration. SYM0890-FA08BA in VSAN 1000 is easier to understand than the same description using just a pWWN. In this naming scheme the model (SYMmetrix), serial number (0890), slot (FA08) and port (BA) are all used in the name to specifically describe the device. (See Figure 1-17.)

Figure 1-17   DPVM Leveraging Device Aliases

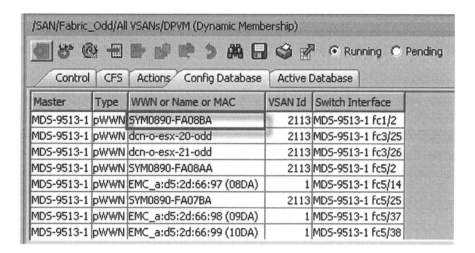

Enabling DCNM-SAN to use Device Aliases

To enable device aliases in DCNM-SAN during installation, check the **Use Global device aliases in place of FC Aliases** check box on the initial installation screen.

To enable device aliases in DCNM-SAN after installation, configure DCNM-SAN by unchecking the **Use FC Alias** check box under **Server -> Admin**.

How to Create a Device Alias for an Existing Device

Before performing any device alias procedures in DCNM-SAN, configure DCNM-SAN to use device aliases. DCNM-SAN can use device aliases to provide plain text names in many locations including the map, zoning, and QoS. However, to do this, DCNM-SAN needs to be configured to use device aliases instead of FC aliases. Device aliases can be enabled either during installation or afterward. See the "Enabling DCNM-SAN to use Device Aliases" section on page 1-53.

These resources are used in the example:

- Host: dcn-o-w2k3-1
- HBA instance: qlc0
- PWWN: 21:00:00:e0:8b:05:48:e9

To create a device alias in DCNM-SAN for a device already logged into the fabric, follow these steps:

Step 1   In DCNM-SAN's **Physical Attributes** pane, expand **End Devices.**

Step 2   Because the WWN corresponds to a host, choose **Hosts**. (For a storage device, you would choose Storage.)

Step 3   In the device alias column, enter the device alias for the corresponding pWWN.

Step 4   Click **Apply Changes**. If CFS is enabled for device-alias, this performs an implicit device-alias commit. (See Figure 1-18.)

Figure 1-18   Creating a Device Alias with DCNM-SAN

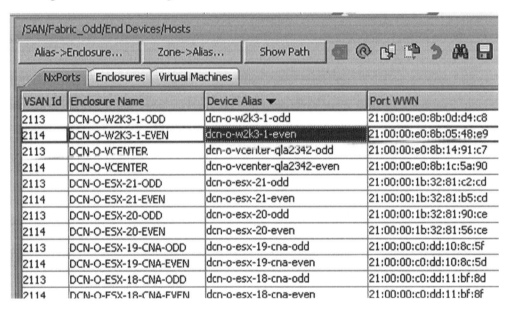

Creating a Device Alias for a New Device

This recipe creates a device alias for a device that is not logged into the switch using CFS. This recipe uses these example resources.

- Device alias HDS10208-LC5G
- Port WWN 50:06:0e:80:04:27:e0:46

To create a device alias for a device that is not logged into the switch using CFS, follow these steps:

Step 1   In the Physical Attributes pane, expand **End Devices** (see Figure 1-19).

Step 2   Choose **Device Alias** (see Figure 1-19).

Step 3   Choose the **Configuration** tab (see Figure 1-19).

Figure 1-19   Creating a New Device Alias

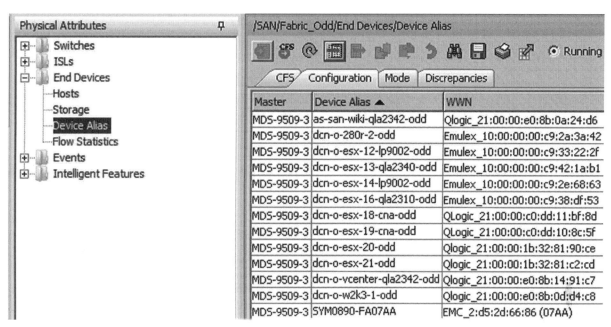

Step 4   Click **Create Row...**

Step 5   Enter the device alias and WWN in the corresponding fields.

Step 6   Click **Create**.

Step 7   When all device aliases have been created, click **Close**.

Step 8   Click **Apply Changes**.

Step 9   If CFS is enabled click **Commit CFS Pending Changes**.

Automating Switch Configuration Backups

In addition to the CLI scheduler-based recipe provided in "Automated Switch Configuration Backup" section on page 1-20, one can also leverage DCNM to backup the switch configuration via the web interface.

The prerequisite to set up switch configuration backup from the DCNM web interface requires a Secure FTP (sftpd) server to be installed on DCNM server. There are many sftpd software packages available. Install the Secure FTP server on the DCNM server and configure a user name and password that will be used to back up the configuration on the switches in the fabric.

The configuration can be backed up at regular intervals and will be backed up into the DCNM database. The DCNM interface supports various functions like viewing the current config configuration, view differences between versions of the configurations backed up and apply one the backed up configuration back to the switch can be performed.

Note   This feature requires a DCNM SAN server license for all the SAN switches in the fabric. Switches that do not have DCNM SAN license will not be backed up.

The recipe below details the steps to automate the daily backup of all the switches in the selected fabric.

Step 1   Log on to the Web interface of the DCNM server. This is done by accessing the server name to its IP address in a web browser.

Step 2   From the Admin drop down (Highlighted in red) select "SFTP Credentials" highlighted in blue in Figure 1-20.

Figure 1-20   Select SFTP credential setup from Admin drop down

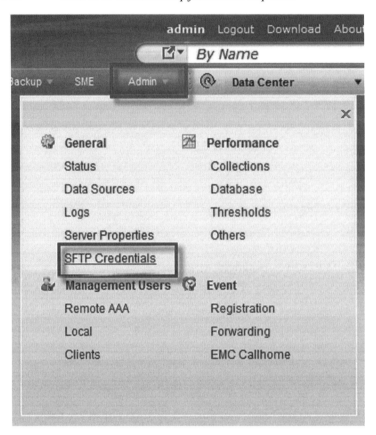

Step 3   Enter the sftp user name and password created when configuring the sftpd server on the DCNM server. The required fields are shown in Figure 1-21. Ensure that you have configured a valid root directory for the sftpd server on the DCNM server. Click verify and apply button highlighted with a red box in Figure 1-21. Upon successfully verifying and applying the above credentials a success popup is displayed.

Best Practice   Ensure that the steps 1 thru 3 are successfully completed before automated switch configuration backup can be configured from DCNM's web interface.

Figure 1-21   Enter sftpd credentials in the DCNM web form

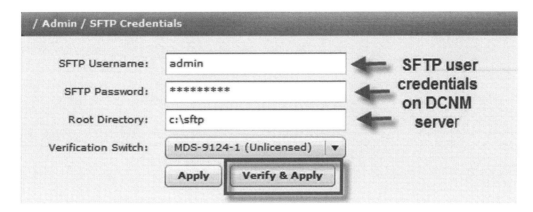

Step 4   Select Backup --> Create from the DCNM Wen Interface. This is shown in Figure 1-22.

Figure 1-22   Backup Job Create drop down

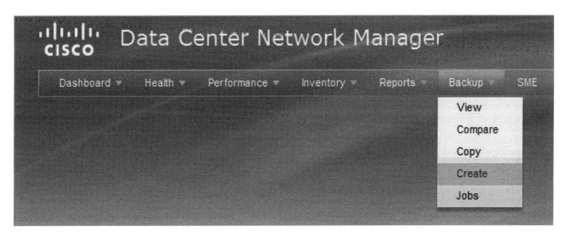

Step 5   In the resulting dialog box select the schedule, the time of backup and the duration of the schedule and then click create. Also the running or the startup configuration of the switches can be backed up. In this example it is configured to perform daily backups for a year daily at 4: 20 pm. The startup configuration is backed up in this recipe. The form is as shown in Figure 1-23. Click create to create the job. This results in a results popup dialogue as seen in Figure 1-24.

Figure 1-23   Backup Job details

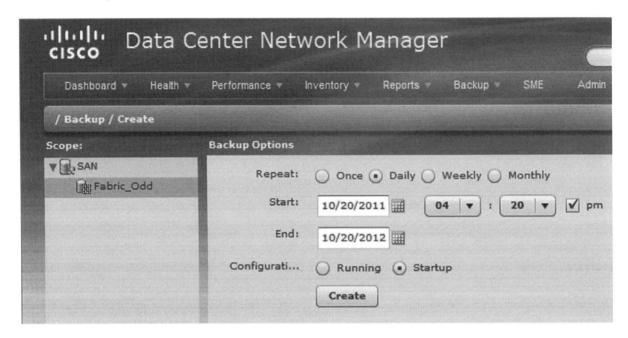

Figure 1-24   Backup job create result

Now the backup job is successfully created and will run every day at 4:20 pm for a year.

Step 6   The backed up configuration files can be viewed by selecting Backup -->View as shown in Figure 1-25

Figure 1-25   View backed up files select

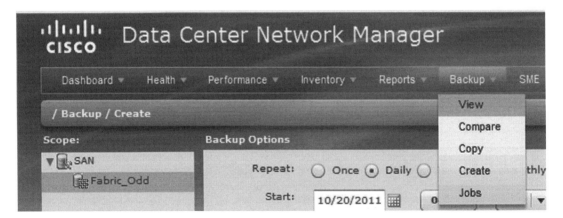

Step 7   In the resulting Backup/View mode Select a fabric in **Scope**--> Select a switch under **Switch** --> Select a configuration file and use the **View, Delete** and other button to perform various configuration file house keeping details. This is shown in Figure 1-26 below.

Figure 1-26   *Select configuration file to manage*

CHAPTER 2

Security and Access Management

Due to the criticality of the role of the Storage Area Network (SAN), care must be taken to prevent end devices from accessing each other's storage. However, switch security itself is often overlooked, such that in many environments default usernames and passwords are used or all storage administrators use the same user account to perform their tasks, which makes it impossible to create an accounting log of who did what task and at what time.

Switches are no different from servers in that they must adhere to an Authentication, Authorization, and Accounting (AAA) policy. This AAA policy can be further defined as:

- **Authentication:** Is this user allowed to access a resource?

- **Authorization:** What level of rights or privileges does the user have?

- **Accounting:** The user's activity on the resource is logged.

An MDS/Nexus switch should be a self-defending resource, such that it must be able to prevent access from unauthorized users and allow authorized users to make configuration changes that their role permits. With the critical role of the SAN in the larger picture of the data center, small SAN mistakes can lead to much larger impacting events.

Within an organization, there are many different roles that work with the SAN. While some just monitor it from within a Network Operations Center (NOC) and do not make changes, others perform the daily routine of enabling servers to access their storage with zones, while still others may be creating VSANs when a new switch is deployed. It is important to identify these different roles required within an organization and create a security policy, that enables a user to have enough privileges on an MDS/Nexus switch to perform their job. For example, an engineer within the NOC should be assigned read-only access to an MDS switch, because their job does not require making configuration changes.

Identifying and using the right features and functionality of the MDS/Nexus switch in creating a secure deployment within your environment can significantly increase uptime.

This chapter contains recipes dealing with managing users, security and access levels within NX-OS.

NX-OS based switches do not have an existing or default admin password. One needs to be chosen the first time the switch is booted. NX-OS enforces strong passwords with the following restrictions:

- At least eight characters long

- Not too many consecutive characters

- Not too many repeated characters

- No easily-guessed dictionary words

Best Practice   Use the admin account only during initial setup. After setup, create other user accounts. Each administrator should have their own individual account. Grant users the minimum rights or abilities needed for their job function. Implementing TACACS+ (see Configuring TACACS+ with Cisco SecureACS 4, page 2-8) eliminates the need for password recovery on the switch.

Creating a User Role

Roles provide a container for rights, privileges or abilities. These abilities are called rules, and so a role contains multiple rules. By default, the MDS switch has two default roles: network-admin and network-operator. Network-admin has write privileges to all parts of the switch, while network-operator has read-only access to the switch. The Nexus 7000 platform has three defined roles: network-admin, network-operator and vdc-admin, The network-admin and the network-operator roles are similar to that of the MDS platform in that it provides either global read/write access (network-admin) or global read-only access (network-operator). The vdc-admin enables read/write privileges within a specific Virtual Device Context (VDC) on this platform. For more information on VDC refer to the section in Chapter 9, "Configuring a Storage VDC on Nexus 7K to support FCoE". Later, you may want to create a user with write access to only specific areas of the switch (see the example in the "Creating a Role with Device Manager" section on page 2-2).

The MDS switch has two predefined roles:

- **Network-admin** is the role assigned to an administrator. A network-admin can perform any modification to an MDS switch. There are no restrictions on this user.

- **Network-operator** is a read-only role. A network operator cannot make modifications to the switch.

Best Practice   Provide each user with a role that provides them with the minimum abilities needed. Use the network-operator role for users who do not need to modify the switch. VSAN- based roles allow administrators to have complete control over their VSANs while having read-only or no access to other VSANs.

Creating a Role with Device Manager

This example shows how to create a role with the ability to modify only the zoning configuration on the switch. To create this role, follow these steps:

Step 1   In DCNM-SAN, enable role distribution for all switches in the fabric. In the **Physical Attributes** pane, by choose **Switches > Security > Users and Roles** (see Figure 2-1). In the Feature Admin column, change the cells to **enable**, and then click **Apply**. For the rest of this procedure, DCNM-SAN is no longer needed.

Figure 2-1   *Enabling CFS Distribution for Roles*

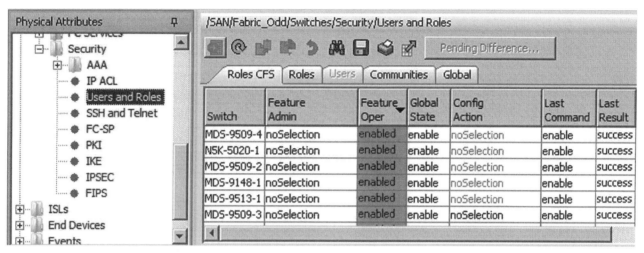

Step 2   Open Device Manager (DM) from any of the switches that are enabled for Cisco Fabric Services (CFS) distribution of roles.

Step 3   Choose **Security** >**Roles**. You see the screen in Figure 2-2.

Step 4   When Device Manager informs you that CFS is enabled, click **Continue**.

Figure 2-2   *Initial Roles Screen*

Name	Description	VSAN Scope Enable	VSAN Scope List
priv-0	This is a system defined privilege role.	☐	
priv-1	This is a system defined privilege role.	☐	
priv-2	This is a system defined privilege role.	☐	
priv-3	This is a system defined privilege role.	☐	
priv-4	This is a system defined privilege role.	☐	
priv-5	This is a system defined privilege role.	☐	
priv-6	This is a system defined privilege role.	☐	
priv-7	This is a system defined privilege role.	☐	
priv-8	This is a system defined privilege role.	☐	
priv-9	This is a system defined privilege role.	☐	
priv-10	This is a system defined privilege role.	☐	
priv-11	This is a system defined privilege role.	☐	
priv-12	This is a system defined privilege role.	☐	
priv-13	This is a system defined privilege role.	☐	
priv-14	This is a system defined privilege role.	☐	
priv-15	This is a system defined privilege role.	☐	
default-role	This is a system defined role and applies to all users.	☐	

| Rules... | CFS ▼ | Create... | Delete | Apply | Refresh | Help | Close |

17 row(s)

Step 5   Click **Create**.

Figure 2-3   *Create Common Roles*

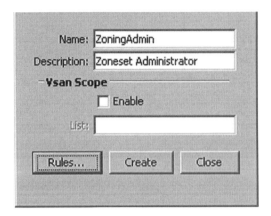

Step 6   Provide a name and description (no spaces) for the role (see Figure 2-3).

Note   This example does not specify a VSAN scope, but you could optionally create a VSAN scope limiting this specific role to a subset of VSANs. For example, a zoning admin role could be created for zone admins who can only modify VSANs 1–10. Adding a VSAN scope requires the installation of the **Enterprise Package license**.

Step 7   Click **Rules...** to define what this role can and cannot do within the optional VSAN scope (see Figure 2-3). The Create Common Rules screen shown in Figure 2-4 appears.

Figure 2-4   *Create Common Role Rules*

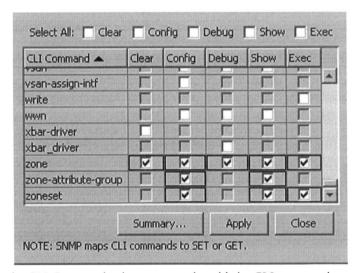

Step 8   Choose the CLI Command column to sort the table by CLI command.

Step 9   Check the **Show** check box at the top of the screen to enable show for all commands.

Step 10   Scroll down and check all of the **zone, zone-attribute-group, zoneset** options. Plus any others that may be appropriate (show fcns, flogi, interface etc..)

Step 11   Check **copy** so that the zoning admin can save the configuration.

Step 12   Select the **Summary...** button to see a listing of what will be configured.

Step 13   Click **Apply** (see Figure 2-4).

Step 14 Click **Create** (see Figure 2-5). This saves the role configuration to the CFS pending database. Not until the CFS **commit** command is executed will this role become part of the running configuration of the switches in the fabric.

Figure 2-5 *Create Common Roles*

Name: ZoningAdmin

Description: Zoneset Administrator

Vsan Scope

☐ Enable

List:

Rules...   Create   Close

Step 15 Click **Close** (see Figure 2-5) to return to the original Roles screen (see Figure 2-6). The ZoningAdmin role now exists only in the pending database.

Figure 2-6 *Display Roles*

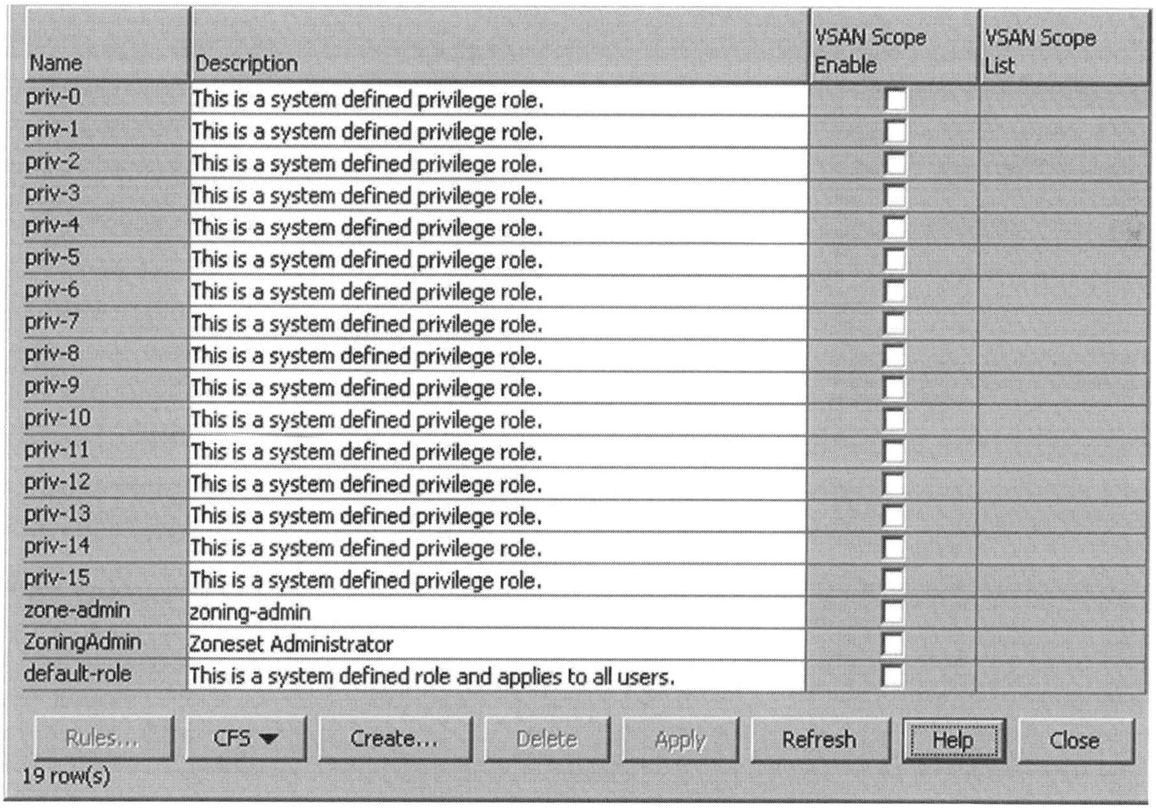

Name	Description	VSAN Scope Enable	VSAN Scope List
priv-0	This is a system defined privilege role.	☐	
priv-1	This is a system defined privilege role.	☐	
priv-2	This is a system defined privilege role.	☐	
priv-3	This is a system defined privilege role.	☐	
priv-4	This is a system defined privilege role.	☐	
priv-5	This is a system defined privilege role.	☐	
priv-6	This is a system defined privilege role.	☐	
priv-7	This is a system defined privilege role.	☐	
priv-8	This is a system defined privilege role.	☐	
priv-9	This is a system defined privilege role.	☐	
priv-10	This is a system defined privilege role.	☐	
priv-11	This is a system defined privilege role.	☐	
priv-12	This is a system defined privilege role.	☐	
priv-13	This is a system defined privilege role.	☐	
priv-14	This is a system defined privilege role.	☐	
priv-15	This is a system defined privilege role.	☐	
zone-admin	zoning-admin	☐	
ZoningAdmin	Zoneset Administrator	☐	
default-role	This is a system defined role and applies to all users.	☐	

Rules...   CFS ▼   Create...   Delete   Apply   Refresh   Help   Close

19 row(s)

Step 16 Commit the changes by expanding **CFS** (see Figure 2-6) and selecting **Commit**.

To abort the changes and flush the pending database, expand **CFS** (see Figure 2-6) and select **Abort**.

To see the status of the CFS operation, from the main window click **Admin > CFS (Cisco Fabric Services)**. The status of the Created Roles CFS commit is shown in Figure 2-7.

Figure 2-7   Created Roles

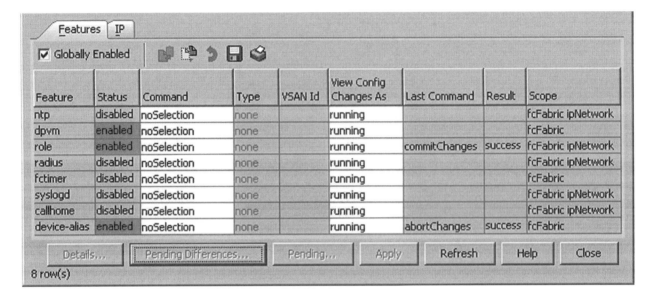

Creating a Role with CLI

Leveraging CFS, the roles configuration can be distributed across the fabric, thereby saving the user from having to individually configure roles on each switch in the fabric.

To use the CLI to distribute roles throughout the physical fabric, follow these steps:

Step 1   Enter configuration mode and enable CFS distribution (**role distribute**) for roles on each switch that should receive this role. This is the only step that must be done individually for all switches. The other steps do not need to be repeated on each switch.

```
MDS-9513-1# conf t
Enter configuration commands, one per line. End with CNTL/Z.
MDS-9513-1(config)# role distribute
```

Step 2   Create the ZoningAdmin role with the **role name** command, describe the role with **description** command, and add rules to it with **rule** command.

```
MDS-9513-1(config)#role name ZoningAdmin
MDS-9513-1(config-role)#   description Zoneset_Administrator
MDS-9513-1(config-role)#   rule 1 permit show
MDS-9513-1(config-role)#   rule 2 permit config feature zoneset
MDS-9513-1(config-role)#   rule 3 permit exec feature zoneset
MDS-9513-1(config-role)#   rule 4 permit clear feature zone
MDS-9513-1(config-role)#   rule 5 permit config feature zone
MDS-9513-1(config-role)#   rule 6 permit debug feature zone
MDS-9513-1(config-role)#   rule 7 permit exec feature zone
MDS-9513-1(config-role)#   rule 8 permit exec feature copy
```

Step 3 Commit the role and distribute it to the other switches with the **role commit** command.

```
MDS-9513-1(config)# role commit
```

Step 4 (Optional) Create a user zoning_user and assign the new ZoningAdmin role to that user.

```
MDS-9513-1# config terminal
MDS-9513-1(config)# username zoning_user password g0s0x456 role ZoningAdmin
```

Step 5 Save the configuration fabric-wide with the **copy running-config startup-config fabric** command.

```
MDS-9513-1(config)# copy running-config startup-config fabric
[########################################] 100%
```

Creating User Accounts

To access an MDS switch, create at least one user. This section explains how to create an user.

Best Practice Use TACACS+ servers to centrally manage user accounts instead of managing them locally on each switch, especially if there multiple users and multiple MDS/Nexus switches. See "Configuring TACACS+ with Cisco SecureACS 4" on page 8.

Creating a User Account via Command-Line

To create a user from the CLI, follow these steps:

Step 1 Enter configuration submode with the **config terminal** command.

```
MDS-9513-1# config terminal
```

Step 2 Create the user with the syntax **username** *username* **password** *password* **role** *role*.

```
MDS-9513-1(config)# username fedona password sox2004ch@mps role network-admin
```

At this point, the user "fedona" can access the switch with the password sox2004ch@mps. Access can be with console, SSH, Telnet, or SNMP.

Creating User Accounts via DCNM

To create a user from DCNM-SAN, follow these steps:

Note Creating a user with DCNM-SAN *requires* that you previously logged into DCNM-SAN using a privacy password, which provides additional security when using SNMPv3.

Step 1 In the Physical Attributes pane, select **Switches**.

Step 2   Select **Security**.

Step 3   Select **Users and Roles**

Step 4   In the top pane, select the **Users** tab. (If the Users tab is grayed out, select the Roles tab first, then select the Users tab.)

Step 5   Click **Create Row...**. See Figure 2-8.

Figure 2-8   Creating a User in DCNM-SAN

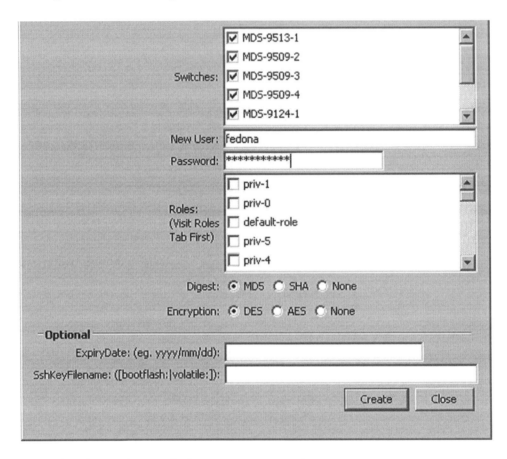

Step 6   Select the switches on which you want to create the user.

Step 7   Fill in the username and password. The password will not be displayed.

Step 8   Select the roles for this user.

Step 9   Select **Create...**

Configuring TACACS+ with Cisco SecureACS 4

Cisco's SecureACS product enhances MDS/Nexus switch management security and provides centralized authentication, authorization, and accounting of users.

Best Practice   It is recommend that a TACACS+ server be used for authentication, authorization and accounting. With TACACS+ implemented, you do not have to perform password recovery on the MDS switch.

Authentication and Authorization with TACACS+

Configuring an MDS/Nexus switch to use TACACS+ allows centralized account management of the switch. This centralized user management eliminates the need to create and maintain usernames and passwords on individual switches. The SecureACS server provides the authentication to a switch login as well as role assignment for the user. A shared secret key is used to provide encryption and authentication between the TACACS+ client (MDS-9500) and the TACACS+ server (Cisco SecureACS). The TACACS+ server does not have a definition for what a specific user can or cannot do, as defined by the role's rules, but it does determine what role a given user is assigned to. For example, it can inform the MDS/Nexus switch that a given user has the role "ZoningAdmin" but does not know exactly what abilities that user has.

In this example, these resources are used:

- The TACACS+ server is Cisco Secure ACS v4.0
- The switch's IP address is 172.22.36.142.
- The TACACS+ server's IP address is 172.22.36.10.
- The TACACS+ shared secret key is WarEagle.

Note   If SecureACS v5 is being used, consult your SecureACS administration team as the deployment model between SecureACS v4 and v5 has changed. However, the cisco av-pair specified in Step 3 g.on page 13 will still need to be passed back to the MDS/Nexus switch from the SecureACS server. The MDS/Nexus switch can be configured with the recipe Configuring TACACS+ on the MDS Switch, page 2-14

Configuring the SecureACS v4 Server

Before configuring the switch, configure the SecureACS server with Cisco SecureACS. After completing this recipe continue on to the recipe Configuring TACACS+ on the MDS Switch, page 2-14

To configure the SecureACS server with Cisco SecureACS, follow these steps:

Step 1   Configure SecureACS to allow modification of advanced TACACS+ settings.

   a. On the left pane of the main screen, choose **Interface Configuration**.

   b. Select the link **TACACS+ (Cisco IOS)**. You see the Interface Configuration screen shown in Figure 2-9.

Figure 2-9   *SecureACS Configure Display*

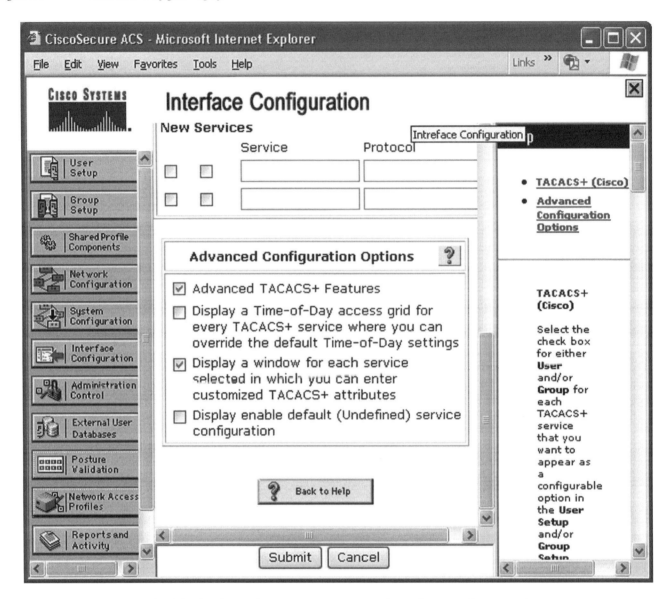

c. Check both **Advanced TACACS+ Features** and **Display a window...** attributes.

d. Click **Submit** to save the changes.

Step 2   Use SecureACS to define the switch for the TACACS+ server. This allows the MDS switch to be authenticated by the server.

    a. In the left pane, click **Network Configuration** > **Add Entry.** You then see the Network Configuration screen shown in Figure 2-10.

    b. Provide the MDS switch IP address **172.22.36.142** and the shared secret key **WarEagle** as shown in Figure 2-10.

Figure 2-10   *SecureACS Client Setup*

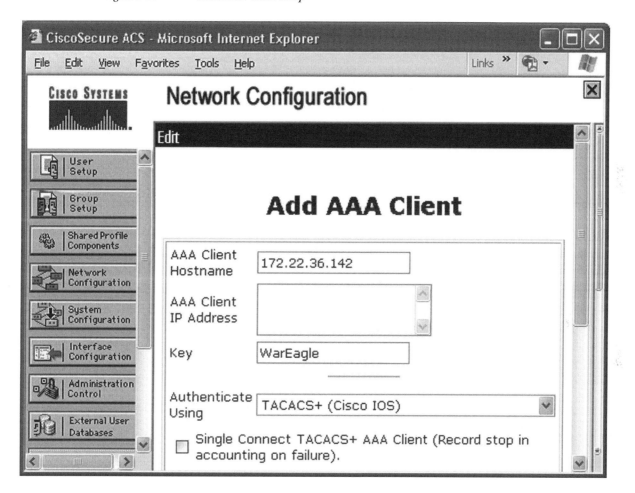

    c. Click **Submit** to save the information.

Step 3   Define a group so you can assign the same role to multiple users without having to modify the attributes of each user individually.

Note   The name of the TACACS+ group is not related to the role of the MDS users. The role that is assigned to the MDS users is a **property** of the TACACS+ group or the TACACS+ user.

a.   In the left pane, click **Group Setup.** The Group Setup screen appears (see Figure 2-11).

Figure 2-11   *SecureACS: Group Setup*

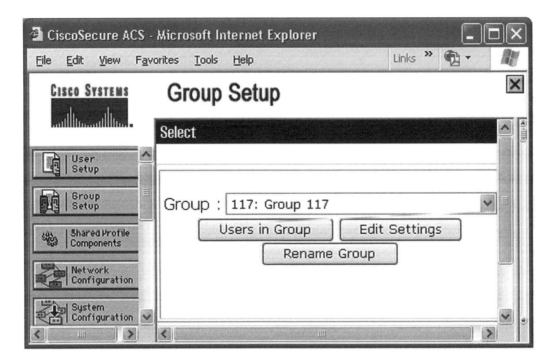

b.   Select an available group and click **Rename Group** (see Figure 2-11).

c.   Enter a new name for this group.

Best Practice   Use the same SecureACS group name as the role name to ease creation of TACACS+-based users. Names such as MDS_Zoning_Admin can aid in determining what the role is without looking at the role's rules.

d.   Click **Submit** to save the name change.

e.   Select the newly renamed group and click **Edit Settings**.

f.   Scroll to the section labeled TACACS+ Settings, then check the **Shell** and **Custom attributes** (see Figure 2-12).

Figure 2-12   SecureACS Adding MDS Switch Role

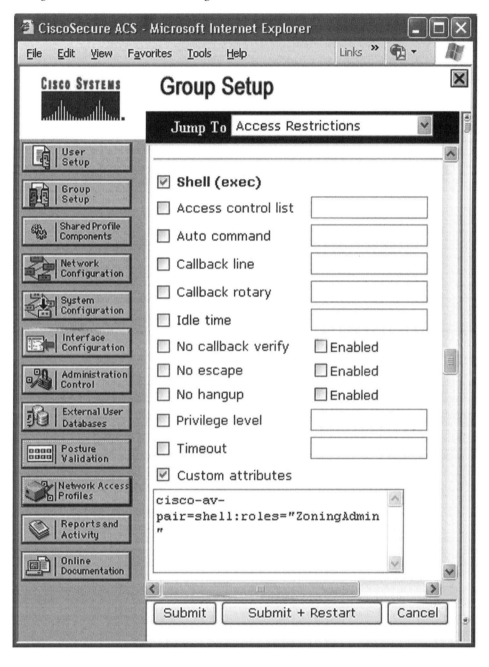

g. In the Custom attributes field, enter the av-pair string corresponding to the role defined on the switch for users. The syntax is **cisco-av-pair=shell:roles="<role1> <role2>"** (see Figure 2-12)

h. Click **Submit + Restart** (see Figure 2-12) to save and apply the configuration.

Step 4 Define a user using these steps:

a. Click **User Setup** in the left pane. You then see the User Setup screen.

b. Enter a new or existing user name.

c. Click **Add/Edit**.

d. Provide the information for the fields **Password**, **Confirm Password** and **Group to which user is assigned** (see Figure 2-13).

Figure 2-13   SecureACS Creating TACACS+ User

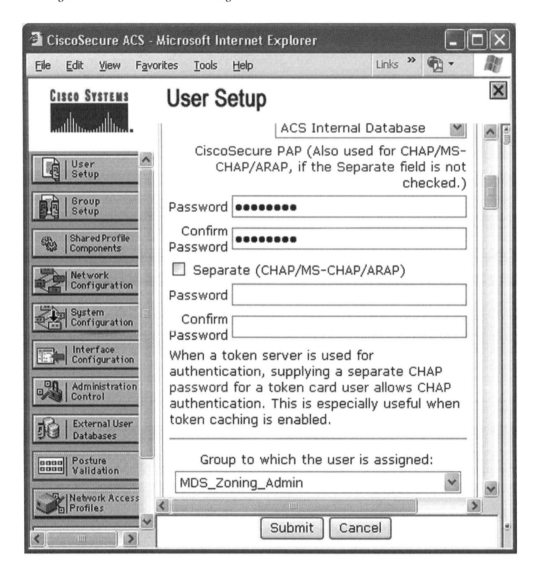

Configuration of the SecureACS server is complete. Next, configure the MDS switch itself.

Configuring TACACS+ on the MDS Switch

You can configure an MDS switch from the CLI or using SNMP.

To configure the switch from the CLI, follow these steps:

Step 1   Enter configuration mode, and then enable TACACS+.

```
MDS-9513-1# conf t
```

```
Enter configuration commands, one per line. End with CNTL/Z.
MDS-9513-1(config)# feature tacacs+
```

Step 2   Define the TACACS+ server 172.22.36.10 and the corresponding shared secret key WarEagle.

```
MDS-9513-1(config)# tacacs-server host 172.22.36.10 key WarEagle
```

Step 3   Define a group of authentication servers to use, and then add the TACACS+ server to the group.

```
MDS-9513-1(config)# aaa group server tacacs+ tacacs-group1
MDS-9513-1(config-tacacs+)# server 172.22.36.10
```

Step 4   Define the authentication method for the switch's Telnet, SSH, or SNMP access.

```
MDS-9513-1(config)# aaa authentication login default group tacacs-group1
```

Step 5   Use **show** commands to display and check the configuration:

```
MDS-9513-1# show tacacs-server

timeout value:5
total number of servers:1

following TACACS+ servers are configured:
        172.22.36.10:
                available on port:49
                TACACS+ shared secret:********
MDS-9513-1# show aaa authentication
        default: group tacacs-group1
        console: local
        iscsi: local
        dhchap: local

MDS-9513-1# show user-account
user:admin
        this user account has no expiry date
        roles:network-admin

user:fedona
        expires on Fri Jun 18 23:59:59 2011
        roles:ZoningAdmin
account created through REMOTE authentication
Local login not possible
```

Note   The user fedona is not available locally on the switch and yet is a member of the group/role network-admin. This means fedona was authenticated by the TACACS server and not by the switch.

Accounting with TACACS+

Cisco's SecureACS server can provide a command history of users and their actions. This information is similar to that provided by the CLI command **show accounting log.** However, by placing the information on a remote system, the logs can be independently examined and are available if the switch is inaccessible. This configuration builds upon the configuration defined in Authentication and Authorization with TACACS+, page 2-9.

Configuring the MDS Switch to Use TACACS Accounting

Because this procedure builds on the configuration defined in Authentication and Authorization with TACACS+, page 2-9, only small modifications need to be made.

To configure the switch to use a TACACS+ server for accounting, follow these steps:

Step 1 Enter configuration mode.

Step 2 Configure the switch to use the tacacs-group1 server group. The local keyword indicates local logging on the switch if all servers listed in the server group are unavailable. If the server group is available, commands and events are **not** logged locally.

```
switch# conf t
switch(config)# aaa accounting default group tacacs-group1 local
```

Configuring SecureACS v4 to Receive TACACS+ Accounting

To configure SecureACS v4 to receive TACACS+ accounting, follow these steps:

Step 1 Configure the SecureACS server to monitor Update/Watchdog packets by modifying the client configuration.

   a. In the SecureACS left pane, click **Network Configuration** (see Figure 2-14)

   b. Select the client to be modified.

   c. Check the **Log Update/Watchdog Packets from this AAA Client** check box (see Figure 2-14).

   d. Click **Submit.**

Figure 2-14   *Enabling Accounting on the SecureACS server*

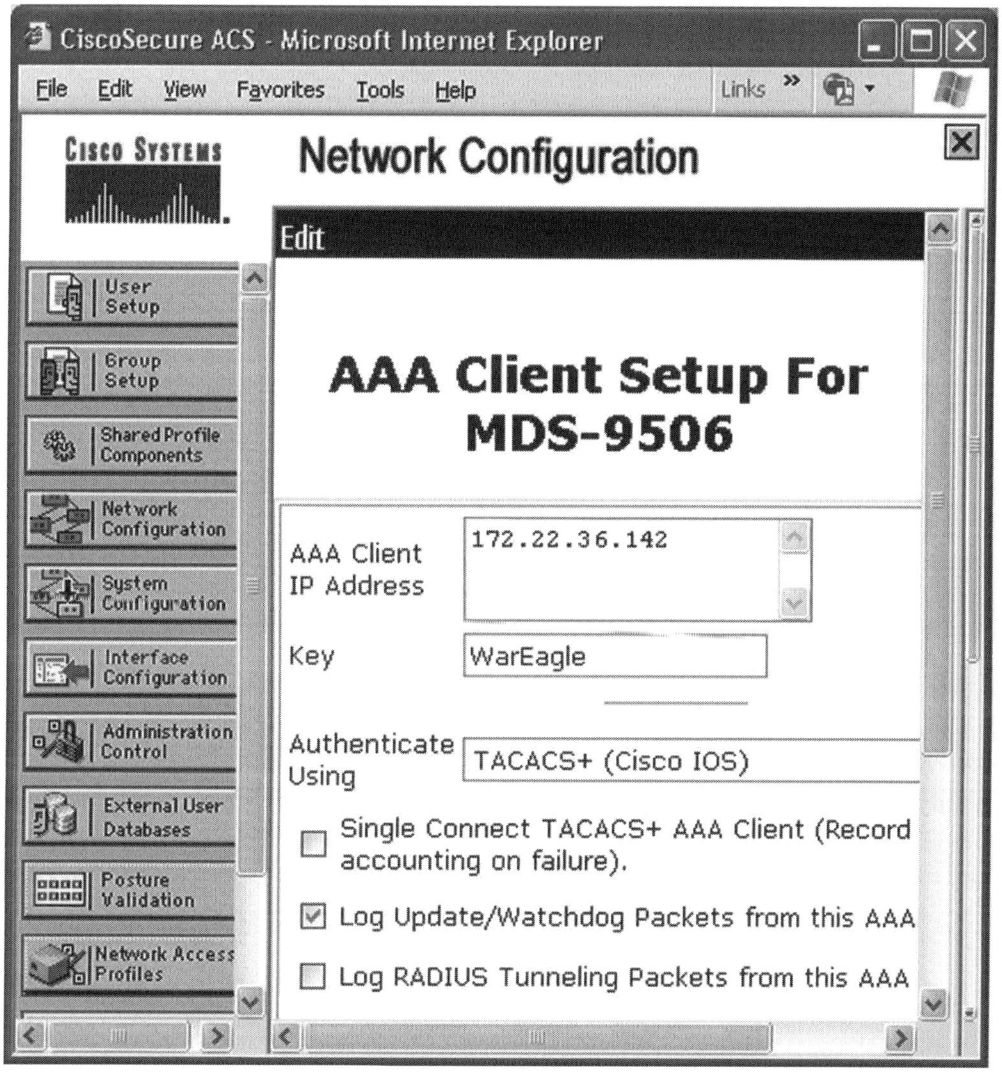

Step 2   Configure SecureACS to display commands.

    a.   Click **System Configuration** in the left pane.

    b.   Click **Logging**.

    c.   Select **CSV TACACS+ Accounting**.

    d.   Add the column **err_msg**.

    e.   Check the **Log to CSV TACACS+ Accounting report** box (see Figure 2-15).

    f.   Click **Submit**.

Figure 2-15   Add MDS Command Logging to the Report

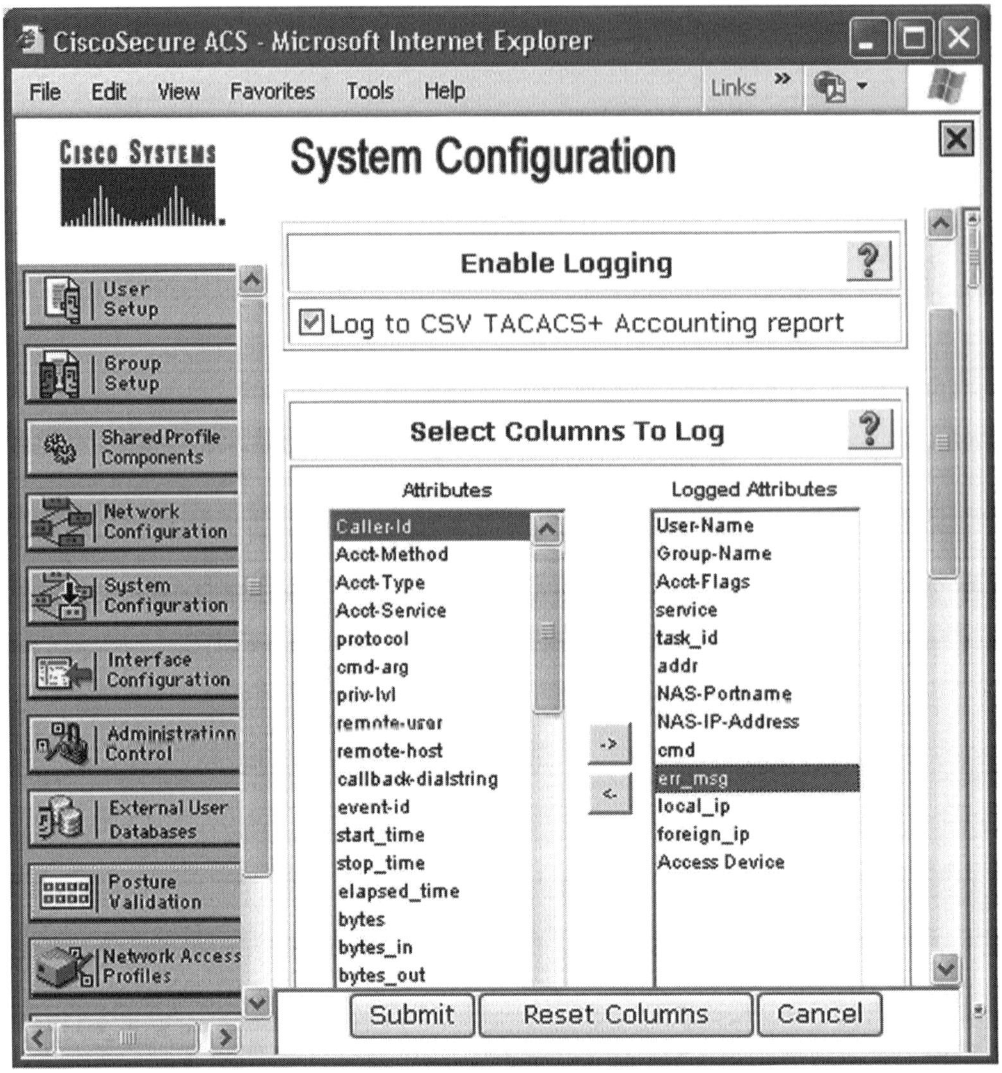

Step 3   View the accounting report.

   a. Click **Reports and Activity** in the left pane (see Figure 2-15).

   b. Select **TACACS+ Accounting**.

   c. In the right pane, select the day to view (see the result in Figure 2-16).

     The current day is called **TACACS+ Accounting active.csv**.

Figure 2-16   SecureACS Accounting Log

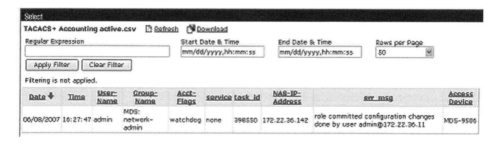

Providing Password-Free Access Using SSH

You can allow switch access with no password from automated scripts or agents. Providing a null password or hard-coding the password into the script or agent could be considered a weak security practice. However, using the private/public key infrastructure of SSH maintains a secure environment. SSH uses a private/public key exchange; the switch knows only the public key while the host knows both the public and private keys. Access is only granted if the user comes from a host that knows both the public and private keys

This procedure includes creating the appropriate key on a host, then adding the key to a new read-only (network-operator) user.

Best Practice   Assign password-free logins to either a read-only role like network-operator or to a role with a minimal set of privileges from a trusted system.

Caution   Having only the public key does not trigger the switch to grant access. The private key must also be on the host. Treat the private key like a password.

To create a key on a host and then add the key to a read-only user, follow these steps:

Step 1   Create an SSH RSA1 public/private key on the host.

```
$ /usr/bin/ssh-keygen -t rsa1
Generating public/private rsa1 key pair.
Enter file in which to save the key (/users/testuser/.ssh/identity):
/users/testuser/.ssh/identity already exists.
Overwrite (y/n)? y
Enter passphrase (empty for no passphrase):
Enter same passphrase again:
Your identification has been saved in /users/testuser/.ssh/identity.
Your public key has been saved in /users/testuser/.ssh/identity.pub.
The key fingerprint is:
c2:4d:6d:26:21:9d:79:9b:c3:86:dc:a5:07:d2:62:d4 testuser@host
```

On the host, the file **/users/testuser/.ssh/identity.pub** is the SSH public key that is encrypted using the RSA1 algorithm. The contents of this file are used in the creation of the MDS switch user. In this example, the file looks like this:

```
$ cat /users/testuser/.ssh/identity.pub
1024 35
1391986772647321648581534763577479260246565482337450270063811786219920835240379062117142411
4504365470196042145303540708736242692836406130584706151706499634146350368596283440051422278
8863181341221261531829067404184490980478279617682141489367526314824591300566032684042565221
91410368204629699075809390037814979061 testuser@host
```

Step 2   On the switch, create all of the SSH keys, even though in this case the client is using RSA1.

```
MDS-9513-1# conf t
Enter configuration commands, one per line. End with CNTL/Z.

MDS-9513-1(config)# ssh key rsa1
generating rsa1 key(1024 bits).....
generated rsa1 key

MDS-9513-1(config)# ssh key dsa
generating dsa key(1024 bits).....
generated dsa key

MDS-9513-1(config)# ssh key rsa
generating rsa key(1024 bits).....
generated rsa key
```

Step 3   Enable SSH on the switch.

```
MDS-9513-1(config)# feature ssh
```

Step 4   On the switch, create the user, pasting in the contents of the identity.pub file after the SSH key parameter.

```
MDS-9513 1# conf t
Enter configuration commands, one per line.  End with CNTL/Z.
MDS-9513-1(config)# username testuser role network-operator
warning: password for user:testuser not set. S/he cannot login currently
MDS-9513-1(config)# username testuser sshkey 1024 35
1391986772647321648581534763577479260246565482337450270063811786219920835240379062117142411
4504365470196042145303540708736242692836406130584706151706499634146350368596283440051422278
8863181341221261531829067404184490980478279617682141489367526314824591300566032684042565221
91410368204629699075809390037814979061 testuser@host
172.22.36.11(config)# end
```

Step 5   Examine the configuration of the user with the **show user-account** command.

```
MDS-9513-1# show user-account testuser
user: testuser
        this user account has no expiry date
        roles:network-operator
no password set. Local login not allowed
Remote login through RADIUS/TACACS+ is possible
        ssh public key: 1024 35 1391986772647321648581534763577479260246565482337
45027006381178621992083524037906211714241450436547019604214530354070873624269286
63406130584706151706499634146350368596283440051422278863181341221261531829067404
18449098047827961768214148936752631482459130056603268404256522191410368204629699
07580939003781497906061 testuser@host
```

Step 6   Test the login process from the host with the **testuser** command.

```
$ ssh testuser@MDS-9513-1
Cisco Nexus Operating System (NX-OS) Software
TAC support: http://www.cisco.com/tac
Copyright (c) 2002-2011, Cisco Systems, Inc. All rights reserved.
The copyrights to certain works contained in this software are
owned by other third parties and used and distributed under
license. Certain components of this software are licensed under
the GNU General Public License (GPL) version 2.0 or the GNU
```

```
Lesser General Public License (LGPL) Version 2.1. A copy of each
such license is available at
http://www.opensource.org/licenses/gpl-2.0.php and
http://www.opensource.org/licenses/lgpl-2.1.php
MDS-9509-2#
```

If the same user tries logging in from another host without both the private key file
(/users/testuser/.ssh/identity) and the public key file (/users/testuser/.ssh/identity), then access to the switch
is denied. The fact that the public key has **testuser@host** included does not tie it to a specific host, but does
allow an administrator to determine from which host it was generated.

.ılıílıı

Best Practice   A simple way to use this feature is to schedule a nightly backup (using cron, for example) for the switch
configuration using SSH. The following backup example works as long as the specified user has the privilege
to enter the **copy** command. An alternative approach, using the MDS's scheduler ability is shown in
"Automated Switch Configuration Backup" section on page 1-20.

```
#!/bin/sh
#####################################################
#
#/usr/local/bin/backup_mds_config.sh

# This is used for a cron entry. No arguments are
# allowed in cron.Absolute paths to commands must
# be specified to ssh for it to work properly
# ssh key exchange must be separately configured
# for the account "USER"
#
# Adjust the variables for your host and switch
#####################################################

DIR=/mds_config
DATE=`date "+%m%d%y_%H%M%S"`
SWITCH_NAME=beat_bama
FILE=$SWITCH_NAME"_run_cfg_"$DATE
USER=testuser
COMMAND1="copy running-config startup-config"
COMMAND2="show startup-config"

#Copy running to startup-config
/usr/local/bin/ssh -l $USER $SWITCH_NAME $COMMAND1
#Backup MDS config to local file
/usr/local/bin/ssh -l $USER $SWITCH_NAME $COMMAND2 > $DIR/$FILE
```

Set up cron to execute the script. The cron job must be run by the user specified in the script. Configure the
crontab for the user. This example runs at 11:00pm every Sunday:

```
#Backup MDS config:
00 23 * * 0 /usr/local/bin/backup_mds_config.sh > /mds_logs/beat_bama1/
```

Disabling the Web Server

On an MDS switch, a built-in web server provides a method for downloading and installing Device Manager. After installation of these tools, the web server is no longer needed. For configuration and notification, the MDS switch does not rely on HTTP for communication to the switch.

To increase the security of the MDS platform, IP ACLs can be used to block access to TCP port 80 of the switch or one can disable it completely.

The IP access control list (ACL) that is set up in this recipe denies access to TCP port 80 on the switch but allows access to all other TCP ports.

Instead of blocking access to the web server on TCP port 80, the follow commands can be used to turn it off completely:

```
MDS-9513-1# conf terminal
Enter configuration commands, one per line.  End with CNTL/Z.
MDS-9513-1(config)# no feature http-server
```

Caution   IP ACLs have an implicit DENY ALL added to the end of an ACL, so at least one permit statement must be used. Otherwise, all traffic is denied, and the user can be locked out of the switch.

Best Practice   Whenever using ACLs on the mgmt0 interface, first test it using a switch that has console access, in case a typo occurs. The commands in this recipe can be integrated into a script by copying the bold commands and pasting them into a CLI session.

To create an IP ACL filter and apply it to the mgmt0 interface from the CLI, follow these steps:

Step 1   Enter configuration mode and then create an access list called **disable_webserver**. The second entry for the access list is a permit any statement.

```
MDS-9513-1#conf t
MDS-9513-1(config)#ip access-list disable_webserver deny tcp any any eq port www
MDS-9513-1(config)#ip access-list disable_webserver permit ip any any
```

Step 2   Apply the access list to mgmt0.

```
MDS-9513-1(config)#interface mgmt0
MDS-9513-1(config-if)#ip access-group disable_webserver in
```

CHAPTER 3

Managing DCNM Server

Managing DCNM

The recipes in this section are for configuring DCNM Client and Server application rather than for configuring the switch. The other chapters in this book cover those "on switch" functions.

Optimizing DCNM Server Performance

When deploying DCNM Server, further optimizations can be done to the platform to enhance the performance and stability of the platform. As your fabric increases in size, the number of ports, flows and end devices being monitored by the DCNM Server are primary factors when determining the size of the server that is hosting DCNM.

Optimizing the performance of DCNM Server often requires tuning the Java Runtime Environment, DCNM Server, and the database that it uses.

Performance Manager Database Sizing

DCNM Server provides persistent monitoring, which means that it continues to monitor or poll the fabric even after the DCNM Client is closed. When setting up DCNM for persistent monitoring, be aware of the disk space that the DCNM database uses. When Performance Manager is enabled, it provides DCNM Server with the ability to collect performance statistics on ports, ISLs, or flows (end device-to-end device traffic).

DCNM Server stores its data in a round-robin database (RRD). RRD is a database that contains a fixed number of records. When the last record in the database has been written, the next record to be written overwrites or updates the first record, which keeps the size of the database under control. Also, as data points get older, the granularity of those points becomes less relevant and the trend of those points becomes more important. Performance Manager keeps its rrd files in C:\Program Files (x86)\Cisco Systems\dcm\fm\pm\db directory on Windows.

Table 3-1 lists the default polling values for DCNM. To understand the table, read it in the following manner: "X days of polling, every Y (interval), results in Z samples." Or you can read it this way: "If I take Z samples every Y interval, I'll have that granularity for X days." Increasing the number of days to keep a sample will increase the size of the database. These values can be modified through the Performance Manager web GUI, under the **Admin** tab. Follow the resulting screen on the left menu to **Performance**, **Database**.

Table 3-1   Performance Sample Sizes

Day	Interval	Samples
2.0	5 min	600
15.4	30 min	700
64	2 hour	775
300	1 day	300

For the purpose of this chapter, default values are used to calculate the required disk space. The default values for Performance Manager require the following amount of space:

- **77KB** per port/ISL/flow traffic monitored.

- **39KB** per error/discards if enabled.

A 1000 port fabric with 10 ISLs, with 4:1 hba:target fanout (which is used to determine the number of flows) would use the following amount of disk space:

- 800 zones, and if configured, 800 flows. (800 x 77 KB) = 61600 KB.

- 1000 port traffic and errors/discards (1000 x 77 KB+1000 x 39 KB) = 116000 KB.

- 10 ISL traffic and error files (10 x 77 KB+10 x 39 KB) = 1160 KB.

This DCNM Server would require 74360 KB (~74 MB of disk space) consumed in 1820 RRD files. Although this is a trivial amount of storage in disk drives of today, the number of RRD files could create a bottleneck for the DCNM Server because it would need to update all 1820 RRD files every five minutes. It is important to locate the RRD files on fast storage. It is not the throughput (MB/s) of the storage device that is important but the number of I/O /sec that can be performed. A RAID-1 array for writes, performs exactly the same as a single disk device. Just mirroring the internal disk for the DCNM Server may not increase the write performance of this task.

Configuring DCNM to Use an External Oracle Database

DCNM Server supports the ability to connect to an external Oracle 11i database server to host its database. This is a different database from the one used for Performance Manager as discussed in Performance Manager Database Sizing, page 3-1. This database, instead of holding performance data, contains the inventory, fabric configuration, and the states of the ports within the fabric.

Best Practice   To maximize scalability and performance, use Oracle 11i for the back-end database instead of the bundled postgres SQL database.

To configure DCNM Server to use an external Oracle 11i server, follow these steps:

Step 1   Obtain from your Oracle database administrator the database URL, username and password. These are required during DCNM installation to access the database and create the necessary tables.

Step 2   Install DCNM-SAN and choose Oracle 11i as the database.

Adjusting Memory Usage of DCNM

By default, DCNM Server can use up to 1 GB of RAM; however, for larger installations, it is recommended to increase the amount of memory that DCNM can address. To adjust the maximum amount of memory, modify the file **C:\Program Files (x86)\Cisco Systems\dcm\fm\conf\FMServer.conf** and then restart the DCNM service.

```
:# Initial Java Heap Size (in MB)
wrapper.java.initmemory=6
wrapper.java.maxmemory=4096
```

Note   DCNM Server only uses memory if it needs it. So, for example, allocating 2048MB of memory when the DCNM Server only needs 1024 MB will not increase performance.

Authenticating DCNM Through TACACS

To provide authentication to users accessing DCNM, an external TACACS+ or RADIUS server can be leveraged. If an existing TACACS+ or RADIUS environment provides authentication services for your switches, the same TACACS+ or RADIUS servers can be used to provide authentication for the DCNM Server.

In this recipe, the following information came from the team that manages the TACACS+ environment:

- Primary TACACS+ IP address: 192.168.1.1
- Primary server TACACS+ secret: g0s0x!
- Authentication method: pap
- Secondary TACACS+ IP address: 192.168.1.2
- Secondary server TACACS+ secret: f@z3d@z3
- Authentication method: pap

Best Practice   Use at least two AAA servers. If you have just one server and it is not reachable, you will not be able to log into DCNM Server unless you switch back to local authentication.

While you can perform the following procedure during installation of DCNM, this method does it after DCNM is installed.

To configure TACACS+ authentication services, follow these steps:

Step 1   Log in via the web to the DCNM server.

Step 2   Select the **Admin** pull down menu

Step 3   Under Management Users, select **Remote AAA**.

Step 4   Select the radio bullet for the method to be used, in this case **TACACS+**

Step 5   Fill in the server IP address and Secret for the primary server

Step 6   Select **Test...** This should result in a popup box showing the role and av-pair that was configured on the TACACS+ server. If no role is defined, the user will be assigned to network-operator, and if the av-pair isn't defined at all, an av-pair undefined message will appear.

Step 7   Repeat for the optional Secondary or Tertiary servers.

Step 8   Select **Apply**

At this point, when a user logs into DCNM Server, you will see entries in **C:\Program Files (x86)\Cisco Systems\dcm\fm\logs\fmserver.log** logging their success or failure to log into DCNM Server authenticated by the TACACS+ server.

Measuring End-Device Performance with DCNM

Performance Manager is a licensed feature that is part of DCNM Server. Performance Manager provides historical analysis of SAN statistics and is displayed graphically to a web browser.

Note   Performance Manager requires the FM_Server_Pkg License. This license is required for all switches on which performance data is gathered.

DCNM Server must be configured to run Performance Manger. Select a host that is always up and has enough storage to gather and store the performance data.

Flows are the term used to describe the "flow" of data between two end devices, typically a server HBA and a storage port within a fabric. Measuring the traffic sent and received by the end devices helps to determine how much bandwidth the flow is consuming, compared with the bandwidth used by the port itself.

Best Practice   If you are upgrading from FabricManager 3.1(x) or earlier, you should recreate your flows. Recreating them will remove old flows and by not choosing to "Create flows on all cards" you can optimize your flow collection and reduce the load on both the switch and the DCNM Server.

Creating Flows Within DCNM

To create a flow with DCNM, follow these steps:

Step 1   Within DCNM, select the **Performance pull down** menu and then choose **Create flows...** as shown in Figure 3-1.

Figure 3-1   *DCNM Performance --> Create Flows*

This selection launches the Define Traffic Flows screen shown in Figure 3-2. From this screen, you can select the types of flows to be gathered. You can gather flows from Host to Storage, Storage to Host, Storage to Storage, or All flows.

Step 2   Select the VSAN to create the flows for as in Figure 3-2.

Figure 3-2   Define Traffic Flows

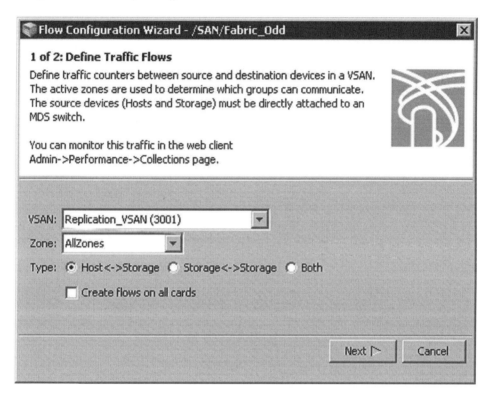

Step 3   Click **Next** to see all the possible flows in Figure 3-3. The Review Traffic Flows screen lists all the discovered flows that can be monitored. Remove any that do not need to be monitored.

Figure 3-3   Review Flows

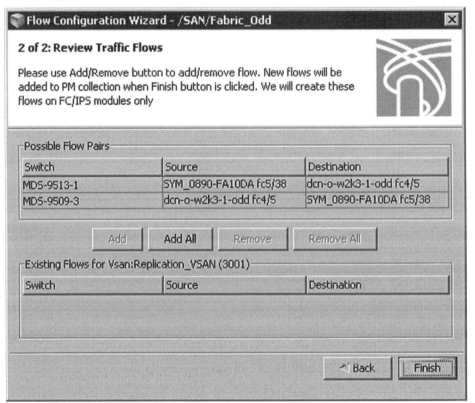

Note   If you are using device aliases, the device alias will be displayed instead of the world-wide name (WWN).

Step 4   Select the flows to be created, and select **Add** or **Add All** if all flows should be added.

Step 5   Click **Finish** to create the flows for all the entries listed in the Review Traffic Flows on the appropriate switches.

Repeat this procedure for every VSAN in which you want flows to be created. Or you can add new devices to a VSAN.

If a collection in the DCNM web GUI has not already been created, proceed with "Creating a Collection in Performance Manager" section on page 3-6.

Creating a Collection in Performance Manager

A collection is a container within Performance Manager that determines what types of objects (flows, interfaces, ISLs) to monitor. Perform the following procedure after creating flows in the recipe "Creating Flows Within DCNM" section on page 3-4. The procedure instructs DCNM to begin populating its database with performance data for flows, end devices, and ISLs.

To create a collection, follow these steps:

Step 1   Log into DCNM by pointing your web browser at the DCNM Server.

Step 2   Select the **Admin** tab.

Step 3   Select **Collections** under the Performance heading.

Step 4   At the bottom of the screen, select the **Add...** button. See Figure 3-4

Figure 3-4   Create Collection

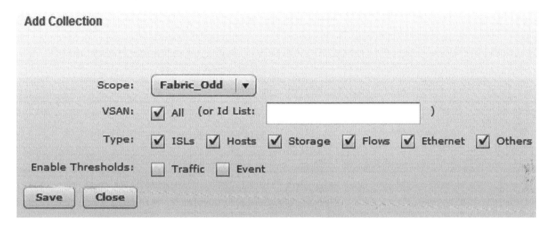

Step 5   Select the appropriate Fabrics, VSANs and statistics to capture and select **Save**.

Step 6   The dialog will be dismissed and DCNM will prompt you to restart Performance Manager (PM).

Step 7   Click **OK** to restart PM.

Note   If you need to create multiple collections because of multiple fabrics, do not restart Performance Manager when prompted. Instead, create the rest of your collections and then restart Performance Manager.

At this point, DCNM is starting to collect performance data, on the collection(s) you defined. It can take some time for the flows to start to appear in the web page.

Figure 3-5   List Collections

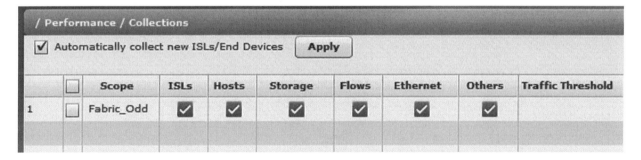

Depending on the size of the fabric and the number of objects to be collected (hosts, storage and ISLs), it can take some time for the performance data to appear in the various web pages. By default, the shortest period of time collected is five minutes.

CHAPTER 4

Physical Interfaces

The MDS switch is a multi-protocol switch. It supports Fibre Channel (FC), Fibre Channel Over Ethernet (FCoE), and Gigabit Ethernet interfaces in the same switch. The Fibre Channel interfaces support Fibre Channel as well as FICON. The FCoE ports support the fibre channel Over Ethernet protocol. The Gigabit Ethernet ports support FCIP and iSCSI protocols. In this section, different interface modes and protocol options that are used to configure the Fibre Channel (FC), FCoE and Gigabit Ethernet ports are detailed.

An MDS switch running NX-OS 5.2 and above will not support Generation-1 modules. These include the 16-port and 32-port Fibre Channel switching modules, the SSM, Supervisor-1, the MPS-14/2, and the IPS-8 and IPS-4 storage services modules.

The 8-Gb/s Generation-3 modules include the DS-X9224-96K9 and the DS-X9248-96K9 which are 24 and 48 port FC modules respectively. The Generation-3 24 port module supports line rate on all 24 ports at 2 and 4-Gb/s and is 2:1 over subscribed at 8-Gb/s. The Generation-3 48 port module is over subscribed 2:1 at 4-Gb/s on and 4:1 oversubscribed at 8-Gb/s.

The 8Gb/s Generation- 4 modules include the DS-X9232-256K9 and the DS-X9248-256-K9 which have 32 and 48 ports respectively. The Generation-4 32 ports module supports 1/2/4/8-Gb/s line rate on all 32 ports. While the Generation-4 48 port module supports line rate at 1/2/4-Gb/s and is oversubscribed 1.5:1 at 8-Gb/s for all 48 ports. The ports can auto negotiate to 1, 2, 4 or 8-Gb/s. Additionally, the Generation-4 modules also support up to 24 10-Gb/s FC ports at line rate. The Figure 4-1 shows the various MDS line cards, the speeds and the oversubscription if any.

For supporting multi-protocol applications there is the Multi-Protocol Services Module (MSM) and the Storage Services Node (SSN-16). The MSM 18+4 module has 18 2 and 4-Gb/s FC ports with 4 Gigabit Ethernet ports for FCIP and iSCSI. The SSN-16 module has 16 Gigabit Ethernet ports for FCIP and iSCSI connectivity

Additionally, the MSM 18+4 and the SSN-16 modules can run intelligent storage applications in addition to providing FCIP/iSCSI connectivity. While the MSM has one application engine, the SSN-16 has four. If SAN Extension is required, the application engines can be configured for FCIP with compression, Write Acceleration and encryption or the transport agnostic IO Acceleration (IOA). For environments requiring data migration Data Mobility Manager (DMM) can be enabled. While backup administrators needing tape encryption can configure Storage Media Encryption (SME).

Note   Each intelligent engine on the MSM 18+4 or SSN-16 modules can only be use for one intelligent application at a time. On the SSN-16 different engines can be configured to run different applications.

Figure 4-1   *MDS line cards, speeds and oversubscription*

Line Cards	Speeds and Over Subscription				
	1-Gb/s	2-Gb/s	4-Gb/s	8-Gb/s	10-Gb/s
DS-X9248-48K9 [4/44]-Port LC	1:1 (line rate)	2:1	4:1	8:1	Not Supported
DS-X9224-96K9 24-Port LC	1:1 (line rate)	1:1 (line rate)	1:1 (line rate)	2:1	Not Supported
DS-X9248-96K9 48-Port LC	1:1 (line rate)	1:1 (line rate)	2:1	4:1	Not Supported
DS-X9232-256K9 32-Port LC	1:1 (line rate)	1:1 (line rate)	1:1 (line rate)	1:1 (line rate)	24 ports 1:1 (line rate)
DS-X9248-256K9 48-Port LC	1:1 (line rate)	1:1 (line rate)	1:1 (line rate)	1:1.5	24 ports 1:1 (line rate)
DS-X9704 4-Port LC	Not Supported	Not Supported	Not Supported	Not Supported	1:1 (line rate)
DS-X9304-18K9 18 + 4 IP-Port LC	1:1 line rate	1:1 (line rate)	2:1	Not Supported	Not Supported
DS-X9316-SSNK9 16 IP Port LC	1:1 (line rate)	Not Supported	Not Supported	Not Supported	Not Supported

The recipes in this chapter show how to configure various parameters and modes for different physical ports supported on the MDS switches.

Configuring Fibre Channel Ports

This section describes how to configure Fibre Channel ports.

Port Description

A port description provides a plain text description for the interface of a port on a switch. In this example, the Fibre Channel interface fc 1/1 is given the description "storage array 17 port 1."

```
MDS-9509-2# conf t
Enter configuration commands, one per line.  End with CNTL/Z.
MDS-9509-2(config)# interface fc 1/1
MDS-9509-2(config-if)# switchport description "storage array 17 port 1"
MDS-9509-2(config-if)# end
MDS-9509-2#
```

Port Speed

This example sets the port speed for fc 1/1 to either 2-Gb/s, 4-Gb/s, 8-Gb/s, or an automatically negotiated speed.

Note   A port can be set to only one speed at a time. The default port speed is auto.

```
MDS-9509-2# conf t
Enter configuration commands, one per line.  End with CNTL/Z.
MDS-9509-2(config)# interface fc 1/1
MDS-9509-2(config-if)# switchport speed 1000 <- port speed set to 1 Gbits/sec
MDS-9509-2(config-if)# switchport speed 2000 <- port speed set to 2 Gbits/sec
MDS-9509-2(config-if)# switchport speed 4000 <- port speed set to 4 Gbits/sec
MDS-9509-2(config-if)# switchport speed 8000 <- port speed set to 8 Gbits/sec
MDS-9509-2(config-if)# switchport speed auto <- port speed set to auto negotiate
MDS-9509-2(config-if)# exit
MDS-9509-2#
```

Port Mode Auto

Note   A Fibre Channel port can be set to only one port mode at a time.

Setting port mode to auto allows the port to negotiate to either F port mode, FL port mode or E port mode. It cannot negotiate to ST port mode, SD port mode, or TL port mode.

In this example, fc 1/1 is set to auto port mode. This is the default setting for all ports on a 16-port module.

```
MDS-9509-2# conf t
Enter configuration commands, one per line.  End with CNTL/Z.
MDS-9509-2(config)# interface fc 1/1
MDS-9509-2(config-if)# switchport mode auto
MDS-9509-2(config-if)# end
MDS-9509-2#
```

Port Mode E

Setting port mode to E restricts the port to operating as an E port; the port can be either a trunking or non-trunking port, depending on the trunk port mode. E port mode is used when the port talks to another port of a different switch forming an ISL. In this example, fc 1/1 is set to E port mode.

The following example shows the configuration steps for 12- and16-port modules.

```
MDS-9509-2# conf t
Enter configuration commands, one per line.  End with CNTL/Z.
MDS-9509-2(config)# interface fc 1/1
MDS-9509-2(config-if)# switchport mode E
MDS-9509-2(config-if)# end
```

Configuring an E Port on 24- and 48-Port Modules

On 24- and 48-port modules, all ports by default use rate-mode as shared. This means that a port is not guaranteed a specific amount of bandwidth and will share the bandwidth the other ports in the port group. To make one of the ports on a 24- or a 48-port modules an E port, the rate-mode for the port has to be configured as dedicated, which means it is guaranteed the negotiated bandwidth amount. Then the port has to be configured as an E port. These two additional steps are required before the ports on these module can function as an E port. The default speed on 24- and 48-port modules is 4 or 8-Gb/s depending on whether it is a Generation-2 or Generation-3 module.

The following example shows the configuration details for 24- and 48-port modules.

```
MDS-9509-2# conf t
Enter configuration commands, one per line.  End with CNTL/Z.
MDS-9509-2(config)# interface fc 2/1
MDS-9509-2(config-if)# switchport rate-mode dedicated
MDS-9509-2(config-if)# switchport speed 8000
MDS-9509-2(config-if)# end
MDS-9509-2#
```

Configuring Trunking E Ports

A trunking port is used to carry VSAN-enabled frames between switches. The following section shows various configuration options for a trunking port.

Note The same commands apply to port-channels. Specify the port channel interface using the command **interface port-channel 1** rather than an individual link **interface fc 1/1**.

Trunk Port Mode

This example sets interface fc 1/1's trunk port mode to auto, on, and off. The default mode is auto. One end of an ISL should be set to on when connected between two MDS switches, while the other end can be either on or auto. When connecting to a non-Cisco switch, the trunk mode should be set to either off or auto.

```
MDS-9509-2# conf t
Enter configuration commands, one per line.  End with CNTL/Z.
MDS-9509-2(config)# interface fc 1/1
MDS-9509-2(config-if)# switchport trunk mode auto <- auto negotiates trunk port mode
MDS-9509-2(config-if)# switchport trunk mode on   <- sets trunk port mode to on
MDS-9509-2(config-if)# switchport trunk mode off  <- sets trunk port mode to off
MDS-9509-2(config-if)# exit
MDS-9509-2#
```

Configuring Trunk Ports to Filter-Specific VSANs

The recipe details the configuration steps required to allow selected VSAN traffic to pass through the interface fc 1/1. The **all** keyword allows all VSAN traffic to go through the port. The **add 2** portion of the **switchport trunk allowed vsan add 2** command adds VSAN 2 to the list of VSANs allowed through the port. Similarly **add 2-4** portion of the **switchport trunk allowed vsan add 2-4** command adds VSAN range, 2 through 4 to the list of VSANs allowed through the port. Default mode is to allow all VSAN traffic to pass through the port.

```
MDS-9509-2# conf t
Enter configuration commands, one per line.  End with CNTL/Z.
MDS-9509-2(config)# interface fc 1/1
```

```
MDS-9509-2(config-if)# switchport trunk allowed vsan all     <- all VSAN traffic
MDS-9509-2(config-if)# switchport trunk allowed vsan add 2   <- only VSAN 2 traffic
MDS-9509-2(config-if)# switchport trunk allowed vsan add 2-4 <- VSAN 2 to 4 traffic
MDS-9509-2(config-if)# ^Z
MDS-9509-2#
```

Port Mode F

Setting port mode to F restricts the port to operating as an F port only. F port mode is used for end devices that can only communicate in point-to-point mode. This mode allows the FC ports on the switch to connect to an end -device namely, a host HBA or a storage port or a tape device. In this example, fc 1/1 is set to F port mode.

```
MDS-9509-2# conf t
Enter configuration commands, one per line.  End with CNTL/Z.
MDS-9509-2(config)# interface fc 1/1
MDS-9509-2(config-if)# switchport mode F
MDS-9509-2(config-if)# end
MDS-9509-2#
```

Port Mode FL

Setting port mode to FL restricts the port to operating as an FL port. FL port mode is used for end devices that is a Fibre Channel arbitrated loop (FCAL) device. In this example, fc 1/1 is set to FL port mode.

```
MDS-9509-2# conf t
Enter configuration commands, one per line.  End with CNTL/Z.
MDS-9509-2(config)# interface fc 1/1
MDS-9509-2(config-if)# switchport mode FL
MDS-9509-2(config-if)# end
MDS-9509-2#
```

Port Mode Fx

Setting port mode to Fx restricts the port to operating as either an F or FL port. Fx port mode is used exclusively for end devices and prevents a port from auto negotiating to an E port. In this example, fc 1/1 is set to Fx port mode.

```
MDS-9509-2# conf t
Enter configuration commands, one per line.  End with CNTL/Z.
MDS-9509-2(config)# interface fc 1/1
MDS-9509-2(config-if)# switchport mode Fx
MDS-9509-2(config-if)# end
MDS-9509-2#
```

Port Mode SD

Setting port mode to SD configures the port as the span destination (SD) port of a span session. This is used in conjunction with the port analyzer adapter (PAA) to span a port and obtain FC traces without a FC analyzer. In this example, fc 1/1 is set to SD port mode.

```
MDS-9509-2# conf t
Enter configuration commands, one per line.  End with CNTL/Z.
MDS-9509-2(config)# interface fc 1/1
```

```
MDS-9509-2(config-if)# switchport mode SD
MDS-9509-2(config-if)# end
```

Port Mode ST

Setting port mode to ST configures the port as the span tunnel (ST) port of a remote span session. This is used to set up a remote SPAN session to a remote switch in which a PAA or protocol analyzer is connected. In this example, fc 1/1 is set to ST port mode.

```
MDS-9509-2# conf t
Enter configuration commands, one per line.  End with CNTL/Z.
MDS-9509-2(config)# interface fc 1/1
MDS-9509-2(config-if)# switchport mode ST
MDS-9509-2(config-if)# end
MDS-9509-2#
```

Enabling Port Beaconing

Using the **switchport beacon** command shown in this example causes the LEDs below port fc 1/1 to start flashing. This is useful in identifying a port for physical cabling or troubleshooting.

```
MDS-9509-2# conf t
Enter configuration commands, one per line.  End with CNTL/Z.
MDS-9509-2(config)# interface fc 1/1
MDS-9509-2(config-if)# switchport beacon
MDS-9509-2(config-if)# end
```

Oversubscription Management or Ports and Rate Limiting

This section describes oversubscription on a 24-port and 48-port modules. The bandwidth management using the rate-limiting feature can be used to effectively manage the available bandwidth to ports in a port group on these modules.

The Generation-2 can operate at 1/2/4-Gb/s. The DS-X9124, 24-port module is oversubscribed 2:1 at 4-Gb/s speeds and the DS-X9148 48-port modules is oversubscribed 2:1 at 2-Gb/s and 4:1 at 4-Gb/s speeds.

On a 24-port module, there are four groups of 6 ports. Each group of 6 ports has 12.8-Gb/s to the crossbar. Similarly, on a 48-port module there four groups of 12 ports each. Each group of 12 ports has 12.8-Gb/s to the crossbar. By default, the rate-mode on all the ports on the 24 and 48-port modules set to shared. The rate-limiting feature allows the user to decide which port gets how much of the bandwidth in a port group.

On a 24-port module or a 48-port module, a maximum of 3 ports from each of the 4 port groups can be configured to operate at 4-Gb/s each. This essentially permits only 0.8-Gb/s for the remaining ports in the port group which is insufficient to operate the other ports in that group. In order to get 3 ports of the 6 ports in a port group of a 24-port module and 3 ports of the 12 ports in the port group of a 48-port modules to get dedicated 4-Gb/s of bandwidth, the remaining ports in the port group need to be set to out-of-service or put into shared mode with a maximum speed of 1-Gb/s, or one port could be at 2-Gb/s shared and 2 other ports in out-of-service mode.

The Generation-3 modules can operate at 1/2/4/8-Gb/s. The DS-X9224-96K9, 24-port module is line rate at 4-Gb/s and oversubscribed 2:1 at 8-Gb/s. The DS-X9248-96K9, 48-port module is 2:1 oversubscribed at 8-Gb/s.

On a 24-port module, there are eight groups of 3 ports. Each group of 3 ports has 12.8-Gb/s to the crossbar. Similarly, on a 48-port module there six groups of 6 ports each. Each group of 6 ports has 12.8-Gb/s to the crossbar. By default, the rate-mode on all the ports on the 24- and 48-port modules set to shared. The rate-limiting feature allows the user to decide which port gets how much of the bandwidth in a port group.

The Generation-4 modules can operate at 1/2/4/8/10-Gb/s. The DS-X9232-256K9, 32-port module is line rate at 2/4/8-Gb/s. The DS-X9248-256K9, 48 port module is line rate at 1/2/4-Gb/s and 1:1.5 oversubscribed at 8-Gb/s. On both the modeules 24 ports can operate at 10 Gb/s.

On a 32-port module, there are eight groups of 4 ports. Each group of 4 ports has 32-Gb/s to the crossbar. all ports on this line card operate at line rate at 1/2/4/8-Gb/s. Similarly, on a 48-port module there eight groups of 6 ports each. Each group of 6 ports has 32-Gb/s to the crossbar. By default, the rate-mode on all the ports on the 32 and 48-port modules set to shared.

Figure 4-2 shows the various line cards, their per port group bandwidth, the number of ports per port group and how many 4-Gb/s or 8-Gb/s or 10-Gb/s port each port group can support.

Figure 4-2   Port group lookup table

Line Cards	Bandwidth per port group	Total Ports per port group	Dedicated 4-Gb/s ports per port group	Dedicated 8-Gb/s ports per port group	Dedicated 10 Gb/s ports per port group
DS-X9124 24-Port LC	12.8-Gb/s	6 ports	3 ports	Not Supported	Not Supported
DS-X9148 48-Port LC	12.8-Gb/s	12 ports	3 ports	Not Supported	Not Supported
DS-X9248-48K9 (4/44)-Port LC	12.8-Gb/s	12 ports	3 ports	1 port	Not Supported
DS-X9224-96K9 24-Port LC	12.8-Gb/s	3 ports	3 ports	1 port	Not Supported
DS-X9248-96K9 48-Port LC	12.8-Gb/s	6 ports	3 ports	1 port	Not Supported
DS-X9232-256K9 32-port LC	32-Gb/s	4 ports	4 ports	4 ports	3 ports
DS-X9248-256K9 48-Port LC	32-Gb/s	6 ports	6 ports	4 ports	3 ports

There are two modes of oversubscription enforcement on the 24- and 48-port modules: strict mode oversubscription and unlimited mode oversubscription.

In the strict mode oversubscription, oversubscription ratios are enforced. In the unlimited oversubscription mode, no specific oversubscription is enforced, which means that if certain ports have been allocated dedicated bandwidth but are not currently using it, the spare bandwidth can be used by the ports that do not have dedicated bandwidth.

The **show port-resource module** *slot* command lists the current status of the bandwidth allocation and the rate-mode for each port group.

```
MDS-9509-2# show port-resources module 2
Module 2
Available dedicated buffers are 5400

 Port-Group 1
  Total bandwidth is 12.8 Gbps
  Total shared bandwidth is 12.8 Gbps
  Allocated dedicated bandwidth is 0.0 Gbps
  ------------------------------------------------------------------
  Interfaces in the Port-Group        B2B Credit  Bandwidth  Rate Mode
                                      Buffers     (Gbps)
  ------------------------------------------------------------------
  fc2/1                                 16          2.0      shared
  fc2/2                                 16          2.0      shared
  fc2/3                                 16          4.0      shared
  fc2/4                                 16          4.0      shared
  fc2/5                                 16          4.0      shared
  fc2/6                                 16          4.0      shared

 Port-Group 2
  Total bandwidth is 12.8 Gbps
  Total shared bandwidth is 12.8 Gbps
  Allocated dedicated bandwidth is 0.0 Gbps
  ------------------------------------------------------------------
  Interfaces in the Port-Group        B2B Credit  Bandwidth  Rate Mode
                                      Buffers     (Gbps)
  ------------------------------------------------------------------
  fc2/7                                 16          4.0      shared
  fc2/8                                 16          4.0      shared
  fc2/9                                 16          4.0      shared
  fc2/10                                16          4.0      shared
  fc2/11                                16          4.0      shared
  fc2/12                                16          4.0      shared

 Port-Group 3
  Total bandwidth is 12.8 Gbps
  Total shared bandwidth is 12.8 Gbps
  Allocated dedicated bandwidth is 0.0 Gbps
  ------------------------------------------------------------------
  Interfaces in the Port-Group        B2B Credit  Bandwidth  Rate Mode
                                      Buffers     (Gbps)
  ------------------------------------------------------------------
  fc2/13                                16          2.0      shared
  fc2/14                                16          2.0      shared
  fc2/15                                16          4.0      shared
  fc2/16                                16          4.0      shared
  fc2/17                                16          4.0      shared
  fc2/18                                16          4.0      shared

 Port-Group 4
  Total bandwidth is 12.8 Gbps
  Total shared bandwidth is 12.8 Gbps
  Allocated dedicated bandwidth is 0.0 Gbps
  ------------------------------------------------------------------
  Interfaces in the Port-Group        B2B Credit  Bandwidth  Rate Mode
                                      Buffers     (Gbps)
  ------------------------------------------------------------------
  fc2/19                                16          4.0      shared
  fc2/20                                16          4.0      shared
  fc2/21                                16          4.0      shared
  fc2/22                                16          4.0      shared
```

```
       fc2/23                                          16       4.0   shared
       fc2/24                                          16       4.0   shared

    MDS-9509-2#
```

Strict Oversubscription Mode Recipes

The following two recipes describe strict oversubscription mode in the 24- and 48-port modules. A strict 4:1 oversubscription ration on the 24-port module and a 5:1 oversubscription ration on the 48-port module is enforced in this mode.

The following recipes use 24-port modules. The same procedure applies for configuring a 48-port module also.

To configure three ports in the first port group to have 4-Gb/s bandwidth, follow these steps:

Step 1   Choose three ports that require dedicated bandwidth, ports 2/2, 2/3, 2/5.

Step 2   Set the other three ports (2/1, 2/4 , 2/6) to out-of-service.

Step 3   Set the rate-mode on the three ports that require dedicated bandwidth to dedicated.

Step 4   Set the bandwidth on the three ports to 4-Gb/s.

Step 5   Enable the ports.

The following example shows the preceding steps. It dedicates 3 ports on the first group of 6 ports on a 24-port modules to have 4-Gb/s dedicated bandwidth and the remaining ports are set to out-of-service.

```
MDS-9509-2# conf t
Enter configuration commands, one per line.  End with CNTL/Z.
MDS-9509-2(config-if)# interface fc 2/4
MDS-9509-2(config-if)# out-of-service force
MDS-9509-2(config-if)# interface fc 2/6
MDS-9509-2(config-if)# out-of-service force
MDS-9509-2(config-if)# interface fc 2/2
MDS-9509-2(config-if)# interface fc 2/2
MDS-9509-2(config-if)# switchport rate-mode dedicated
MDS-9509-2(config-if)# switchport speed 4000
MDS-9509-2(config-if)# interface fc 2/3
MDS-9509-2(config-if)# switchport rate-mode dedicated
MDS-9509-2(config-if)# switchport speed 4000
MDS-9509-2(config-if)# interface fc 2/5
MDS-9509-2(config-if)# switchport rate-mode dedicated
MDS-9509-2(config-if)# switchport speed 4000
MDS-9509-2(config)# interface fc 2/2-3, fc 2/5
MDS-9509-2(config-if)# no shut
MDS-9509-2(config-if)# end
MDS-9509-2#
```

The **show port-resource module** 2 command shows the status of the ports in port group 1.

```
MDS-9509-2# show port-resources module 2
Module 2
Available dedicated buffers are 5478

 Port-Group 1
  Total bandwidth is 12.8 Gbps
  Total shared bandwidth is 0.8 Gbps
  Allocated dedicated bandwidth is 12.0 Gbps
```

```
----------------------------------------------------------------
Interfaces in the Port-Group       B2B Credit  Bandwidth  Rate Mode
                                   Buffers     (Gbps)
----------------------------------------------------------------
fc2/1 (out-of-service)
fc2/2                                  16        4.0    dedicated
fc2/3                                  16        4.0    dedicated
fc2/4 (out-of-service)
fc2/5                                  16        4.0    dedicated
fc2/6 (out-of-service)
```

The following recipe shows how to configure the same port group to operate all six ports in that group with the following combination: three ports have dedicated 4-Gb/s bandwidth and the three other ports can operate at 1-Gb/s shared instead of being shut down. When the 12-Gb/s bandwidth is allocated to three of the six ports, the remaining bandwidth is just 0.8-Gb/s with 4:1 over subscription. This is enforced at a maximum of 0.8 * 4 = 3.2-Gb/s bandwidth that can be supported on the remaining three ports. If the remaining three ports need to operate, they can do so with a maximum bandwidth of 1-Gb/s each in shared mode.

To configure all six ports in the first port group to have a combination dedicated and shared bandwidth as described in the preceding paragraph, follow these steps:

Step 1   Set the port speed of the three ports to 1-Gb/s (2/1, 2/4, 2/6)

Step 2   Set the rate-mode to dedicated on the port that requires dedicated bandwidth.

Step 3   Enable the port in that port group.

The following example shows the preceding steps.

```
MDS-9509-2# conf t
Enter configuration commands, one per line.  End with CNTL/Z.
MDS-9509-2(config)# interface fc 2/1, fc 2/4, fc 2/6
MDS-9509-2(config-if)# switchport speed 1000
MDS-9509-2(config-if)# interface fc 2/2-3, fc 2/5
MDS-9509-2(config-if)# switchport rate-mode dedicated
MDS-9509-2(config-if)# no shut
MDS-9509-2(config-if)# exit
MDS-9509-2(config)# interface fc 2/1, fc 2/4, fc 2/6
MDS-9509-2(config-if)# no shut
MDS-9509-2(config-if)# end
MDS-9509-2#
```

The **show port-resource module 2** command lists the status of the ports in port groups on module 2.

```
MDS-9509-2# show port-resources module 2
Module 2
Available dedicated buffers are 5391

  Port-Group 1
   Total bandwidth is 12.8 Gbps
   Total shared bandwidth is 0.8 Gbps
   Allocated dedicated bandwidth is 12.0 Gbps
  ----------------------------------------------------------------
  Interfaces in the Port-Group       B2B Credit  Bandwidth  Rate Mode
                                     Buffers     (Gbps)
  ----------------------------------------------------------------
  fc2/1                                  16        1.0    shared
  fc2/2                                  16        4.0    dedicated
  fc2/3                                  16        4.0    dedicated
```

```
fc2/4                                      16        1.0  shared
fc2/5                                      16        4.0  dedicated
fc2/6                                      16        1.0  shared
```

Unlimited Oversubscription Mode Recipe

The next two recipes describe how unlimited oversubscription mode is configured in the 24- and 48-port modules. There are three ports in the first port group with 4-Gb/s bandwidth dedicated and the remaining three ports, also configured for 4-Gb/s, are in shared mode. The three ports that are configured for shared bandwidth may use the bandwidth in the pool and any unused bandwidth that is not being used by the dedicated ports.

Note   Only unused bandwidth from the ports with dedicated bandwidth can be used by the ports configured with the shared bandwidth. This mode of oversubscription is available in Cisco SAN-OS Release 3.1(x) and higher.

The following recipes use a 24-port modules, but the same procedure applies for configuring a 48-port module.

The command **no rate-mode oversubscription-limit module** enables the unlimited oversubscription mode in that module. In this configuration all the ports can operate at 4-Gb/s but only interfaces fc 2/2, 2/3 and 2/5 are guaranteed 4-Gb/s bandwidth.

To configure three ports in the first port group with 4-Gb/s dedicated bandwidth and the remaining three ports with 4-Gb/s in shared mode, follow these steps:

Step 1   Use the **shutdown** command on all the ports in the port group (2/1-2/6).

Step 2   Set the rate mode dedicated on the interfaces that need dedicated 4-Gb/s (2/2, 2/3, 2/5) bandwidth.

Step 3   Use the **no shutdown** command all the ports in the port group.

The following example shows the preceding steps:

```
MDS-9509-2# conf t
Enter configuration commands, one per line.  End with CNTL/Z.
MDS-9509-2(config)# interface fc 2/1-6
MDS 9509-2(config-if)# shut
MDS-9509-2(config-if)# no rate-mode oversubscription-limit module 2
MDS-9509-2(config)# interface fc 2/2-3, fc 2/5
MDS-9509-2(config-if)# switchport rate-mode dedicated
MDS-9509-2(config-if)# exit
MDS-9509-2(config)# interface fc 2/1-6
MDS-9509-2(config-if)# no shut
MDS-9509-2(config-if)# end
MDS-9509-2#
```

The **show port-resources module 2** command lists oversubscription related data.

```
MDS-9509-2# show port-resources module 2
Module 2
  Available dedicated buffers are 5391

 Port-Group 1
  Total bandwidth is 12.8 Gbps
  Total shared bandwidth is 0.8 Gbps
```

```
        Allocated dedicated bandwidth is 12.0 Gbps
        -----------------------------------------------------------------
        Interfaces in the Port-Group        B2B Credit  Bandwidth  Rate Mode
                                            Buffers     (Gbps)
        -----------------------------------------------------------------
        fc2/1                                    16       4.0   shared
        fc2/2                                    16       4.0   dedicated
        fc2/3                                    16       4.0   dedicated
        fc2/4                                    16       4.0   shared
        fc2/5                                    16       4.0   dedicated
        fc2/6                                    16       4.0   shared
```

Local Switching

This section details local switching that is available on the MDS platform with the DS-X9232-256K9 and DS-X9248-256K9 modules. This functionality requires NX-OS 5.2(1) and above version of NX-OS software.

Local switching is a feature that enables all the ports on a line card to switch fibre channel frames with the other ports on the same line cards independent of the switch's back plane. Local switching provides line-rate switching performance independent of the backplane bandwidth.

Local switching could potentially benefit in a high-density virtualized data center deployments of virtual machine clusters or other high bandwidth applications. Local switching can be enabled on any Cisco MDS 9000 Family director-class chassis (9506, 9509, 9513) using the DS-X9232-256K9 and DS-X9248-256K9 modules.

Best Practice   Local switching is recommended on MDS 9506 and MDS 9509 chassis which can only support 96-Gb/s per slot to the backplane. For the MDS 9513 directors it is recommended to upgrade to the fabric 3 modules to utilize 256-Gb/s per slot capability.

On the MDS platform local switching is disabled by default. It can be enabled on a per-line-card basis. However, enabling and disabling local switching may be disruptive.

Best Practice   It is recommended that all the ports on the line card where local switching is needed should be shutdown before enabling local switching.

When local switching is enabled on a line card:

- The ports on the line card do not support dedicated mode. This will prevent the ports from becoming an ISL.
- 10-Gb/s operating mode cannot be enabled.

Enabling Local Switching

The recipe below details the procedure to enable local switching on supported line cards. The recipe assumes that:

- The 32 port Advanced FC switching module is in use in slot 1.
- No dedicated ports are enabled on the line card.
- No 10 Gb ports are configured on the line card.

Step 1   Shutdown all the ports on the line card.

```
MDS-9509-2# conf t
Enter configuration commands, one per line.  End with CNTL/Z.
MDS-9509-2(config)# interface fc 1/1-32
MDS-9509-2(config-if)# shutdown
MDS-9509-2(config-if)# end
MDS-9509-2#
```

Step 2   Enable local switching on the line card

```
MDS-9509-2# conf t
Enter configuration commands, one per line.  End with CNTL/Z.
MDS-9509-2(config)# local-switching module 1
It is recommended that all the ports on this module be shut first as moving to and out of
local switching mode may be disruptive.
Do you wish to proceed with enabling local switching (y/n)  [n] Y
local switching is supported by this card and enabled <-- reports if it is supported
MDS-9509-2(config)# end
MDS-9509 2#
```

To check which line cards have local switching enabled on the switch use the **show system internal xbar local-switching** command.

```
MDS-9509-2#show system internal xbar local-switching
```

```
---------------------------------
| Slot | Local-switching enabled |
---------------------------------
|  1  |          yes            |
|  2  |          no             |
|  3  |          no             |
|  4  |          no             |
|  7  |          no             |
|  8  |          no             |
|  9  |          no             |
---------------------------------
```

The status of local switching is highlighted in bold in the above output.

Configuring 10 Gigabit Fibre Channel Ports

The ports on DS-X9232-256K9 and DS-X9248-256K9 line cards can be configured to support 2/4/8 or 10-Gb/s fibre channel speed. Configuring 10-Gb/s ports on these line cards require the configuration to be applied to a group of ports on each line card. On the 32-port line card the 10-Gb/s configuration is applied to a group of 8 ports. On the 48-port line card the configuration is applied to a group of 12 ports. The port layout is listed in Figure 4-3. The 10-Gb/s fibre channel configuration is automatically applied to the port groups. As part of the 10-Gb/s port configuration 2 to 6 ports in a group of ports being configured for 10 bps is automatically put into out of service stated to provide full 10-Gb/s bandwidth to the remaining ports in the port group.

Figure 4-3   *Port grouping for configuring 10 Gb/s fibre Channel ports*

Line Cards	Port Range for 10-Gb/s Configuration	10-Gb/s ports	Out of Service ports
DS-X9232-256K9 32-port LC	1 – 8 9 – 16 17 - 24 25 - 32	6 ports	2 ports
DS-X9248-256K9 48-Port LC	1 – 12 13 – 24 25 - 36 37 - 48	6 ports	6 ports

The recipe below shows configuration of ports 1-8 on a 32-port line card to operate at 10-Gb/s. As explained above, two of the six ports are put in to out of service mode to ensure bandwidth for the remaining 6 ports.

Step 1   Select a port range on the line card that needs to have 10-Gb/s ports. Ensure that the ports are not in use or are shutdown before conversion. Also, Local switching cannot be enabled on these line cards.

```
MDS-9509-4# conf t
Enter configuration commands, one per line.  End with CNTL/Z.
MDS-9509-4(config)# interface fc 4/1-8
```

Step 2   Enable 10-Gb/s speed on the ports using the command **10G-speed-mode**.

```
MDS-9509-4(config-if)# 10G-speed-mode
This command will disrupt traffic
Do you wish to continue(y/n)? [n] y
MDS-9509-4(config-if)# end
MDS-9509-4
```

This enables 10-Gb/s port speed for the allowed ports in port range specified above, In this example, six ports in the port group of 1 thru 8 will be operating at 10-Gb/s.

The "**show interface fc 4/1-8 brief**" command is used to show the status of the ports.

```
MDS-9509-4# show interface fc4/1-8 brief
```

```
-------------------------------------------------------------------------------
Interface  Vsan   Admin   Admin   Status       SFP   Oper   Oper    Port
                  Mode    Trunk                      Mode   Speed   Channel
                          Mode                              (Gbps)
-------------------------------------------------------------------------------
fc4/1      1      FX      on      outOfServc   --    --     --      --
fc4/2      1      FX      on      up           swl   FX     10      --
fc4/3      1      FX      on      up           swl   FX     10      --
fc4/4      1      FX      on      up           swl   FX     10      --
fc4/5      1      FX      on      up           swl   FX     10      --
fc4/6      1      FX      on      up           swl   FX     10      --
fc4/7      1      FX      on      outOfServc   --    --     --      --
fc4/8      1      FX      on      up           swl   FX     10      --
```

4-14

Configuring Gigabit Ethernet Ports

The following section describes configuring of Gigabit Ethernet ports.

Configuring VRRP

Virtual Router Redundancy Protocol (VRRP) allows two Gigabit Ethernet interfaces to provide fail over capability for an IP address. The two interfaces form an active/passive or master/backup state in which one interface services requests for the shared IP address, while the other remains in a backup or standby state. It is ideal for providing port level redundancy in iSCSI configurations. A Gigabit Ethernet port can still have its own IP address while participating in a VRRP configuration.

A VRRP session has an ID assigned to it and the two interfaces use it to communicate to identify its peer. The same ID must be used on both switches. The procedure for having both members of the VRRP pair on the same switch would be the same as if the two members were on different switches.

Best Practice   To have one interface become the master interface whenever it is online (preemption), set the Gigabit Ethernet interface to have the same IP address as the VRRP IP address.

In this example, the following resources are used to show how VVRP can be configured.:

- VRRP ID: 1
- VRRP IP address (common address): 192.168.1.40
- MDS-9509-2: Interface gige3/3 (192.168.1.20)
- MDS-9509-4: Interface gige4/1 (192.168.1.30)

To configure VRRP, follow these steps:

Step 1   Configure IP addresses on the two Gigabit Ethernet interfaces.

```
MDS-9509-2# config terminal
Enter configuration commands, one per line.  End with CNTL/Z.
MDS-9509-2(config)# interface gigabitethernet 3/3
MDS-9509-2(config-if)# ip address 192.168.1.20 255.255.255.0
MDS-9509-2(config-if)# no shut

MDS-9509-4# config terminal
Enter configuration commands, one per line.  End with CNTL/Z.
MDS-9509-4(config)# interface gigabitethernet 4/1
MDS-9509-4(config-if)# ip address 192.168.1.30 255.255.255.0
MDS-9509-4(config-if)# no shut
```

At this point, it is a good idea to verify that a host on the local subnet can ping both IP addresses (192.168.1.20 and 192.168.1.30). Alternatively, the **ips measure-rtt** command can be used to test network connectivity between the gigabit Ethernet interfaces.

```
MDS-9509-2# ips measure-rtt 192.168.1.30 interface gigabitethernet 3/3
Round trip time is 172 micro seconds (0.17 milli seconds)
```

Step 2   Configure the VRRP session on both switches using the VRRP id (1).

```
MDS-9509-2# conf t
```

```
Enter configuration commands, one per line.  End with CNTL/Z.
MDS-9509-2(config)# interface gigabitethernet 3/3
MDS-9509-2(config-if)# vrrp 1
MDS-9509-2(config-if-vrrp)# address 192.168.1.40
MDS-9509-2(config-if-vrrp)# no shut
MDS-9509-2(config-if-vrrp)# end

MDS-9509-4# conf t
Enter configuration commands, one per line.  End with CNTL/Z.
MDS-9509-4(config)# interface gigabitethernet 4/1
MDS-9509-4(config-if)# vrrp 1
MDS-9509-4(config-if-vrrp)# address 192.168.1.40
MDS-9509-4(config-if-vrrp)# no shut
MDS-9509-4(config-if-vrrp)# end
```

Step 3   Verify that the VRRP session is up and determine which interface has become the master with the **show vrrp vr** command.

```
MDS-9509-2# show vrrp vr 1
                        Interface    VR      Status
-------------------------------------------------------
            GigabitEthernet3/3       1       master

MDS-9509-2# show vrrp vr 1 interface gig3/3 status
vr id 1 status
MAC address 00:00:5e:00:01:01
Operational state: master
Up time 8 sec
MDS-9509-4# show vrrp vr 1
                        Interface    VR      Status
-------------------------------------------------------
            GigabitEthernet4/1       1       backup

MDS-9509-4# show vrrp vr 1 interface gig3/3 status
vr id 1 status
MAC address 00:00:5b:00:01:01
Operational state: backup
Up time 10 sec
```

View the configuration with the **show vrrp vr** command.

```
MDS-9509-2# show vrrp vr 1 interface gigabitethernet 3/3 configuration
vr id 1 configuration
admin state up
priority 100
associated ip: 192.168.1.40
no authentication
advertisement-interval 1
preempt no
protocol IP
```

CHAPTER 5

Logical Interfaces

Port-channels

Port-channels aggregate multiple FC or FCIP links into a single, high-speed, fault-tolerant logical link between a given pair of switches. A Port-channel has the same configuration options as a single link Fibre Channel or FCIP ISL. However, building, modifying and reducing port-channels is different from working with a single link Fibre Channel or FCIP ISL. This section discusses these different Port-Channel operations.

Best Practice   A port-channel should use interfaces on multiple modules to protect the port-channel against module failure.

The same channel group number should be used on both ends of a port-channel. This aids in troubleshooting and identifying the corresponding channel group on the other switch.

A port-channel, like all other interfaces, can have a description. Use the description field to specify exactly what switches the port-channel connects.

Port-channels can use any port on the switch and connect to any other port on the second switch.

Set the initial VSAN Allowed List before bringing up the port-channel. This prevents VSANs from merging during the port-channel start up.

DCNM SAN port-channel recipes

The recipes below describe in detail the creation and modification of port-channels on the MDS platforms.

Creating a port-channel Using DCNM SAN

This DCNM SAN recipe creates a port-channel from three existing ISLs. Because converting all ISLs between two switches into one port-channel can be disruptive, this procedure first creates a port-channel with two of the three ISL links between the switches MDS-9509-2 and MDS-9509-4, In a separate step a third link is added into the port-channel. If traffic disruption is not a concern, then all three ISLs can be added to the port-channel in one go.

The topology and the ISL port mappings used in the recipe is shown in Figure 5-1.

Figure 5-1   Topology used to create port-channel with DCNM SAN

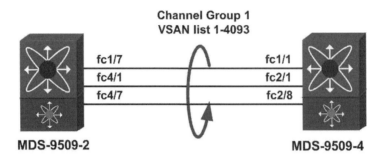

To create a port-channel from DCNM SAN, open the topology map and follow these steps:

Step 1   From DCNM SAN click the port-channel create wizard highlighted in red in Figure 5-2 to launch it.

Figure 5-2   DCNM SAN FCIP Wizard

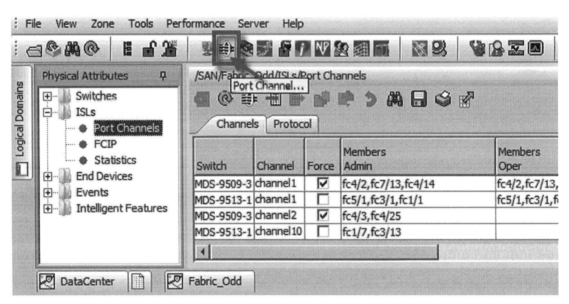

Step 2   In the resulting wizard select two of the three ISLs are shown in Figure 5-3 below.

Best Practice   If there are two or more ISLs that need to be configured into a port-channel, it is recommended to always leave at least one of the ISL out of the initial configuration. This make the port-channel creation no disruptive to the traffic flow in the SAN. I.e. for example if there are two ISLs between the switches configure only one ISL into the port-channel and then add the second to it.

In this display the ISLs are displayed in the available column. Now select 2 of the 3 ISLs highlighted using a red box (see Figure 5-3). Then click the button highlighted in blue to select the ISLs that will be configured into a port-channel.

Figure 5-3   ISL selection to create a port-channel

Figure 5-3   ISL selection to create a port-channel

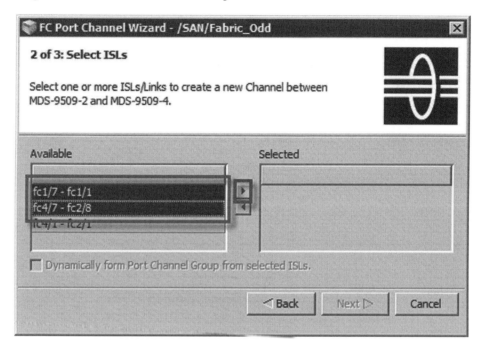

The selected ISLs appear in the **Selected** column while any other available or candidate links appear in the Available column. This is shown in Figure 5-4 and the select ISLs are highlighted using a blue rectangle. As explained in the Cisco Best Practice above only two of the three ISLs will be configured into a port-channel to avoid traffic disruption in the SAN.

Figure 5-4   ISLs Selected for port-channel configuration

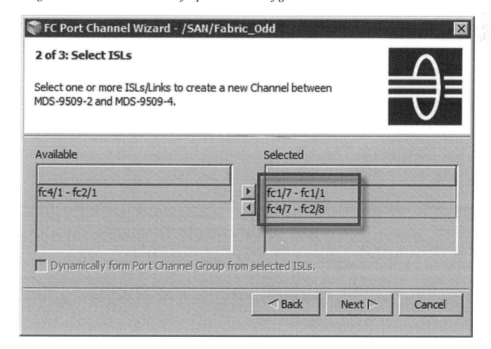

Step 3   Click **Next** to proceed.

Step 4   In the resulting create port-channel dialogue screen (see Figure 5-5) make sure that the

- Channel IDs are the same on both switches. Channel ID is 2 in this recipe. (highlighted with red boxes in Figure 5-5)

- Descriptions fully identify the port-channel (highlighted with blue boxes in Figure 5-5)

- Channel attributes section the port VSAN defaults to 1 (highlighted using a brown box in Figure 5-5)

- VSAN allowed list is modified as required. In this recipe all VSANs are allowed. (highlighted using a black box in Figure 5-5)

- Trunk mode is set to trunk. (highlighted in purple in Figure 5-5)

- Speed is set appropriately. In this recipe it is set to 4Gb/s as all the ISLs operate at 4 Gb. If using 8 Gb ISL set it to 8 Gb. (highlighted with a green circle in Figure 5-5)

- Force option is select (highlighted in orange in Figure 5-5)

Figure 5-5   Port-channel properties input configuration

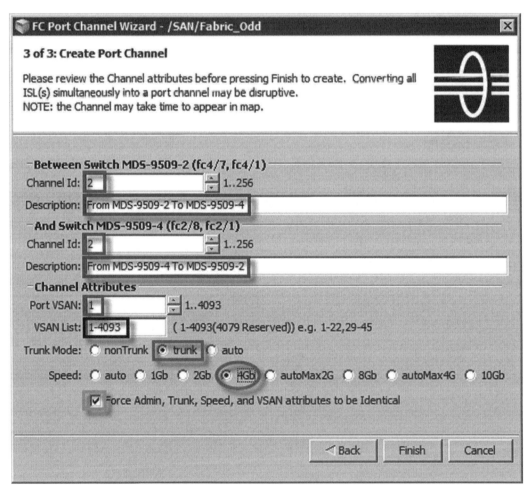

Step 5   Click **Finish** to complete the port-channel configuration.

Step 6 A warning is displayed stating that converting ISLs into port-channel may be disruptive.(see Figure 5-6). Because only two of the three ISLs will be converted into a port-channel, the other untouched ISL continues to carry SAN traffic. (Fabric Shortest Path First (FSPF) load balances around this link.) Click **Yes** to continue to create port-channel 2.

Figure 5-6   *Port-channel Creation Warning*

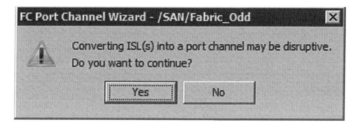

On the DCNM SAN map, the links selected to become a port-channel momentarily go down and then comes back up as a port-channel represented by a thicker line in the topology map.

The remaining steps detail the process of adding the third ISL into the port-channel with out disrupting the SAN traffic in the fabric.

Adding a new member to a port-channel using DCNM SAN

Continuing from the above recipe this recipe shows the configuration steps to add an ISL into an existing port-channel. The topology used is shown in Figure 5-7.

Figure 5-7   *Topology to add new ISL to an existing port-channel*

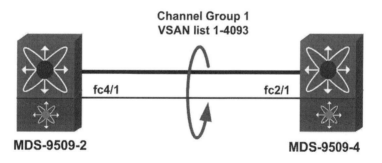

Step 1   Select the Port-channel create wizard highlighted using a red box as shown in Figure 5-8.

Figure 5-8   Port-channel create wizard

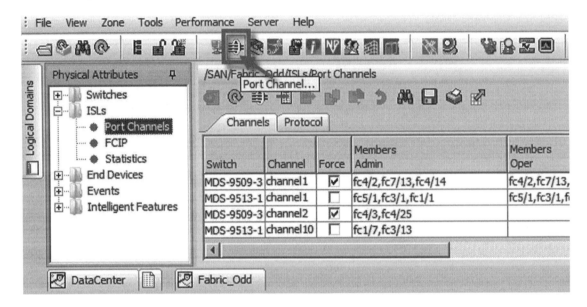

- In the wizard select the port-channel in the list. In this recipe **port-channel 2** will be modified to add the third ISL. This is highlighted using a red box in Figure 5-9. Also make sure that the "**Edit Existing**" option is selected shown using a blue box in Figure 5-9.

Figure 5-9   Select port-channel to add the additional ISL

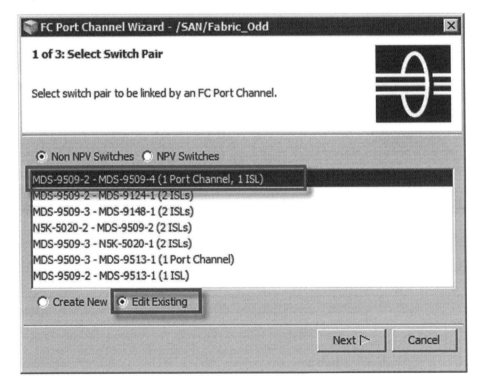

Step 2   Click **Next** to continue. This will bring up a screen to confirm the port-channel selected to edit. This is shown in Figure 5-10

Figure 5-10   *Port-channel edit confirmation window*

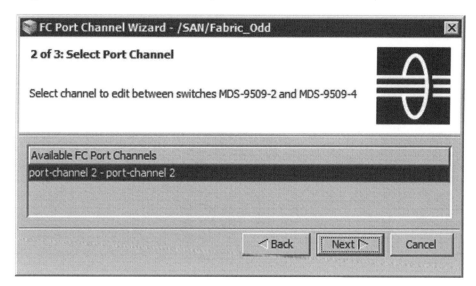

- Click Next to continue to launch the ISL selection screen shown in Figure 5-11. Here select the ISL (fc4/1 - fc2/1) in the available column. This is highlighted using a red box in Figure 5-11. Then click the button highlighted in blue to move it from available to the selected column.

Figure 5-11   *Additional ISL select window*

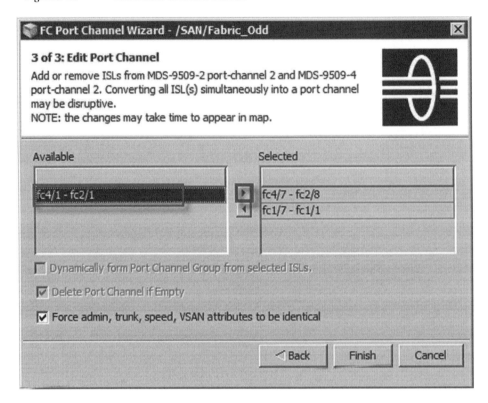

The moved ISL is shown in Figure 5-12 with a reds box.

Figure 5-12   ISL in the selected column

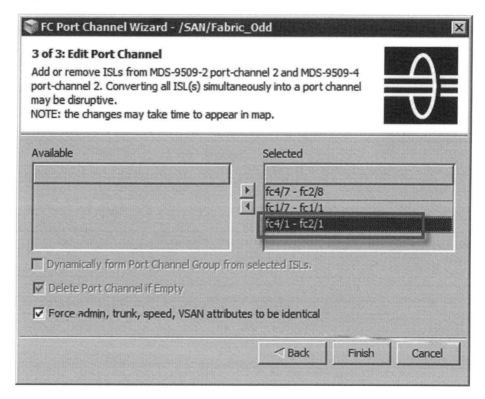

Step 3   Click **Finish** to add the ISL to the port-channel.

Step 4   A warning is displayed about adding an ISL into port-channels (see Figure 5-13). Since we are adding a link, the port-channel is not affected. The SAN traffic is automatically routed over the previously created port-channel. Click **Yes** to continue to add the ISL to the port-channel 2.

Figure 5-13   Port Modification Warning

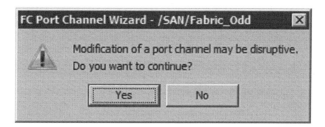

As before, the newly added ISL goes down when it joins the port-channel. This is now a part of port-channel 2.

Modifying the VSAN allowed list on a port-channel using DCNM SAN

To modify the VSAN allowed list for a port-channel in DCNM SAN, follow these steps (this is the same procedure as the one used to modify a standard trunking E port (TE port)):

Step 1   In DCNM SAN, double click the port-channel in the map This should bring up the port-channel attributes screen. This is shown in Figure 5-14

Figure 5-14   *Port-channel Attributes*

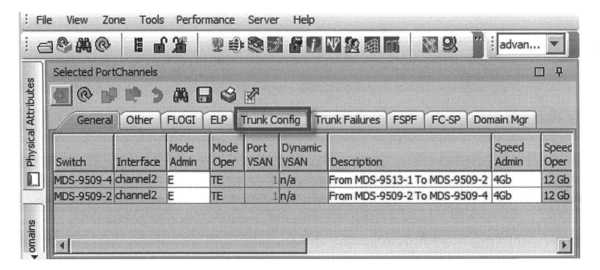

Step 2   Choose the **Trunk Config** tab. this is shown using a blue box in Figure 5-14.

Figure 5-15   *Modify VSAN Allowed List for a port-channel*

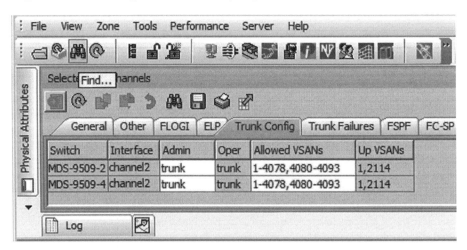

Step 3   Modify the **Allowed VSANs** column for both rows, as each row represents the configuration of the port-channel on each switch.(see Figure 5-15)

Figure 5-16   Modify VSAN allowed list

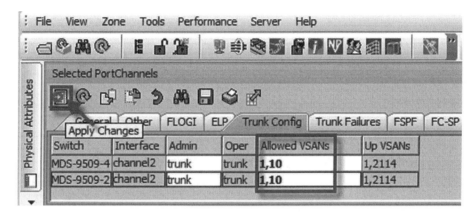

Step 4 Modify the VSAN allowed list to the required VSAN (see blue box Figure 5-16) IN this example only VSAN 1 and VSAN 10 are allowed through port-channel 2. Click **Apply Changes**. (shown using a red box in the Figure 5-16) to change the VSAN allowed list for the port-channel.

Port-channel configuration using CLI

The section below details the CLI configuration steps that are required to create and modify port-channels on the MDS platform.

Creating a port-channel from the CLI

This procedure below used CLI to create a port-channel between switches MDS-9509-3 and MDS-9513-1.

The following resources are used in this example:

- MDS-9509-3: Channel Group 2 and Interfaces fc1/1 and fc2/1
- MDS-9513-1: Channel Group 2 and Interfaces: fc1/1 and fc2/1
- Allowed VSANs: 1,10
- The topology used in this recipe is shown in Figure 5-17

Figure 5-17   port-channel Topology

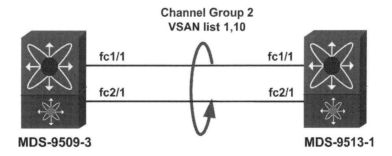

To create a port-channel using the CLI, follow these steps:

Step 1   Create the port-channel on MDS-9509-3 with the **channel-group** command. Create a description for the port with the **switchport description** command.

```
MDS-9509-3# config terminal
Enter configuration commands, one per line.  End with CNTL/Z.
MDS-9509-3(config)# interface fc1/1, fc2/1
MDS-9509-3(config-if)# channel-group 2
fc1/1 fc2/1 added to port channel 2 and disabled
please do the same operation on the switch at the other end of the port channel,
then do "no shutdown" at both ends to bring them up
MDS-9509-3(config-if)# switchport description "From MDS-9509-3 To MDS-9513-1
port-channel2"
MDS-9509-3(config)# switchport speed 4000
MDS-9509-3(config)# switchport mode E
MDS-9509-3(config)# switchport rate-mode dedicated
MDS-9509-3(config)#end
MDS-9509-3#
```

Step 2   Enable trunking and set the VSAN allowed list on MDS-9509-3.

Best Practice

It is recommended to allow port-channel protocol (PCP) to manage the links in a port-channel for optimal performance and load balancing. Write acceleration is one feature that need PCP to manage links in a port-channel to be able to work seamlessly across a port-channel. This enabled using the **channel mode active** commend for the port-channel interface.

```
MDS-9509-3# config terminal
MDS-9509-3(config)# interface port channel 2
MDS-9509-3(config-if)# switchport trunk mode on
MDS-9509-3(config-if)# switchport trunk allowed vsan 1
MDS-9509-3(config-if)# switchport trunk allowed vsan add 10
MDS-9509-3(config-if)# channel mode active <-- allows port-channel protocol to manage the
links in the port-channel
MDS-9509-3(config)#end
MDS-9509-3#
```

Step 3   Create the port-channel on MDS-9513-1 with the **channel-group** command. Create a description for the port with the **switchport description** command.

```
MDS-9513-1# config terminal
Enter configuration commands, one per line.  End with CNTL/Z.
MDS-9513-1(config)# interface fc1/1, fc2/1
MDS-9513-1(config-if)# channel-group 2
fc1/1 fc2/1 added to port channel 2 and disabled
please do the same operation on the switch at the other end of the port channel,
then do "no shutdown" at both ends to bring them up
MDS-9513-1(config-if)# switchport description "From MDS-9513-1 To MDS-9509-3
port-channel2"
MDS-9513-1(config-if)# switchport speed 4000
MDS-9513-1(config-if)# switchport mode E
MDS-9513-1(config-if)# switchport reate-mode dedicated
MDS-9513-1(config)#end
MDS-9513-1#
```

Step 4   Enable trunking (TE) and set the VSAN allowed list on MDS-9509-3.

```
MDS-9513-1# config terminal
MDS-9513-1(config)# interface port channel 2
MDS-9513-1(config-if)# switchport trunk mode on
MDS-9513-1(config-if)# switchport trunk allowed vsan 1
MDS-9513-1(config-if)# switchport trunk allowed vsan add 10
MDS-9513-1(config-if)# channel mode active <-- allows port-channel protocol to manage the
links in the port-channel

MDS-9513-1(config)#end
MDS-9513-1#
```

Step 5   Enable MDS-9509-3 interfaces with the **interface** command.

```
MDS-9509-3# config terminal
Enter configuration commands, one per line.   End with CNTL/Z.
MDS-9509-3(config)# interface fc1/1, fc2/1
MDS-9509-3(config-if)# no shut
MDS-9509-3(config)#end
MDS-9509-3#
```

Step 6   Enable MDS-9513-1 interfaces with the **interface** command.

```
MDS-9513-1# config terminal
Enter configuration commands, one per line.   End with CNTL/Z.
MDS-9513-1(config)# interface fc1/1, fc2/1
MDS-9513-1(config-if)# no shut
MDS-9513-1(config)#end
MDS-9513-1#
```

Step 7   Verify that the port-channel has come up using the **show interface port channel** command.

```
MDS-9509-3# show interface port channel 2
port channel 2 is trunking
    Port description is From MDS-9509-2 To MDS-9513-1 port-channel2
    Hardware is Fibre Channel
    Port WWN is 24:02:00:0c:85:e9:d2:c0
    Admin port mode is E, trunk mode is on
    Port mode is TE
    Port vsan is 1
    Speed is 8 Gbps
    Trunk vsans (admin allowed and active) (1,10)
    Trunk vsans (up)                       (1,10)
    Trunk vsans (isolated)                 ()
    Trunk vsans (initializing)             ()
    5 minutes input rate 64 bits/sec, 8 bytes/sec, 0 frames/sec
    5 minutes output rate 56 bits/sec, 7 bytes/sec, 0 frames/sec
      78296342 frames input, 72311141128 bytes
        0 discards, 0 errors
        0 CRC,  0 unknown class
        0 too long, 0 too short
      56299070 frames output, 26061293700 bytes
        0 discards, 0 errors
      0 input OLS, 2 LRR, 0 NOS, 0 loop inits
      4 output OLS, 2 LRR, 0 NOS, 0 loop inits
    Member[1] : fc1/1
    Member[2] : fc2/1
    iSCSI authentication: None
```

Adding New Members to a port-channel from the CLI

This recipe adds a new member to a port-channel using the CLI. This example uses the following resources:

- MDS-9509-3 and MDS-9513-1
- Existing interfaces fc1/1 and fc2/1 that are already in a port-channel (port-channel 2) on both switches
- New interface fc3/1 that will be added to the port-channel2

To add a new member to a port-channel from the CLI, follow these steps:

Step 1   Use the **force** keyword with the **channel-group** command to add the new member to MDS-9509-3. This makes a new link inherit the parameters of the existing links in channel group 2.

```
MDS-9509-3# conf t
MDS-9509-3(config)# interface fc3/1
MDS-9509-3(config-if)# channel-group 2 force
fc3/1 added to port channel 2 and disabled
please do the same operation on the switch at the other end of the port channel,
then do "no shutdown" at both ends to bring them up
MDS-9509-3(config-if)# no shut
MDS-9509-3(config)#end
MDS-9509-3#
```

Step 2   Use the **force** keyword with the **channel-group** command to add the new member to MDS-9513-1. This makes a new link inherit the parameters of the existing links in channel group 2.

```
MDS-9513-1# conf t
MDS-9513-1(config)# interface fc3/1
MDS-9513-1(config-if)# channel-group 2 force
fc3/1 added to port channel 2 and disabled
please do the same operation on the switch at the other end of the port channel,
then do "no shutdown" at both ends to bring them up
switch3(config-if)# no shut
MDS-9513-1(config)#end
MDS-9513-1#
```

Step 3   Verify that the port-channel now has three members. Use the **show interface port channel** command.

```
MDS-9509-3# show interface port channel 2
port channel 2 is trunking
    Port description is To MDS-9513-1 port-channel2
    Hardware is Fibre Channel
    Port WWN is 24:02:00:0c:85:e9:d2:c0
    Admin port mode is E, trunk mode is on
    Port mode is TE
    Port vsan is 1
    Speed is 12 Gbps
    Trunk vsans (admin allowed and active) (1,10)
    Trunk vsans (up)                       (1,10)
    Trunk vsans (isolated)                 ()
    Trunk vsans (initializing)             ()
    5 minutes input rate 64 bits/sec, 8 bytes/sec, 0 frames/sec
    5 minutes output rate 56 bits/sec, 7 bytes/sec, 0 frames/sec
      78296342 frames input, 72311141128 bytes
        0 discards, 0 errors
        0 CRC,  0 unknown class
        0 too long, 0 too short
      56299070 frames output, 26061293700 bytes
        0 discards, 0 errors
      0 input OLS, 2 LRR, 0 NOS, 0 loop inits
      4 output OLS, 2 LRR, 0 NOS, 0 loop inits
    Member[1] : fc1/1
```

```
      Member[2] : fc2/1
      Member[3] : fc3/1
      iSCSI authentication: None
MDS-9509-3#
```

Modifying the VSAN Allowed List on a port-channel From the CLI

The following example modifies the VSAN allowed list for a port-channel and adds VSAN 17 to port-channel 2 with the **switchport trunk allowed** command. (This is the same process used for a standard, single link TE port.)

```
MDS-9509-3# config terminal
MDS-9509-3(config)# interface port channel 2
MDS-9509-3(config-if)# switchport trunk allowed vsan add 17
MDS-9509-3(config)#end
MDS-9509-3#
```

Remove VSAN 17 from port-channel 2 using the **no switchport trunk allowed** command.

```
MDS-9513-1# config terminal
MDS-9513-1(config)# interface port channel 2
MDS-9513-1(config-if)# switchport trunk allowed vsan add 17
MDS-9513-1(config)#end
MDS-9513-1#
```

Configuring TF links and F port-channels

For steps on how to create a TF links and F port-channels please refer to the recipe in Chapter 10, "Configuring MDS ToR switch in NPV mode" for FC switches and Chapter 10, "Configuring a Nexus 5000 switch to support FCoE (NPV mode)" for FCoE Tor Switches to MDS switches.

CHAPTER 6

VSANs

A virtual SAN (VSAN) is a logical grouping of ports in a single switch or across multiple switches that are inter connected forming a single fabric. A VSAN is completely isolated from other VSANs in terms of traffic, security, and has it's own fabric services. This level of isolation ensures that changes made to one VSAN do not affect the other VSAN, even though they are share the same physical SAN infrastructure hardware.

VSANs provide the capability to host, multiple logical SANs on the same physical SAN hardware infrastructure. A VSAN lends itself to SAN island consolidation on a higher port density physical switch, while still maintaining traffic isolation and providing increased security that was available in SAN islands. Once a VSAN is created, it has all the properties and functions of a SAN switch.

Multiple VSANs can be defined on a physical switch. Each VSAN requires its own domain_ID. A single VSAN can span 239 physical switches (a Fibre Channel standards limit). At the current time, a maximum of 256 VSANs can be created in a physical switch.

Using VSANs provides some important advantages:

- VSAN traffic stays within the VSAN boundaries. Any devices can be part of only one VSAN at any given time.

- VSANs allow the creation of multiple logical SAN instances on top of a physical SAN infrastructure. This allows for the consolidation of multiple SAN islands onto a physical SAN infrastructure, which reduces the hardware requirement in the Data Center.

- Each VSAN has it own set of fabric services, which allows the SAN infrastructure to be scalable and highly available.

- Additional SAN ports can be added to and removed from each VSAN as needed without impacting VSAN ports that are already in use. Moving ports between VSANs is as simple as assigning the port to a different VSAN.

VSANs are numbered from 1 through 4094. VSAN 1 and VSAN 4094 are predefined and have very specific pre-defined roles. The user-specified VSAN range is from 2 through 4093. VSAN 1 is the default VSAN that contains all ports by default. VSAN 1 and VSAN 4094 cannot be deleted.

VSAN 1 is used as a management VSAN. VSAN 4094 is the isolated VSAN into which all orphaned ports (when a VSAN with ports is deleted) are assigned. Devices that are part of VSAN 4094 cannot communicate with each other.

Best Practice   It is recommended to use VSAN 1 strictly as a management VSAN. It is recommended not to use VSAN 1 to connect production end devices to it.

Creating a VSAN and adding interfaces in CLI

The recipe below details the steps needed to configure VSAN 1000 on two switches MDS-9509-3 and MDS-9513-1 using the CLI. VSAN 1000 is created on the two inter-connected switches and has unique Domain IDs on each switch. This allows the VSAN to merge and span both the switches.

Best Practice   When the same VSAN is created on multiple inter-connected switches ensure that the VSAN has unique Domain IDs for that VSAN on each switch.

The recipe will create VSAN 1000 on the two switches assign unique Domain IDs on each switch and add one interface on each switch to VSAN 1000. The resources used in this recipe are:

- MDS-9509-3:
    - VSAN 1000
    - Domain ID: 10
    - interface fc 4/6
- MDS-9513-1:
    - VSAN 1000
    - Domain ID: 11
    - interface fc 5/14

To create a VSAN on two inter-connected switches following are the steps.

Step 1   Create VSAN 1000 on MDS-9509-3

```
MDS-9509-3# conf t
Enter configuration commands, one per line.  End with CNTL/Z.
MDS-9509-3(config)# vsan database
MDS-9509-3(config-vsan-db)# vsan 1000 name VSAN1000 <-- Created VSAn 1000
MDS-9509-3(config-vsan-db)# end
MDS-9509-3
#
```

Step 2   Assign Domain ID 10 to VSAN 1000 on MDS-9509-3.

```
MDS-9509-3# conf t
Enter configuration commands, one per line.  End with CNTL/Z.
MDS-9509-3(config)# fcdomain domain 10 static vsan 1000 <-- Assigns Domain ID 10
MDS-9509-3(config)# end
MDS-9509-3
```

Best Practice   It is always recommended to make **Domain IDs static**. This ensures that fabric events do not change Domain IDs causing disruption to the SAN service.

Note   Domain ID has to be unique for a VSAN on each inter-connected switch, on which the same VSAN exists.

Step 3   Restart VSAN 1000 for the Domain ID to take effect.

```
MDS-9509-3# conf t
Enter configuration commands, one per line.  End with CNTL/Z.
MDS-9509-3(config)# vsan database
MMDS-9509-3(config-vsan-db)# vsan 1000 suspend <-- Suspend the VSAN (Stop VSAN)
MDS-9509-3(config-vsan-db)# no vsan 1000 suspend <-- Un Suspend VSAN (Restart VSAN)
MDS-9509-3(config-vsan-db)# end
MDS-9509-3
```

Step 4   Check to see that the new Domain ID is in effect using the "**show fcdomain vsan 1000**" command.

```
MDS-9509-3# show fcdomain vsan 1000
The local switch is the Principal Switch. <-- indicates the principal Switch

Local switch run time information:
        State: Stable
        Local switch WWN:    23:e8:00:05:30:00:18:a3
        Running fabric name: 23:e8:00:05:30:00:18:a3
        Running priority: 128
        Current domain ID: 0x0a(10) <-- Current Domain ID

Local switch configuration information:
        State: Enabled
        FCID persistence: Enabled
        Auto-reconfiguration: Disabled
        Contiguous-allocation: Disabled
        Configured fabric name: 20:01:00:05:30:00:28:df
        Optimize Mode: Disabled
        Configured priority: 128
        Configured domain ID: 0x0a(10) (static) <-- Configured Domain ID

Principal switch run time information:
        Running priority: 128
MDS-9509-3#
```

The configured and running Domain ID is highlighted in bold in the above output.

Step 5   Add interface fc 4/6 to VSAN 1000.

```
MDS-9509-3# conf t
Enter configuration commands, one per line.  End with CNTL/Z.
MDS-9509-3(config)# vsan database
MDS-9509-3(config-vsan-db)# vsan 1000 interface fc 4/6 <-- Add interface fc 4/6
Traffic on fc4/6 may be impacted. Do you want to continue? (y/n) [n] y
MDS-9509-3(config-vsan-db)# end
MDS-9509-3
```

Step 6   Use the command "**show vsan membership**" to verify that the interface is now part of VSAN 1000

```
MDS-9509-3# show vsan 1000 membership
vsan 1000 interfaces:
    fc4/6

MDS-9509-3#
```

Step 7   Create VSAN 1000 on MDS-9513-1

```
MDS-9513-1# conf t
Enter configuration commands, one per line.  End with CNTL/Z.
MDS-9513-1(config)# vsan database
MDS-9513-1(config-vsan-db)# vsan 1000 name VSAN1000 <-- Created VSAn 1000
MDS-9513-1(config-vsan-db)# end
MDS-9513-1
```

Step 8 Assign Domain ID 11 to VSAN 1000 on MDS-9513-1.

```
MDS-9513-1# conf t
Enter configuration commands, one per line.  End with CNTL/Z.
MDS-9513-1(config)# fcdomain domain 11 static vsan 1000 <-- Assigns Domain ID 11
MDS-9513-1(config)# end
MDS-9513-1
```

Step 9 Restart VSAN 1000 for the Domain ID to take effect.

```
MDS-9513-1# conf t
Enter configuration commands, one per line.  End with CNTL/Z.
MDS-9513-1(config)# vsan database
MMDS-9513-1(config-vsan-db)# vsan 1000 suspend <-- Suspend the VSAN (Stop VSAN)
MDS-9513-1(config-vsan-db)# no vsan 1000 suspend <-- Un Suspend VSAN (Restart VSAN)
MDS-9513-1(config-vsan-db)# end
```

Step 10 Check to see that the new Domain ID is in effect using the "**show fcdomain vsan 1000**" command.

```
MDS-9513-1# show fcdomain vsan 1000
The local switch is a Subordinated Switch. <-- A subordinate switch
Local switch run time information:
        State: Stable
        Local switch WWN:    23:e8:00:0d:ec:6d:50:41
        Running fabric name: 23:e8:00:05:30:00:18:a3
        Running priority: 128
        Current domain ID: 0x0b(11) <-- Current Domain ID

Local switch configuration information:
        State: Enabled
        FCID persistence: Enabled
        Auto-reconfiguration: Disabled
        Contiguous-allocation: Disabled
        Configured fabric name: 20:01:00:05:30:00:28:df
        Optimize Mode: Disabled
        Configured priority: 128
        Configured domain ID: 0x0b(11) (static) <-- COnfigured Domain ID

Principal switch run time information:
        Running priority: 2
MDS-9513-1#
```

The configured and running Domain ID is highlighted in bold in the above output.

Step 11 Add interface fc 5/14 to VSAN 1000.

```
MDS-9513-1# conf t
Enter configuration commands, one per line.  End with CNTL/Z.
MDS-9513-1(config)# vsan database
MDS-9513-1(config-vsan-db)# vsan 1000 interface fc 5/14 <-- Add interface fc 5/14
Traffic on fc4/6 may be impacted. Do you want to continue? (y/n) [n] y
MDS-9513-1(config-vsan-db)# end
MDS-9513-1
```

Step 12 Use the command "**show vsan membership**" to verify that the interface is now part of VSAN 1000

```
MDS-9513-1# show vsan 1000 membership
vsan 1000 interfaces:
    fc5/14

MDS-9513-1#
```

VSAN Recipes using DCNM SAN

The section below details various VSAN recipes using the DCNM SAN client.

Creating a new VSAN

This recipe creates a VSAN (1500) on MDS-9509-3 and MDS-9513-1 and adds an interface fc 4/6 on MDS-9509-3 and interface fc 5/14 on MDS-9513-1 to the VSAN on each switch.

Note   Moving a port from one VSAN to another does not change its configuration (F, FL, TL), its speed, or its administrative state (shut/noshut). However, any device attached to the port needs to do a fabric login (FLOGI) back into the switch.

To create a VSAN from DCNM SAN, follow these steps:

Step 1   On the toolbar, click the **Create VSAN** icon (see Figure 6-1).

Figure 6-1   *Create VSAN using DCNM SAN*

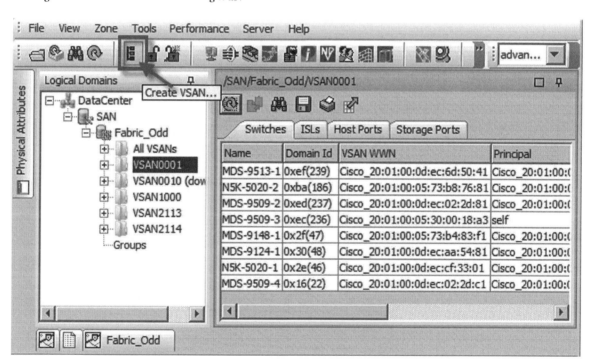

Step 2   Select the switch(es) for the VSAN. The switches are highlighted using red boxes in Figure 6-2.

Step 3   Enter the VSAN ID in **Create VSAN** dialog box (see Figure 6-2). In this recipe VSAN 1500 is being created.

Step 4   Enter the VSAN id 1500. it is shown using a green oval in Figure 6-2.

Step 5   Enter a name for the VSAN. the VSAN name used in this recipe is VSAN1500. highlighted using a blue box in Figure 6-2.

Step 6   Select the static domain ID option shown using a brown box in Figure 6-2.

Step 7 Assign static domain IDs highlighted in black in Figure 6-2. In this recipe the VSAN 1500 on switch MDS-9513-1 get Domain ID 11 and on switch MDS-9509-3 it gets Domain ID 10.

Note You can specify a static domain_ID for a VSAN at the time of creation. Otherwise, you can follow the recipe in Converting an Existing VSAN to Static Domain ID and Enabling a Persistent FCID Using the CLI, page 6-17 to specify the new domain_ID.

Figure 6-2   VSAN create attributes wizard

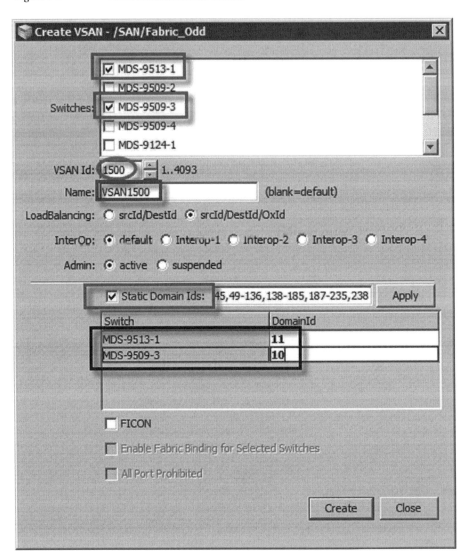

Step 8 Click **Create** to create VSAN 1500 on the two selected switches.

Step 9 Select **Logical Domain** -->**VSAN 1500** (highlighted in the blue box in Figure 6-3. This should show the switches in the newly created VSAN and their domain IDs shown using a black box in Figure 6-3.

Figure 6-3   *VSAN create status screen*

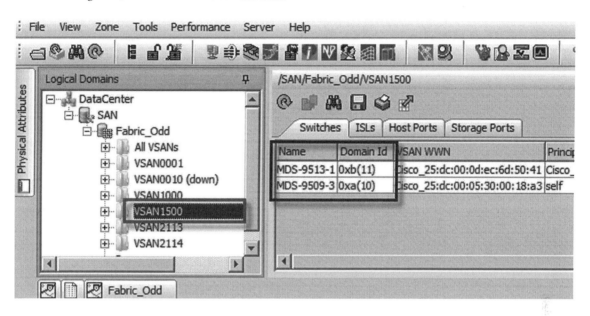

Adding an interface to the VSAN

To add interfaces to the new VSAN using DCNM SAN, follow these steps:

Step 1   In DCNM SAN select the **Physical Attributes** pane, expand **Switches -> FC Interfaces -> Physical.** shown using a black box in Figure 6-4.

Figure 6-4   *Change Port VSAN Membership*

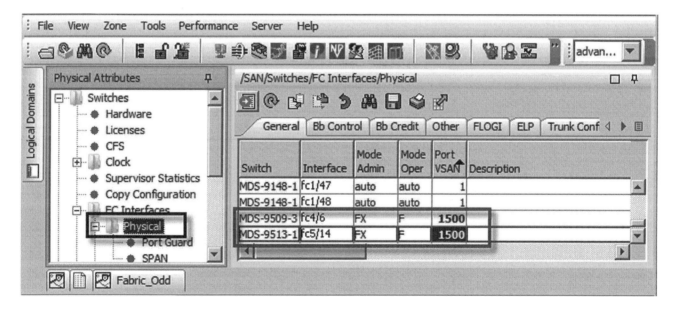

Step 2 Modify the **Port VSAN** field for both the switch interfaces that need to be moved to the specified VSAN. In this case to VSAN 1500. (See blue box in Figure 6-4)

Step 3 Click **Apply Changes....**

A warning is displayed that moving a port between two VSANs can be disruptive to that port.

Caution The port that is moved will have to log in again to the fabric and will no longer have access to resources in the previous VSAN.

Step 4 Click **Yes** to move the ports to the new VSAN. (see Figure 6-5)

Figure 6-5 Move Port to New VSAN Confirmation

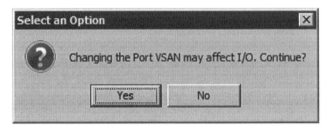

Modifying VSAN Attributes

These recipes modify the attributes of a VSAN using DCNM SAN Client. The attributes of a VSAN include:

- VSAN name
- Load balancing (src/dst or src/dst/ox-id)
- Administrative state (suspended or active)
- Interoperability mode to work with third-party switches
- Order delivery

To modify the attributes of a VSAN, follow these steps:

Step 1 Select Logical Domains pane.

Step 2 Expand the **VSAN** to be modified (VSAN 1500 in Figure 6-6).

Step 3 Choose **VSAN Attributes**.

Step 4 Make changes to the desired fields.

Note Standard editing keyboard shortcuts (Ctrl+X to cut, Ctrl+C to copy, and Ctrl+V to paste) can be used to edit the text fields.

Step 5 Click **Apply Changes....** for the configuration changes to take effect.(see red box in Figure 6-6)

Figure 6-6   Modify VSAN Attributes

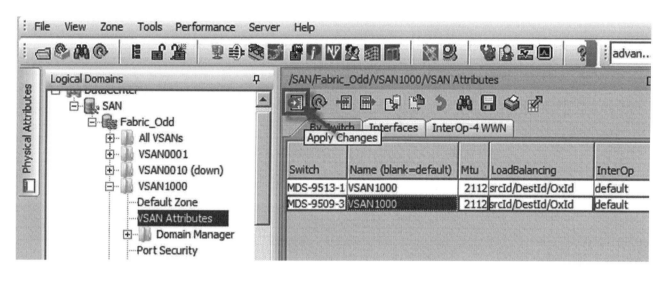

Changing Domain ID and related configuration of a VSAN

Within a VSAN, the domain manager process on the principal switch in a fabric is responsible for assigning a domain ID to a switch joining the fabric. When a switch boots up or joins a new fabric, it can request a specific domain ID or accept any available domain ID assigned to it by the principal switch.

A domain ID can be configured in two ways:

- **Preferred:** The new switch requests a specific domain ID. However, if it receives a different domain ID, it accepts it.

- **Static:** The new switch requests a specific domain ID. If it receives a different domain ID, it isolates itself from the fabric.

Best Practice   It is recommend to use static domain IDs on all VSANs.

After obtaining the domain ID from the principal switch in the VSAN, the local switch assigns Fibre Channel Identifiers (FC IDs) to each end device as they log into the fabric. This process is known as FLOGI.

Best Practice   HPUX and AIX are two operating systems that use a FC ID in the device path to storage. For the switch to always assign the same FC ID to a device across switch reboots, configure a persistent FC ID and static domain ID for the VSAN.

Caution   If an FC ID changes for a storage device accessed by either an AIX or a HPUX host, the host will lose access to the device.

By default, the switch assigns the same FC ID to a device. However, if the switch is rebooted this database of port world-wide name (pWWN)/FC ID mapping is not statically maintained. Enabling persistent FC IDs will make this database persistent across reboots.

A persistent FC ID can be configured two ways:

- **Dynamic:** The FC ID is determined and assigned by the switch and if the persistent FC ID database is manually purged by the user this entry will be deleted. These entries are persistent across reboots of the switch and are VSAN specific.

- **Static:** The FC ID is determined by the user before attaching the device to the switch. If the persistent FC ID database is manually purged by the user these entries will not be removed. These entries are persistent across reboots of the switch and are VSAN-specific.

When a persistent FC ID is enabled for a VSAN, the switch makes persistent FC ID of all the devices in that VSAN. The system automatically assigns a FC ID and make it permanent. This feature is the default behavior on MDS switches.

The recipe below shows changing the Domain ID for VSAN 1000 on switches MDS-9509-3 and MDS-9513-1 and setting the FC ID to be persistent for the same VSAN.

To change the Domain ID for a VSAN and set the FC ID to be persistent for the same VSAN, follow these steps:

Step 1 Select Logical Domains.

Step 2 Expand the **VSAN 1500** whose attribute needs to be modified and select **Domain Manager.** (see blue box inFigure 6-7) This brings up the current domain_ID of the VSAN 1500. See Figure 6-7.)

Figure 6-7   *Current Domain ID and config type of VSAN 1500*

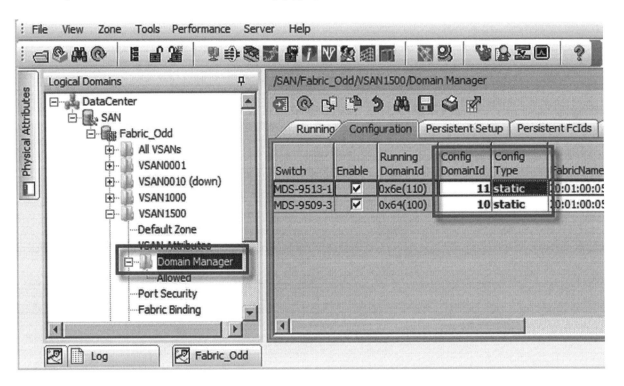

Step 3   Select the **Configuration** tab on the right-hand side. Then edit the Domain ID of the required switches in the **Config Domain Id** field. (see red box in Figure 6-7). Here the Domain ID for VSAN 1500 on MDS-9513-1 is set to 11 and on MDS-9509-3 is set to 10.

Step 4   Change the **Config Type** field, from **preferred** to **static.** (see red box in Figure 6-8.)

Best Practice   The domain IDs can range between 1 through 239 in a Fibre Channel environment. When a VSAN spans multiple switches, the domain ID for the VSAN in each switch that it spans also has to be unique.

Caution   Changing domain IDs changes the FC IDs for a device. This is disruptive, as an end device will be logged out of the fabric and has to log back in again to the fabric (FLOGI) to obtain a new FC ID. However, just making a domain ID static without changing its value is not disruptive.

Step 5   Click the green **Apply changes** button for the conf io gu ration to take effect.

Step 6   Then in the logical pane select **VSAN1500 --> VSAN Attributes** (seeFigure 6-8)

Step 7   In the Admin field drop down box select suspended on both the switches where the Domain ID was changed. (see blue box in Figure 6-8)

Figure 6-8   Suspend VSAN 1500 on the switches where Domain ID was changed

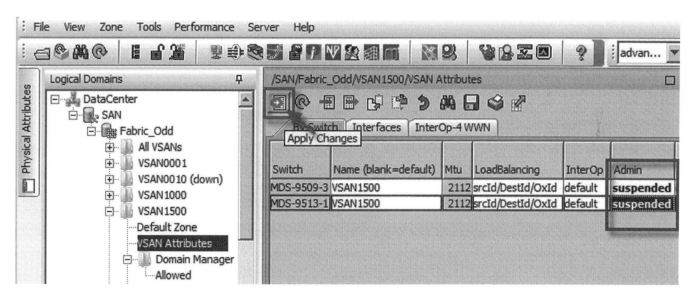

Step 8   Click the **Apply Changes** button highlighted in a red box in Figure 6-8. This will bring up a warning about disruption to the VSAN on the switches. (see This only affects the VSAN 1500 on the two switches.

Figure 6-9   VSAN suspend warning message

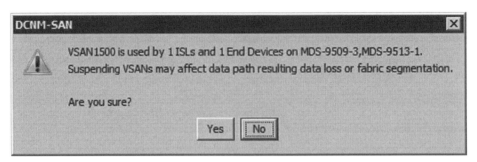

Step 9   Select **Yes** to apply the changes.

Step 10   Again in the same screen in the **Admin** Field drop down box select **active**. (see red box in Figure 6-10)

Figure 6-10   Activate VSAN to apply Domain ID Changes

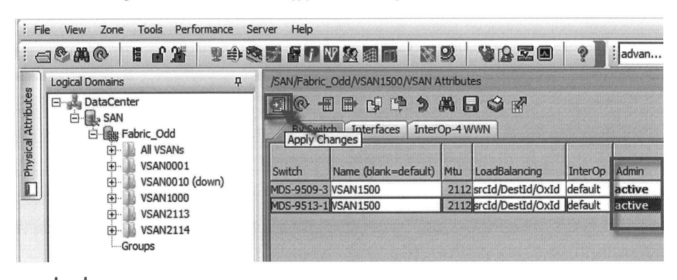

Best Practice   When the domain ID of a VSAN changes, it is recommended to suspend and un suspend the VSAN on the switches where the Domain ID of the VSAn was changed. This forces all logged in devices to log out and log back in. At that time, new FC IDs are allocated to all the devices in that VSAN on the affected switches.

Step 11   Click **Apply Changes** to apply the configuration. This should apply the Domain ID changes to VSAN 1500

Changing the FCID Configuration of VSAN

Step 1   Select Logical Domains pane.

Step 2   Expand the **VSAN 1000** --> **Domain Manager.** (This brings up the current domain_ID of the VSAN 1000.) See Figure 6-11.

Step 3   Select the **Persistent Setup** tab on the right-hand side. The **enable** check box should be selected for all the switches visible here. This is enabled by default on the MDS platform. (see red box in Figure 6-11.)

Figure 6-11   *Persistent FC ID setup*

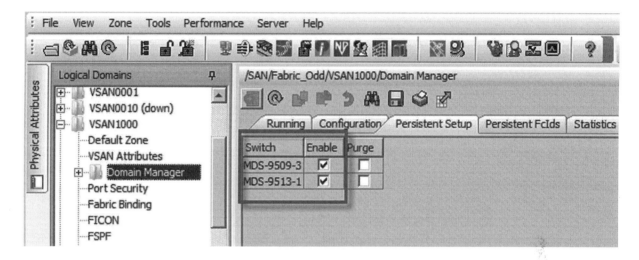

Step 4   If not enabled select the **enable** check box and click **Apply changes** to apply the changes.

At this point, the domain ID is statically set and FC IDs will remain persistent across reboots for VSAN 1000 on the switches MDS-9509-3 and MDS-9513-1. The persistent FC ID database can be viewed in the **Persistent FCIDs** tab (see Figure 6-12).

Figure 6-12   *Persistent FC ID Database*

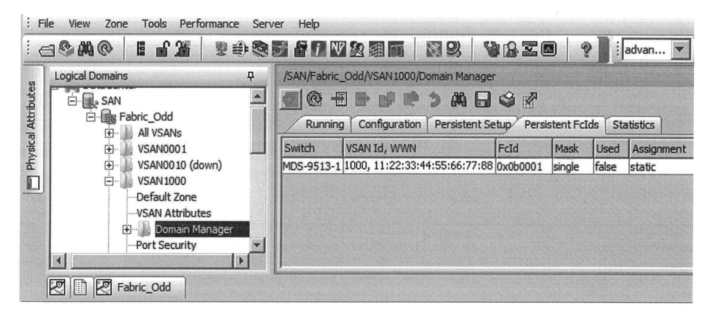

Modifying VSAN Attributes with the CLI

These recipes modify the attributes of a VSAN using the CLI. This includes interop modes, load balancing, and setting static Domain IDs and persistent FC IDs.

Setting VSAN Interop Mode

Set Interop mode for VSANs that need to interact with other third-party switches. Different interop modes are required for various 3rd party switches. The various modes are shown in Figure 6-13.

Best Practice   Configuring the MDS fabric switch or a 3rd Party fabric switch into NPV mode as outlined in Chapter 10, "Top of Rack (ToR) Switches"and connecting it to an NPIV enabled core switch, will eliminate the need to configure the VSAN for interoperability. Switches configured for NPV mode log into the core switch as an F-Port and not as an E-Port.

Figure 6-13   Interop Modes

Interop Mode	When to use it
Mode 1	**Required when all vendor switches are set in their respective interop modes. In interop mode 1, only Domain IDs 97 to 127 are allowed**
Mode 2	**Required when VSAN has to work with a Brocade 2800/3800 switch in native corePID 0 mode**
Mode 3	**Required when the VSAN has to work with a Brocade switch running in corePID 1 mode**
Mode 4	**Required when the VSAN has to work with a Mcdata switch. Only domain IDs 1 through 31 are allowed.**

For more information, refer to the *Cisco MDS 9000 Family Switch-to-Switch Interoperability Configuration Guide* on http://www.cisco.com. Consult this manual before doing interoperability tasks; it explains the different Interop modes.

The following examples shows how set interop modes to 1, 2,3 and 4 for a VSAN.

Interop Mode 1

Interop mode 1 is required when all vendor switches are set in their respective interop modes. This mode only supports Domain IDs between 97 and 127. Ensure that the domain_ID of the VSAN is between 97 and 127 for mode 1 to work. Change the interop mode with the **vsan interop** command.

```
MDS-9513-1# conf t
MDS-9513-1(config)# vsan database
MDS-9513-1(config-vsan-db)# vsan 200 interop 1
MDS-9513-1(config-vsan-db)# end
MDS-9513-1#
```

Interop Mode 2

Interop mode 2 is required when a VSAN has to work with a Brocade 2800/3800 switch in corePID 0 mode. Change the interop mode with the **vsan interop** command.

```
MDS-9513-1# conf t
Enter configuration commands, one per line.  End with CNTL/Z.
MDS-9513-1(config)# vsan database
MDS-9513-1(config-vsan-db)# vsan 200 interop 2
MDS-9513-1(config-vsan-db)# end
MDS-9513-1#
```

Interop Mode 3

Interop mode 3 is required when a VSAN has to work with a Brocade switch running in corePID 1. Change the interop mode with the **vsan interop** command.

```
MDS-9513-1# conf t
Enter configuration commands, one per line.  End with CNTL/Z.
MDS-9513-1(config)# vsan database
MDS-9513-1(config-vsan-db)# vsan 200 interop 3
MDS-9513-1(config-vsan-db)# end
MDS-9513-1#
```

Interop Mode 4

Interop mode 4 is required when a VSAN has to work with a McData switch. Change the interop mode with the **vsan interop** command.

```
MDS-9513-1# conf t
Enter configuration commands, one per line.  End with CNTL/Z.
MDS-9513-1(config)# vsan database
MDS-9513-1(config-vsan-db)# vsan 200 interop 4
MDS-9513-1(config-vsan-db)# end
MDS-9513-1#
```

Note Besides setting the VSAN in interop mode 4, additional configurations are required to successfully bring up the VSAN to operate in interop mode 4. Refer to the *Cisco MDS 9000 Family Switch-to-Switch Interoperability Configuration Guide* on http://www.cisco.com for more comprehensive instructions.

Changing the Load-Balancing method for a VSAN

Configure the load-balancing scheme with VSAN S_ID (source id), D_ID (destination id)-based load-balancing, and the exchange level (S_ID, D_ID, OX_ID) on the switch.

These recipes configure load-balancing for VSAN 200.

Sequence Level Load-Balancing (Source_ID, Destination_ID)

Change the load-balancing method for VSAN 200 to S_ID, D_ID mode with the **vsan loadbalancing** command.

```
MDS-9513-1# conf t
Enter configuration commands, one per line.  End with CNTL/Z.
MDS-9513-1(config)# vsan database
MDS-9513-1(config-vsan-db)# vsan 200 loadbalancing src-dst-id
MDS-9513-1(config-vsan-db)# end
MDS-9513-1#
```

Exchange Level Load-Balancing (S_ID, D_ID, OX_ID)

Change the load-balancing method for VSAN 200 to S_ID, D_ID, and OX_ID modes with the **vsan loadbalancing** command. This is the default load-balancing method for VSANs.

```
MDS-9513-1# conf t
Enter configuration commands, one per line.  End with CNTL/Z.
MDS-9513-1(config)# vsan database
MDS-9513-1(config-vsan-db)# vsan 200 loadbalancing src-dst-ox-id
MDS-9513-1(config-vsan-db)# end
MDS-9513-1#
```

Converting an Existing VSAN to Static Domain ID and Enabling a Persistent FCID Using the CLI

This recipe configures a static domain ID for a VSAN and enables a persistent FC ID for VSAN 3000 on switch MDS-9513-1.

In this recipe an existing VSAN (3000) on switch MDS-9513-1with domain ID 239 is statically configured and the persistent FC ID is enabled. This recipe does not alter the running domain ID.

To configure a static domain ID for a VSAN and enable a persistent FC ID for a VSAN, follow these steps:

Step 1   Get the current domain ID for VSAN 3000 using the command **show domain-list**.

```
MDS-9513-1# show fcdomain domain-list vsan 3000
Number of domains: 2
Domain ID          WWN
---------          -----------------------
0xef(239)     2b:b8:00:05:30:00:68:5f [Local] [Principal]
```

Step 2   Configure the static domain_ID with the **domain static** command.

```
MDS-9513-1# conf t
Enter configuration commands, one per line.  End with CNTL/Z.
MDS-9513-1(config)# fcdomain domain 239 static vsan 3000
```

Step 3   Enable persistent FC ID with **fcid persistent**.

```
MDS-9513-1(config)# fcdomain fcid persistent vsan 3000
MDS-9513-1(config)# end
```

Step 4   Save the configuration.

```
MDS-9513-1# copy running-config startup-config
[#######################################] 100%
MDS-9513-1#
```

Note   If the domain ID of VSAN 200 is different from what is currently running, then the VSAN has to be suspended and un-suspended before configuration changes to the domain ID can take effect.

Caution   Changing domain IDs changes the FC IDs for a device. This is disruptive, as an end device will be logged out of the fabric and has to log back in again to the fabric (FLOGI) to obtain a new FC ID. However, just making a domain ID static without changing its value is not disruptive.

Changing the Domain ID in a VSAN and Making It Static

Sometimes the VSAN on a switch needs a specific domain ID for various operational requirements. If the domain ID of the VSAN needs to be changed from its current running domain ID, the VSAN has to be restarted (**using suspend and no suspend commands**) for the new domain ID to take effect.

To configure the domain ID of VSAN 200 from it running domain ID 145 to 229, follow these steps:

Step 1   List the current domain_ID of VSAN 200.

```
MDS-9513-1# show fcdomain domain-list vsan 200
Number of domains: 1
Domain ID          WWN
---------     -----------------------
0x91(145)     20:c8:00:0d:ec:24:5e:c1 [Local] [Principal]
MDS-9513-1#
```

Step 2   Change the domain_ID of VSAN 200 to 229 and make it static.

```
MDS-9513-1# conf t
Enter configuration commands, one per line.  End with CNTL/Z.
MDS-9513-1(config)# fcdomain domain 229 static vsan 200
MDS-9513-1(config)# end
MDS-9513-1#
```

Step 3   Restart VSAN 200 for the new domain_ID to take effect using **vsan suspend** command.

```
MDS-9513-1# conf t
Enter configuration commands, one per line.  End with CNTL/Z.
MDS-9513-1(config)# vsan database
MDS-9513-1(config-vsan-db)# vsan 200 suspend
MDS-9513-1(config-vsan-db)# no vsan 200 suspend
MDS-9513-1(config-vsan-db)# end
MDS-9513-1#
```

Step 4   List the current running domain_ID of the VSAN 200 to verify the Domain ID changes.

```
MDS-9513-1# show fcdomain domain-list vsan 200
Number of domains: 1
Domain ID          WWN
---------     -----------------------
0xe5(229)     20:c8:00:0d:ec:24:5e:c1 [Local] [Principal]
MDS-9513-1#
```

Assigning a Predetermined FC ID to a pWWN

When performing a migration or host bus adapter (HBA) replacement, the FC ID may need to be reassigned to the new pWWN. This recipe assigns a predetermined FC ID to a specific pWWN.

Best Practice   A new FC ID cannot be assigned to a pWWN that is logged into the fabric. Before assigning a new FC ID, log the device out of the fabric. You can log out the device by shutting down the Fibre Channel interface.

FC ID 0x160000 will be assigned to pWWN 50:06:0b:82:bf:d1:db:cd permanently. When the pWWN logs into the switch (FLOGI), it receives this assigned FC ID.

Note   The FC ID to be assigned (0x160000) should contain the same domain_ID (0x16) as the currently running domain in the VSAN.

To assign a predetermined FC ID to a specific pWWN, follow these steps:

```
MDS-9513-1# conf t
Enter configuration commands, one per line.  End with CNTL/Z.
MDS-9513-1(config)# fcdomain fcid database
MDS-9513-1(config-fcid-db)# vsan 22 wwn 50:06:0b:82:bf:d1:db:cd fcid 0x160000 dynamic
MDS-9513-1(config-fcid-db)# end
MDS-9513-1#
```

Note   If the device is currently logged in, you cannot change the FC ID of the device. To change the FCID, the switch port to which it is connected has to be shut down and the current FC ID, if persistent, needs to be purged from the FC ID database and the new FC ID for that interface has to be configured. This procedure for a currently logged in device is disruptive only to the device.

Assigning a new predetermined FCID to a currently logged in pWWN

The following recipe describes the steps required to change the FC ID of the device that is logged into the fabric. The device with pWWN 50:06:0e:80:03:4e:95:33 has a FCID 0x7b0002 and needs to be changed to 0x7b0010.

To change the FC ID of a device currently logged in to the fabric, follow these steps:

Step 1   Get the port on the switch that the device is connected to and its current FCID on the switch to which the device is connected using the "**show flogi database**" command.

```
MDS-9509-2# show flogi database vsan 3000
---------------------------------------------------------------------
INTERFACE VSAN    FCID        PORT NAME            NODE NAME
---------------------------------------------------------------------
fc1/1     3000   0x7b0002    50:06:0e:80:03:4e:95:33  50:06:0e:80:03:4e:95:33
                             [storage-CL4D]
fc1/9     3000   0x7b0003    10:00:00:00:c9:3b:54:78  20:00:00:00:c9:3b:54:78
                             [sjc7-pc-9-emlx]

Total number of flogi = 2.
MDS-9509-2#
```

Step 2   Shut down the interface on the switch to which the device is connected.

```
MDS-9509-2# conf t
Enter configuration commands, one per line.  End with CNTL/Z.
MDS-9509-2(config)# interface fc 1/1
MDS-9509-2(config-if)# shutdown
MDS-9509-2(config-if)# exit
MDS-9509-2#
```

Step 3   Purge the FC ID database for this device.

```
MDS-9509-2# conf t
Enter configuration commands, one per line.  End with CNTL/Z.
MDS-9509-2(config)# fcdomain fcid database
MDS-9509-2(config-fcid-db)# no vsan 3000 wwn 50:06:0e:80:03:4e:95:33 <-- clears persistent
FCID
MDS-9509-2(config-fcid-db)# end
MDS-9509-2#
```

Step 4   Verify that the FC ID is gone from the database using the "**show fcdomain**" command.

```
MDS-9509-2# show fcdomain fcid persistent vsan 3000 <-- lists the current persistent FCIDs
Total entries 1.
Persistent FCIDs table contents:
VSAN            WWN                     FCID        Mask         Used    Assignment
----     ----------------------    --------    ----------    ----    ----------
3000     10:00:00:00:c9:3b:54:78   0x7b0003    SINGLE FCID    YES     DYNAMIC
MDS-9509-2#
```

Step 5   Configure the new FC ID for the device.

```
MDS-9509-2# config t
MDS-9509-2(config)# fcdomain fcid database
MDS-9509-2(config-fcid-db)# vsan 3000 wwn 50:06:0e:80:03:4e:95:33 fcid 0x7b0010 dynamic
MDS-9509-2(config-fcid-db)#end
mMDS-9509-2#
```

Step 6   Enable the port fc 1/1.

```
MDS-9509-2# conf t
Enter configuration commands, one per line.  End with CNTL/Z.
MDS-9509-2(config)# interface fc 1/1
MDS-9509-2(config-if)# no shutdown
MDS-9509-2(config-if)# exit
MDS-9509-2#
```

Step 7   Use the "**show fcdomain**" command to verify that the new entry is configured properly.

```
MDS-9509-2# show fcdomain fcid persistent vsan 3000 <-- lists all the persistant FCIDs
Total entries 2.

Persistent FCIDs table contents:
VSAN            WWN                     FCID        Mask         Used    Assignment
----     ----------------------    --------    ----------    ----    ----------
3000     50:06:0e:80:03:4e:95:33   0x7b0010    SINGLE FCID    NO      DYNAMIC
3000     10:00:00:00:c9:3b:54:78   0x7b0003    SINGLE FCID    YES     DYNAMIC
MDS-9509-2#
```

Step 8   Use the **show FLOGI database** command to see the new FC ID of the logged in port.

```
MDS-9509-2# show flogi database
--------------------------------------------------------------------------------
INTERFACE  VSAN    FCID        PORT NAME               NODE NAME
--------------------------------------------------------------------------------
fc1/1      3000    0x7b0010    50:06:0e:80:03:4e:95:33 50:06:0e:80:03:4e:95:33
                               [storage-CL4D]
fc1/9      3000    0x7b0003    10:00:00:00:c9:3b:54:78 20:00:00:00:c9:3b:54:78
                               [sjc7-pc-9-emlx]

Total number of flogi = 2.
MDS-9509-2#
```

## CHAPTER 7

Zoning

Zones are the basic form of data path security in a Fibre Channel environment. Zones are used to define which end devices (two or more) in a VSAN can communicate with each other. Zones are grouped together into zone sets. For the zones to be active, the zone set to which the zones belong needs to be activated. Individual zone members can be part of multiple zones. Zones can be part of multiple zone sets. Multiple zone sets can be defined in a VSAN. However, at any given time, only one zone set can be active per VSAN.

If zoning is not activated in a fabric, all the end devices are part of the default zone. If zoning is activated, any end devices that are not part of an active zone are part of the default zone. The default zone policy is set either to deny (none of the end devices that are part of the default zone can communicate with each other) or permit (all the devices that are part of the default zone can communicate with each other).

Best Practice It is recommended that you set the default zone policy to deny. This is the default setting on MDS 9000 series switches and directors.

Figure 7-1 shows the basic zoning flow.

Enhanced Zoning

Figure 7-1   *Basic Zoning Flow*

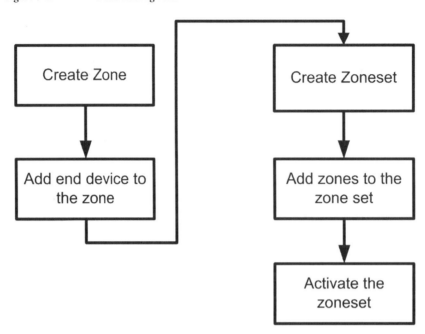

The MDS series products support two modes of zoning: basic zoning (FC-GS-3) and enhanced zoning (FC-GS-4). Both basic zoning and enhanced zoning (introduced in Cisco SAN-OS Release 2.0) use the concepts of zones and zone sets.

Best Practice   It is recommended to use Enhanced zoning over basic zoning.

Enhanced Zoning

Enhanced zoning, introduced in Cisco SAN-OS Release 2.0, was defined in the FC-GS-4 and FC-SW-3 standards. It provides significant enhancements to basic zoning.

Enhanced zoning has the following features:

- Has a VSAN scope, so that while VSAN X is using enhanced zoning, other VSANs can continue to use basic zoning.

- Is IVR compatible.

- Provides session locking, so that two SAN administrators cannot simultaneously modify a zoning database within a VSAN.

- Provides implicit full zone set distribution, so that the zone set database local to each switch remains in sync when a zone set is modified.

- Allows full zone set changes to be distributed without having to activate a zone set. You can use this to ready features in the daytime and activate the zone set at night.

- Stages modifications until they are explicitly committed or aborted, allowing the SAN administrator to review changes before activation.

- Can control how a zone merge is done. Merging can be accomplished either by performing a union of two zone sets according to the same rules as basic zoning, or by merging only identical active zone sets. The latter method prevents accidental merging.

Enhanced zoning uses the same techniques and tools as basic zoning, with a few added commands that are covered in these recipes. The flow of enhanced zoning, however, differs from that of basic zoning. For one thing, a VSAN-wide lock, if available, is implicitly obtained for enhanced zoning. Second, all zone and zone set modifications for advanced zoning include activation. Last, changes are either committed (put into production) or aborted (pending changes are scrapped) with advanced zoning. The flow is illustrated in Figure 7-2.

Figure 7-2　　Enhanced Zoning Flowchart

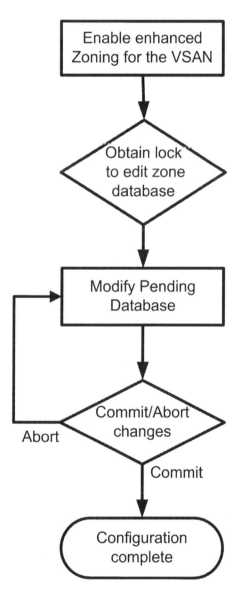

- Only done once to enable enhanced zoning mode for the VSAN.
- Full zoneset from enabling switch will overwrite other switch's full zoneset, so choose carefully which switch to enable enhanced zoning from

- Lock Implicitly obtained when first configuration command is attempted.

- Create Zones and Zonesets
- Add Zones to Zonesets
- Activate Zoneset

- Abort command deletes the pending changes.
- Commit command puts commands into production and adds to running-configuration.
- Doing neither command leaves them in the pending database.

- Exiting the configuration mode releases the lock on the application.

Enabling Enhanced Zoning

Enhanced zoning, with its VSAN scope, requires that all switches in a VSAN be capable of enhanced zoning and have enhanced zoning enabled later on. Due to its distributed architecture and abilities, enhanced zoning is enabled only on one switch in the VSAN. Commands are then propagated to other switches in the VSAN. The rules for enabling enhanced zoning with DCNM are as follows:

- Enhanced zoning is enabled on just one switch in the VSAN. Attempting to enable it on multiple switches in the same VSAN can result in a failure to activate.

- Enabling enhanced zoning does not trigger a zone set activation.

- The switch chosen to perform migration distributes its full zone database to other switches in the VSAN, which overwrites the destination switches' full zone set database.

Caution   It is critical that to select the switch with the correct full zone database for enhanced zoning; otherwise, you can accidentally delete the wrong full zone set database.

Enabling Enhanced Zoning with the CLI

To enable enhanced zoning with the CLI, follow these steps:

Step 1   Enter configuration mode and enable enhanced zoning with the **zone mode enhanced** command.

```
MDS-9513-1# conf t
Enter configuration commands, one per line.  End with CNTL/Z.
MDS-9513-1(config)# zone mode enhanced vsan 3000
WARNING: This command would distribute the zoning database
         of this switch throughout the fabric.
Please enter yes to proceed.(y/n) [n]? y
Set zoning mode command initiated. Check zone status
MDS-9513-1(config)# end
MDS-9513-1#
```

Step 2   Display the zoning status with the **show zone status** command.

```
MDS-9513-1# show zone status vsan 3000
VSAN: 3000 default-zone: deny distribute: full Interop: default
    mode: enhanced merge-control: allow
    session: none
    hard-zoning: enabled broadcast: enabled
Default zone:
    qos: none broadcast: disabled ronly: disabled
Full Zoning Database :
    DB size: 44 bytes
    Zonesets:0  Zones:0 Aliases: 0 Attribute-groups: 1
Active Zoning Database :
    Database Not Available
Status: Set zoning mode complete at 21:51:46 UTC Oct 13 2011
```

Enabling Enhanced Zoning with DCNM

To enable enhanced zoning with DCNM, follow these steps:

Step 1 In the Logical Domains pane, choose a VSAN and then choose the folder corresponding to the name of the active zone set (see Figure 7-3). If no active zone set exists, choose Default Zone.

Step 2 Choose the **Enhanced** Tab (see Figure 7-3).

Step 3 In the Action column for the enabling switch, change the cell to **Enhanced** and save the configuration using the green Apply Changes button (see Figure 7-3). From now on, this switch distributes its full zone database for this VSAN, overwriting all other switches in the enhanced zone database.

Figure 7-3   *Enabling Enhanced Zoning with DCNM*

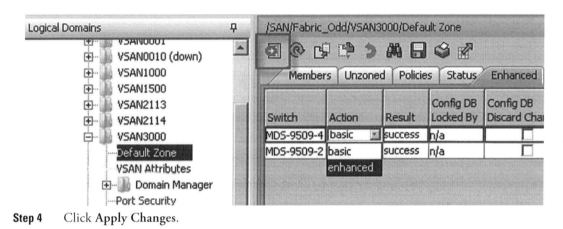

Step 4 Click **Apply Changes**.

Displaying the User with the Current Lock in CLI and DCNM

With enhanced zoning, only one user at a time can make changes to the zone database within a VSAN. The database is implicitly locked.

To determine who has the database locked using the CLI, use the **show zone status** command.

```
MDS-9513-1# show zone status vsan 3000
VSAN: 3000 default-zone: deny distribute: full Interop: default
    mode: enhanced merge-control: allow
    session: cli [admin]
    hard-zoning: enabled broadcast: enabled
Default zone:
    qos: none broadcast: disabled ronly: disabled
Full Zoning Database :
    DB size: 44 bytes
    Zonesets:0  Zones:0 Aliases: 0 Attribute-groups: 1
Active Zoning Database :
    Database Not Available
Status: Set zoning mode complete at 21:51:46 UTC Oct 13 2011
```

To determine who has this lock in DCNM, follow these steps:

Step 1 Choose the Logical Domains Pane (see Figure 7-4).

Step 2 Choose the VSAN to be investigated (see Figure 7-4).

Step 3 Choose the name of the zone set, or Default Zone if there is no active zone set. (See Figure 7-4.)

Step 4   Click the **Enhanced** tab (see Figure 7-4).

The user is displayed in the **Config DB Locked By** column as shown in Figure 7-4.

Figure 7-4   Displaying the Enhanced Zoning Lock

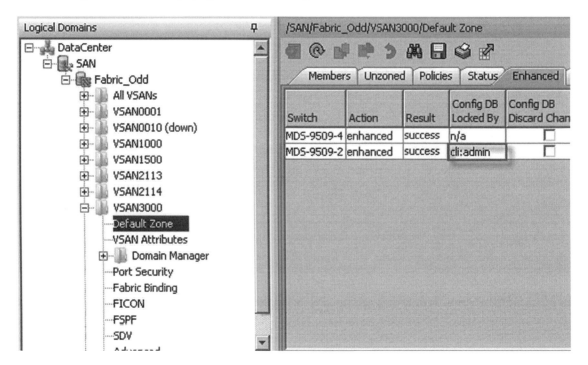

Zonesets

Zone sets are containers for zones. There are two types of zone sets on MDS switches: active zone sets and local zone sets.

- **Active zone set:** It provides the rules by which the MDS platform enforces its zoning security policy. It cannot be modified and it is distributed to all switches in the VSAN. There are specific rules for merging the active zone set when two switches are connected by an ISL as set by the Fibre Channel standards. There is only one active zoneset per VSAN.

- **Local zone set(s):** They are contained in the full zone set database on the switch. The zone sets are edited directly and then activated to become the active zone set. They can optionally be distributed to other switches in the same VSAN, either manually or when a zone set is activated. There can be multiple local zone sets in a VSAN.

Distributing Zonesets in Basic Zoning Mode

The zone set in the full zone set database can be distributed to other switches either during activation or manually when basic zoning is enabled. When enhanced zoning is enabled, the full zone set is always distributed when changes are committed to the full zone set database.

Best Practice   This feature should be enabled on all switches in the VSAN, and can be specified in the initial setup script. This feature is implicitly used if Enhanced Zoning is configured.

Distributing Zone Sets Automatically

Enabling automatic full zone set distribution distributes the local zone set to all other switches in the VSAN when a zone set is activated.

Note   When two VSANs with full zone set distribution enabled are merged, they try to merge the full zone set database according to standard zone set merge rules. *Failure to merge the full zone set database does not isolate the ISL*; only failing to merge the active zone set can results in an isolated ISL. This failure to merge the full zone set database produces the following syslog error message:

```
2007 May 31 14:35:59 MDS-9513-1 %ZONE-2-ZS_MERGE_FULL_DATABASE_MISMATCH: %$VSAN 1000%$
Zone merge full database mismatch on interface fc1/1
```

Distributing Zone sets Automatically with the CLI

To automatically distribute the full zoneset from the CLI when the zoneset is activated, use the **zoneset distribute** command:

```
MDS-9513-1# conf t
Enter configuration commands, one per line.  End with CNTL/Z.
MDS-9513-1(config)# zoneset distribute full vsan 3000
```

Distributing Zone Sets Automatically with DCNM

To automatically distribute the full zoneset when the zoneset is activated using DCNM, follow these steps:

Step 1   In the Logical Domains window, choose the correct fabric.

Step 2   Choose the VSAN to be modified.

Step 3   Select the **name** of the Active Zone set (or default zone if none is active).

Step 4   Click the **Policies** tab.

Step 5   Change the Propagation field to **FullZoneSet** for all switches in that VSAN.

Step 6   Click the green **Apply Changes** icon.

Distributing Zone Sets Manually

You can manually distribute the full zone set database to other switches without activating a zone set. Do this when a new switch is brought into the fabric and the zone set with its zones and Fibre Channel aliases need to be distributed. This **zoneset distribute** command overwrites the existing zone set database in the target switch.

```
MDS-9513-1# zoneset distribute vsan 3000
Zoneset distribution initiated. check zone status
```

Zones

In order for two devices to communicate, they must be in the same zone. Valid members of a zone are:

- Port WWN
- FC alias
- FC ID
- FWWN (WWN of a FC interface)
- Switch interface (fc X/Y)
- Symbolic node name
- Device alias

The four most common zone member types are the port world-wide name (pWWN), device alias, FC alias, and the switch interface.

Best Practice   Create device aliases (see "Device Aliases" section on page 1-47) for the pWWNs prior to creating the zones. This will provide hardware-enforced zoning and associate a zone member to a specific pWWN rather than to the switch port. Also, device aliases have the added benefit of being VSAN-independent and are based on an easy-to-understand name rather than a cryptic pWWN.

Equally important is the name of the zone. Environments use many different zone names. However, all name formats should provide relevant information as to their contents. Names like "Zone1" or "TapeZone" do not provide sufficient information about their contents.

Examples of recommended naming conventions would include the name of the host and the hba instance (host123_lpfc0) for single-initiator multi-target zones, while single-initiator, single-target zones could contain both the initiator and target's device-alias (host123_lpfc0_HDS7890_10B)

Creating a Zone and Adding It to a Zone Set with DCNM

This recipe creates a zone set, creates zones, adds them to the zone set, and then activates the zone set. The method used is the same for both basic zoning and enhanced zoning. The following topology is used:

Figure 7-5   DCNM Zoning Topology

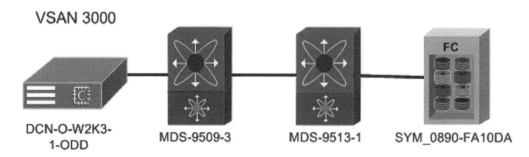

In addition, these resources are used in this example:

- Zone set: ZS_cookbook
- W2k3 host: DCN-O-W2k3-1-ODD
- Storage array: SYM_0890-FA10DA
- Zoning Mode: Enhanced

Creating a Zone Set

To create a zone set, follow these steps:

Step 1   In the Logical Domains pane, right-click the VSAN, and select **Edit Local Full Zone Database**. To see the screen shown in Figure 7-6.

Figure 7-6   Edit Local Full Zone Database

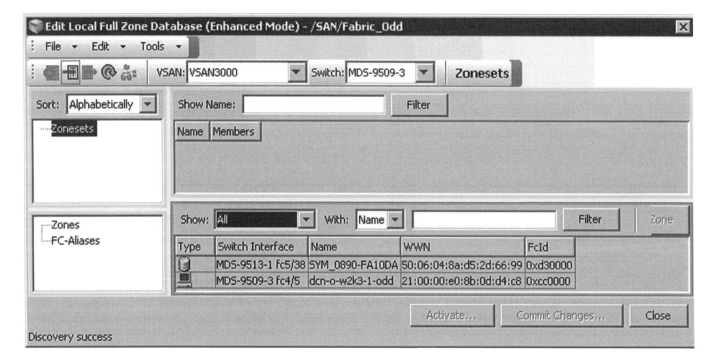

Note
- The VSAN field displays the VSAN whose database is to be modified.
- The Switch field displays the switch being edited.
- The Name column lists either FC aliases or Device Aliases (Device Aliases, page 1-47) if they are used.
- If Full Zone Set Distribution is enabled, the left column lists existing zone sets and zones. If Active Zone Set Distribution is enabled, choose the switch that contains the Full Zone Database.

Step 2   In the left pane, right-click **Zonesets**.

Step 3   In the resulting pop-up menu, select **Insert...**

Step 4   Enter a zone set name, such as ZS_cookbook, as shown in Figure 7-7, and then click **OK**.

Figure 7-7   *Create Zone Set*

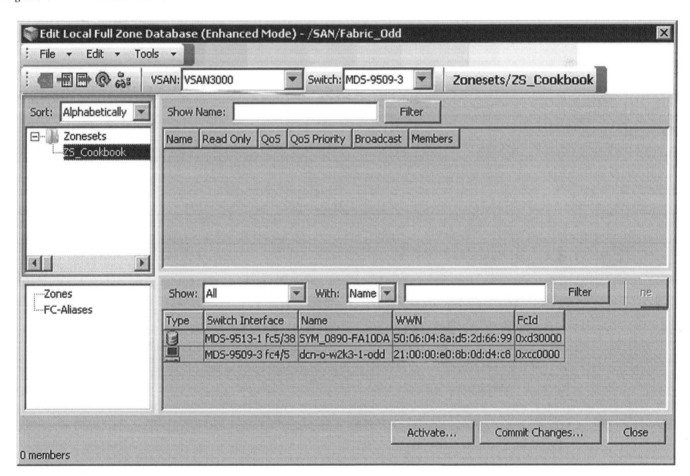

At this point a zone set has been created. The next phase is to create a zone and add members to it.

Creating a Zone and Adding Members

To create a zone and add members to it from DCNM, follow these steps:

Step 1   Right click **Zones.**

Step 2   In the resulting pop-up menu, select **Insert...**

Step 3   Enter a meaningful zone name such as **Z_DCN-O-W2k3-1-ODD** to represent both the initiator and target in the name.

Step 4   Click **OK.**

You see the dialog box in Figure 7-8.

Figure 7-8   Zone Database after Creating Zone Set and Zones

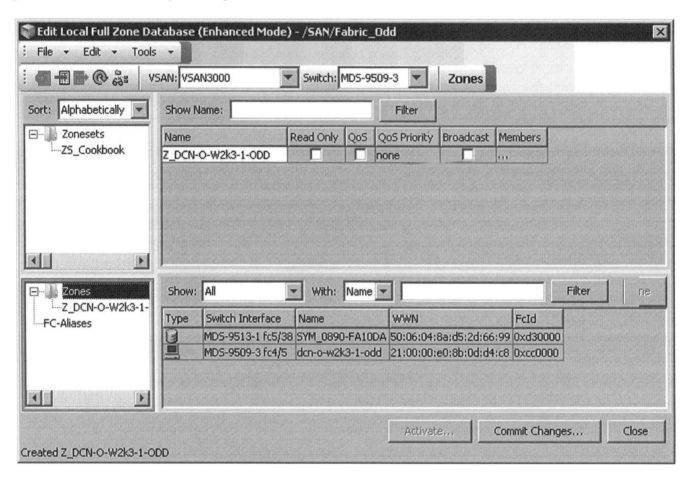

Step 5   Drag the two end devices from the bottom pane into the new zone. This creates a pWWN-based zone. If non-pWWN zone members (such as interface, FCID, or Global Device Alias) are needed, refer to Creating Non-pWWN-Based Zones, page 7-15 to specify these member types before continuing.

Figure 7-9   *Zone with Newly Added Members*

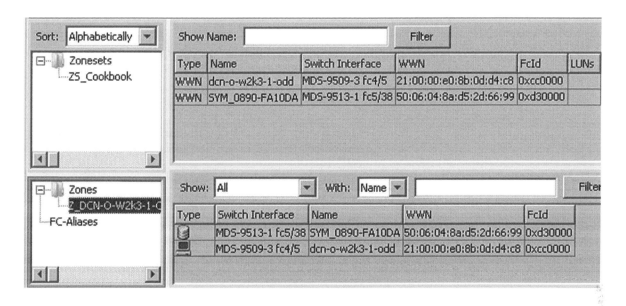

This zone is created populated with the two zone members, as shown in Figure 7-9. Next, add the zone to the zone set.

Adding the Zone to the Zone Set and Activating It

To add the zone to the zone set, follow these steps:

Step 1   In the left pane, drag the zone (Z_sjc7-pc-9-emlx_storage-CL4D) into the zone set (ZS_cookbook). The zone set's icon changes by appending a folder icon, and it expands with the newly added zone underneath it. (Figure 7-10)

Figure 7-10   Zone Added to Zone Set

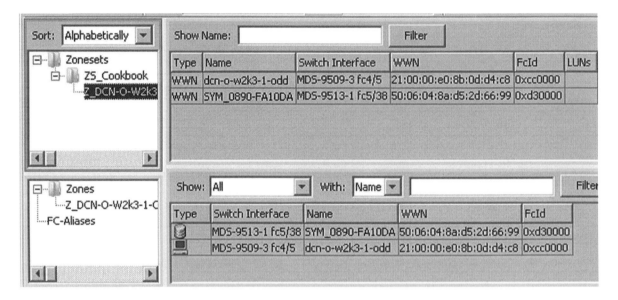

Now activate the new zone set. This instructs the switch program to update its Access Control Lists, and modify the running configuration of the zone server to allow the two devices to communicate. When enhanced zoning is enabled, clicking **Activate** commits the changes as well.

Step 2   In the left pane, right-click the zone set (ZS_Cookbook) and choose **Activate....** Since Enhanced Zoning is configured, DCNM-SAN performs an *implicit* Commit

   a. If the current Active zone set is empty, click **Continue Activation....**

   b. If the current Active zone set is not empty, DCNM prompts the user with the option to view the differences between the active zone set and zone set that is being activated. If you Select **YES**, the DCNM displays what is being added or removed from the active zone set. You see a dialog box showing the added or removed zones and members. Click **close** and then select **Continue Activation....**

The Zone Set activation results dialog is as shown in Figure 7-11.

Figure 7-11   Zoneset Activation Results

```
MDS-9509-3:Activating ZS_Cookbook
MDS-9509-3:checking status, elapsed time:0 sec activating ZS_Cookbook
MDS-9509-3:ZS_Cookbook Activation success
MDS-9509-3:commiting full zone configuration 3000.
MDS-9509-3:checking status, elapsed time:0 sec commiting zone configuration changes
MDS-9509-3: Commit success
MDS-9509-3:Finished
Success
```

`                                                                    Close`

The zone set is now active and the two end devices can communicate.

Creating Non-pWWN-Based Zones

This recipe creates a zone that is not based on pWWN. The procedure is the same for either basic or enhanced zoning.

To create the zones, follow these steps:

Step 1   In the Logical Domains pane, right-click the VSAN, and select **Edit Local Full Zone Database.**

Step 2   In the resulting dialog box, right-click **Zones** and select **Insert....**

Step 3   Specify a zone name and click **OK.**

Step 4   Right-click the newly created zone and select **Insert...** You see the options shown in Figure 7-12.

Figure 7-12   Possible Zone Member Types

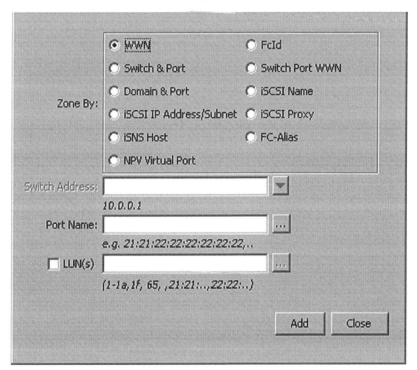

Step 5   Select the type of zone member require. This selection changes the rest of the screen. For example, if **Switch & Port** is selected, the text boxes change to **Switch Interface** (for example, fc1/1) and **Switch Address** (for example, 192.168.1.2). Also, the meaning of the boxes with "..." and the pull-down menus change depending on the zone member type.

Note   • Domain and Port zoning should only be done when working in interop mode 2 or 3. See the section Setting VSAN Interop Mode, page 6-14 for more information about interop modes.

• Alias refers to both FC Alias and Global Device Alias, depending on which mode DCNM is in.

The resulting zone still must be added to a zone set and the zone set activated, which is described in Creating a Zone and Adding It to a Zone Set with DCNM, page 7-9.

Creating a Device Alias-Based Zone with the CLI

This example uses device alias as zone members. This recipe would be the same if device aliases were in basic or in enhanced mode. In this example, device alias is operating in enhanced mode. The recipe will first create the device aliases and then zone them together.

Obtain pWWNs either from the device itself or from the **show fcns database vsan 3000** command.

Note   When using device alias in enhanced mode and doing zoning using device alias, if the pWWN of a device changes (HBA replacement) and if the device alias of the device is not suitably changed in the device alias database, the zone information will not automatically change to reflect the new pWWN. The device alias has to be updated with the new pWWN for the changes to propagate to the zones.

```
MDS-9513-1# show fcns database vsan 3000

VSAN 3000:
-------------------------------------------------------------------------
FCID        TYPE    PWWN                      (VENDOR)      FC4-TYPE:FEATURE
-------------------------------------------------------------------------
0xcc0000    N       21:00:00:e0:8b:0d:d4:c8  (Qlogic)      scsi-fcp:init
0xd30000    N       50:06:04:8a:d5:2d:66:99  (EMC)         scsi-fcp 253

Total number of entries = 2
#
```

The topology in Figure 7-14 is used in the example.

Figure 7-13   Standalone Zoning Topology

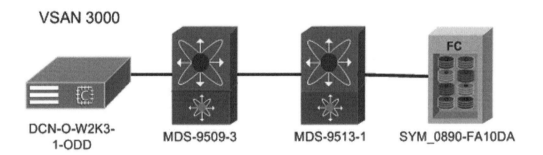

These resources are also used in this example:

- Zone set: ZS_cli_cookbook
- Device Alias for host: DCN-O-W2K3-1-ODD
- Device Alias for storage: SYM_0890-FA10DA
- Device Aliases are in Enhanced Mode

To create a single zone for a host with a disk storage port, follow these steps:

Step 1   Create the device alias for the host HBA and the storage port using the device alias database commands.

```
MDS-9513-1# config t
MDS-9513-1(config)# device-alias database
MDS-9513-1(config-device-alias-db)# device-alias name SYM_0890-FA10DA pwwn
50:06:04:8a:d5:2d:66:99
MDS-9513-1(config-device-alias-db)# device-alias name dcn-o-w2k3-1-odd pwwn
21:00:00:e0:8b:0d:d4:c8
MDS-9513-1(config-device-alias-db)# exit
MDS-9513-1(config)# device-alias commit
```

Note   A device alias commit is required to store the device alias into the device alias database.

The device aliases can be verified with the **show fcns database command**:

```
MDS-9513-1# show fcns database vsan 3000

VSAN 3000:
-------------------------------------------------------------------------
FCID        TYPE  PWWN                     (VENDOR)      FC4-TYPE:FEATURE
-------------------------------------------------------------------------
0xcc0000    N     21:00:00:e0:8b:0d:d4:c8 (Qlogic)      scsi-fcp:init
                  [dcn-o-w2k3-1-odd]
0xd30000    N     50:06:04:8a:d5:2d:66:99 (EMC)         scsi-fcp 253
                  [SYM_0890-FA10DA]

Total number of entries = 2
```

Step 2   Create the zone with the **zone name** command. Use a zone name that reflects the names of the members. Then add members to the zone with the **member device-alias** command.

```
MDS-9513-1# conf t
Enter configuration commands, one per line.  End with CNTL/Z.
MDS-9513-1(config)# zone name Z_dcn-o-w2k3-1-odd vsan 3000
MDS-9513-1(config-zone)# member device-alias dcn-o-w2k3-1-odd
```

```
MDS-9513-1(config-zone)# member device-alias SYM_0890-FA10DA
MDS-9513-1(config-zone)# exit
MDS-9513-1(config)#
```

Step 3   Add the zone to the zone set with the **zoneset name** command.

```
MDS-9513-1(config)# zoneset name ZS_cli_cookbook vsan 3000
MDS-9513-1(config-zoneset)# member Z_dcn-o-w2k3-1-odd
MDS-9513-1(config-zoneset)# exit
MDS-9513-1(config)# exit
```

Step 4   Display the zone set with the **show zoneset name** command.

```
MDS-9513-1# show zoneset name ZS_cli_cookbook vsan 3000
zoneset name ZS_cli_cookbook vsan 3000
  zone name Z_dcn-o-w2k3-1-odd vsan 3000
    device-alias dcn-o-w2k3-1-odd
    device-alias SYM_0890-FA10DA
```

Step 5   Put the zone set into production with the command **zoneset activate name ZS_cli_cookbook vsan 3000**. This activates all the zones in the zone set, not just the new one.

```
MDS-9513-1(config)# zoneset activate name ZS_cli_cookbook vsan 3000
```

Step 6   If you are using enhanced zoning, the zone has to be committed to the database using the command **zone commit vsan 3000**.

```
MDS-9513-1(config)# zone commit vsan 3000
Commit operation initiated. Check zone status
```

Note   Only when the commit is complete does the zone set become active.

Step 7   Display the zone set with the **show zoneset** command. The pWWNs are not displayed since the zone members are device aliases running in enhanced mode.

```
MDS-9513-1# show zoneset active v 3000
zoneset name ZS_cli_cookbook vsan 3000
  zone name Z_dcn-o-w2k3-1-odd vsan 3000
  * fcid 0xd80000 [device-alias SYM_0890-FA10DA]
  * fcid 0xd80001 [device-alias DCN-O-W2K3-1-ODD]
MDS-9513-1#
```

Creating a pWWN-based Zone with the CLI

This example uses pWWNs as zone members. You can obtain pWWNs either from the device itself or from the **show flogi database vsan 3000** command run from the switch where the device is connected to. Device Aliases have already been created for these devices for ease of comprehension.

The topology in Figure 7-14 is used in the example.

Figure 7-14   *pWWN-based Zoning Topology*

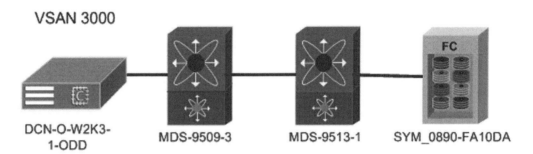

These resources are also used in this example:

- Zone set: ZS_cli_cookbook
- Server HBA's pWWN: 10:00:00:00:c9:3b:54:78
- Storage port's pWWN: 50:06:0e:80:03:4e:95:33

To create a single zone for the host with a disk storage port, follow these steps:

Step 1   Create the zone with the **zone name** command. Use a zone name that reflects the names of the members. Then add members to the zone with the **member pwwn** command.

```
MDS-9513-1# conf t
Enter configuration commands, one per line.  End with CNTL/Z.
MDS-9513-1(config)# zone name Z_dcn-o-w2k3-1-odd vsan 3000
MDS-9513-1(config-zone)# member pwwn 50:06:0e:80:03:4e:95:33
MDS-9513-1(config-zone)# member pwwn 10:00:00:00:c9:3b:54:78
MDS-9513-1(config-zone)# exit
MDS-9513-1(config)#
```

Step 2   Add the zone to the zone set with the **zoneset name** command.

```
MDS-9513-1(config)# zoneset name ZS_cli_cookbook vsan 3000
MDS-9513-1(config-zoneset)# member Z_dcn-o-w2k3-1-odd
MDS-9513-1(config-zoneset)# exit
```

Step 3   Display the zone set with the **show zoneset name** command.

```
MDS-9513 1(config)# show zoneset name ZS_cli_cookbook vsan 3000
zoneset name ZS_cli_cookbook vsan 3000
  zone name Z_dcn-o-w2k3-1-odd vsan 3000
    pwwn 50:06:0e:80:03:4e:95:33 [SYM_0890-FA10DA]
    pwwn 10:00:00:00:c9:3b:54:78 [dcn-o-w2k3-1-odd]
```

Step 4   Put the zone set into production with the **zoneset activate name ZS_cli_cookbook vsan 3000** command. This activates all the zones in the zone set, not just the new one.

```
MDS-9513-1(config)# zoneset activate name ZS_cli_cookbook vsan 3000
```

Step 5   If you are using enhanced zoning, the zone has to be committed to the database using the **zone commit vsan 3000** command.

```
MDS-9513-1(config)# zone commit vsan 3000
Commit operation initiated. Check zone status
```

Note   With Enhanced zoning, only when the commit is complete does the zone set become active.

Step 6   Display the zone set with the **show zoneset** command.

```
MDS-9513-1# show zoneset active v 3000
zoneset name ZS_cli_cookbook vsan 3000
  zone name Z_dcn-o-w2k3-1-odd vsan 3000
  * fcid 0xd80000 [pwwn 50:06:0e:80:03:4e:95:33] [SYM_0890-FA10DA]
  * fcid 0xd80001 [pwwn 10:00:00:00:c9:3b:54:78] [dcn-o-w2k3-1-odd]
MDS-9513-1#
```

Creating a Zone and Adding it to a Zone Set with the CLI In line Method

This procedure creates a single zone for a Windows host and a storage port, then adds the zone to the zone set ZS_Engr_primary. Using the in line method automatically adds the zone to the zone set upon creation of the zone, and removes the manual step of having to add the zone to the zoneset at the end of the procedure. Device aliases have already been created for the two devices to aid with comprehension.

The procedure is the same for both basic zoning and enhanced zoning, with one exception. With enhanced zoning, the pending database must be committed at the end.

This example uses pWWNs as zone members. You can obtain pWWNs either from the device itself or from the **show flogi database vsan 3000** command run from the switch where the device is connected to.

The topology in Figure 7-15 is used in the example.

Figure 7-15   *In line Zoning Topology*

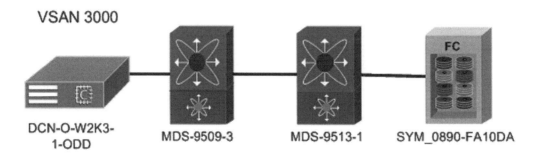

VSAN 3000

DCN-O-W2K3-1-ODD   MDS-9509-3   MDS-9513-1   SYM_0890-FA10DA

The following resources are also used in this example:

- Zone set: ZS_cli_cookbook
- Server HBA pWWN: 10:00:00:00:c9:3b:54:78
- Storage port pWWN: 50:06:0e:80:03:4e:95:33

To create a single zone for a server and a disk storage port, follow these steps:

Step 1   Enter the sub mode of the zone set with the **zoneset name** command.

```
MDS-9513-1# config terminal
Enter configuration commands, one per line.  End with CNTL/Z.
MDS-9513-1(config)# zoneset name ZS_cli_cookbook vsan 3000
```

Step 2   Create the zone with the **zone name** command.

```
MDS-9513-1(config-zoneset)# Z_dcn-o-w2k3-1-odd vsan 3000
```

Step 3   Add members to the zone with the **member** command.

```
MDS-9513-1(config-zoneset-zone)# member pwwn 50:06:0e:80:03:4e:95:33
MDS-9513-1(config-zoneset-zone)# member pwwn 10:00:00:00:c9:3b:54:78
```

Step 4   For basic zoning, put the zone set into production with the **zoneset activate** command. This activates all zones in the zone set, not just the new one. For enhanced zoning, in addition to activating the zone set, you must commit it in Step 5.

```
MDS-9513-1(config)# zoneset activate name ZS_cli_cookbook vsan 3000
```

Step 5   If enhanced zoning is used, explicitly commit the zone set with **zoneset commit** command.

```
MDS-9513-1(config)# zone commit vsan 3000
```

Step 6   Display the local zone set with the **show zoneset** command.

```
MDS-9513-1# show zoneset name ZS_cli_cookbook vsan 3000
zoneset name ZS_cli_cookbook vsan 3000
  zone name Z_dcn-o-w2k3-1-odd vsan 3000
    pwwn 50:06:0e:80:03:4e:95:33 [SYM_0890-FA10DA]
    pwwn 10:00:00:00:c9:3b:54:78 [DCN-O-W2K3-1-ODD]
```

Step 7   Display the active zone set with the **show active zoneset** command.

```
MDS-9513-1# show zoneset active vsan 3000
zoneset name ZS_cli_cookbook vsan 3000
  zone name Z_dcn-o-w2k3-1-odd vsan 3000
  * fcid 0xd80000 [pwwn 50:06:0e:80:03:4e:95:33] [SYM_0890-FA10DA]
  * fcid 0xd80001 [pwwn 10:00:00:00:c9:3b:54:78] [DCN-O-W2K3-1-ODD]
```

Creating a FC Alias-Based Zone with the CLI

Fibre Channel aliases let the administrator assign a plain text, human readable name to a pWWN, FC ID interface, IP address, nWWN, or symbolic nodename. FC aliases are restricted to the VSAN where they were created. The most common and recommended method of naming is using the pWWN, which is demonstrated in this procedure.

Best Practice   Use device aliases instead of FC aliases.

FC Aliases are distributed with the full zone set database, so if multiple switches are changed, enable full zone set distribution to distribute the aliases.

An alias can be mapped to more than one device, however, we recommend one-to-one mapping.

Use Enhanced zones instead of basic zones.

The topology in Figure 7-16 is used in the example.

Figure 7-16   FC Alias Zoning Topology

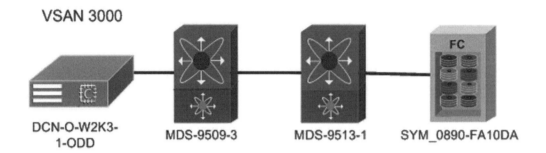

The following resources are also used in this example:

- Zone set: ZS_cli_cookbook
- Server, HBA pWWN: 10:00:00:00:c9:3b:54:78
- Storage port pWWN: 50:06:0e:80:03:4e:95:33

To create an FC alias-based zone, follow these steps:

Step 1   Create an FC alias-to-pWWN mapping for each FC alias, using the **member pwwn** command.

```
MDS-9513-1# config terminal
Enter configuration commands, one per line.  End with CNTL/Z.
MDS-9513-1(config)# fcalias name dcn-o-w2k3-1-odd vsan 3000
MDS-9513-1(config-fcalias)# member pwwn 10:00:00:00:c9:3b:54:78
MDS-9513-1(config-fcalias)# exit
MDS-9513-1(config)# fcalias name SYM_0890-FA10DA vsan 3000
MDS-9513-1(config-fcalias)# member pwwn 50:06:0e:80:03:4e:95:33
MDS-9513-1(config-fcalias)# end
```

Step 2   Display the newly created FC aliases with the **show fcalias** command.

```
MDS-9513-1# show fcalias vsan 3000
fcalias name dcn-o-w2k3-1-odd vsan 3000
  pwwn 10:00:00:00:c9:3b:54:78

fcalias name SYM_0890-FA10DA vsan 3000
  pwwn 50:06:0e:80:03:4e:95:33
```

Step 3   Create an alias-based zone in the zone set with the **zone name** command. Add members to the zone using the **member fcalias** command and the names of the FC aliases. This example uses the in-line method for zone creation.

```
MDS-9513-1# config terminal
Enter configuration commands, one per line.  End with CNTL/Z.
MDS-9513-1(config)# zoneset name Zs_cli_cookbook vsan 3000
MDS-9513-1(config-zoneset)# zone name Z_dcn-o-w2k3-1-odd vsan 3000
MDS-9513-1(config-zone)# member fcalias dcn-o-w2k3-1-odd
MDS-9513-1(config-zone)# member fcalias SYM_0890-FA10DA
MDS-9513-1(config-zone)# exit
```

Step 4   Optionally, display the local zone set with the **show zoneset** command.

```
MDS-9513-1# show zoneset vsan 3000
zoneset name ZS_cli_cookbook vsan 3000
  zone name Z_sjc7-pc-9-emlx_storage-CL4D vsan 3000
    fcalias name sjc7-pc-9-emlx vsan 3000
      pwwn 10:00:00:00:c9:3b:54:78

    fcalias name storage_CL4D vsan 3000
      pwwn 50:06:0e:80:03:4e:95:33
```

Step 5   Activate the zone set with the **zoneset activate** command.

```
MDS-9513-1# conf t
Enter configuration commands, one per line.  End with CNTL/Z.
MDS-9513-1(config)# zoneset activate name ZS_cli_cookbook vsan 3000
Zoneset activation initiated. check zone status
```

Step 6   If enhanced zoning is enabled, commit the configuration with the **zone commit** command.

```
MDS-9513-1(config)# zone commit vsan 3000
```

Creating an Interface-Based Zone with the CLI

This procedure creates a zone based on the physical interface (fc X/Y) of the switch. The procedure is the same for both basic zoning and enhanced zoning with one exception. With enhanced zoning, you must commit the pending database at the end. Run the show flogi database command to see which switch ports the host and storage ports have logged into. The storage port is logged into port fc 1/1 and the host port is logged into port fc 1/9.

The below flogi database output is used for this example.

```
MDS-9509-3# show flogi database vsan 3000
--------------------------------------------------------------------------
INTERFACE  VSAN   FCID       PORT NAME            NODE NAME
--------------------------------------------------------------------------
fc1/9      3000   0xd80001   10:00:00:00:c9:3b:54:78  20:00:00:00:c9:3b:54:78
                             [dcn-o-w2k3-1-odd]
Total number of flogi = 1.


MDS-9513-1# show flogi database vsan 3000
----  ---------------------------------------------------------------------
INTERFACE  VSAN   FCID       PORT NAME            NODE NAME
--------------------------------------------------------------------------
fc1/1      3000   0xd80000   50:06:0e:80:03:4e:95:33  50:06:0e:80:03:4e:95:33
                             [SYM_0890-FA10DA]
Total number of flogi = 1.
```

The switch's wwn is required to identify the switch where the interface exists and can be obtained using the command **show wwn switch**. Omitting the swwn assumes the local switch.

```
MDS-9513-1# show wwn switch
Switch WWN is 20:00:00:0d:ec:6d:50:40
```

Best Practice   Use interface-based zoning when a zone must be created before the HBA is connected to the fabric. After the HBA is connected to the fabric, convert the zone member to a pWWN-based member.

To create an interface-based zone with the CLI, follow these steps:

Step 1   Create the zone using the **zone name** command. Add members with the **member interface** command.

```
MDS-9513-1# config terminal
Enter configuration commands, one per line.  End with CNTL/Z.
MDS-9513-1(config)# zoneset name ZS_cli_cookbook vsan 3000
MDS-9513-1(config-zoneset)# zone name Z_dcn-o-w2k3-1-odd vsan 3000
MDS-9513-1(config-zoneset-zone)# member interface fc1/1 swwn 20:00:00:0d:ec:6d:50:40
MDS-9513-1(config-zoneset-zone)# member interface fc1/9 swwn 20:00:00:05:30:00:18:a3
```

Step 2   Optionally, display the zone set with the **show zoneset** command.

```
MDS-9513-1# show zoneset vsan 3000
zoneset name ZS_cli_cookbook vsan 3000
  zone name Z_dcn-o-w2k3-1-odd vsan 3000
    interface fc1/1 swwn 20:00:00:0c:85:e9:d2:c0
    interface fc1/9 swwn 20:00:00:0c:85:e9:d2:c0
```

Activate the zone set with the **zoneset activate** command.

```
MDS-9513-1# conf t
Enter configuration commands, one per line.  End with CNTL/Z.
MDS-9513-1(config)# zoneset activate name ZS_cli_cookbook vsan 3000
Zoneset activation initiated. check zone status
```

Step 3   If enhanced zoning is enabled, then commit the configuration.

```
MDS-9513-1(config)# zone commit vsan 3000
```

Inter-VSAN Routing

Inter-VSAN Routing (IVR), which was first introduced into the MDS platform in Cisco SAN-OS Release 1.3(1), the precursor to NX-OS, enables devices in different VSANs to communicate. The classic example is a shared tape library in one VSAN which is being accessed by servers which are in different VSANs. Another common implementation is allowing disk subsystems to communicate over WAN without having to merge large zoneset databases.

With the introduction of NX-OS 5.0(1), the initial version of IVR (aka IVR-1) was deprecated, leaving the much improved second version of IVR which is often referred to as IVR NAT (Network Address Translation) or IVR-2. IVR NAT has actually been around since SAN-OS 2.1, and the advantages of IVR NAT far outweigh those of IVR-1. For example, IVR-1 required unique domain IDs in the source and destination VSANs, and secondly, the two VSANs could not have the same number.

IVR-2 continues to leverage the same basic principles as in IVR-1, such as IVR topologies, IVR zones, and IVR zone sets as well as transit VSANs. However, the disadvantages with regards to IVR-1 were resolved. Starting with Cisco SAN-OS Release 2.1, IVR has had the ability to perform Network Address Translation (NAT) on the device's FCID and VSAN ID.

In addition to the FC-NAT capabilities, IVR also leverages Cisco Fabric Services (CFS) (introduced in Cisco SAN-OS Release 2.0(1)) and auto topology (introduced in Cisco SAN-OS Release 2.1(1)), both of which ease the tasks of configuring and managing an IVR deployment.

When planning an IVR deployment, careful consideration should be given to determine which switches will have IVR enabled on them, which VSANs will be routed, and which devices will require IVR to access their targets. While IVR solves many problems in today's multi-VSAN fabrics, it should not be used as a sole replacement for solid designs and zoning.

Best Practice

The preferred method of configuring IVR is to use IVR-2 with CFS. Even in previous versions of NX-OS, where IVR-1 is still supported, IVR-2 should be used with CFS. CFS eases topology configuration and reduces the number of configuration steps and potential configuration errors. See IVR with CFS, page 8-5

IVR Core Components

This section provides background information about IVR topology, IVR zones and zone sets, and how IVR interacts with CFS.

IVR Topology

An IVR topology is a set of VSANs that can have their devices routed between them by an IVR enabled switch. The VSANs specified in the topology can either contain end devices or connect two IVR-enabled switches through a common VSAN, which does not contain any end devices. This second type of VSAN is referred to as a transit VSAN (Transit VSANs, page 8-3). Each IVR-enabled switch does not have to include all VSANs in the fabric, however, it does need to contain any locally defined VSAN that participates in the define IVR topology. The topology database must be the same, or in sync, on all switches.

For example, in Table 8-1, the switch MDS-9509-3 can route between VSANs 1, 3000, 3001 and 3002; while switch MDS-9513-1 can route between VSANs 1, 3001 and 3003.

Table 8-1   Example IVR Topology

IVR Enabled Switch	VSANs to Route
MDS-9509-3	1,3000-3002
MDS-9513-1	1,3001, 3003

If a new VSAN is created on switch MDS-9509-3, it could not be routed between the new VSAN and one of the VSANs in the existing topology until the new VSAN is added into the topology and the database is distributed to all the IVR enabled switches.

Best Practice   Only add those VSANs to the IVR topology that should have devices routed between them.

Auto Topology

Configuring IVR to use automatic topology discovery (auto topology) frees the user from having to configure IVR topology or maintain the IVR topology database. You only need to create IVR zones and zone sets. The MDS fabric creates, distributes, and synchronizes the IVR topology database automatically. When you create or remove a VSAN from an IVR-enabled switch, the new VSAN is added and via CFS it is distributed to the IVR topology database on the local and remote IVR enabled switches.

Even if an end device exists in a VSAN that is in the IVR topology database, it cannot access any other devices until it is part of an IVR zone.

IVR's auto topology does have its drawbacks, which should not be overlooked. Auto topology adds every VSAN in every IVR-enabled switch into the topology. This can result in VSANs being unintentionally used as transit VSANs or devices being routed between via user errors. See Q.If I have multiple parallel transit VSANs, which VSAN is used?, page 8-3.

Some recipes in this chapter create topology manually, for example, Configuring Two IVR Switches Separated by a Transit VSAN Topology, page 8-11, and some use auto topology, such as Configuring a Single Switch with Two VSANs, page 8-8.

Best Practice   It is recommended to use manual topology with CFS.

Transit VSANs

When creating an IVR topology, you may need to specify additional VSANs in addition to the source and destination VSANs. These additional VSANs that do not necessarily contain any actual end devices may be required in the IVR topology. These VSANs are known as transit VSANs and their sole purpose is connecting two VSANs together when no one switch contains both the source and destination VSANs. The most common example for using a transit VSAN is to configure the transit VSAN to span across a WAN link and not extend either the source or destination VSANs across the it.

In the example below, VSANs 1 and 3001 could be used as a transit VSAN. These two VSANs are the only common VSANs between the two MDS switches, so they can and will be used as transit VSANs. (The IVR topology in Figure 8-1 corresponds to the information in Table 8-2)

Table 8-2   Example IVR Topology

VSAN Route Switch	VSANs to Route
MDS-9509-3	1,3000-3002
MDS-9513-1	1,3001, 3003

Figure 8-1   Example Topology Using a Transit VSAN

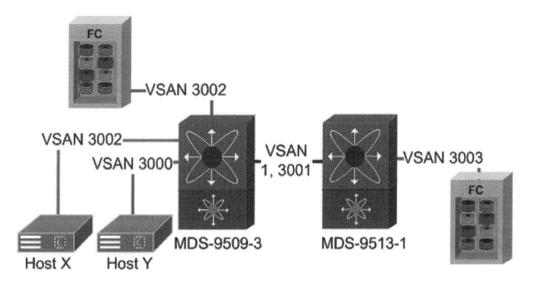

To specify a particular VSAN as a transit VSAN, no special configuration is required. The VSAN only needs to be part of the IVR topology to be used. It does not need to be empty, nor does it need to be in any specific Interop mode. It can have a mix of E and TE ports and can potentially contain non-MDS switches.

Note

Q. If I have multiple parallel transit VSANs, which VSAN is used?

A. The most direct path is used, that is, the path that uses the fewest VSAN hops. For example, a path that requires a frame to go through two different transit VSANs to reach the destination VSAN will not be chosen if there is a path that only requires one VSAN. This applies regardless of the Fabric Shortest Path First (FSPF) cost of the links inside the VSANs.

If there are two VSANs that have the same VSAN hop count (VSANs 1 and 3001 in Figure 8-1), then the one with the lowest VSAN ID is used. In the Figure 8-1 example, VSAN 1 would be used as the transit VSAN to go from VSAN 3002 to VSAN 3003.

IVR does not load balance across transit VSANs, so IVR would use only VSAN 1 as the transit, unless VSAN 1 failed or became isolated.

Best Practice   Only allow the transit VSAN to be trunked across the ISL. Otherwise a different VSAN could be used as the transit VSAN.

Leverage multiple paths within the transit VSAN with port-channels and use FSPF to route around path failures.

IVR Zones and Zonesets

IVR zones and zone sets, the objects that allow an end device in one VSAN to communicate with an end device in another VSAN, have the same features and functionality as a regular zone or zoneset with one exception: the zone members are in different VSANs.

Members of IVR zones can be pWWNs or device aliases. Registered State Change Notifications (RSCNs) are restricted to the device within the IVR zone that triggered the RSCN. IVR zone names automatically have the prefix "IVRZ_" added to them so they are easily identified in an active zone set. Adding "IVR_" to a non-IVR zone does not make it an IVR zone.

```
MDS-9513-1: show zoneset active vsan 3000
zoneset name ZoneSet1 vsan 3000
zone name Zone1 vsan 3000
    pwwn 50:06:0e:80:03:4e:95:23 [HDS20117-c20-9]
    pwwn 21:00:00:e0:8b:09:78:88 [ca-aix_lpfc0]
zone name IVRZ_IvrZone1 vsan 3000
    pwwn 50:06:0e:80:03:4e:95:23 [HDS20117-c20-9]
    pwwn 21:00:00:e0:8b:09:78:47 [ca-sun2_qlc0]
```

IVR zones must be members of IVR zonesets just as regular zones must be members of regular zonesets. An IVR zoneset must also be activated in order to be part of the running configuration. There is still only one active zoneset at activation, consisting of regular zones and IVR zones, so a switch that is not IVR-enabled (either a non-IVR enabled MDS or a third-party switch) can still receive and apply the new active zoneset.

Best Practice   Both VSANs referenced in an IVR zone must be in the IVR topology to communicate.

If there are devices in the VSAN that require IVR access, the IVR-enabled switch should be used for all zoning, including non IVR zoning, because the resulting active zoneset is a union of the regular zoneset and the IVR zoneset.

Do not use IVR zones to provide access between devices in the same VSAN. Use regular zones.

Do not use regular zones to provide access between a real device and the pseudo device created by IVR.

IVR with CFS

Before Cisco SAN-OS Release 2.x, IVR topology had to be defined on each switch using either DCNM or the CLI. If a new switch was going to perform IVR, the entire IVR topology had to be manually entered on the new switch, then the other switches participating in the topology had to be modified to include the new switch. For example, in the old method, a fabric with two switches required four individual entries into the topology database (2 switches with IVR * 2 VSAN route switches).

Figure 8-2 is an example of a two-switch topology configuration without CFS. There are two switches with IVR times two VSAN route switches for a total of four entries.

Figure 8-2   IVR Topology without CFS

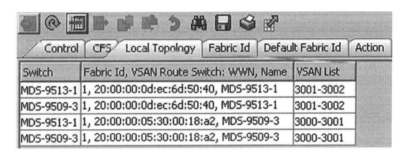

Modifying a topology is still a manual operation, but you no longer need to modify each switch individually. With CFS support for IVR, a single topology is maintained and CFS distributes changes to other IVR switches in the fabric. If a new switch is added to the fabric, CFS automatically synchronizes the new switch with the existing IVR topology.

The topology described in Figure 8-2 is illustrated in Figure 8-3 and shown again, using CFS this time, in Figure 8-4.

Figure 8-3   *CFS Reference Topology*

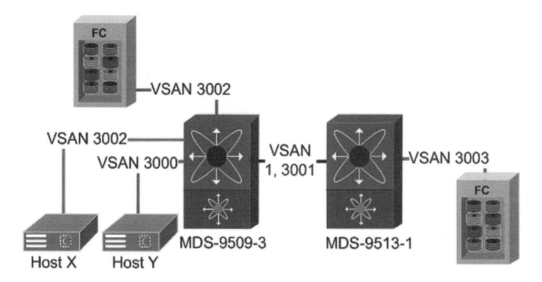

The two-switch configuration with CFS has one row for each VSAN Route Switch as shown in Figure 8-4.

Figure 8-4   *IVR Topology with CFS*

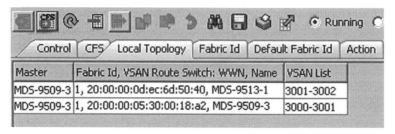

The topology using CFS is easier to comprehend, since only one row per IVR-enabled switch is displayed. The first column represents the switch that DCNM uses to perform CFS operations. Columns two and three describe the routes. MDS-9513-1 routes between VSANs 3001 and 3002, while switch MDS-9509-3 routes between 3000 and 3001. CFS prevents duplicate information from being displayed as the topology is managed on a fabric basis rather than a per switch basis.

Note
- If CFS is to be used with IVR, all IVR enabled switches must have CFS distribution for IVR enabled.

- Conversely, If CFS is not going to be used for IVR, then all of the IVR enabled switches should have CFS distribution for IVR disabled.

Enabling IVR with CFS and Auto Topology

This recipe uses DCNM to enable IVR with CFS and auto topology discovery.

Note   In a multi switch topology, repeat these steps for each switch in the fabric. Remember, that CFS commands (for example, adding NAT and auto topology) only have to be done from one switch as CFS informs the other switches.

To enable IVR with CFS and auto topology discovery, follow these steps:

Step 1   In the Logical Domains pane, expand **All VSANs**, then select **IVR** as shown in Figure 8-5.

Step 2   Under the Control tab, change the Command column entry to **enable** for switches that should have IVR enabled.

Step 3   Click the green **Apply Changes** icon shown in Figure 8-5.

The Status field entries change from disabled to **enabled** for the switches you selected in Step 2.

Figure 8-5   Enable IVR in DCNM

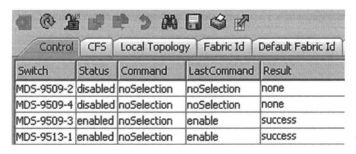

At this point, IVR is enabled.

Step 4   To Enable CFS distribution for IVR following these steps:

    a.   Choose the **CFS** tab.

    b.   Under Feature Admin, change noSelection (shown in Figure 8-6) to enable.

    c.   Click the green **Apply Changes** icon. The Last Result changes to success as shown in Figure 8-6.

Figure 8-6   Enable CFS Distribution for IVR

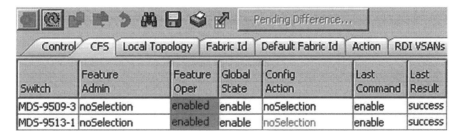

Note   Auto topology is not required for IVR-2 with FC NAT. If you do not enable it, manually define the topology. In this example, if you do not use auto topology, skip Step 6.

Step 5   Enable the FC NAT function of IVR by selecting the **Action** tab and checking the **Enable IVR NAT** check box (see Figure 8-7).

Step 6   Enable the auto topology discovery function of IVR by checking the **Automatically Discover Topology** check box (see Figure 8-7)

Step 7   Click the green **Apply Changes** icon (see Figure 8-7). Remember that the configuration is not active until it has been CFS committed.

Figure 8-7   *Enabling IVR-2's FC NAT and Auto Topology Discovery*

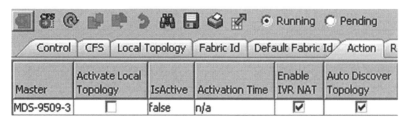

Step 8   Click **CFS Commit Pending Changes** button. The message **CFS (ivr): Committed** should be displayed in the bottom left hand corner.

Step 9   Choose the **Active Topology** tab to see the active topology as shown in Figure 8-8.

Figure 8-8   *IVR-2 FC NAT Auto Discovered Topology*

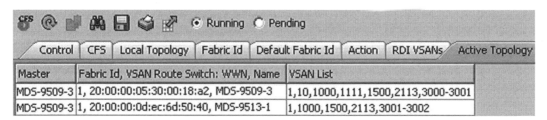

At this point IVR is enabled for CFS distribution, NAT, and auto topology discovery.

Configuring a Single Switch with Two VSANs

In this example, a simple two VSAN configuration is done with one switch (see Figure 8-9). Only IVR-2 with FC NAT works for this example. The topology cannot be done with IVR-1 because the domain IDs are the same between the two VSANs, and the devices themselves have exactly the same FC ID.

Figure 8-9   *IVR-2 Single Switch Example Topology*

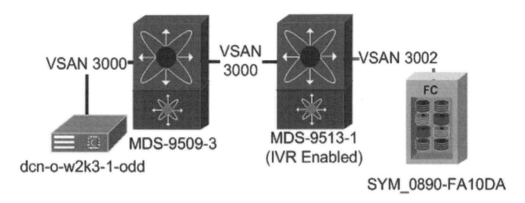

To configure two VSANs with one IVR enabled switch using DCNM, follow these steps:

Step 1   Enable IVR with CFS, IVR-NAT and auto topology discovery as described in Enabling IVR with CFS and Auto Topology, page 8-7.

Step 2   Create the IVR zones and zone set.

    a. In the Logical Domains pane, select the fabric and expand **All VSANs**.

    b. Right-click **IVR** and choose **Edit Full Local Zone Database**.

Figure 8-10   *IVR-2 Create a Zone Set*

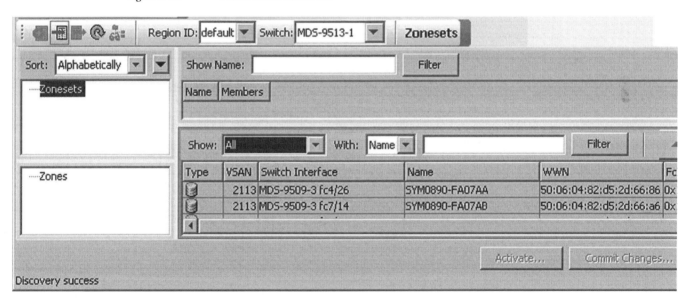

Step 3   Create the IVR zone set.

    a. Right-click **Zonesets** in the left pane and choose **Insert**.

    b. Type a name for the zone set and click **OK**.

The resulting zone set appears in the left hand pane.

Step 4   Create the IVR zone.

    a. Right-click **Zone** in the left pane and choose **Insert**.

b. Enter a meaningful zone name and click **OK.**

Step 5 Add the members to be zoned from the bottom pane into the newly created zone by dragging them into the zone or clicking the **Add to Zone** button.

Step 6 In the left pane, drag the zone into the zone set. The pane should now look like Figure 8-11.

Figure 8-11   Single Switch IVR-2, Create Zoneset

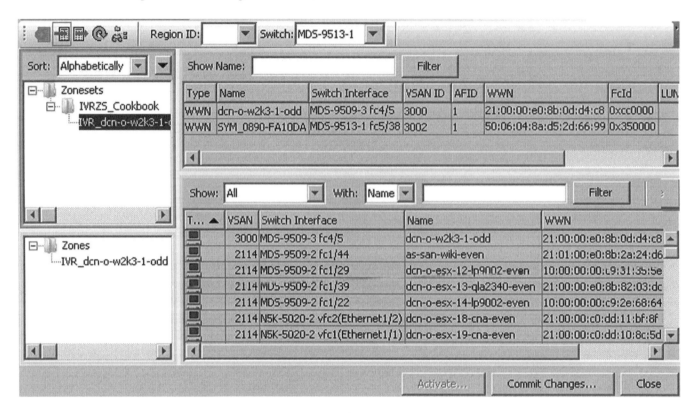

Step 7 Activate the zone set which implicitly performs CFS commit it (see Figure 8-12).

a. Right-click the zone set in the left pane and choose **Activate.**

b. Click **Continue Activation.** A pop-up window will display a status log of the activation similar to the following:

```
MDS-9513-1:Activating IVRZS_Cookbook
MDS-9513-1:checking status, elapsed time:0 sec activating IVRZS_Cookbook
commiting zone configuration changes
MDS-9513-1:checking status, elapsed time:3 sec activating IVRZS_Cookbook
commiting zone configuration changes
MDS-9513-1:checking status, elapsed time:6 sec activating IVRZS_Cookbook
MDS-9513-1:checking status, elapsed time:6 sec activating IVRZS_Cookbook
MDS-9513-1:MDS-9513-1:Commit Successful
MDS-9513-1:checking status, elapsed time:12 sec activating IVRZS_Cookbook
MDS-9513-1:IVRZS_Cookbook Activation success
MDS-9513-1:Save running configuration to Startup
MDS-9513-1:Save running configuration to Startup on Enhanced MDS-9513-1
MDS-9513-1:Save running configuration to Startup on Enhanced MDS-9509-3
MDS-9513-1:Saved running configuration to Startup
MDS-9513-1:Finished
Success
```

c. Click **Close** to return to the main DCNM window.

Figure 8-12   Single Switch IVR-2, Display IVR Zoneset

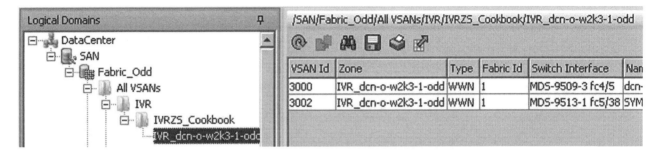

At this point, the host dcn-o-w2k3-1-odd in VSAN 3000 can access the storage on SYM_0890_FA10DA in VSAN 3002.

Configuring Two IVR Switches Separated by a Transit VSAN Topology

This recipe configures the IVR topology for a configuration with two IVR switches using a single transit VSAN (see Figure 8-13). The example uses CFS to distribute the topology. IVR has already been enabled on both switches. Additionally it is leveraging IVR-2 with FC NAT and a manual topology.

Best Practice   Instead of using multiple transit VSANs, use a single transit VSAN extended over multiple switches. It simplifies the topology while providing the isolation of a transit VSAN.

Figure 8-13   Two Switch, Transit VSAN IVR Topology.

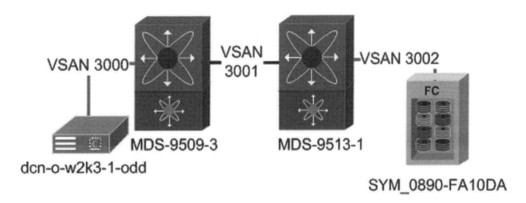

Before configuring a topology, decide what is needed. By examining the diagram in Figure 8-13, you can determine that the entries in Table 8-3 need to be configured.

Table 8-3   *IVR VSANs*

VSAN Route Switch	VSANs to Route
MDS-9509-3	3000, 3001
MDS-9513-1	3001, 3002

Best Practice   Table 8-3 provides simple documentation that can be easily added to an implementation plan, detailed design document or run book.

To configure the topology, follow these steps:

Step 1   In the DCNM **Logical Domains** pane, select a fabric, then **All VSANs**, then **IVR**.

Step 2   Choose the **CFS** tab to activate the other tabs.

Step 3   Choose the tab **Local Topology** (see Figure 8-14).

Figure 8-14   *Local Topology Tab*

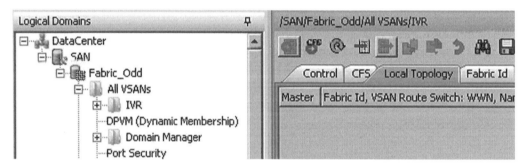

Step 4   Click the blue **Create Row...** icon (see Figure 8-14).

Step 5   In the resulting pop up box, from the **Switch** pull-down menu, select the first switch (MDS-9509-3) and its associated VSAN list. (This is part of the plan shown in Table 8-3 on page 8-12.)

Step 6   Complete the switch's **VSAN List** (3000, 3001) as shown in Figure 8-15.

Figure 8-15   *Create Topology*

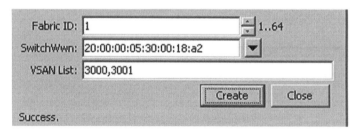

Step 7   Click **Create**.

Step 8   Repeat this procedure for the second and third switch in Table 8-3 on page 8-12, and then close the dialog box. The local topology should look like the one in Figure 8-16.

Figure 8-16   Local Topology

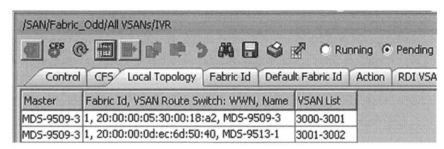

Step 9   Choose the **Action** tab.

Step 10   Check the **Activate Local** check box, and then click the green **Apply Changes** icon.

Step 11   Click **Apply CFS** (green circle with CFS written above it). The message **CFS(ivr):Committed** appears in the bottom left corner of DCNM.

Step 12   To verify the topology, choose the **Active Topology** tab. You see the topology in Figure 8-17.

Figure 8-17   Active Topology

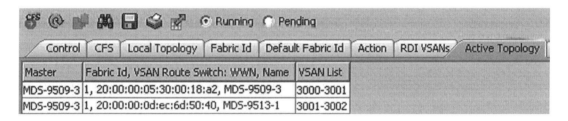

At this point, the topology is correctly defined and the active topology contains the correct information. When this topology is configured and distributed by CFS, the **Discrepancies** tab will have no entries.

Now IVR zone sets and zones can be defined to provide connectivity between the two end devices. For a detailed example, see "Step 2Create the IVR zones and zone set." section on page 8-9.

Advanced IVR Procedures

This section contains IVR related procedures that are not commonly performed.

Upgrading from IVR-1 to IVR-2

This recipe upgrades an IVR-1 configuration to IVR-2 using both CFS and auto topology. This recipe should be performed before upgrading to NX-OS 5.x.

Best Practice   If using IVR-1 in the configuration, it needs to be upgraded to IVR-2 before upgrading to NX-OS 5.x

Caution   Upgrading from IVR-1 to IVR-2 disrupts IVR-based traffic, but does not disrupt non IVR traffic such as non-IVR zones contained in a VSAN.

Upgrading from IVR-1 to IVR-2 with NAT may change the FC IDs of virtual devices, which requires FC ID dependent hosts, such as HPUX and AIX, to re-scan for the devices.

Note   IVR-1 cannot coexist with IVR-2 within a single physical fabric. IVR enabled switches must be either in IVR-1 mode or IVR-2 mode. Mixed configurations are not supported. Use CFS to ensure that all switches are running the same configuration.

To upgrade an IVR-1 configuration to IVR-2 using both CFS and auto topology, follow these steps:

Step 1   Back up all MDS switch configurations using a procedure similar to Copying Files to and from a Switch, page 1-22.

Step 2   Upgrade all IVR border switches to a common level of NX-OS. Switches not acting as IVR border switches are not required to be upgraded, but we recommended that you upgrade them. For upgrading SAN-OS firmware directions, see Firmware Upgrades and Downgrades, page 1-26.

Step 3   Deactivate the IVR zone set using DCNM. This does not delete the IVR zone set from the local database as it is reactivated once IVR-2 has been enabled.

    a.   In the Logical Domains pane, select a fabric and expand **All VSANs.**

    b.   Right-click **IVR** and choose **Deactivate Zoneset**. A pop-up window opens.

    c.   Click **OK**.

    All devices are now isolated from devices in other VSANs.

    d.   Close the pop-up window.

Step 4   Enable CFS for IVR for all switches that will perform IVR, using DCNM.

    a.   In the Logical Domains pane, select a fabric, expand **All VSANs** and select IVR.

    b.   Choose the **CFS** tab in the top pane (see Figure 8-18).

    c.   In the Feature Admin column, change the field from noSelection to **enable.**

    d.   Click the green **Apply Changes** icon. The Last Command columns should now display enable and success (see Figure 8-18).

Figure 8-18   Enable CFS

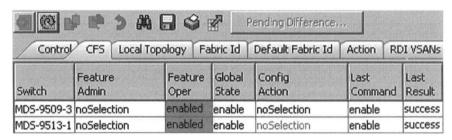

Step 5   Enable FC NAT and auto topology.

    a.   Click the **CFS** tab to determine the CFS master switch.

b. Click the **Action** tab. Only one switch should be listed here, the switch that DCNM will use to perform configuration distribution.

c. Check both the **Enable IVR NAT** and the **Automatically Discover Topology** check boxes.

d. Click the green **Apply Changes** icon.

Note   A local topology may still be present on the switch. Auto topology modifies the local topology database.

Step 6   Click **CFS Commit Pending Changes**. **CFS (ivr): Committed** should be displayed in the bottom left-hand corner.

Step 7   Activate the IVR zone set.

a. In the Logical Domains pane, select the fabric and expand **All VSANs**.

b. Right-click **IVR** and choose **Edit Local Full Zone Database**.

Step 8   Right-click the zone set that was deactivated in Step 3 and choose **Activate**.

Step 9   Click **Continue Activation** in the resulting confirmation window. It takes a few seconds to commit the changes and save the running-configuration to startup.

Step 10   Click **Close** to return to the main DCNM window.

At this point the switches are upgraded to IVR-2 with FC NAT, CFS and auto topology. Further firmware upgrades to the IVR enabled switches may be performed and HPUX and AIX hosts with disks associated with the FC ID may need to re scan for the new FC IDs.

Configuring Persistent FC IDs in IVR from the CLI

Virtual devices created by an IVR with NAT configuration can have associated persistent FC IDs. This feature, similar to the persistent FC ID feature discussed in Chapter 6, "VSANs" for actual devices, enables a virtual device to receive the same FC ID across reboots of the switch.

Best Practice   HPUX and AIX are two operating systems that use FC IDs in device paths to storage. If the FC ID changes for a device accessed by either an AIX or a HPUX host, the host might lose access to the device. Configure persistent FC IDs for IVR to have a switch assign the same FC ID to a virtual device across switch reboots.

This example configures a storage device to use a specific FC ID in the host's VSAN. The actual devices are already logged into the fabric and the IVR topology has been created to include VSANs 3000 and 3002. In addition, this example uses these resources:

- IVR features enabled: CFS and IVR with NAT.

- Host with pWWN: 10:00:00:00:c9:32:8b:a8 and VSAN 3002.

- Storage with pWWN: 50:06:0e:80:03:4e:95:33, VSAN 3000, Real FC ID: 0xef0002, and FC ID to be configured in Host VSAN: 0x630063.

- IVR topology:

```
AFID   SWITCH WWN                 Active   Cfg. VSANS
----------------------------------------------------------
   1   20:00:00:05:30:00:68:5e *  yes     yes   3000,3002
```

To configure a storage device to use a specific FC ID in the host VSAN, follow these steps:

Step 1 Enter IVR FC domain configuration mode for the autonomous fabric ID (AFID) and VSAN for the location of the virtual device. In this case it is the AFID and VSAN where the storage will be virtual.

```
MDS-9513-1# conf t
MDS-9513-1(config)# ivr fcdomain database autonomous-fabric-num 1 vsan 3002
MDS-9513-1(config-fcdomain)#
```

Step 2 Enter the native AFID, VSAN of the storage device, and domain to be used in the host's VSAN. CFS is enabled for IVR so any changes must be committed later. The domain ID in this command is in decimal format.

```
MDS-9513-1(config-fcdomain)# native-autonomous-fabric-num 1 native-vsan 3000 domain 99
fabric is locked for configuration. Please commit after configuration is done.
MDS-9513-1(config-fcdomain-fcid)#
```

Step 3 Specify the pWWN and FC ID to be used. (A device-alias can be used instead of a pWWN.) The virtual domain and FC IDs are not created until the zone set is activated.

```
MDS-9513-1(config-fcdomain-fcid)# pwwn 50:06:0e:80:03:4e:95:33 fcid 0x630063

The FCID should correspond to virtual domain 99 specified earlier for this mode
MDS-9513-1(config-fcdomain-fcid)#
```

Step 4 Create the IVR zone sets and zones with **ivr zoneset** commands.

```
MDS-9513-1(config-fcdomain-fcid# ivr zoneset name IVR_Zoneset1
MDS-9513-1(config-ivr-zoneset)# zone name IVRZ_host1_lpfc0_Array1_port12
MDS-9513-1(config-ivr-zoneset-zone)# member pwwn 10:00:00:00:c9:32:8b:a8 vsan 3002
MDS-9513-1(config-ivr-zoneset-zone)# member pwwn 50:06:0e:80:03:4e:95:33 vsan 3000
MDS-9513-1(config-ivr-zoneset-zone)# ivr zoneset activate name IVR_Zoneset1
```

Step 5 CFS commit the changes for IVR to activate both the IVR zone set and the modifications to the IVR persistent FC ID database.

```
MDS-9513-1(config)# ivr commit
commit initiated. check ivr status
```

Step 6 Verify FC IDs and active zone set with the **show** command.

```
MDS-9513-1(config)# show ivr fcdomain database
---------------------------------------------------
 AFID  Vsan  Native-AFID  Native-Vsan  Virtual-domain
---------------------------------------------------
   1   3002       1         3000         0x63(99)

Number of Virtual-domain entries: 1


---------------------------------------------------
 AFID  Vsan        Pwwn          Virtual-fcid
---------------------------------------------------
   1   3002  50:06:0e:80:03:4e:95:33  0x630063
              [HDS20117-c20-8]

Number of Virtual-fcid entries: 1
```

```
switch# show fcns database vsan 3002

VSAN 3002:
--------------------------------------------------------------------------
FCID        TYPE   PWWN                            (VENDOR)      FC4-TYPE:FEATURE
--------------------------------------------------------------------------
0x1c0003    N      10:00:00:00:c9:32:8b:a8 (Emulex)             scsi-fcp
                   [ca-sun1_lpfc0]
0x630063    N      50:06:0e:80:03:4e:95:33                      scsi-fcp
                   [HDS20117-c20-8]

Total number of entries = 2

switch# show zoneset active vsan 3002
zoneset name ZS_test vsan 3002
  zone name zone1 vsan 3002
    pwwn 50:06:0e:80:03:4e:99:99
    pwwn 50:06:0e:80:03:4e:98:98

  zone name IVRZ_IVRZ_host1_lpfc0_Array1_port12 vsan 3002
  * fcid 0x630063 [pwwn 50:06:0e:80:03:4e:95:33] [HDS20117-c20-8]
  * fcid 0x1c0003 [pwwn 10:00:00:00:c9:32:8b:a8] [ca-sun1_lpfc0]
```

Configuring Persistent FC IDs in IVR Using DCNM

Virtual devices created by an IVR with NAT configuration can have associated persistent FC IDs. This feature, similar to the persistent FC ID feature discussed in Chapter 6, "VSANs" for actual devices, enables a virtual device to receive the same FC ID across reboots of the switch.

Best Practice

HPUX and AIX are two operating systems that use FC IDs in device paths to storage. If the FC ID changes for a device accessed by either an AIX or a HPUX host, the host may lose access to the device. Configure persistent FC IDs for IVR to have a switch assign the same FC ID to a virtual device across switch reboots.

This example configures a storage device to use a specific FC ID in the host's VSAN. The actual devices are already logged into the fabric and the IVR topology has been created to include VSANs 3000 and 3002. In addition, this example uses these resources:

- IVR features enabled: CFS and IVR with NAT.
- Host with pWWN: 21:00:00:e0:8b:0d:d4:c8 and VSAN 3002.
- Storage with pWWN: 50:06:04:8a:d5:2d:66:99, Real VSAN 3000, Real FC ID: 0x350000, and FC ID to be configured in Host VSAN: 0x630063.
- IVR topology:

```
MDS-9509-3# show ivr vsan-topology

AFID  SWITCH WWN                   Active   Cfg.  VSANS
--------------------------------------------------------------
   1  20:00:00:05:30:00:18:a2 *    yes      yes   3000-3001
   1  20:00:00:0d:ec:6d:50:40      yes      yes   3001-3002

Total:   2 entries in active and configured IVR VSAN-Topology
```

To configure a storage device to use a specific FC ID in the host VSAN, follow these steps:

Step 1   In DCNM, in the Logical Domains pane, select the fabric, All VSANs, then IVR. At the far right of the top pane, select the **Domains** tab. The window may need to be scrolled to the right by clicking on the small arrows next to the tabs.

Step 2   Click **Create Row**....

Step 3   Enter the following values:

- **Current Fabric number** (AFID where the virtual domain will be created).
- **Current VSAN** (where the Virtual Domain will be created).
- **Native Fabric** (AFID where the device actually exists).
- **Native VSAN** (where the device actually exists).
- **Domain ID** (this is the virtual domain ID that will be created, in decimal equivalent of the hex value).

Figure 8-19   Create IVR Domain

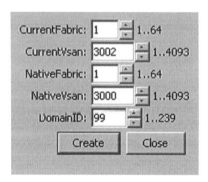

Step 4   Select **Create** and **Close**.

Step 5   Select the **CFS Commit Pending Changes** button.

At this point, the domain ID will be displayed in the **Domains** tab along with the Fabric and VSAN IDs.

To create the IVR Persistent FC ID, follow these steps:

Step 1   With the IVR folder selected in the Logical Domains pane, select the **FCID** tab.

Step 2   Click **Create Row**...

Step 3   Fill in the following information:

- **Current Fabric** (AFID where the virtual device will exist).
- **Current VSAN** (VSAN where the virtual device will exist).
- **PWWN**: (PWWN of virtual device).
- **FCID**: (FC ID for the virtual device). The pull-down arrow automatically inserts the domain ID corresponding to the virtual domain configured. Edit the domain ID as in Figure 8-20.

Figure 8-20   Create IVR Persistent FCID

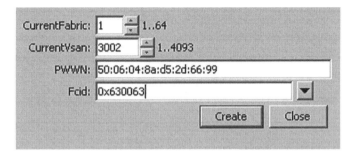

Step 4   Click **Create** and **Close**.

Step 5   Click **CFS Commit Pending Changes** and **CFS(ivr):Committed** should be displayed in the bottom left corner of DCNM.

At this point the IVR zones and zone sets can be created as per IVR Zones and Zonesets, page 8-4.

Adding a New IVR-Enabled Switch to an Existing Topology

This recipe adds a new switch to an existing IVR-2 configuration with CFS and auto topology. It builds on the configuration described in Configuring a Single Switch with Two VSANs, page 8-8. The topology is shown in Figure 8-21. The new switch has the IP address 172.22.36.9.

Figure 8-21   Topology for Adding a New IVR-2 Switch

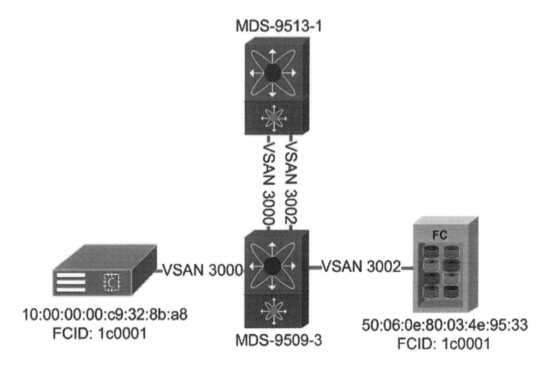

In this configuration, the switch MDS-9509-3 is currently performing IVR-FC NAT between the host in VSAN 3000 and the storage in VSAN 3002. You will add the new switch MDS-9513-1 without impacting the currently running configuration.

Best Practice   When multiple IVR-2 capable switches are configured, one switch can take over the routing functionality of another, provided it can directly see both the source and destination VSANs. With this recipe, if IVR-2 was disabled on MDS-9509-3, switch MDS-9513-1 could automatically take over the routing. This is not possible with IVR-1.

To add a new switch, first enable IVR in DCNM, follow these steps:

Step 1   In the Logical Domains pane, choose a fabric, expand **All VSANs,** and then select **IVR**.

Step 2   Click the **Control** tab.

Step 3   In the Command column, change the MDS-9513-1 switch entry to **enable**.

Step 4   Click the green **Apply Changes** icon.

The status column entry changes from a yellow progress box, to the word **Success**.

Step 5   Click the **CFS** tab.

Step 6   In the Enable Admin column, change the MDS-9513-1 switch entry to **enable**.

Step 7   Click the green **Apply Changes** icon.

The Last Result column changes from inProgress to **Success**.

Step 8   Click the Active Topology column to see a topology that includes both switches, even though only the MDS-9509-3 switch is performing any IVR.

Step 9   Save the configuration of both switches.

Note   By having CFS for IVR already enabled on the first switch (MDS-9509-3) and enabling IVR and CFS on the second switch (MDS-9513-1), the second switch learned what configuration parameters (FC NAT and auto topology) to enable. There is no need to enable FC NAT and auto topology on the second switch.

Best Practice   One of the primary advantages of CFS is the fact that the configuration of the first switch is communicated to the second switch. This is more apparent when the first switch configuration is more complex. In addition, as the topology grows larger and the number of switches, devices and VSANs increase, adding a single switch to an IVR-enabled configuration requires changes to be made to more and more switches, increasing the possibility for human error if done manually.

## CHAPTER 9

Fibre Channel Over Ethernet (FCoE)

Fibre Channel over Ethernet (FCoE) is an INCITS T11 industry standard that allows Fibre Channel protocol to be carried over an Ethernet infrastructure. The primary goal of FCoE is to consolidate I/O (network and block storage) over Ethernet which can result in reduced network complexity in the Data Center. FCoE relies on the a reliable and loss less 10 Gigabit ethernet infrastructure in the Data center to deliver an unified I/O. FCoE could potentially consolidate SAN and LAN infrastructure into a single unified I/O infrastructure supporting both network and block I/Os.

Fibre Channel over Ethernet (FCoE) maps the Fibre Channel over a full duplex loss less Ethernet. FC frame is carried over Ethernet with out being modified. This enables FCoE networks to inter operate into existing FC SAN infrastructure that is in place today.

Traditionally the Data Center network comprises of two separate network infrastructure, one for Network I/O (server to server, server to client, server management, network File access and backup) and one for block I/O (block storage (scsi disk), tape, etc.). To access these two diverse infrastructures servers require one or more network interface cards (NIC) to access the LAN and at least two host bus adapters (HBA) to access the SAN storage.

FCoE enables a server in the Data Center to use a pair of converged network adapters (CNA) to access both LAN and SAN resources. This results in consolidation of LAN and SAN switching infrastructure into a single infrastructure. This reduces the number of switches required, lowering Data Center space, power and cooling requirements.

The Ethernet network that supports FCoE is required to be a loss less. The Ethernet infrastructure devices (switches) must support no-drop packet and network flow control mechanisms that allow loss less traffic over it enabling FC to be transported over Ethernet.

FCoE is supported on Cisco Nexus 7000 series, Nexus 5000 series, Nexus 4000 series, Nexus 2000 series and MDS 9500 series switches. The above platforms support host, storage and inter switch connectivity using FCoE.

The recipes in this section details FCoE and FCoE switch related configurations.

FCoE and port-channel commands

Nexus and the MDS platforms support multiple protocols (Ethernet and Fibre Channel). To provide redundancy between interconnected switches these platforms support bundling of multiple ISL links in to a single logical link called port-channels. The Nexus 5000 and the MDS platform today support native fibre channel ports. the Nexus platform and MDS platform support FCoE ethernet ports.

The fibre channel ISLs between Nexus 5000 and MDS family of switches can be configured into a fibre channel port-channel. These switch families along with the Nexus 7000 series of switches thane FCoE ethernet port that can be configured as ISL between them. These Ethernet ISLs can be configured into a ethernet port-channel. the creation of fibre channel and ethernet port-channels require different command. The matrix below in Figure 9-1 shows the command syntax used to create the two types of port-channels on the two platforms. These commands are later used in the various recipes to create the appropriate port-channels.

Figure 9-1   *Port-channel command matrix for Nexus and MDS platforms*

Protocol	Nexus 7000	MDS	Nexus 5000
Fibre Channel	Not Supported	port-channel	san-port-channel
Ethernet	port-channel	ethernet-port-channel	port-channel

Configuring the Nexus 5000 switch with FCoE

The following recipes provide information on how to configure the Nexus 5000 series switch to support Fibre Channel over Ethernet (FCoE) in both switch mode and NPV mode.

Configuring a Nexus 5000 switch to support FCoE (switch mode)

This recipe details the steps required to configure a pair of Nexus 5020 configured in switch mode to enable a host to connect to it using FCoE. The hosts needs to access fibre channel storage connected to the MDS director. The Nexus 5020 switch is connected through ISL to a MDS switch which has fibre channel storage.

The topology for this recipe is shown in Figure 9-2. The host is dual attached (one connect to each fabric) to the two Nexus 5020. The Nexus 5020 switches are connected to the MDS 9500 directors as shown.

The Nexus 5020 switches are configured in **switch mode**. (i.e. the VSANs created to support devices need to be configured with unique Domain ID). The storage is connected to the MDS directors. The devices involved in this recipe are:

- N5K-5020-1: ethernet interface 1/1, vfc 1 and fibre channel expansion module
- N5k-5020-2: ethernet interface 1/1, vfc 1 and fibre channel expansion module
- MDS-9509-2
- MDS-9509-3
- Server
- FC Storage

Figure 9-2   *FCoE topology*

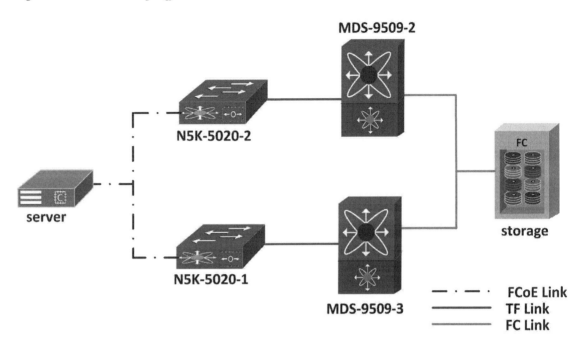

This configuration assumes that the nexus switches are configured in switch mode.

Step 1   Enable FCoE on N5K-5020-1 switch. NX-OS 5.x and above the enabling FCoE is non disruptive.

```
N5K-5020-1# conf t
N5K-5020-1(config)# feature fcoe
FC license checked out successfully
fc_plugin extracted successfully
FC plugin loaded successfully
FCoE manager enabled successfully
FC enabled on all modules successfully
N5K-5020-1(config)# end
N5K-5020-1
```

Step 2   Configure the QoS for FCoE on the N5K-5020-1

```
N5K-5020-1# conf t
N5K-5020-1(config)# system qos
N5K-5020-1(config-sys-qos)# service-policy type qos input fcoe-default-in-policy
N5K-5020-1(config-sys-qos)# service-policy type queuing input fcoe-default-in-policy
N5K-5020-1(config-sys-qos)# service-policy type queuing output fcoe-default-out-policy
N5K-5020-1(config-sys-qos)# service-policy type network-qosfcoe-default-nq-policy
N5K-5020-1(config)# end
N5K-5020-1
```

Step 3   Create VSAN 2113 on the N5K-5020-1.

```
N5K-5020-1# conf t
N5K-5020-1(config)# vsan database
N5K-5020-1(config-vsan-db)# vsan 2113 name FCoE_VSAN2113
N5K-5020-1(config-vsan-db)# end
N5K-5020-1#
```

Step 4   Map a VSAN for fcoe traffic to a VLAN In this recipe VSAN 2113 is mapped to VLAN 2113 for FCoE traffic.

Best Practice   It is recommended to keep the VLAN and VSAN number same in the above mapping configuration.

```
N5K-5020-1# conf t
N5K-5020-1(config)# vlan 2113
N5K-5020-1(config)# fcoe vsan 2113
N5K-5020-1(config)@ end
N5K-5020-1#
```

Step 5   Enable the ethernet interface, configure and enable vfc interface and bind it to a underlining ethernet interface. Modify the ethernet port characteristics; set trunk mode on and spanning tree mode to edge type trunk

Note   Without the Ethernet interface spanning-tree port type being defined as edge trunk the flogi process will not complete and the end device will not be able to communicate through the network. This configuration needs to be applied to every ethernet interface that will have an FCoE capable end device connected to it. This should not be performed for ethernet interfaces that are part of a port-channel.

```
N5K-5020-1# conf t
N5K-5020-1(config)# interface ethernet 1/1
N5K-5020-1(config-if)# no shutdown
N5K-5020-1(config-if)# switchport mode trunk
N5K-5020-1(config-if)# spanning-tree port type edge trunk
Warning: Edge port type (portfast) should only be enabled on ports connected to a single
  host. Connecting hubs, concentrators, switches, bridges, etc... to this
  interface  when edge port type (portfast) is enabled, can cause temporary bridging loops.
  Use with CAUTION

N5K-5020-1(config-if)@ interface vfc 1
N5K-5020-1(config-if)# bind interface ethernet 1/1 <-- Binds the vfc to the ethernet
interface
N5K-5020-1(config-if)# no shut
N5K-5020-1(config-if)# end
N5K-5020-1#
```

Step 6   Add the vfc1 interface on N5K-5020-1 switch VSAN 2113.

Caution   Ensure that the VSAN 2113 has an unique Domain ID so that it can merge with VSAN 2113 on the MDS director.

```
N5K-5020-1# conf t
N5K-5020-1(config)# vsan database
N5K-5020-1(config-vsan-db)# vsan 2113 interface vfc1
N5K-5020-1(config-vsan-db)# end
N5K-5020-1#
```

Step 7   Enable FCoE on N5K-5020-2 switch.

```
N5K-5020-2# conf t
N5K-5020-2(config)# feature fcoe
FC license checked out successfully
fc_plugin extracted successfully
FC plugin loaded successfully
FCoE manager enabled successfully
FC enabled on all modules successfully
N5K-5020-2(config)# end
N5K-5020-2
```

Step 8   Configure the QoS for FCoE on the N5K-5020-1

```
N5K-5020-2# conf t
N5K-5020-2(config)# system qos
N5K-5020-2(config-sys-qos)# service-policy type qos input fcoe-default-in-policy
N5K-5020-2(config-sys-qos)# service-policy type queuing input fcoe-default-in-policy
N5K-5020-2(config-sys-qos)# service-policy type queuing output fcoe-default-out-policy
N5K-5020-2(config-sys-qos)# service-policy type network-qosfcoe-default-nq-policy
N5K-5020-2(config)# end
N5K-5020-2
```

Step 9   Configure VSAN 2114 on switch N5K-5020-2

```
N5K-5020-2# conf t
N5K-5020-2(config)# vsan database
N5K-5020-2(config-vsan-db)# vsan 2114 name FCoE_VSAN2114
N5K-5020-2(config-vsan-db)# end
N5K-5020-2#
```

Step 10   Map a VSAN for fcoe traffic to a VLAN. In this recipe VSAN 2114 is mapped to VLAN 2114 for FCoE traffic.

Caution   Ensure that the VSAN 2114 has an unique Domain ID so that it can merge with VSAN 2114 on the MDS director.

```
N5K-5020-2# conf t
N5K-5020-2(config)# vlan 2114
N5K-5020-2(config-vlan)# fcoe vsan 2114
N5K-5020-2(config)@ end
N5K-5020-2#
```

Step 11   Enable the Ethernet interface, configure and enable vfc interface and bind it to an ethernet interface. Modify the ethernet port characteristics; set trunk mode on and spanning tree mode to edge type trunk.

Note   Without the Ethernet interface **spanning-tree port type being defined as edge trunk** the flogi process will not complete and the host's CNA will not be able to access storage.

```
N5K-5020-2# conf t
N5K-5020-2(config)# interface ethernet 1/1
N5K-5020-2(config-if)# no shutdown
N5K-5020-2(config-if)# switchport mode trunk
N5K-5020-2(config-if)# spanning-tree port type edge trunk
Warning: Edge port type (portfast) should only be enabled on ports connected to a single
  host. Connecting hubs, concentrators, switches, bridges, etc... to this
  interface  when edge port type (portfast) is enabled, can cause temporary bridging loops.
  Use with CAUTION

N5K-5020-2(config-if)@ interface vfc 1
N5K-5020-2(config-if)# bind interface ethernet 1/1 <-- Binds the vfc to the ethernet
interface
N5K-5020-2(config-if)# no shut
N5K-5020-2(config-if)# end
N5K-5020-2#
```

Step 12   Add interface vfc1 on N5K-5020-2 to VSAN 2114.

```
N5K-5020-2# conf t
N5K-5020-2(config)# vsan database
N5K-5020-2(config-vsan-db)# vsan 2114 interface vfc1
N5K-5020-2(config-vsan db)# end
N5K-5020-2#
```

The host's CNA should now log on to the Nexus 5020 on both the fabrics. Run **show flogi database** command to verify that the host is indeed logged on to the fabric.

Connect two of the fibre channel port in the expansion slots on both the Nexus 5020 switches to the respective MDS switches in their fabrics for ISL connectivity to the storage. Then configure a port-channel between the N5K-5020-1 and MDS-9513-1. (refer to Creating a port-channel Using DCNM SAN, page 5-1) Similarly configure another port-channel using the two ISL between N4K-5020-2 and MDS-9509-2.

Create a zone and activate the zoneset in VSAN 2114 and VSAN 2113 that allows the server to access the fibre channel storage on the MDS directors.

Configuring a Nexus 5000 switch to support FCoE (NPV mode)

This recipe details the steps required to configure Nexus 5020 configured in NPV mode to enable a host to connect to it using FCoE. The Nexus 5020 switch is connected to MDS using TF ports to a MDS switch which has fibre channel storage. The **NPV feature** needs to be enabled on **N5K-5020-1 and on N5K-5020-2** switches. The **NPIV** feature needs to be enabled on **MDS-9509-2 and MDS-9509-3** directors.

Figure 9-3   NPV Nexus 5020 FCoE topology

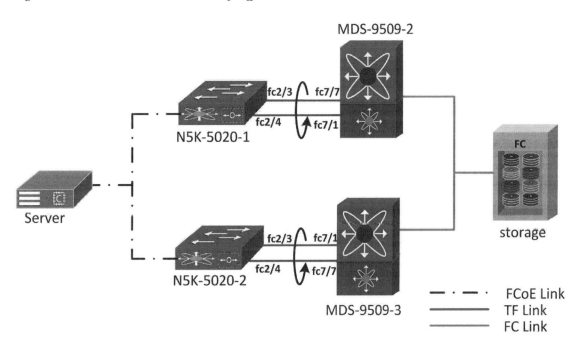

The topology for this recipe is shown in Figure 9-3. The host is dual attached (one connect to each fabric) to the two Nexus 5020. The Nexus 5020 switches are connected to the MDS 9500 directors as shown in Figure 9-3 using **TF links**.

The Nexus 5020 switches are configured in **NPV Mode**. The storage is connected to the MDS directors. The devices involved in this recipe are:

*   N5K-5020-1: ethernet interface 1/1, vfc 1 and fibre channel expansion module
*   N5k-5020-2: ethernet interface 1/1, vfc 1 and fibre channel expansion module
*   MDS-9509-2
*   MDS-9509-3
*   Server
*   FC Storage

This configuration recipe requires the Nexus 5020 to be configured in NPV mode. NPV mode configuration will erase existing configuration on the Nexus 5020 and reboot the switch.

Best Practice   It is recommended to backup the Nexus 5000 switch configuration before running the command "**feature NPV**". It is recommended to copy the current configuration to the bootflash or to an external server.

For this recipe both the Nexus 5020 will be configured in NPV mode. They will connect up to the MDS switches with two NP links. These NP links will be port-channeled. The server has redundant CNA' and will connect into the Nexus 5020 switches using FCoE.

Step 1   Configure N5K-5020-1 in NPV mode. This will erase the nexus 5020's configuration and reload the switch.

```
N5K-5020-1# conf t
N5K-5020-1(config)# feature npv
Verify that boot variables are set and the changes are saved. Changing to npv mode erases
the current configuration and reboots the switch in npv mode. Do you want to continue?
(y/n):y
2011 Oct 15 03:10:14 N5K-5020-1 Oct 15 03:10:14 %KERN-0-SYSTEM_MSG: Shutdown Ports.. -
kernel

Broadcast message from root (Sat Oct 15 03:10:14 2011):

The system is going down for reboot NOW!
```

The switch will erase all configuration and reboot and come up in NPV mode.

Step 2   Configure VSAN 2113, VLAN 2113 and map FCoE VSAN on M5K-5020-1.

```
N5K-5020-1# conf t
N5K-5020-1(config)# vsan database
N5K-5020-1(config-vsan-db)# vsan 2113 name FCoE_VSAN2113
N5K-5020-1(config-vsan-db)# vlan 2113
N5K-5020-1(config-vlan)# fcoe vsan 2113
N5K-5020-1(config-vlan)# end
N5K-5020-1#
```

Step 3   Configure **san-port-channel** 20 on N5K-5020-1

Note   On the Nexus platform to create FC port-channel use the **san-port-channel** command. **port-channel** command will create ethernet port-channel on the Nexus platform.

```
N5K-5020-1# conf t
N5K-5020-1(config)# interface san-port-channel 20 <-- san-port-channel is the FC
port-channel equivalent command on the nexus platform.
N5K-5020-1(config-if)# switchport mode NP <-- ensure that the switch port mode is NP
N5K-5020-1(config-if)# switchport speed 2000
N5K-5020-1(config-if)# switchport trunk mode on
N5K-5020-1(config-if)# channel mode active
N5K-5020-1(config-if)# no shut
N5K-5020-1(config-if)# end
N5K-5020-1#
```

Step 4   Configure the ethernet ports to which the vfc interfaces will be bound to. The trunk mode needs to be turned on and the spanning-tree port type needs to be set to edge trunk. This will allow the flogi to complete.

Note   Without the Ethernet interface spanning-tree port type being defined as edge trunk the flogi process will not complete and the end device will not be able to communicate with other end devices in the network. This configuration needs to be applied to every ethernet interface that will have an FCoE capable end device connected to it.

```
N5K-5020-1# conf t
N5K-5020-1(config)# interface ethernet 1/1
N5K-5020-1(config-if)# switchport mode trunk
N5K-5020-1(config-if)# spanning-tree port type edge trunk
Warning: Edge port type (portfast) should only be enabled on ports connected to a single
 host. Connecting hubs, concentrators, switches, bridges, etc... to this
 interface  when edge port type (portfast) is enabled, can cause temporary bridging loops.
 Use with CAUTION

N5K-5020-1(config-if)# end
N5K-5020-1#
```

Step 5   Configure the NP ports on N5K-5020-1 with, trunk mode on and their speed configured and assigned to channel group 20 (port-channel 20 is used in this recipe. the NP ports used in this recipe are fc2/3 and fc 2/4.

```
N5K-5020-1# conf t
N5K-5020-1(config)# interface fc 2/3-4
N5K-5020-1(config-if)# switchport speed 2000
N5K-5020-1(config-if)# switchport trunk mode on
N5K-5020-1(config-if)# channel-group 20 force <-- use the force command
N5K-5020-1(config-if)# no shut
N5K-5020-1(config-if)# end
N5K-5020-1#
```

Step 6   On MDS 9509-3 enable the fport-channel-trunk feature. This is need to configure port-channel of TF ports.

```
MDS-9509-3# conf t
MDS-9509-3(config)# feature npiv <-- with out this feature the links between the switches
will not come up.
MDS-9509-3(config)# feature fport-channel-trunk
Admin trunk mode has been set to off for
1- Interfaces with admin switchport mode F,FL,FX,SD,ST in admin down state
2- Interfaces with operational switchport mode F,FL,SD,ST.
MDS-9509-3(config)# end
MDS-9509-3#
```

Step 7   Create port-channel 20 on MDS-9509-3

```
MDS-9509-3# conf t
MDS-9509-3(config)# interface port-channel 20
MDS-9509-3(config-if)# switchport mode F
MDS-9509-3(config-if)# switchport trunk mode on
MDS-9509-3(config-if)# swithport speed 2000
MDS-9509-3(config-if)# swithport rate-mode dedicated
MDS-9509-3(config-if)# channel mode active
MDS-9509-3(config-if)# no shut
MDS-9509-3(config-if)# end
MDS-9509-3#
```

Step 8   Configure the ports fc 7/1 and 7/7 on the MDS-9509-3 as F ports. From Figure 9-3 the fc interfaces 7/1 and 7/7 on MDS-9509-3 needs to be configured as F ports. Add the ports to the channel-group 20.

```
MDS-9509-3# conf t
MDS-9509-3(config)# interface fc 7/1, fc 7/7
MDS-9509-3(config-if)# switchport mode F
MDS-9509-3(config-if)# switchport trunk mode on
MDS-9509-3(config-if)# switchport speed 2000
MDS-9509-3(config-if)# channel group 20 force
MDS-9509-3(config-if)# no shut
MDS-9509-3(config-if)# end
MDS-9509-3#
```

Repeat the same process on the N5k-5020-2 and MDS-9509-2 to complete the NPV setup process

Step 9   Configure N5K-5020-2 in NPV mode. This will erase the nexus 5020's configuration and reload the switch.

```
N5K-5020-2# conf t
N5K-5020-2(config)# feature npv
Verify that boot variables are set and the changes are saved. Changing to npv mode erases
the current configuration and reboots the switch in npv mode. Do you want to continue?
(y/n):y
2011 Oct 15 03:10:14 N5K-5020-2 Oct 15 03:10:14 %KERN-0-SYSTEM_MSG: Shutdown Ports.. -
kernel

Broadcast message from root (Sat Oct 15 03:10:14 2011):

The system is going down for reboot NOW!
```

The switch will erase all configuration and reboot and come up in NPV mode

Step 10   Configure VSAN 2114, VLAN 2114 and map FCoE VSAN on M5K-5020-2.

```
N5K-5020-2# conf t
N5K-5020-2(config)# vsan database
N5K-5020-2(config-vsan-db)# vsan 2114 name FCoE_VSAN2114
N5K-5020-2(config-vsan-db)# vlan 2114
N5K-5020-2(config-vlan)# fcoe vsan 2114
N5K-5020-2(config-vlan)# end
N5K-5020-2#
```

Step 11   Configure **san-port-channel** 21 on N5K-5020-2

Note   On the Nexus platform to create FC port-channel use the **san-port-channel** command. **port-channel** command will create ethernet port-channel on the Nexus platform.

```
N5K-5020-2# conf t
N5K-5020-2(config)# interface san-port-channel 21 <-- san-port-channel is the FC
port-channel equivalent command on the nexus platform.
N5K-5020-2(config-if)# switchport mode NP <-- ensure that the switch port mode is NP
N5K-5020-2(config-if)# switchport speed 2000
N5K-5020-2(config-if)# switchport trunk mode on
N5K-5020-2(config-if)# channel mode active
N5K-5020-2(config-if)# no shut
N5K-5020-2(config-if)# end
N5K-5020-2#
```

Step 12 Configure the Ethernet port to which the vfc interfaces will be bound to. The trunk mode needs to be turned on and the spanning-tree port type needs to be set to edge trunk. This will allow the flogi to complete.

Note Without the Ethernet interface spanning-tree port type being defined as edge trunk the flogi process will not complete and the end device will not be able to communicate through the network. This configuration needs to be applied to every ethernet interface that will have an FCoE capable end device connected to it. This should not be performed for ethernet interfaces that are part of a port-channel.

```
N5K-5020-2# conf t
N5K-5020-2(config)# interface ethernet 1/1
N5K-5020-2(config-if)# switchport mode trunk
N5K-5020-2(config-if)# spanning-tree port type edge trunk
Warning: Edge port type (portfast) should only be enabled on ports connected to a single
 host. Connecting hubs, concentrators, switches, bridges, etc... to this
 interface  when edge port type (portfast) is enabled, can cause temporary bridging loops.
 Use with CAUTION

N5K-5020-2(config-if)# end
N5K-5020-2#
```

Step 13 Configure the NP ports on N5K-5020-2 with, trunk mode on and their speed configured and assigned to channel group 21 (port-channel 21 is used in this recipe. the NP ports used in this recipe are fc2/3 and fc 2/4.

```
N5K-5020-2# conf t
N5K-5020-2(config)# interface fc 2/3-4
N5K-5020-2(config-if)# switchport speed 2000
N5K-5020-2(config-if)# switchport trunk mode on
N5K-5020-2(config-if)# channel-group 21 force <-- use the force command
N5K-5020-2(config-if)# no shut
N5K-5020-2(config-if)# end
N5K-5020-2#
```

Step 14 On MDS 9509-2 enable the fport-channel-trunk feature. This is need to configure port-channel of TF ports.

```
MDS-9509-2# conf t
MDS-9509-2(config)# feature npiv <-- with out this feature the links between the switches
will not come up.
MDS-9509-2(config)# feature fport-channel-trunk
Admin trunk mode has been set to off for
1- Interfaces with admin switchport mode F,FL,FX,SD,ST in admin down state
2- Interfaces with operational switchport mode F,FL,SD,ST.
MDS-9509-2(config)# end
MDS-9509-2#
```

Step 15 Create port-channel 20 on MDS-9509-2

```
MDS-9509-2# conf t
MDS-9509-2(config)# interface port-channel 21
MDS-9509-2(config-if)# switchport mode F
MDS-9509-2(config-if)# switchport trunk mode on
MDS-9509-2(config-if)# swithport speed 2000
MDS-9509-2(config-if)# swithport rate-mode dedicated
MDS-9509-2(config-if)# channel mode active
MDS-9509-2(config-if)# no shut
MDS-9509-2(config-if)# end
MDS-9509-2#
```

Step 16   Configure the ports fc 7/1 and 7/7 on the MDS-9509-2 as F ports. From Figure 9-3 the fc interfaces 7/1 and 7/7 on MDS-9509-2 needs to be configured as F ports. Add the ports to the channel-group 21.

```
MDS-9509-2# conf t
MDS-9509-2(config)# interface fc 7/1, fc 7/7
MDS-9509-2(config-if)# switchport mode F
MDS-9509-2(config-if)# switchport trunk mode on
MDS-9509-2(config-if)# switchport speed 2000
MDS-9509-2(config-if)# channel group 21 force
MDS-9509-2(config-if)# no shut
MDS-9509-2(config-if)# end
MDS-9509-2#
```

The trunking F port channel should be up and the CNA connected to ethernet 1/1 and vfc 1 should be visible by running the **show flogi database** command.

Create a zone and activate the zoneset in VSAN 2114 and VSAN 2113 that allows the server to access the fibre channel storage on the MDS directors.

Step 17   Run the **show san-port-channel database** command to see the details of the san-port-channel on the N5K-5020-1 switch.

```
N5K-5020-2# show san-port-channel database
san-port-channel 20
    Last membership update is successful
    2 ports in total, 2 ports up
    First operational port is fc2/3
    Age of the port-channel is 0d:01h:33m:19s
    Ports:   fc2/3              [up] *
             fc2/4              [up]

N5K-5020-2#
```

Step 18   Run the **show port-channel database** command on MDS-9509-3 directors to see the details on the other side of the port-channel.

```
MDS-9509-3# show port-channel database
port-channel 21
    Administrative channel mode is active
    Operational channel mode is active
    Last membership update succeeded
    First operational port is fc7/1
    2 ports in total, 2 ports up
    Ports:   fc7/1   [up] *
             fc7/7   [up]

MDS-9509-3#
```

Configuring a Storage VDC on Nexus 7K to support FCoE

The Virtual Device Context (VDC) feature on the Nexus 7000 platform is used to virtualize the switch to enable presented itself as multiple logical switches. VDCs allow the switches to be virtualized at the device level. Each configured VDC appears as an unique device (switch) within the framework of the chassis. Each VDC runs as a separate logical switch within the physical switch, maintaining its own set of running processes, configuration and access methods which are independent of the other configured VDCs on that physical switch.

Today the Nexus 7000 platform supports up to four VDCs. Each VDC can contain its own unique and independent set of network functions (VLAN, VRFs) or storage functions (FCoE). Each VDC can be assigned physical ports, thus allowing for the hardware data plane to be virtualized. Additionally, each VDC can be managed independent of the other VDCs thereby allowing the separation of the management plane as well.

Of the four VDCs that can be created, only one of then can be a used to support FCoE.

The recipes below detail the steps required to configure a FCoE VDC on a Nexus 7000 switch and assign ports to it. Once the FCoE VDC is configured it functions and behaves as a separate switch that supports the FCoE enabled ports.

Creating a storage VDC and allocating ethernet interfaces

The recipe below details the steps needed to create a storage VDC on a Nexus 7000 platform. It is assumed that the default VDC is up and running.

Step 1   Enable the FCoE and related features on the Nexus 7010 switch. The FCoE capable module is in slot 10.

- Enable the FCoE feature-set

- Enable the feature LACP

- Enable the feature LLDP

- License fcoe for the correct module

```
N7K-7010-1# config t
N7K-7010-1(config)# install feature-set fcoe
N7K-7010-1(config)# feature lacp
N7K-7010-1(config)# feature lldp
N7K-7010-1(config)# license module 10 <-- FCoE module in slot 10
N7K-7010-1(config)# end
N7K-7010-1#
```

Step 2   Configure the correct QoS policies to support FCoE

```
N7K-7010-1# config t
N7K-7010-1(config)# system qos
N7K-7010-1(config-sys-qos)# service-policy type network-qos default-nq-7e-policy no-drop
N7K-7010-1(config-sys-qos)# 2011 Oct 17 23:34:20 N7K-7010-1 %$ VDC-1 %$
%IPQOSMGR-2-QOSMGR_NETWORK_QOS_POLICY_CHANGE: Policy default-nq-7e-policy is now active
N7K-7010-1(config-sys-qos)# end
N7K-7010-1#
```

Step 3   Create the storage VDC called FCoE_VDC on the Nexus 7010 switch.

```
N7K-7010-1# config t
N7K-7010-1(config)# vdc FCoE_VDC type storage id 4 <-- storage VDC with VDC ID 4
Note:  Creating VDC, one moment please ...
2011 Oct 17 23:38:54 N7K-7010-1 %$ VDC-1 %$ %SYSMGR-STANDBY-2-SHUTDOWN_SYSTEM_LOG: vdc 4
will shut down soon.
N7K-7010-1(config-vdc)# 2011 Oct 17 23:39:14 N7K-7010-1 %$ VDC-1 %$ %VDC_MGR-2-VDC_ONLINE:
vdc 4 has come online
N7K-7010-1(config-vdc)# end
N7K-7010-1#
```

Step 4   Run the "**show vdc**" command to display the status of the VDCs configured.

```
N7K-7010-1# show vdc

vdc_id  vdc_name        state    mac               type       lc
------  --------        -----    ----------        ---------  ------
1       N7K-7010-1      active   00:26:98:02:a3:41 Ethernet   m1 f1 m1xl
4       N7K-FCoE-VDC    active   00:26:98:02:a3:44 Storage    f1

N7K-7010-1#
```

The VDC as shown in the above output is created and active and highlighted in bold.

Step 5   Allocate Ethernet interfaces to the Storage VDC in dedicated mode for ISLs. This needs to be configured from the Default VDC.

Note   Dedicated ethernet interfaces are used for FCoE ISL traffic and for those end devices that do not need access to other VDCs for non-FCoE traffic.

```
N7K-7010-1# config t
N7K-7010-1(config)# vdc FCoE_VDC
N7K-7010-1(config-vdc)# allocate interface ethernet 10/3-4
Moving ports will cause all config associated to them in source vdc to be removed. Are you
sure you want to move the ports (y/n)?  [yes] y
N7K-7010-1(config-vdc)# end
N7K-7010-1#
```

Step 6   Configure the shared ethernet interfaces before they are added to the storage VDC, This configuration happens in the default VDC or the VDC that owns the interfaces.

```
N7K-7010-1# conf t
Enter configuration commands, one per line.  End with CNTL/Z.
N7K-7010-1(config)# interface ethernet 10/1-2
N7K-7010-1(config-if-range)# switchport mode trunk
N7K-7010-1(config-if-range)# switchport trunk allowed vlan 1
N7K-7010-1(config-if-range)# no shut
N7K-7010-1(config-if-range)# end
N7K-7010-1#
```

Step 7 Add Ethernet interfaces in shared mode to support end devices like host CNAs, and storage arrays that require both FCoE access and Ethernet access.

Note Shared interfaces allow the end devices to be part of the Storage VDC for FCoE traffic and to one other VDC for Ethernet traffic. This is only required to be configured explicitly on a Nexus 7000 switch.

```
N7K-7010-1# conf t
Enter configuration commands, one per line.  End with CNTL/Z.
N7K-7010-1(config)# vdc N7K-FCoE-VDC
N7K-7010-1(config-vdc)# allocate shared interface ethernet 10/1-2
Ports that share the port group of the interfaces you have specified will be affected as
well. Continue (y/n)? [yes]
N7K-7010-1(config-vdc)# end
N7K-7010-1#
```

Configuring Interfaces for FCoE end devices

This recipe details the steps required to configure the ethernet interfaces to accept FCoE end devices. This assumes that the storage VDC has been created and the interfaces have been allocated to the storage VDC in shared mode and are ready for further FCoE configuration. Refer to Creating a storage VDC and allocating ethernet interfaces for the steps to configure VDC and to allocate interfaces for end devices.

This recipe assumes that the storage and initiator ports are on the same Nexus 7000 chassis.

Step 1 Configure VSAN 20 in the FCoE VDC.

```
7K-7010-1-N7K-FCoE-VDC# conf t
N7K-7010-1-N7K-FCoE-VDC(config)# vsan database
N7K-7010-1-N7K-FCoE-VDC(config-vsan)# vsan 20
N7K-7010-1-N7K-FCoE-VDC(config-vsan)# end
N7K-7010-1-N7K-FCoE-VDC#
```

Step 2 Create the VLAN to VSAN mapping to facilutate FCoE traffic.

```
N7K-7010-1-N7K-FCoE-VDC# conf t
N7K-7010-1-N7K-FCoE-VDC(config-vsan)# vlan 20
N7K-7010-1-N7K-FCoE-VDC(config-vlan)# fcoe vsan 20
N7K-7010-1-N7K-FCoE-VDC(config-vlan)# end
N7K-7010-1-N7K-FCoE-VDC#
```

Step 3 Allocate FCoE VLAN range from the owner VDC (n7k-7010-1) to the storage VDC (n7k-fcoe-vdc).

Best Practice It is recommended to create VLAN ranges so that so that the shared interfaces configured in various VDCs can avoid VLAN overlap between the primary VDC and the storage VDC. Add the shared interfaces into the FCoE VDC.

```
N7K-7010-1-N7K-FCoE-VDC# conf t
Enter configuration commands, one per line.  End with CNTL/Z.
N7K-7010-1-N7K-FCoE-VDC(config)# vdc N7K-FCoE-VDC
N7K-7010-1-N7K-FCoE-VDC(config-vdc)# allocate fcoe-vlan-range 10-40 from vdcs N7K-7010-1
N7K-7010-1-N7K-FCoE-VDC(config-vdc)# end
N7K-7010-1-N7K-FCoE-VDC#
```

Step 4   Configure the ethernet port that will connect to a FCoE CNA or storage port.

```
N7K-7010-1-N7K-FCoE-VDC# conf t
Enter configuration commands, one per line.  End with CNTL/Z.
N7K-7010-1-N7K-FCoE-VDC(config)# interface ethernet 10/1
N7K-7010-1-N7K-FCoE-VDC(config-if)# switchport trunk allowed vlan 20
N7K-7010-1-N7K-FCoE-VDC(config-if)# spanning-tree port-type edge trunk
Warning: Edge port type (portfast) should only be enabled on ports connected to a single
 host. Connecting hubs, concentrators, switches, bridges, etc... to this
 interface  when edge port type (portfast) is enabled, can cause temporary bridging loops.
 Use with CAUTION
N7K-7010-1-N7K-FCoE-VDC(config-if)# no shut
N7K-7010-1-N7K-FCoE-VDC(config-if)# end
N7K-7010-1-N7K-FCoE-VDC#
```

Step 5   Configure the virtual FC (vFC) interface and bind it to the ethernet interface.

```
N7K-7010-1-N7K-FCoE-VDC# conf t
Enter configuration commands, one per line.  End with CNTL/Z.
N7K-7010-1-N7K-FCoE-VDC(config)# interface vfc 1
N7K-7010-1-N7K-FCoE-VDC(config-if)# switchport mode F
N7K-7010-1-N7K-FCoE-VDC(config-if)# switchport trunk allowed vsan 20
N7K-7010-1-N7K-FCoE-VDC(config-if)# bind interface ethernet 10/1
N7K-7010-1-N7K-FCoE-VDC(config-if)# no shut
N7K-7010-1-N7K-FCoE-VDC(config-if)# end
N7K-7010-1-N7K-FCoE-VDC#
```

Step 6   Create the VSAN and add the interface to the required VSAN. In this recipe it is added to VSAN 20

```
N7K-7010-1-N7K-FCoE-VDC# conf t
Enter configuration commands, one per line.  End with CNTL/Z.
N7K-7010-1-N7K-FCoE-VDC(config)# vsan database
N7K-7010-1-N7K-FCoE-VDC(config-vsan-db)# vsan 20 interface vfc 1
N7K-7010-1-N7K-FCoE-VDC(config-vsan-db)# end
N7K-7010-1-N7K-FCoE-VDC#
```

Use command **show interface vfc1** to see the status of the vfc port. Interface vfc1 should now be visible in VSAN 20 in the storage VDC. The next steps is to create zones required to enable host to target communications in the VSAN. Repeat Steps 4 through Step 6 for any other ports that needs to support FCoE interfaces.

Configuring Virtual FC Port-Channels for FCoE

The following recipes provide procedures on how to configure Virtual Fibre Channel (vFC) interfaces on the Nexus and MDS platforms for carrying FCoE traffic.

Virtual FC port-channel configuration between Nexus 7000 and Nexus 5000

In this recipe virtual FC port-channel configuration steps will be detailed. The topology use is shown in Figure 9-4. N5K-5010-1 which in turn is connected to N7K-7010-1using the ethernet ports. The recipe configures a ethernet port-channel first. Then virtual FC interfaces is configured and bound to the ethernet port-channel to carry FC traffic between the two switches. The various steps required are detailed below. VLAN 20 and FCoE VSAN 20 are used in the configuration. The F1 line card on the Nexus 7010 is in slot 10.

In this recipe the virtual FC port-channel between the N5k-51010-1 and N7K-7101-1 is configured.

Figure 9-4   *Virtual FC port-channel topology between N7K and N5K*

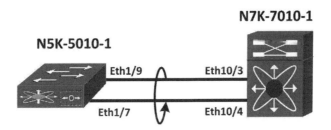

Step 1   Configure and enable FCoE and related features on a Nexus 500 switch N5K-5010-1.

```
N5K-5010-1# config t
N5K-5010-1(config)# feature lacp
N5K-5010-1(config)# feature fcoe
FC license checked out successfully
fc_plugin extracted successfully
FC plugin loaded successfully
FCoE manager enabled successfully
FC enabled on all modules successfully
N5K-5010-1(config)# system qos <-- configure the required qos policies
N5K-5010-1(config-sys-qos)# service-policy type qos input fcoe-default-in-policy
N5K-5010-1(config-sys-qos)# service-policy type queuing input fcoe-default-in-policy
N5K-5010-1(config-sys-qos)# service-policy type queuing output fcoe-default-out-policy
N5K-5010-1(config-sys-qos)# service-policy type network-qosfcoe-default-nq-policy
N5K-5010-1(config-sys-qos)# end
N5K-5010-1#
```

Step 2   Create a storage VDC on N7K-7010-1 switch.

Caution   The user needs to have network-admin privileges on the Nexus 7000 platform to create a VDC.

```
N7K-7010-1# config t
N7K-7010-1(config)# vdc FCoE_VDC type storage id 4 <-- storage VDC with VDC ID 4
Note:  Creating VDC, one moment please ...
2011 Oct 17 23:38:54 N7K-7010-1 %$ VDC-1 %$ %SYSMGR-STANDBY-2-SHUTDOWN_SYSTEM_LOG: vdc 4
will shut down soon.
2011 Oct 17 23:39:14 N7K-7010-1 %$ VDC-1 %$ %VDC_MGR-2-VDC_ONLINE: vdc 4 has come online
N7K-7010-1(config-vdc)#
```

Step 3   Allocate Ethernet dedicated ethernet interfaces to the storage VDC. The ethernet interfaces 10/3 and 10/4 will be use for ISL connectivity to the N5K-5010-1 switch.

Note   There are two types of interfaces that can be allocated to storage VDC, a shared interface and a dedicated interface. The dedicated interfaces is used for ISL/ port-channel connectivity.The shared interfaces (shared between a networking and the storage VDC) is used by end devices for both ethernet and storage traffic.

The allocation of interfaces needs to happen from the default VDC. All interfaces on a Nexus 7000 platform belongs to the default VDC. This task can be performed only by a user with the network-admin role.

Within the FCoE VDC only role defined is the VDC-admin role. This role can configure every feature within that FCoE VDC. The admin account created for the VDC is automatically assigned this role. This role can then allocate the different vfc interfaces to various VSANs instantiated in this FCoE VDC.

```
N7K-7010-1# config t
N7K-7010-1(config)# vdc FCoE_VDC
N7K-7010-1(config-vdc)# allocate interface ethernet 10/3-4
Moving ports will cause all config associated to them in source vdc to be removed. Are you
sure you want to move the ports (y/n)?  [yes] y
N7K-7010-1(config-vdc)# end
N7K-7010-1#
```

Step 4   Configure the lldp and lacp features in the storage VDC. This needs to be performed by logging on to the FCoE VDC's ip address.

```
N7K-7010-1-N7K-FCoE-VDC# conf t
N7K-7010-1-N7K-FCoE-VDC(config)# feature lldp
N7K-7010-1-N7K-FCoE-VDC(config)# feature lacp
N7K-7010-1-N7K-FCoE-VDC(config)# end
N7K-7010-1-N7K-FCoE-VDC#
```

Step 5   Configure VSAN 20 and VLAN 20 for fcoe traffic.

```
N7K-7010-1-N7K-FCoE-VDC# conf t
N7K-7010-1-N7K-FCoE-VDC(config)# vsan database
N7K-7010-1-N7K-FCoE-VDC(config-vsan)# vsan 20
N7K-7010-1-N7K-FCoE-VDC(config-vsan)# vlan 20
N7K-7010-1-N7K-FCoE-VDC(config-vlan)# fcoe vsan 20
N7K-7010-1-N7K-FCoE-VDC(config-vlan)# end
N7K-7010-1-N7K-FCoE-VDC#
```

Step 6 Configure the dedicated interfaces for port-channel on the N7K as shown below.

```
N7K-7010-1-N7K-FCoE-VDC# config t
N7K-7010-1-N7K-FCoE-VDC(config)# interface ethernet 10/3-4
N7K-7010-1-N7K-FCoE-VDC(config-if-range)# switchport mode trunk
N7K-7010-1-N7K-FCoE-VDC(config-if-range)# switchport trunk allowed vlan 20
N7K-7010-1-N7K-FCoE-VDC(config-if-range)# channel-group 20 force mode active
N7K-7010-1-N7K-FCoE-VDC(config-if-range)# no shut
N7K-7010-1-N7K-FCoE-VDC(config-if-range)# end
N7K-7010-1-N7K-FCoE-VDC#
```

Step 7 Configure the ethernet port-channel on the FCoE VDC on the N7K-7010-1 switch

```
N7K-7010-1-N7K-FCoE-VDC# config t
N7K-7010-1-N7K-FCoE-VDC(config)# interface port-channel 20
N7K-7010-1-N7K-FCoE-VDC(config-if)# no shut
N7K-7010-1-N7K-FCoE-VDC(config-if)# end
N7K-7010-1-N7K-FCoE-VDC#
```

Step 8 Configure the interfaces for port-channel on the N5K-5010-1 switch.

```
N5K-5010-1# conf t
Enter configuration commands, one per line.  End with CNTL/Z.
N5K-5010-1(config)# interface ethernet 1/7, ethernet 1/9
N5K-5010-1(config-if-range)# switchport mode trunk
N5K-5010-1(config-if-range)# switchport trunk allowed vlan 20
N5K-5010-1(config-if-range)# channel-group 20 mode active
N5K-5010-1(config-if-range)# no shut
N5K-5010-1(config-if-range)# end
N5K-5010-1#
```

Step 9 Configure the ethernet port-channel on the N5K-5010-1 switch.

```
N5K-5010-1# conf t
Enter configuration commands, one per line.  End with CNTL/Z.
N5K-5010-1(config)# interface port-channel 20
N5K-5010-1(config-if)# no shut
N5K-5010-1(config-if)# end
N5K-5010-1#
```

Step 10 Change the load balancing mechanism on the Nexus 5000 to source-dest-port based load balancing on the port-channel.

Note On the Nexus 5000 the default load balancing mechanism is **source-destination** based load balancing.

٠١|١٠١|١٠

Best Practice It is recommended to change the load balancing to **source-destination-port** based load balancing to allow FCoE traffic to do **Exchange based load balancing** across the ethernet port-channel.

```
N5K-5010-1# conf t
Enter configuration commands, one per line.  End with CNTL/Z.
N5K-5010-1(config)# port-channel load-balance ethernet source-dest-port
5K-5010-1(config)# end
N5K-5010-1#
```

Now the Ethernet port-channel should be up and running between the N7K-7010-1 and N5K-5010 switches.

Step 11 Run the "**show port-channel summary**" command on both switches to ensure that the port-channel 20 is up and running.

```
N7K-7010-1-N7K-FCoE-VDC# show port-channel database
port-channel20
    Last membership update is successful
    2 ports in total, 2 ports up
    First operational port is Ethernet10/4
    Age of the port-channel is 0d:00h:22m:47s
    Time since last bundle is 0d:00h:22m:47s
    Last bundled member is Ethernet10/4
    Ports:   Ethernet10/3    [active ] [up]
             Ethernet10/4    [active ] [up] *

N7K-7010-1-N7K-FCoE-VDC#

N5K-5010-1(config)# show port-channel database
port-channel20
    Last membership update is successful
    2 ports in total, 2 ports up
    First operational port is Ethernet1/7
    Age of the port-channel is 0d:00h:07m:52s
    Time since last bundle is 0d:00h:07m:52s
    Last bundled member is Ethernet1/9
    Ports:   Ethernet1/7     [active ] [up] *
             Ethernet1/9     [active ] [up]

N5K-5010-1(config)#
```

Step 12 Configure the VFC interfaces to build the virtual E port on the N7K-7010-1.

Note It is **critical that the vfc-port-channel number** be the same as the **ethernet-port-channel number** as the system uses this information to bind the VFC interface to the ethernet port-channel automatically.

```
N7K-7010-1-N7K-FCoE-VDC# conf t
Enter configuration commands, one per line.  End with CNTL/Z.
N7K-7010-1-N7K-FCoE-VDC(config)# interface vfc-port-channel 20
N7K-7010-1-N7K-FCoE-VDC(config-if)# switchport mode E
N7K-7010-1-N7K-FCoE-VDC(config-if)# switchport trunk allowed vsan 20
N7K-7010-1-N7K-FCoE-VDC(config-if)# no shut
N7K-7010-1-N7K-FCoE-VDC(config-if)# end
N7K-7010-1-N7K-FCoE-VDC#
```

Step 13 Configure the VFC interface on the N5K-5010-1 switch.

```
N5K-5010-1# config t
N5K-5010-1(config)# interface vfc 20
N5K-5010-1(config-if)# bind interface port-channel 20
N5K-5010-1(config-if)# switchport mode E
N5K-5010-1(config-if)# switchport trunk allowed vsan 20
N5K-5010-1(config-if)# no shut
N5K-5010-1(config-if)# end
N5K-5010-1#
```

Step 14   Run the command **show interface vfc-port-channel <number>** on the N7K-7010-1 switch to see the status of VE port configured and bound to the ethernet port-channel.

```
N7K-7010-1-N7K-FCoE-VDC# show interface vfc-port-channel 20
vfc-po20 is trunking
    Bound interface is port-channel20
    Hardware is Ethernet
    Port WWN is 25:25:00:26:98:02:a3:00
    Admin port mode is E, trunk mode is on
    snmp link state traps are enabled
    Port mode is TE
    Port vsan is 1
    Speed is 20 Gbps
    Trunk vsans (admin allowed and active) (20)
    Trunk vsans (up)                       (20)
    Trunk vsans (isolated)                 ()
    Trunk vsans (initializing)             ()
    1439 fcoe in packets
    161476 fcoe in octets
    1439 fcoe out packets
    128660 fcoe out octets
    Interface last changed at Tue Oct 18 18:04:51 2011

N7K-7010-1-N7K-FCoE-VDC#
```

Step 15   Run the command **show interface vfc <number>** on the N5K-5010 to see the status of the created VE port channel.

N5K-5010-1# show interface vfc 20

```
vfc20 is trunking
    Bound interface is port-channel20
    Hardware is Virtual Fibre Channel
    Port WWN is 20:13:00:05:9b:74:f1:ff
    Admin port mode is E, trunk mode is on
    snmp link state traps are enabled
    Port mode is TE
    Port vsan is 1
    Trunk vsans (admin allowed and active) (20)
    Trunk vsans (up)                       (20)
    Trunk vsans (isolated)                 ()
    Trunk vsans (initializing)             ()
    1 minute input rate 88 bits/sec, 11 bytes/sec, 0 frames/sec
    1 minute output rate 224 bits/sec, 28 bytes/sec, 0 frames/sec
      1511 frames input, 134804 bytes
        0 discards, 0 errors
      1511 frames output, 193748 bytes
        0 discards, 0 errors
    last clearing of "show interface" counters never
    Interface last changed at Tue Oct 18 17:49:01 2011

N5K-5010-1#
```

The above outputs shows the status of the virtual FC port-channel between N5k-5010-1 and N7K-7010-1 switches.

Virtual FC port-channel configuration between MDS and Nexus 5000

In this recipe virtual FC port-channel configuration steps will be detailed. The topology use is shown in Figure 9-5. N5K-5010-1 connects to a MDS-9513-2 using ethernet ports. The recipe configures a ethernet port-channel first. Then virtual FC interfaces is configured and bound to the ethernet port-channel to carry FC traffic between the two switches. The various steps required are detailed below. VLAN 30 and FCoE VSAN 30 are used in the configuration. The 8 port FCoE line card on the MDS is in slot 4. The Ethernet port-channel 300 is created and a virtual FC port-channel 300 is also created.

Figure 9-5   Virtual FC port-channel topology between MDS and N5K

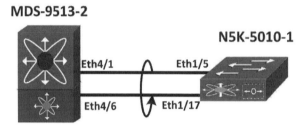

Note   On the MDS platform it is not required to explicitly enable FCoE and related features. When a FCoE card is detected the features are automatically enabled on the MDS.

The following features are enabled on a MDS when a FCoE line card is detected.

- Install feature-set fcoe
- feature-set fcoe
- feature lldp
- feature vlan-vsan-mapping

Step 1   Enable **LACP feature** on the MDS to configure Ethernet port-channels .

```
MDS-9513-2# conf t
Enter configuration commands, one per line.  End with CNTL/Z.
MDS-9513-2(config)# feature lacp
MDS-9513-2(config)# end
MDS-9513-2#
```

Step 2   Enable FCoE and FcoE related features on the N5K-5010-1 switch

```
N5K-5010-1# config t
N5K-5010-1(config)# feature lacp
N5K-5010-1(config)# feature fcoe
FC license checked out successfully
fc_plugin extracted successfully
FC plugin loaded successfully
FCoE manager enabled successfully
FC enabled on all modules successfully
N5K-5010-1(config)# system qos <-- configure the required qos policies
N5K-5010-1(config-sys-qos)# service-policy type qos input fcoe-default-in-policy
N5K-5010-1(config-sys-qos)# service-policy type queuing input fcoe-default-in-policy
N5K-5010-1(config-sys-qos)# service-policy type queuing output fcoe-default-out-policy
N5K-5010-1(config-sys-qos)# service-policy type network-qosfcoe-default-nq-policy
N5K-5010-1(config-sys-qos)# end
```

Step 3   Configure the FCoE VLAN and VSAN mapping on the MDS-9513-2.

```
MDS-9513-2# conf t
Enter configuration commands, one per line.  End with CNTL/Z.
MDS-9513-2(config)# vsan database
MDS-9513-2(config-vsan-db)# vsan 30
MDS-9513-2(config-vsan-db)# vlan 30
MDS-9513-2(config-vlan)# fcoe vsan 30
MDS-9513-2(config-vlan)# end
MDS-9513-2#
```

Step 4 Configure the FCoE VLAN and VSAN mapping on the N5K-5010-1

```
N5K-5010-1# conf t
Enter configuration commands, one per line.  End with CNTL/Z.
N5K-5010-1(config)# vsan database
N5K-5010-1(config-vsan-db)# vsan 30
N5K-5010-1(config-vsan-db)# vlan 30
N5K-5010-1(config-vlan)# fcoe vsan 30
N5K-5010-1(config-vlan)# end
N5K-5010-1#
```

Step 5 Configure the FCoE no-drop QoS policy to 7e on the MDS platform.

Note Configuring the correct QoS policy for FCoE is a critical step for FCoE to work properly on a MDS platform. It needs to be configured at 7e.

```
MDS-9513-2# conf t
MDS-9513-2(config)# system qos
MDS-9513-2(config-sys-qos)# service-policy type network-qos default-nq-7e-policy
MDS-9513-2(config-sys-qos)# end
MDS-9513-2#
```

Step 6 Configure the interfaces for ethernet port-channel (LACP port-channel) on the MDS switch. From the figure above the ethernet interfaces 4/1 and 4/6 on MDS-9513-2 are used for the port-channel.

Note On the MDS switches the Ethernet port-channel on the FCoE line cards can be numbered only from 257 thru 4096,. The first 1-256 are reserved for fibre channel port-channels.

```
MDS-9513-2# conf t
Enter configuration commands, one per line.  End with CNTL/Z.
MDS-9513-2(config)# interface ethernet 4/1, ethernet 4/6
MDS-9513-2(config-if-range)# switchport mode trunk
MDS-9513-2(contig-if-range)# switchport trunk allowed vlan 30
MDS-9513-2(config-if-range)# channel-group 300 mode active
MDS-9513-2(config-if-range)# no shut
MDS-9513-2(config-if-range)# end
MDS-9513-2#
```

Step 7   Configure the ethernet port-channel on the MDS-9513-2.

Note   The command to create an ethernet port-channel on the MDS is **interface ethernet-port-channel <number>**.

```
MDS-9513-2# conf t
Enter configuration commands, one per line.  End with CNTL/Z.
MDS-9513-2(config)# interface ethernet-port-channel 300
MDS-9513-2(config-if)# no shut
MDS-9513-2(config-if)# end
MDS-9513-2#
```

Step 8   Configure the interfaces for ethernet port-channel (LACP port-channel) on the N5K-5010-1 switch. From the figure above the ethernet interfaces 1/5 and 1/17 on N5K-5010-1 are used for the Ethernet port-channel

```
N5K-5010-1# conf t
Enter configuration commands, one per line.  End with CNTL/Z.
N5K-5010-1(config)# interface ethernet 1/5, ethernet 1/17
N5K-5010-1(config-if-range)# switchport mode trunk
N5K-5010-1(config-if-range)# switchport trunk allowed vlan 30
N5K-5010-1(config-if-range)# channel-group 300 mode active
N5K-5010-1(config-if-range)# no shut
N5K-5010-1(config-if-range)# end
N5K-5010-1#
```

Step 9   Configure the port-channel on the N5K-5010-1 switch. Change the load balancing scheme to a source-destination-port based one.

Best Practice   It is recommended to change the load balance on the port-channel to source-dest-port so that Exchange base load balancing is enabled for FCoE traffic.

Note   The default load balancing scheme in the Nexus 5000 platform source destination based load balancing.

```
N5K-5010-1# conf t
Enter configuration commands, one per line.  End with CNTL/Z.
N5K-5010-1(config)# interface port-channel 300
N5K-5010-1(config-if)# no shut
N5K-5010-1(config-if)# port-channel load-balance ethernet source-dest-port
N5K-5010-1(config)# end
N5K-5010-1#
```

Step 10   Configure the VE port for virtual FC port-channel on the MDS09513-1.

```
MDS-9513-2# conf t
Enter configuration commands, one per line.  End with CNTL/Z.
MDS-9513-2(config)# interface vfc-port-channel 300
MDS-9513-2(config-if)# switchport mode E
MDS-9513-2(config-if)# switchport trunk allowed vsan 30
MDS-9513-2(config-if)# no shut
MDS-9513-2(config-if)# end
MDS-9513-2#
```

Step 11   Configure the VE port for the Virtual FC port-channel on the N5k_5010-1

```
N5K-5010-1# conf t
Enter configuration commands, one per line.  End with CNTL/Z.
N5K-5010-1(config)# interface vfc 300
N5K-5010-1(config-if)# bind interface port-channel 300
N5K-5010-1(config-if)# switchport mode E
N5K-5010-1(config-if)# switchport trunk allowed vsan 30
N5K-5010-1(config-if)# no shut
N5K-5010-1(config-if)# end
N5K-5010-1#
```

Step 12   Run the **show interface vfc-port-channel <number>** command on the MDS-9513-2 and the **show interface vfc <number>** command on the N5K-5010-1 to see that the virtual FC port-channel is up and the configured VSAN is being trunked.

```
MDS-9513-2# show interface vfc-port-channel 300
vfc-po300 is trunking
    Bound interface is ethernet-port-channel300
    Hardware is Ethernet
    Port WWN is 25:3d:00:0d:ec:a2:28:c0
    Admin port mode is E, trunk mode is on
    snmp link state traps are enabled
    Port mode is TE
    Port vsan is 1
    Speed is 20 Gbps
    Trunk vsans (admin allowed and active) (30)
    Trunk vsans (up)                       (30)
    Trunk vsans (isolated)                 ()
    Trunk vsans (initializing)             ()
    283 fcoe in packets
    32340 fcoe in octets
    283 fcoe out packets
    29804 fcoe out octets
    Interface last changed at Tue Oct 18 21:20:27 2011
MDS-9513-2#


N5K-5010-1# show interface vfc 300
vfc300 is trunking
    Bound interface is port-channel300
    Hardware is Virtual Fibre Channel
    Port WWN is 21:2b:00:05:9b:74:f1:ff
    Admin port mode is E, trunk mode is on
    snmp link state traps are enabled
    Port mode is TE
    Port vsan is 1
    Trunk vsans (admin allowed and active) (30)
    Trunk vsans (up)                       (30)
    Trunk vsans (isolated)                 ()
    Trunk vsans (initializing)             ()
    1 minute input rate 152 bits/sec, 19 bytes/sec, 0 frames/sec
    1 minute output rate 208 bits/sec, 26 bytes/sec, 0 frames/sec
      293 frames input, 30660 bytes
        0 discards, 0 errors
      293 frames output, 38156 bytes
        0 discards, 0 errors
    last clearing of "show interface" counters never
    Interface last changed at Tue Oct 18 21:00:34 2011
N5K-5010-1#
```

The virtual port-channel between the switches is up and running as seen from the above outputs.

## CHAPTER 10

Top of Rack (ToR) Switches

The Cisco SAN and FCoE portfolio of Top of the Rack switches comprises of MDS 9148, Nexus 5010, Nexus5020, Nexus 5548 and Nexus 5596. These are typically deployed in a Top of Rack (ToR) topology. The host Host Bus Adapters (HBA) and Converged Network Adapters (CNA) attach to the ToR switches which is then connected to the core SAN directors which conn et to storage / tape ports. The core SAN directors could potentially connect to other storage edge directors for storage access in the SAN.

The ToR switches can be deployed in two modes

- Switch mode

- N Port Virtualization mode (NPV)

The ToR are typically deployed as edge switches that provide host connectivity to the SAN. When configured in switch mode the ToR switch has it own SAN services (Fabric login, Port login, name server zoning server etc.), requires a unique Domain ID, and has to be managed separately. The Fibre channel has 239 domain ID, meaning only 239 switches can be inter connected in a fabric. When ToR switches are deployed each rack in the Data center could potentially have two. to support the host in the rack leading to a large scale deployment of ToR switches in the SAN. This greatly increases the SAN management overhead as a large number of switches need to be managed. NPV mode deployment or ToR switches help alleviate this problem. The Tor switches use regular ISL / port-channel to connect to the core switches.

In NPV mode the ToR switches can be managed as extended line cards of the NPIV core switch. When a switch is configured in NPV mode all the control functions (fabric login, FC ID allocation, fibre channel name service, zoning etc.) are provided by another switch to which the ToR switch is connected. The switch providing these function needs to be operating in N Port ID virtualization mode (NPIV). NPV mode make is easier to deploy and manage a large number of ToR switch without having to worry about domain ID limitations that exist in fibre channel protocol. The NPV (ToR) switch uses NP ports to connect to the NPIV core switch.

Configuring MDS ToR switch in NPV mode

This recipe details the steps required to configure MDS switch in NPV mode. The procedure is same for MDS-9124e and MDS 9124. MDS 9134 and MDS 9148 switches. The recipe show the configuration steps required to connect MDS-9148-1 switch in NPV mode to the NPIV core MDS-9509-3 switch. In the recipe the ports used on the MDS-9148-1 switch are FC 1/1 and FC 1/2. Both ports will be configured in NP mode. On the MDS-9509-3 switch the ports used will be fc4/38 and fc 4/41. They will be configured in F port mode. NP links between the switches will be combined into a F-Port channel to protect against link failure and traffic load balancing.

Best Practice   It is recommended to use MDS 9500 series switches as NPIV core switches and use the MDS 9124, MDS 9134 and MDS 9148 and NPV switches.

The port-channel 50 will be configured between the two switches.

The hardware used in the recipe are:

- MDS-9509-3: NPIV switch, ports fc4/38 and fc 4/41
- MDS-9148-2: NPV switch, ports fc 1/1, fc 1/2

The topology used for the recipe is shown in Figure 10-1.

Figure 10-1   MDS 9148 NPV topology

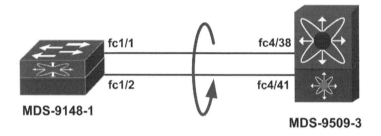

Step 1   Configure NPIV feature on MDS-9509-3

```
MDS-9509-3# conf t
Enter configuration commands, one per line.  End with CNTL/Z.
MDS-9509-3(config)# feature NPIV
MDS-9509-3(config)# end
MDS-9509-3#
```

Step 2   Enable feature fport-channel-trunk on the MDS-9509-3.

Best Practice   The fport-channel-trunk feature needs to be enabled on the NPIV switch to configure trunking of TF ports

```
MDS-9509-3# conf t
Enter configuration commands, one per line.  End with CNTL/Z.
MDS-9509-3(config)# feature fport-channel-trunk
MDS-9509-3(config)# end
MDS-9509-3#
```

Step 3   Configure the interface fc 4/38 and 4/41 as F ports

```
MDS-9509-3# conf t
Enter configuration commands, one per line.  End with CNTL/Z.
MDS-9509-3(config)# interface fc 4/38, fc 4/41
MDS-9509-3(config-if)# switchport mode F
MDS-9509-3(config-if)# switchport trunk mode on
MDS-9509-3(config-if)# shut
MDS-9509-3(config-if)# no shut
MDS-9509-3(config-if)# end
MDS-9509-3#
```

Step 4   Enable NPV mode on MDS-9148-1.

Caution   This operation will **erase all configuration and reboot** the switch.

```
MDS-9148-1# conf t
Enter configuration commands, one per line.  End with CNTL/Z.
MDS-9148-1(config)# feature npv
Verify that boot variables are set and the changes are saved. Changing to npv mode erases
the current configuration and reboots the switch in npv mode. Do you want to continue?
(y/n):y
```

After the reboot log on to the switch and continue the configuration on the MDS 9148 switch.

Step 5   Configure port fc 1/1 and fc 1/2 as NP ports on MDS-9148-1

```
MDS-9148-1# conf t
Enter configuration commands, one per line.  End with CNTL/Z.
MDS-9148-1(config)# interface fc 1/1-2
MDS-9148-1(config-if)# switchport mode NP
DS-9148-1(config-if)# switchport trunk mode on
MDS-9148-1(config-if)# no shut
MDS-9148-1(config-if)# end
MDS-9148-1#
```

This should bring up two TF links between the NPV MDS-9148-1 switch and the MDS-9509-3 switch.

Best Practice   It not recommended to use MDS 9124 and MDS 9134 as NPIV core switches as they will not allow
F-Port-channelling to other NPV mode switches.

Step 6   Add the ports Fc 1/1 and fc 1/2 to the channel group 50.

```
MDS-9148-1# conf t
Enter configuration commands, one per line.  End with CNTL/Z.
MDS-9148-1(config)# interface fc 1/1-2
MDS-9148-1(config-if)# channel-group 50
fc1/1 fc1/2 added to port-channel 50 and disabled
please do the same operation on the switch at the other end of the port-channel,
then do "no shutdown" at both ends to bring it up
MDS-9148-1(config-if)# no shut
MDS-9148-1(config-if)# end
MDS-9148-1#
```

Step 7   Configure port-channel 50 on the MDS-9148-1 switch

```
MDS-9148-1# conf t
Enter configuration commands, one per line.  End with CNTL/Z.
MDS-9148-1(config)# interface port-channel 50
MDS-9148-1(config-if)# switchport mode NP
MDS-9148-1(config-if)# switchport trunk mode on
MDS-9148-1(config-if)# channel mode active
MDS-9148-1(config-if)# switchport speed 4000
MDS-9148-1(config-if)# no shut
MDS-9148-1(config-if)# end
MDS-9148-1#
```

Step 8   Add port fc4/38 and fc 4/41 to the channel group 50

```
MDS-9509-3# conf t
Enter configuration commands, one per line.  End with CNTL/Z.
```

```
MDS-9509-3(config)# interface fc 4/38, fc 4/41
MDS-9509-3(config-if)# channel-group 50
fc4/38 fc4/41 added to port-channel 50 and disabled
please do the same operation on the switch at the other end of the port-channel,
then do "no shutdown" at both ends to bring it up
MDS-9509-3(config-if)# no shut
MDS-9509-3(config-if)# end
```

Step 9   Configure port-channel 50 on MDS-9509-3

```
MDS-9509-3# conf t
Enter configuration commands, one per line.  End with CNTL/Z.
MDS-9509-3(config)# interface port-channel 50
MDS-9509-3(config-if)# switchport mode F
MDS-9509-3(config-if)# switchport trunk mode on
MDS-9509-3(config-if)# channel mode active
MDS-9509-3(config-if)# switchport speed 4000
MDS-9509-3(config-if)# no shut
MDS-9509-3(config-if)# end
MDS-9509-3#
```

This should bring up the F port-channel 50 between the two switches.

Step 10   Run "**show port-channel database**" command to verify the status of the just created port-channel.

```
MDS-9148-1# show port-channel database
port-channel 50
    Administrative channel mode is active
    Operational channel mode is active
    Last membership update succeeded
    First operational port is fc1/1
    2 ports in total, 2 ports up
    Ports:   fc1/1     [up] *
             fc1/2     [up]


MDS-9148-1#


MDS-9509-3# show port-channel database
port-channel 50
    Administrative channel mode is active
    Operational channel mode is active
    Last membership update succeeded
    First operational port is fc4/38
    2 ports in total, 2 ports up
    Ports:   fc4/38    [up] *
             fc4/41    [up]


MDS-9509-3#
```

Configuring a Nexus 5000 switch to support FCoE (NPV mode)

This recipe details the steps required to configure Nexus 5020 configured in NPV mode to enable a host to connect to it using FCoE. The Nexus 5020 switch is connected to MDS using TF ports to a MDS switch which has fibre channel storage. The **NPV feature** needs to be enabled on **N5K-5020-1 and on** N5K-5020-2 switches. The **NPIV** feature needs to be enabled on **MDS-9509-2 and MDS-9509-3** directors.

Figure 10-2   *NPV Nexus 5020 FCoE topology*

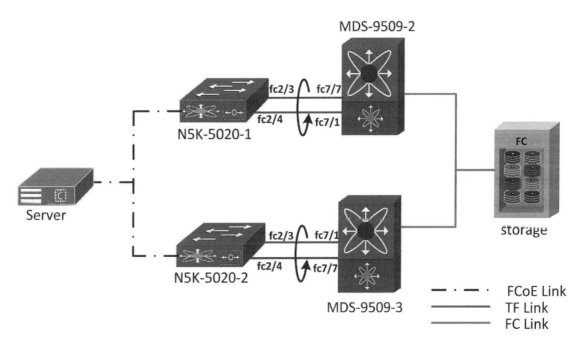

The topology for this recipe is shown in Figure 10-2. The host is dual attached (one connect to each fabric) to the two Nexus 5020. The Nexus 5020 switches are connected to the MDS 9500 directors as shown in Figure 10-2 using **TF links**.

The Nexus 5020 switches are configured in **NPV Mode**. The storage is connected to the MDS directors. The devices involved in this recipe are:

- N5K-5020-1: ethernet interface 1/1, vfc 1 and fibre channel expansion module
- N5k-5020-2: ethernet interface 1/1, vfc 1 and fibre channel expansion module
- MDS-9509-2
- MDS-9509-3
- Server
- FC Storage

This configuration recipe requires the Nexus 5020 to be configured in NPV mode. NPV mode configuration will erase existing configuration on the Nexus 5020 and reboot the switch.

.ı|ıı.ı|ıı

Best Practice   It is recommended to backup the Nexus 5000 switch configuration before running the command "**feature NPV**". It is recommended to copy the current configuration to the bootflash or to an external server

For this recipe both the Nexus 5020 will be configured in NPV mode. They will connect up to the MDS switches with two NP links. These NP links will be port-channeled. The server has redundant CNA' and will connect into the Nexus 5020 switches using FCoE.

Step 1   Configure N5K-5020-1 in npv mode. This will erase the nexus 5020's configuration and reload the switch.

```
N5K-5020-1# conf t
N5K-5020-1(config)# feature npv
Verify that boot variables are set and the changes are saved. Changing to npv mode erases
the current configuration and reboots the switch in npv mode. Do you want to continue?
(y/n):y
2011 Oct 15 03:10:14 N5K-5020-1 Oct 15 03:10:14 %KERN-0-SYSTEM_MSG: Shutdown Ports.. -
kernel

Broadcast message from root (Sat Oct 15 03:10:14 2011):

The system is going down for reboot NOW!
```

The switch will erase all configuration and reboot and come up in NPV mode.

Step 2   Configure VSAN 2113, VLAN 2113 and map FCoE VSAN on M5K-5020-1.

```
N5K-5020-1# conf t
N5K-5020-1(config)# vsan database
N5K-5020-1(config-vsan-db)# vsan 2113 name FCoE_VSAN2113
N5K-5020-1(config-vsan-db)# vlan 2113
N5K-5020-1(config-vlan)# fcoe vsan 2113
N5K-5020-1(config-vlan)# end
N5K-5020-1#
```

Step 3   Configure **san-port-channel** 20 on N5K-5020-1

.ı|ıı.ı|ıı

Best Practice   On the Nexus platform to create FC port-channel use the **san-port-channel** command. **port-channel** command will create ethernet port-channel on the Nexus platform.

```
N5K-5020-1# conf t
N5K-5020-1(config)# interface san-port-channel 20 <-- san-port-channel is the FC
port-channel equivalent command on the nexus platform.
N5K-5020-1(config-if)# switchport mode NP <-- ensure that the switch port mode is NP
N5K-5020-1(config-if)# switchport speed 2000
N5K-5020-1(config-if)# switchport trunk mode on
N5K-5020-1(config-if)# channel mode active
N5K-5020-1(config-if)# no shut
N5K-5020-1(config-if)# end
N5K-5020-1#
```

Step 4 Configure the Ethernet ports to which the vfc interfaces will be bound to. The trunk mode needs to be turned on and the spanning-tree port type needs to be set to edge trunk. This will allow the flogi to complete.

Best Practice With out the Ethernet interface **spanning-tree port type being defined as edge trunk** the flogi process will not complete and the host CAN will not be able to see storage. **This configuration needs to be applied to every ethernet interface that has a vfc interface to talk to an end device (host, storage or tape) port**

```
N5K-5020-1# conf t
N5K-5020-1(config)# interface ethernet 1/1
N5K-5020-1(config-if)# switchport mode trunk
N5K-5020-1(config-if)# spanning-tree port type edge trunk
Warning: Edge port type (portfast) should only be enabled on ports connected to a single
 host. Connecting hubs, concentrators, switches, bridges, etc... to this
 interface  when edge port type (portfast) is enabled, can cause temporary bridging loops.
 Use with CAUTION

N5K-5020-1(config-if)# end
N5K-5020-1#
```

Step 5 Configure the NP ports on N5K-5020-1 with, trunk mode on and their speed configured and assigned to channel group 20 (port-channel 20 is used in this recipe. the NP ports used in this recipe are fc2/3 and fc 2/4.

```
N5K-5020-1# conf t
N5K-5020-1(config)# interface fc 2/3-4
N5K-5020-1(config-if)# switchport speed 2000
N5K-5020-1(config-if)# switchport trunk mode on
N5K-5020-1(config-if)# channel-group 20 force <-- use the force command
N5K-5020-1(config-if)# no shut
N5K-5020-1(config-if)# end
N5K-5020-1#
```

Step 6 On MDS 9509-3 enable the fport-channel-trunk feature. This is need to configure port-channel of TF ports.

```
MDS-9509-3# conf t
MDS-9509-3(config)# feature npiv <-- with out this feature the links between the switches
will not come up.
MDS-9509-3(config)# feature fport-channel-trunk
Admin trunk mode has been set to off for
1- Interfaces with admin switchport mode F,FL,FX,SD,ST in admin down state
2- Interfaces with operational switchport mode F,FL,SD,ST.
MDS-9509-3(config)# end
MDS-9509-3#
```

Step 7 Create port-channel 20 on MDS-9509-3

```
MDS-9509-3# conf t
MDS-9509-3(config)# interface port-channel 20
MDS-9509-3(config-if)# switchport mode F
MDS-9509-3(config-if)# switchport trunk mode on
MDS-9509-3(config-if)# swithport speed 2000
MDS-9509-3(config-if)# swithport rate-mode dedicated
MDS-9509-3(config-if)# channel mode active
MDS-9509-3(config-if)# no shut
MDS-9509-3(config-if)# end
MDS-9509-3#
```

Step 8   Configure the ports fc 7/1 and 7/7 on the MDS-9509-3 as F ports. From Figure 10-2 the fc interfaces 7/1 and 7/7 on MDS-9509-3 needs to be configured as F ports. Add the ports to the channel-group 20.

```
MDS-9509-3# conf t
MDS-9509-3(config)# interface fc 7/1, fc 7/7
MDS-9509-3(config-if)# switchport mode F
MDS-9509-3(config-if)# switchport trunk mode on
MDS-9509-3(config-if)# switchport speed 2000
MDS-9509-3(config-if)# channel group 20 force
MDS-9509-3(config-if)# no shut
MDS-9509-3(config-if)# end
MDS-9509-3#
```

Repeat the same process on the N5k-5020-2 and MDS-9509-2 to complete the NPV setup process

Step 9   Configure N5K-5020-2 in npv mode. This will erase the nexus 5020's configuration and reload the switch.

```
N5K-5020-2# conf t
N5K-5020-2(config)# feature npv
Verify that boot variables are set and the changes are saved. Changing to npv mode erases
the current configuration and reboots the switch in npv mode. Do you want to continue?
(y/n):y
2011 Oct 15 03:10:14 N5K-5020-2 Oct 15 03:10:14 %KERN-0-SYSTEM_MSG: Shutdown Ports.. -
kernel

Broadcast message from root (Sat Oct 15 03:10:14 2011):

The system is going down for reboot NOW!
```

The switch will erase all configuration and reboot and come up in NPV mode.

Step 10   Configure VSAN 2114, VLAN 2114 and map FCoE VSAN on M5K-5020-2.

```
N5K-5020-2# conf t
N5K-5020-2(config)# vsan database
N5K-5020-2(config-vsan-db)# vsan 2114 name FCoE_VSAN2114
N5K-5020-2(config-vsan-db)# vlan 2114
N5K-5020-2(config-vlan)# fcoe vsan 2114
N5K-5020-2(config-vlan)# end
N5K-5020-2#
```

Step 11   Configure **san-port-channel** 21 on N5K-5020-2

ıılıılı.

Best Practice   On the Nexus platform to create FC port-channel use the **san-port-channel** command. **port-channel** command will create ethernet port-channel on the Nexus platform.

```
N5K-5020-2# conf t
N5K-5020-2(config)# interface san-port-channel 21 <-- san-port-channel is the FC
port-channel equivalent command on the nexus platform.
N5K-5020-2(config-if)# switchport mode NP <-- ensure that the switch port mode is NP
N5K-5020-2(config-if)# switchport speed 2000
N5K-5020-2(config-if)# switchport trunk mode on
N5K-5020-2(config-if)# channel mode active
N5K-5020-2(config-if)# no shut
N5K-5020-2(config-if)# end
N5K-5020-2#
```

Step 12 Configure the ethernet port to which the vfc interfaces will be bound to. The trunk mode needs to be turned on and the spanning-tree port type needs to be set to edge trunk. This will allow the flogi to complete.

Best Practice

With out the Ethernet interface **spanning-tree port type being defined as edge trunk** the flogi process will not complete and the host CAN will not be able to see storage. **This configuration needs to be applied to every ethernet interface that has a vfc interface to talk to an end device (host, storage or tape) port**

```
N5K-5020-2# conf t
N5K-5020-2(config)# interface ethernet 1/1
N5K-5020-2(config-if)# switchport mode trunk
N5K-5020-2(config-if)# spanning-tree port type edge trunk
Warning: Edge port type (portfast) should only be enabled on ports connected to a single
 host. Connecting hubs, concentrators, switches, bridges, etc... to this
 interface  when edge port type (portfast) is enabled, can cause temporary bridging loops.
 Use with CAUTION

N5K-5020-2(config-if)# end
N5K-5020-2#
```

Step 13 Configure the NP ports on N5K-5020-2 with, trunk mode on and their speed configured and assigned to channel group 21 (port-channel 21 is used in this recipe. the NP ports used in this recipe are fc2/3 and fc 2/4.

```
N5K-5020-2# conf t
N5K-5020-2(config)# interface fc 2/3-4
N5K-5020-2(config-if)# switchport speed 2000
N5K-5020-2(config-if)# switchport trunk mode on
N5K-5020-2(config-if)# channel-group 21 force <-- use the force command
N5K-5020-2(config-if)# no shut
N5K-5020-2(config-if)# end
N5K-5020-2#
```

Step 14 On MDS 9509-2 enable the fport-channel-trunk feature. This is need to configure port-channel of TF ports.

```
MDS-9509-2# conf t
MDS-9509-2(config)# feature npiv <-- with out this feature the links between the switches
will not come up.
MDS-9509-2(config)# feature fport-channel-trunk
Admin trunk mode has been set to off for
1- Interfaces with admin switchport mode F,FL,FX,SD,ST in admin down state
2- Interfaces with operational switchport mode F,FL,SD,ST.
MDS-9509-2(config)# end
MDS-9509-2#
```

Step 15 Create port-channel 20 on MDS-9509-2

```
MDS-9509-2# conf t
MDS-9509-2(config)# interface port-channel 21
MDS-9509-2(config-if)# switchport mode F
MDS-9509-2(config-if)# switchport trunk mode on
MDS-9509-2(config-if)# swithport speed 2000
MDS-9509-2(config-if)# swithport rate-mode dedicated
MDS-9509-2(config-if)# channel mode active
MDS-9509-2(config-if)# no shut
MDS-9509-2(config-if)# end
MDS-9509-2#
```

Step 16   Configure the ports fc 7/1 and 7/7 on the MDS-9509-2 as F ports. From Figure 10-2 the fc interfaces 7/1 and 7/7 on MDS-9509-2 needs to be configured as F ports. Add the ports to the channel-group 21.

```
MDS-9509-2# conf t
MDS-9509-2(config)# interface fc 7/1, fc 7/7
MDS-9509-2(config-if)# switchport mode F
MDS-9509-2(config-if)# switchport trunk mode on
MDS-9509-2(config-if)# switchport speed 2000
MDS-9509-2(config-if)# channel group 21 force
MDS-9509-2(config-if)# no shut
MDS-9509-2(config-if)# end
MDS-9509-2#
```

Note that the TF port channel should be up and the CNA connected to ethernet 1/1 and VFC 1 should be able to visible by running a "show flogi database command".

Create a zone and activate the zoneset in VSAN 2114 and VSAN 2113 that allows the server to access the fibre channel storage on the MDS directors.

Step 17   Run the "**show san-port-channel database**" command to see the details of the san-port-channel on the N5K-5020-1 switch.

```
N5K-5020-2# show san-port-channel database
san-port-channel 20
    Last membership update is successful
    2 ports in total, 2 ports up
    First operational port is fc2/3
    Age of the port-channel is 0d:01h:33m:19s
    Ports:    fc2/3                [up] *
              fc2/4                [up]

N5K-5020-2#
```

Step 18   Run the "**show port-channel database**" command on MDS-9509-3 directors to see the details on the other side of the port-channel.

```
MDS-9509-3# show port-channel database
port-channel 21
    Administrative channel mode is active
    Operational channel mode is active
    Last membership update succeeded
    First operational port is fc7/1
    2 ports in total, 2 ports up
    Ports:    fc7/1    [up] *
              fc7/7    [up]

MDS-9509-3#
```

Configuring unified ports on the Nexus 5000 UP switches

The **Nexus 5548UP** and **Nexus 5596UP** switches have the unique capability to operate a group of ports either as ethernet (includes FCoE) ports or as pure fibre channel ports. The Nexus 5548UP switch has 32 unified fixed base ports. It also has an expansion slot which will support 16 additional unified ports. The Nexus 5596UP switch has 48 unified fixed base ports. It also has three expansion slots. Each slot will support 16 additional unified ports for a total of 48 expansion ports. The fixed base ports is always slot 1.

As of NX-OS 5.0(3)N2(1) for the Nexus 5000 switches, the configuration of FC and ethernet ports on these switches have to follow certain rules. The rules are:

1. Ethernet ports must be configured from the first port of the base or expansion module

2. The fibre channel port must be configured from the last port of the base or expansion module.

3. By default all ports are ethernet ports on the Nexus 5548UP and 5596UP switches.

4. The ports range selected should be contiguous. (for ports 1-16 can be ethernet and the ports 17-32 can be FC or ports 1-4 can be ethernet and ports 5-32 can be FC.)

5. There cannot be multiple blocks of alternating ethernet and FC ports. (E.g. ports 1-8 as Ethernet ports, ports 9-16 as FC ports and ports 17 - 32ethernet is not allowed)

6. And port re-configuration from Ethernet to FC or FC to Ethernet will require a reload of the base chassis or the module that it is being configured on. If the ports on the expansion module is configured as FC ports only that module needs to be reloaded.

7. Nexus 5596 which 3 expansion modules each can be configured as different port types.

Configuring fixed unified ports on a Nexus 5548 UP switch as FC ports

The recipe details the steps needed to configure ports 17 to 32 in the fixed base as FC ports.

Step 1   Select slot 1 on the Nexus 5548Up switch and configure ports 17 through 32 as FC ports.

```
N5548UP-1# config t
N5548UP-1(config)# slot 1 <-- select the base port which is slot 1
N5548UP-1(config-slot)# port 17-32 type fc <-- converts the ports to FC ports
N5548UP-1(config-slot)# copy running startup
[#######################################] 100%
N5548UP-1(config-slot)# end
N5548UP-1#
```

Step 2   Reboot the switch for the configuration to take effect.

Note   When the base ports are modified the whole switch has to be reloaded.

```
N5548UP-1# config t
N5548UP-1(config)# reload
WARNING: This command will reboot the system
Do you want to continue? (y/n) [n] y
```

Configuring expansion module ports on a 5596 UP switch as FC ports

In this recipe all the ports on the expansion module 2 or Nexus 5596UP switch will be configured as FC ports.

Step 1 Use the **show module** command to list the modules on the Nexus 5548 switch.

```
N5596UP-1# show module
Mod Ports  Module-Type                      Model                   Status
--- -----  -------------------------------  ----------------------  ------------
1   48     O2 48X10GE/Modular Supervisor    N5K-C5596UP-SUP         active *
2   16     O2 16 port flexible GEM          N55-M16UP               ok

Mod Sw             Hw       World-Wide-Name(s) (WWN)
--- -------------  ------   --------------------------------------------------
1   5.0(3)N2(1)    1.0      --
2   5.0(3)N2(1)    1.0      --

Mod MAC-Address(es)                      Serial-Num
--- -----------------------------------  ----------
1   547f.ee23.7c00 to 547f.ee23.7c27     FOC13525VC
2   547f.ee0d.7050 to 547f.ee0d.705f     FOC1251W2V

N5596UP-1#
```

Step 2 Select slot 2 which has the 16 port expansion module and configure all 16 ports as FC ports, save the configuration.

```
N5596UP-1# config t
N5596UP-1(config)# slot 2<-- select the base port which is slot 2
N5596UP-1(config-slot)# port 1-16 type fc <-- converts the ports to FC ports
N5596UP-1(config-slot)# copy running startup
[########################################] 100%
N5596UP-1(config-slot)# end
N5596UP-1#
```

Step 3 Use commands **poweroff module** 2 and **no poweroff module** 2 to restart module 2 for the configuration to take effect.

```
N5596UP-1# config t
N5596UP-1(config)# poweroff module 2
N5596UP-1(config)# no poweroff module 2
N5596UP-1(config)# end
N5596UP-1#
```

CHAPTER 11

FCIP

Fibre Channel over IP (FCIP) is an Internet Engineering Task Force (IETF) standards-based protocol for extending SAN over IP networks (WAN). FCIP has been traditionally used to connect Storage Area Network in Data Centers that are geographically dispersed. FCIP enables data replication, remote tape vaulting and disaster recovery between two or more spread out Data Centers.

The FCIP protocol creates virtual Fibre Channel Tunnels over an IP infrastructure between Data Centers thereby facilitating Fibre channel traffic to seamlessly moved between them. FCIP protocol extends a Fibre Channel SAN transparently over IP networks, while keeping the Fibre Channel fabric services intact. The FCIP protocol uses the underlying TCP/IP protocol for transport.

FCIP encapsulates the Fibre Channel frame into a TCP packet and transports it across the IP infrastructure. Once the FCIP tunnel is established between the SAN islands over an IP network, the FCIP tunnel works like an Inter-Switch Link (ISL) between the SAN islands.

FCIP implementation on MDS switches supports advanced capabilities like compression, read acceleration, write acceleration, tape read acceleration, and tape write acceleration on the FCIP tunnel between the SAN islands. These advanced capabilities on the MDS significantly increase throughput and utilization on the IP network thereby enabling efficient transfer of very large amounts of data between the Data Centers using FCIP.

FCIP links are used between geographically dispersed Data Centers for a wide variety of applications. Some of the well know applications are:

- SAN Extension
- Disaster recovery
- Synchronous data replication
- Asynchronous data replication
- Remote tape backup and Vaulting

On the Cisco MDS platform, FCIP is supported on the MDS 9222i switches, and all the 9500 series directors.

Note   The MDS 9216A switch, IPS-8, IPS-4 and MSM 14+2 line cards are no longer supported as of NX-OS 5.x

On the MDS 9500 series director switches, a Multi Services Module (MSM) 18+4 module or an Storage Services Node (SSN)16 module is required to be installed for configuring FCIP. The MDS 9222i comes with four IP ports built in to the switch. The port capacities and capabilities of the MSM 18+4 and SSN-16 modules are listed in the table below.(See Table 11-1.)

Table 11-1   FCIP Capable Modules for MDS 9000 Series Switches

Modules	Compression in HW	Encryption in HW	I/O Acceleration	IP Ports	FCIP Engines	Throughput w/ Services
MSM 18+4	Yes	Yes	Yes	4	1 Engine (up to 16 FCIP Tunnels)	1-Gb/s on each IP port
SSN 16	Yes	Yes	Yes	16	4 Engines (up to 64 FCIP Tunnels	1-Gb/s on Each IP port

The MSM 18+4 multi services module and the Storage Services Node (SSN 16) modules support both FCIP and iSCSI on the same port at the same time.

The MSM 18+4 module uses hardware to compress and encrypt data. This module has a single engine that can sustain line rate or 1- Gb/s throughput on all the 4 gigabit Ethernet ports while compressing and encrypting data.

The SSN 16 module also does compression and encryption in hardware. This module has 16 IP ports for FCIP configuration and four application engines each managing four of the front end IP ports. This card can deliver line rate FCIP traffic with compression and encryption turned on each of the 16 1GigE ports.

The configuration of the FCIP tunnel requires the configuration of the underlying gigabit Ethernet interfaces. After the gigabit Ethernet interfaces are configured, and can communicated to each other at both ends of the WAN, the FCIP tunnel is configured over this TCP/IP link connecting the two end points. Each of the IP ports can support up to three FCIP tunnels on the same port. The MSM 18+4 module can support up to 4 line rate 1 gigE ports and 12 FCIP tunnels. The SSN 16 module can support up to 16 line rate 1 gigE ports and 48 FCIP tunnels.

Enabling FCIP

Execute the **feature fcip** command before attempting to configure FCIP on the switch.

Note   The **feature fcip** commands needs to be run on the switch before any further FCIP configuration can be performed on that switch. This command enables FCIP feature and configuration options in the CLI.

```
MDS-9513-1# conf t
Enter configuration commands, one per line.  End with CNTL/Z.
MDS-9513-1(config)# feature fcip
MDS-9513-1(config)#exit
MDS-9513-1#
```

Configuring FCIP with the CLI

The recipe below details the FCIP configuration steps on a switch using CLI commands. To successfully configure a FCIP tunnel, the FCIP configuration needs to be performed on two switches; typically one on either side of a Wide Area Network. The topology used in this recipe is as shown in Figure 11-1.

Note   To configure FCIP using **DCNM SAN,** see Configuring FCIP Using DCNM SAN, page 11-23. Configuring IPSec is optional but is illustrated in that recipe.

Figure 11-1   FCIP Topology

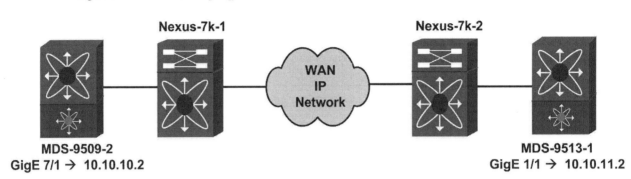

The topology shown in Figure 11-1 consists of two MDS 9509 directors. MDS-9513-1 has a MSM 18+4 module in slot 7 MDS-9509-2 has one MSM-18+4 module also in slot 7. gigabit Ethernet port 7/1 on MDS-9513-1 connects to ethernet switch (Nexus-7k-1) and the gigabit Ethernet port 7/1 on switch MDS-9509-2 connects to another ethernet switch (Nexus-7k-2). The ethernet switches connect to the wide area network (WAN). The gigabit Ethernet port 7/1 on the switch MDS-9513-1 has IP address 10.10.10.2 with subnet mask 255.255.255.0 and gateway address 10.10.10.1. The gigabit Ethernet port 7/1 port on the switch MDS-9509-2 has an IP address 10.10.11.2 with a subnet 255.255.255.0 and the gateway address 10.10.11.1. In the recipe, an FCIP tunnel is established between the switch MDS-9513-1 (gigabit Ethernet port 7/1) and MDS-9509-2 (gigabit Ethernet port 7/1).

Caution   The **IP addresses** for the gigabit Ethernet ports on the MSM 18+4 and SSN-16 modules must be in a **different subnet** than the management interface. This is a requirement for FCIP to function properly.

The FCIP-related configuration needs to be performed on both the switches.

To configure an FCIP tunnel, follow these steps:

Step 1   Configure the gigabit Ethernet interfaces on the MDS switches.

Assign the gigabit Ethernet interface on the MDS switch MDS-9513-1 an IP address and a subnet mask. This allows the gigabit Ethernet interface to communicate with the network.

```
MDS-9513-1# conf t
Enter configuration commands, one per line.  End with CNTL/Z.
MDS-9513-1(config)# interface gigabitethernet 7/1
MDS-9513-1(config-if)# ip address 10.10.10.2 255.255.255.0
MDS-9513-1(config-if)# no shut
MDS-9513-1(config-if)# end
MDS-9513-1#
```

Assign the gigabit Ethernet interface on the MDS switch MDS-9513-1 an IP address and a subnet mask. This allows the gigabit Ethernet interface to communicate with the network.

```
MDS-9509-2# conf t
Enter configuration commands, one per line.  End with CNTL/Z.
MDS-9509-2(config)# interface gigabitethernet 7/1
MDS-9509-2(config-if)# ip address 10.10.11.2 255.255.255.0
MDS-9509-2(config-if)# no shut
MDS-9509-2(config-if)# end
MDS-9509-2#
```

Step 2   Configure an IP route so that the two gigabit Ethernet interfaces can communicate.

An IP route needs to be configured to allow the two gigabit Ethernet interfaces on switches MDS-9513-1 and MDS-9509-2 to communicate with each other. In this recipe, the gigabit Ethernet interfaces are in two different subnets, so an explicit route needs to be configured for the interfaces to communicate with each other.

Best Practice   It is recommended to create a **host route** to each of the two gigabit Ethernet interface with a subnet mask of 255.255.255.255. This allows just the two gigabit Ethernet interfaces to communicate with each other for the purpose of creating the FCIP tunnel.

For the gigabit Ethernet interface 7/1 on MDS-9513-1 to communicate with the gigabit Ethernet interface 7/1 on MDS-9509-2, create the route configuration shown below on MDS-9513-1.

```
MDS-9513-1# conf t
Enter configuration commands, one per line.  End with CNTL/Z.
MDS-9513-1(config)# ip route 10.10.11.2 255.255.255.255 10.10.10.1 interface
gigabitethernet 7/1
MDS-9513-1(config)# end
MDS-9513-1#
```

The above configuration provides the following information:

To reach ip address 10.10.11.2, use ip address 10.10.10.1 as the gateway and use the gigabit Ethernet interface 7/1 on MDS-9513-1 for this (FCIP) traffic.

For the gigabit Ethernet interface 7/1 on MDS-9509-2 to communicate with gigabit Ethernet interface 7/1 on switch MDS-9513-1, apply the below route configuration on MDS-9509-2.

```
MDS-9509-2# conf t
Enter configuration commands, one per line.  End with CNTL/Z.
MDS-9509-2(config)# ip route 10.10.10.2 255.255.255.255 10.10.11.1 interface
gigabitethernet 7/1
MDS-9509-2(config-if)# end
MDS-9509-2#
```

The configuration above provides the following information:

To reach ip address 10.10.10.2, use ip address 10.10.11.1 as the gateway and use the gigabit Ethernet interface 7/1 on switch MDS-9509-2. for this (FCIP) traffic

Step 3   Ping the gigabit Ethernet interfaces to ensure that they can communicate with each other.

From the switch MDS-9513-1, ping the IP address of the gigabit Ethernet interface 7/1 on switch MDS-9509-2 using the gigabit Ethernet interface 7/1. Similarly, ping the IP address of the interface gigabit Ethernet 7/1 on switch MDS-9513-1 from switch MDS-9509-2 using the interface gigabit Ethernet 7/1. This should be done from the switch command prompt.

Note   Before SAN-OS release 3.x, the only option was to ping the IP address of the remote gigabit Ethernet interface. From SAN-OS 3.x, NX-OS 4.x and higher, the interface to be used to perform the ping the remote gigabit Ethernet interface can also be specified.

```
MDS-9513-1# ping 10.10.11.2 interface gigabitethernet 7/1
PING 10.10.11.2 (10.10.11.2) from 10.10.10.2 gige7-1: 56(84) bytes of data.
64 bytes from 10.10.11.2: icmp_seq=1 ttl=254 time=0.637 ms
64 bytes from 10.10.11.2: icmp_seq=2 ttl=254 time=0.610 ms
64 bytes from 10.10.11.2: icmp_seq=3 ttl=254 time=0.596 ms
64 bytes from 10.10.11.2: icmp_seq=4 ttl=254 time=0.611 ms

--- 10.10.11.2 ping statistics ---
4 packets transmitted, 4 received, 0% packet loss, time 3016ms
rtt min/avg/max/mdev = 0.596/0.613/0.637/0.028 ms
MDS-9513-1#

MDS-9509-2# ping 10.10.10.2 interface gigabitethernet 7/1
PING 10.10.10.2 (10.10.10.2) from 10.10.11.2 gige7-1: 56(84) bytes of data.
64 bytes from 10.10.10.2: icmp_seq=1 ttl=254 time=0.688 ms
64 bytes from 10.10.10.2: icmp_seq=2 ttl=254 time=0.606 ms
64 bytes from 10.10.10.2: icmp_seq=3 ttl=254 time=0.566 ms
64 bytes from 10.10.10.2: icmp_seq=4 ttl=254 time=0.590 ms

--- 10.10.10.2 ping statistics ---
4 packets transmitted, 4 received, 0% packet loss, time 3001ms
rtt min/avg/max/mdev = 0.566/0.612/0.688/0.052 ms
MDS-9509-2#
```

Best Practice   Always verify the IP connectivity between the two gigabit Ethernet interfaces on the MSM and/or SSN-16 modules on both the switches before proceeding further. A ping test is sufficient to check connectivity.

Step 4   Measure the round trip time (RTT) between the two gigabit Ethernet interfaces. The RTT value is required for configuring the FCIP profile in the next step.

```
MDS-9513-1# ips measure-rtt 10.10.11.2 interface gigabitethernet 7/1
Round trip time is 425 micro seconds (0.42 milli seconds)
MDS-9513-1#

MDS-9509-2# ips measure-rtt 10.10.10.2 interface gigabitethernet 7/1
Round trip time is 425 micro seconds (0.42 milli seconds)
MDS-9509-2#
```

Best Practice   FCIP by default uses TCP port 3225. If there is a firewall between the two switches that need to be connected through FCIP, then port 3225 needs to opened up in the firewall for the FCIP tunnel to come up.

Step 5   Configure FCIP profiles on both switches.

A FCIP profile must be created on both the switches for each FCIP tunnel. The FCIP profile defines the characteristics of the FCIP tunnel. The profile typically specifies the maximum tunnel bandwidth, the minimum bandwidth and the round trip time between the two switches gigabit Ethernet ports.

The IP address assigned to the gigabit Ethernet ports on the switch is used in the profile configuration.

The round trip time measured in the previous step is needed for profile configuration. In this case, the time was 425 microseconds.

Best Practice   It is recommended that the same FCIP profile number be used on both switches.

```
MDS-9513-1# conf t
Enter configuration commands, one per line.  End with CNTL/Z.
MDS-9513-1(config)# fcip profile 1 <-- use the same fcip profile ID on both switches
MDS-9513-1(config-profile)# ip address 10.10.10.2
MDS-9513-1(config-profile)# tcp max-bandwidth-mbps 1000 min-available-bandwidth-mbps 500
round-trip-time-us 425
MDS-9513-1(config-profile)# end
MDS-9513-1#


MDS-9509-2# conf t
Enter configuration commands, one per line.  End with CNTL/Z.
MDS-9509-2(config)# fcip profile 1 <-- use the same fcip profile ID on both switches
MDS-9509-2(config-profile)# ip address 10.10.11.2
MDS-9509-2(config-profile)# tcp max-bandwidth-mbps 1000 min-available-bandwidth-mbps 500
round-trip-time-us 425
MDS-9509-2(config-profile)# end
MDS-9509-2#
```

The FCIP profile 1 has now been defined on switches MDS-9513-1 and MDS-9509-2.

Step 6   Configure the FCIP interface on both switches.

In the FCIP interface configuration, the profile to be used and the peer information (remote gigabit Ethernet ip address) are configured. Additionally, compression and write acceleration can be configured on the FCIP interface.

```
MDS-9513-1# conf t
Enter configuration commands, one per line.  End with CNTL/Z.
MDS-9513-1(config)# interface fcip 1
MDS-9513-1(config-if)# peer-info ipaddr 10.10.11.2
MDS-9513-1(config-if)# use-profile 1
MDS-9513-1(config-if)# no shutdown
MDS-9513-1(config-if)# end
MDS-9513-1#


MDS-9509-2# conf t
Enter configuration commands, one per line.  End with CNTL/Z.
MDS-9509-2(config)# int fcip 1
MDS-9509-2(config-if)# use-profile 1
MDS-9509-2(config-if)# peer-info ipaddr 10.10.10.2
MDS-9509-2(config-if)# no shut
MDS-9509-2(config-if)# end
MDS-9509-2#
```

Step 7   The FCIP tunnel should be up and running. Use the **show fcip summary** command to see the status of the FCIP link between the two switches.

```
MDS-9513-1# show fcip summary
-----------------------------------------------------------------------
Tun prof    Eth-if    peer-ip      Status T W T Enc Comp  Bandwidth   rtt
                                          E A A           max/min     (us)
-----------------------------------------------------------------------
1    1    GE7/1    10.10.11.2    TRNK  Y N N  N   N    1000M/500M  425

MDS-9513-1#

MDS-9509-2# show fcip summary

-----------------------------------------------------------------------
Tun prof    Eth-if    peer-ip      Status T W T Enc Comp  Bandwidth   rtt
                                          E A A           max/min     (us)
-----------------------------------------------------------------------
1    1    GE7/1    10.10.10.2    TRNK  Y N N  N   N    1000M/500M  425

MDS-9509-2#
```

Enabling FCIP Write Acceleration

Both MSM 18+4 and SSN-16 modules support write acceleration to help alleviate the effects of network latency. Write acceleration helps significantly in improving the write performance for applications transparently over a wide area network (WAN). Write acceleration helps in maximizing the WAN throughput by reducing the effects of WAN latency on the writes that need to go across the WAN.

Write acceleration needs to be enabled on both ends of the FCIP tunnel, otherwise it will fail to function properly.

Note   Enable Write Acceleration across port-channel, the port-channel needs to be managed by port-channel protocol (PCP).

Step 1   Enable write acceleration on the interface FCIP 1 on switch MDS-9513-1.

```
MDS-9513-1# conf t
Enter configuration commands, one per line.  End with CNTL/Z.
MDS-9513-1(config)# interface fcip 1
MDS-9513-1(config)# write-accelerator
MDS-9513-1(config)# end
MDS-9513-1#
```

Step 2   Enable write acceleration on the interface FCIP 1 on switch MDS-9509-2.

```
MDS-9509-2# conf t
Enter configuration commands, one per line.  End with CNTL/Z.
MDS-9509-2(config)# interface fcip 1
MDS-9509-2(config)# write-accelerator
MDS-9509-2(config)# end
MDS-9509-2#
```

Step 3   Use the **show fcip summary** command to see the status of the FCIP link between the two switches with write acceleration turned on.

```
MDS-9513-1# show fcip summary

-------------------------------------------------------------------------------
Tun prof   Eth-if   peer-ip      Status T W T Enc Comp  Bandwidth  rtt
                                        E A A            max/min    (us)
-------------------------------------------------------------------------------
1   1      GE7/1    10.10.11.2   TRNK   Y Y N  N    N   1000M/500M  425

MDS-9513-1#

MDS-9509-2# show fcip summary

-------------------------------------------------------------------------------
Tun prof   Eth-if   peer-ip      Status T W T Enc Comp  Bandwidth  rtt
                                        E A A            max/min    (us)
-------------------------------------------------------------------------------
1   1      GE7/1    10.10.10.2   TRNK   Y Y N  N    N   1000M/500M  425

MDS-9509-2#
```

Enabling FCIP Compression

The MSM-18+4 and SNN-16 modules supports hardware-based compression. The MSM 18+4 and SSN-16 modules Which have four and sixteen IPS ports, perform hardware compression at the line rate of 1-Gb/s per port.

In in the 5.x revision of NX-OS, there are two IP compression modes, which are listed below:

- **Auto** (default) provides compression suitable for most environments or those that have latency sensitive applications such as synchronous replication.

- **Mode2** provides the best compression when MSM 18+4 and SSN-16 modules are used, however, it adds about 3 milliseconds of latency. It should be used in those scenarios where the applications are not sensitive to latency such as asynchronous replication, streaming IO or where the latency is significantly higher than 3 milliseconds.

Best Practice   It is recommended to use compression "**mode 2**" for the best compression in a FCIP tunnel built using MSM 18+4 or SSN-16 modules.

⚠
Caution   The MPS 14/2 line cards are supported up to NX-OS 4.x. They are not supported in NX-OS 5.x. The only way to establish a FCIP tunnel between a MPS 14/2 module and the MSM 18+4 or SSN-16 modules **is without compression** on the FCIP tunnel. It is recommended to replace the 14+2 with MSM 18+4 or a SSN16 module for optimal FCIP performance.

Note   A link will not come up if its compression mode is configured incorrectly. Compression needs to be enabled on both sides of a link. Also, ensure that the compression modes on both sides match.

Use the chart in Figure 11-2 as a guide to determine which compression mode is most appropriate for the line card combination in use in the FCIP configuration.

Figure 11-2   *FCIP compression modes for various line card combinations*

Destination line Cards

Line Cards	MSM 18+4	SSN - 16
MSM 18+4	Auto / Mode 2	Auto / Mode 2
SSN - 16	Auto / Mode 2	Auto / Mode 2

Caution   MDS 9216A switch, IPS-8, IPS-4 are and MSM 14+2 line cards are no longer supported as of NX-OS 5.x. If using one of the above cards the switch should be running 4.x or lower version of the code. The compression mode that should be used is auto.

The recipe below shows how compression is enabled on the FCIP tunnel.

Enable compression on the interface fcip 1 on switch MDS-9513-1. The mode of compression used is mode2.

Step 1   MDS-9513-1# **conf t**

```
Enter configuration commands, one per line.  End with CNTL/Z.
MDS-9513-1(config)# interface fcip 1
MDS-9513-1(config-if)# ip-compression mode2
MDS-9513-1(config-if)# end
MDS-9513-1#
```

Step 2   Enable compression on the interface fcip 1 on switch MDS-9509-2. The mode of compression used is mode2.

```
MDS-9509-2# conf t
Enter configuration commands, one per line.  End with CNTL/Z.
MDS-9509-2(config)# interface fcip 1
MDS-9509-2(config-if)# ip-compression mode2
MDS-9509-2(config-if)# end
MDS-9509-2#
```

Step 3   Use the **show fcip summary** command to see the status of the FCIP link between the two switches after compression is enabled.

```
MDS-9513-1# show fcip summary

----------------------------------------------------------------------------
Tun prof    Eth-if    peer-ip       Status  T W T  Enc  Comp  Bandwidth   rtt
                                            E A A              max/min    (us)
----------------------------------------------------------------------------
1    1      GE7/1     10.10.10.2    TRNK    Y Y N  N    M2    1000M/500M  425

MDS-9513-1#

MDS-9509-2# show fcip summary

----------------------------------------------------------------------------
Tun prof    Eth-if    peer-ip       Status  T W T  Enc  Comp  Bandwidth   rtt
                                            E A A              max/min    (us)
----------------------------------------------------------------------------
1    1      GE7/1     10.10.11.2    TRNK    Y Y N  N    M2    1000M/500M  425

MDS-9509-2#
```

Enabling Tape Acceleration

The tape acceleration feature is similar to write acceleration. Tape acceleration alleviates latency associated issues with backing up to tape drives through FCIP tunnels over long-distance WAN links.

Caution   FCIP tape acceleration does not work if an FCIP tunnel is part of a port-channel, nor if there are multiple equal cost paths between the backup host and the tape device.

Best Practice   It is recommend to use **I/O Acceleration (IOA)** when multiple equal cost FCIP links are available between the host and the tape deices. IOA allows multiple FCIP links to be configured into a port-channel and use the entire bandwidth to accelerate the tape traffic between the media servers and tape device across the port-channel.

When multiple equal cost multiple paths exists between the backup server and the tape devices, and when not using IOA it is recommend that the multiple paths be configured with varying FSPF costs. This ensures that only one link at a time is used for tape acceleration and the remaining FCIP links provide fail over if the primary link fails.

Enabling Tape Acceleration from the CLI

Tape acceleration, like write acceleration, needs to be enabled on both sides of the FCIP tunnel. Tape acceleration is a sub command of write acceleration.

Step 1   Enable tape acceleration on switch MDS-9513-1 for the interface fcip1.

```
MDS-9513-1# conf t
Enter configuration commands, one per line.  End with CNTL/Z.
MDS-9513-1(config)# int fcip1
MDS-9513-1(config-if)# write-accelerator tape-accelerator
MDS-9513-1(config-if)# end
MDS-9513-1#
```

Step 2   Enable tape acceleration on switch MDS-9509-2 for the interface fcip1.

```
MDS-9509-2# conf t
Enter configuration commands, one per line.  End with CNTL/Z.
MDS-9509-2(config)# int fcip1
MDS-9509-2(config-if)# write-accelerator tape-accelerator
MDS-9509-2(config-if)# end
MDS-9509-2#
```

Step 3   Use the **show fcip summary** command to see the status of the FCIP link between the two switches after tape acceleration is enabled.

```
MDS-9513-1# show fcip summary
-------------------------------------------------------------------------------
Tun prof   Eth-if    peer-ip        Status T W T Enc Comp Bandwidth   rtt
                                           E A A            max/min    (us)
-------------------------------------------------------------------------------
1   1      GE7/1     10.10.10.2     TRNK   Y Y Y  N  M2    1000M/500M  425
MDS-9513-1#
```

```
MDS-9509-2# show fcip summary

-------------------------------------------------------------------------------
Tun prof   Eth-if    peer-ip        Status T W T Enc Comp Bandwidth   rtt
                                           E A A            max/min    (us)
-------------------------------------------------------------------------------
1   1      GE7/1     10.10.11.2     TRNK   Y Y Y  N  M2    1000M/500M  425
```

```
MDS-9509-2#
```

Step 4   Use the **show interface FCIP** command to see the status of the link and the configuration of the FCIP tunnel.

```
MDS-9513-1# show interface fcip 1
fcip1 is trunking
    Hardware is gigabitEthernet
    Port WWN is 21:94:00:0d:ec:02:2d:80
    Peer port WWN is 21:94:00:0d:ec:02:2d:80
    Admin port mode is auto, trunk mode is on
    snmp traps are enabled
    Port mode is TE
    Port vsan is 1
    Speed is 1 Gbps
    Trunk vsans (admin allowed and active) (1)
    Trunk vsans (up)                       (1)
    Trunk vsans (isolated)                 ()
    Trunk vsans (initializing)             ()
    Using Profile id 1  (interface gigabitEthernet7/1)
    Peer Information
      Peer Internet address is 10.10.11.2 and port is 3225
    Write acceleration mode is configured on; operationally on
    Tape acceleration mode is configured on; operationally on
    Tape read acceleration mode is operationally on
    Tape Accelerator flow control buffer size is automatic
    FICON XRC Accelerator is configured off
    Ficon Tape acceleration configured off for all vsans
```

```
IP Compression is enabled and set for mode2
Maximum number of TCP connections is 2
QOS control code point is 0
QOS data code point is 0
TCP Connection Information
  2 Active TCP connections
      Control connection: Local 10.10.10.2:65507, Remote 10.10.11.2:3225
      Data connection: Local 10.10.10.2:65509, Remote 10.10.11.2:3225
  14 Attempts for active connections, 2 close of connections
TCP Parameters
  Path MTU 1500 bytes
  Current retransmission timeout is 200 ms
  Round trip time: Smoothed 0 ms, Variance: 0 Jitter: 150 us
  Advertized window: Current: 54 KB, Maximum: 24580 KB, Scale: 4
  Peer receive window: Current: 1023 KB, Maximum: 1023 KB, Scale: 4
  Congestion window: Current: 20 KB, Slow start threshold: 852 KB
  Current Send Buffer Size: 54 KB, Requested Send Buffer Size: 0 KB
  CWM Burst Size: 50 KB
  Measured RTT : 500000 us Min RTT: 289 us Max RTT: 0 us
5 minutes input rate 312 bits/sec, 39 bytes/sec, 0 frames/sec
5 minutes output rate 280 bits/sec, 35 bytes/sec, 0 frames/sec
  52245 frames input, 4823468 bytes
      52245 Class F frames input, 4823468 bytes
      0 Class 2/3 frames input, 0 bytes
      0 Reass frames
      0 Error frames timestamp error 0
  52253 frames output, 4816800 bytes
      52253 Class F frames output, 4816800 bytes
      0 Class 2/3 frames output, 0 bytes
      0 Error frames
MDS-9513-1#
```

In the above output from MDS-9513-1, the link properties are in bold.

```
MDS-9509-2# show int fcip 1
fcip1 is trunking
    Hardware is gigabitEthernet
    Port WWN is 20:10:00:0d:ec:24:5e:80
    Peer port WWN is 20:42:00:0d:ec:24:5e:c0
    Admin port mode is auto, trunk mode is on
    snmp traps are enabled
    Port mode is TE
    Port vsan is 1
    Speed is 1 Gbps
    Trunk vsans (admin allowed and active) (1)
    Trunk vsans (up)                        (1)
    Trunk vsans (isolated)                  ()
    Trunk vsans (initializing)              ()
    Using Profile id 1   (interface gigabitEthernet7/1)
    Peer Information
      Peer Internet address is 10.10.10.2 and port is 3225
    Write acceleration mode is configured on; operationally on
    Tape acceleration mode is configured on; operationally on
    Tape read acceleration mode is operationally on
    Tape Accelerator flow control buffer size is automatic
    FICON XRC Accelerator is configured off
    Ficon Tape acceleration configured off for all vsans
    IP Compression is enabled and set for mode2
    Maximum number of TCP connections is 2
    Time Stamp is disabled
    QOS control code point is 0
    QOS data code point is 0
    B-port mode disabled
    TCP Connection Information
      2 Active TCP connections
        Control connection: Local 10.10.11.2:65428, Remote 10.10.10.2:3225
        Data connection: Local 10.10.11.2:65430, Remote 10.10.10.2:3225
      54 Attempts for active connections, 29 close of connections
    TCP Parameters
      Path MTU 1500 bytes
      Current retransmission timeout is 200 ms
      Round trip time: Smoothed 0 ms, Variance: 0 Jitter: 150 us
      Advertized window: Current: 49 KB, Maximum: 49 KB, Scale: 4
      Peer receive window: Current: 55 KB, Maximum: 55 KB, Scale: 4
      Congestion window: Current: 18 KB, Slow start threshold: 50 KB
      Current Send Buffer Size: 49 KB, Requested Send Buffer Size: 0 KB
      CWM Burst Size: 50 KB
    5 minutes input rate 0 bits/sec, 0 bytes/sec, 0 frames/sec
    5 minutes output rate 0 bits/sec, 0 bytes/sec, 0 frames/sec
      5775 frames input, 570892 bytes
          5775 Class F frames input, 570892 bytes
          0 Class 2/3 frames input, 0 bytes
          0 Reass frames
          0 Error frames timestamp error 0
      5788 frames output, 673640 bytes
          5788 Class F frames output, 673640 bytes
          0 Class 2/3 frames output, 0 bytes
          0 Error frames

MDS-9509-2#
```

In the above output from MDS-9509-2, the link properties are in bold.

Tuning FCIP

Configuring and bringing up an FCIP tunnel establishes an ISL over the WAN link between two switches. To achieve greater efficiency and utilization of the FCIP link, the link parameters can be tuned and optimized. The optimization described in this section is specific to FCIP links between switches. Optimization for a FCIP link over a slow 1.54 Mb/s connection is very different than that for a FCIP link over a 1-Gb/s connection with very low latency.

Note   The results may vary due to network conditions (existing link utilization and quality) as well as the storage array and host type using the FCIP tunnel.

TCP Tuning: Latency and Available Bandwidth

The latency of a FCIP link is the amount of time it takes a packet to go from one end of the link to the other. Latency is affected by many factors including distance and the number of devices that it must traverse. Even the fastest routers and switches incur some latency.

Even though latency cannot be eliminated, protocols can be tuned and the features of an MDS switch (such as FCIP write acceleration) can be enabled to minimize its effect. These features are enabled in the FCIP profile.

Best Practice   If the underlying link is dedicated to FCIP, the minimum and maximum available bandwidth values should be the same.If there are multiple FCIP links Sharing the WAN bandwidth, the maximum bandwidth value should be equally split between all the FCIP tunnels. The combined minimum bandwidth of all the FCIP tunnels should be less than the total bandwidth of the WAN link.

Available bandwidth is the amount of bandwidth that the FCIP link can use on the network. The maximum and a minimum value of bandwidth for the FCIP link is specified in the FCIP profile associated with the tunnel.

- The maximum available bandwidth value is the maximum amount of bandwidth that the FCIP link can use on the network.

- The minimum available bandwidth value is used as a guideline for the minimum value. If there are serious problems on the network (dropped packets, congestion), the link goes slower than the minimum value. It is recommend that the minimum value be set (at least) to the minimum required by applications. (EMC SRDF, IBM PPRC, Hitachi's TrueCopy, etc.).

Table 11-2 contains some common WAN links and their speeds. These circuits are most often used as the underlying network for a FCIP link. For example, the underlying network may be an OC3, but the bandwidth allocated for FCIP link may only be 100 Mb of that link.

Table 11-2   ***Common WAN Link Speeds***

Circuit Name	Link Speed
T1	1.544-Mb/s
T3	44.736-Mb/s
OC3	155-Mb/s
OC12	622-Mb/s
OC24	1.244-Gb/s
OC48	2.488-Gb/s
OC192	10-Gb/s
OC 768	40-Gb/s

Best Practice   When deploying FCIP, It Is best to involve the LAN and WAN teams. Those teams will be able to provide more information about the WAN /LAN connections that are to be used for FCIP configuration. If there are performance issues, the LAN/WAN teams can often help troubleshoot the network (LAN/WAN).

Configuring Multiple FCIP Tunnels Using a Single gigabit Ethernet Port

This recipe describes the method to create multiple FCIP tunnels using a single gigabit Ethernet interface on a MSM 18+4 or SSN-16 modules, meaning that a single gigabit Ethernet port on a MDS switch is used to create two separate tunnels to two different gigabit Ethernet ports on two remote MDS switches. This is accomplished in a couple of ways.

1. Using different TCP ports to establish the separate FCIP tunnels to the local switch to the two remote switches.

2. Using 802.1q interfaces to create separate tunnels from the local switch to the two remote switches.

Note   Each gigabit Ethernet port on the MSM 18+4 and SSN-16 modules can support a maximum of three FCIP tunnels.

This recipe describes a method to create two FCIP tunnels in a single gigabit Ethernet interface using two different TCP ports. The various gigabit Ethernet connections are described below.

MDS-9513-1:

- gigabit Ethernet interface 7/1 connects to the gigabit Ethernet interface 7/1 on the switch MDS-9509-2 using the default FCIP TCP port 3225 (fcip1).

- gigabit Ethernet interface 7/1 connects to the gigabit Ethernet interface 1/1 on MDS-9509-3 using TCP port 3500(fcip2).

MDS-9509-2:

- gigabit Ethernet interface 7/1 connects to the gigabit Ethernet interface 7/1 on the switch MDS-9513-1 using the default FCIP TCP port 3225 (fcip1).

MDS-9509-3:

- the same gigabit Ethernet interface 1/1 connects to the gigabit Ethernet interface 7/1 on MDS-9513-1 using TCP port 3500(fcip2).

This topology illustrating the three way FCIP configuration is diagrammed in Figure 11-3.

The first FCIP tunnel fcip1 is configured between gigabit Ethernet interface 7/1 on MDS-9513-1 and the gigabit Ethernet interface 7/1 on MDS-9509-2. This FCIP tunnel; fcip1 uses the default FCIP TCP port 3225. The second FCIP tunnel fcip2 is configured between gigabit Ethernet port 7/1 on MDS-9513-1 and gigabit Ethernet port 1/1 on MDS-9509-3. The FCIP tunnel (fcip2) is configured to use TCP port 3500.

Figure 11-3   FCIP Three-way Topology using different TCP ports

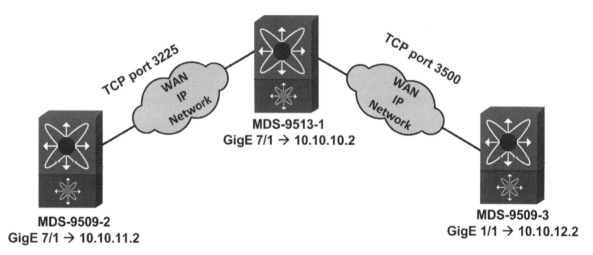

Note   In this configuration the bandwidth available to the gigabit Ethernet port 7/1 on the switch MDS-9513-1 has to be shared between the two FCIP tunnels, fcip1 and fcip2 that are configured to switches MDS-9509-2 and MDS-9509-3.

The configuration steps for the above described topology is as follows:

Step 1   Configure the gigabit Ethernet interface on the MDS switches MDS-9513-1 and MDS-9509-2.

Assign the gigabit Ethernet interface on the MDS switch MDS-9513-1 an IP address and a subnet mask. This allows the gigabit Ethernet interface to communicate with the network.

```
MDS-9513-1# conf t
Enter configuration commands, one per line.  End with CNTL/Z.
MDS-9513-1(config)# interface gigabitethernet 7/1
MDS-9513-1(config-if)# ip address 10.10.10.2 255.255.255.0
MDS-9513-1(config-if)# no shut
MDS-9513-1(config-if)# end
MDS-9513-1#
```

Assign the gigabit Ethernet interface on the MDS switch MDS-9509-2 an IP address and a subnet mask. This allows the gigabit Ethernet interface to communicate with the network.

```
MDS-9509-2# conf t
Enter configuration commands, one per line.  End with CNTL/Z.
MDS-9509-2(config)# interface gigabitethernet 7/1
MDS-9509-2(config-if)# ip address 10.10.11.2 255.255.255.0
MDS-9509-2(config-if)# no shut
MDS-9509-2(config-if)# end
MDS-9509-2#
```

Step 2   Configure an IP route so that the two gigabit Ethernet interfaces can communicate.

An IP route needs to be configured to allow the two gigabit Ethernet interfaces on switches MDS-9513-1 and MDS-9509-2 to communicate with each other. In this recipe, the gigabit Ethernet interfaces are in two different subnets, so an explicit ip route needs to be configured for the two interfaces to be able to communicate with each other.

Best Practice   It is recommended to create a host route to each of the two gigabit Ethernet interface with a subnet mask of 255.255.255.255. This allows just the two gigabit Ethernet interfaces to communicate with each other to enable creation of the FCIP tunnel.

For the gigabit Ethernet interface 7/1 on MDS-9513-1 to communicate with the gigabit Ethernet interface 7/1 on switch MDS-9509-2, apply the following route configuration on switch MDS-9513-1.

```
MDS-9513-1# conf t
Enter configuration commands, one per line.  End with CNTL/Z.
MDS-9513-1(config)# ip route 10.10.11.2 255.255.255.255 10.10.10.1 interface
gigabitethernet 7/1
MDS-9513-1(config)# end
MDS-9513-1#
```

For the gigabit Ethernet interface 7/1 on switch MDS-9509-2 to communicate with gigabit Ethernet interface 7/1 on switch MDS-9513-1, apply the below route configuration on switch MDS-9509-2.

```
MDS-9509-2# conf t
Enter configuration commands, one per line.  End with CNTL/Z.
MDS-9509-2(config)# ip route 10.10.10.2 255.255.255.255 10.10.11.1 interface
gigabitethernet 7/1
MDS-9509-2(config-if)# end
MDS-9509-2#
```

Step 3 Ping the gigabit Ethernet interfaces to ensure that they can communicate with each other.

From the switch MDS-9513-1, ping the IP address of the gigabit Ethernet interface 1/1 on switch MDS-9509-2 using the gigabit Ethernet interface 2/1. Similarly, ping the IP address of the interface gigabit Ethernet 2/1 on switch MDS-9513-1 from switch MDS-9509-2 using the interface gigabit Ethernet 1/1. Do this from the switch prompt.

Note Before SAN-OS release 3.x, the only option was to ping the IP address of the remote gigabit Ethernet interface. From SAN-OS 3.x, NX-OS 4.x and higher, the interface to be used to perform the ping the remote gigabit Ethernet interface can also be specified.

```
MDS-9513-1# ping 10.10.11.2 interface gigabitethernet 7/1
PING 10.10.11.2 (10.10.11.2) from 10.10.10.2 gige7-1: 56(84) bytes of data.
64 bytes from 10.10.11.2: icmp_seq=1 ttl=254 time=0.637 ms
64 bytes from 10.10.11.2: icmp_seq=2 ttl=254 time=0.610 ms
64 bytes from 10.10.11.2: icmp_seq=3 ttl=254 time=0.596 ms
64 bytes from 10.10.11.2: icmp_seq=4 ttl=254 time=0.611 ms

--- 10.10.11.2 ping statistics ---
4 packets transmitted, 4 received, 0% packet loss, time 3016ms
rtt min/avg/max/mdev = 0.596/0.613/0.637/0.028 ms
MDS-9513-1#

MDS-9509-2# ping 10.10.10.2 interface gigabitethernet 7/1
PING 10.10.10.2 (10.10.10.2) from 10.10.11.2 gige7-1: 56(84) bytes of data.
64 bytes from 10.10.10.2: icmp_seq=1 ttl=254 time=0.688 ms
64 bytes from 10.10.10.2: icmp_seq=2 ttl=254 time=0.606 ms
64 bytes from 10.10.10.2: icmp_seq=3 ttl=254 time=0.566 ms
64 bytes from 10.10.10.2: icmp_seq=4 ttl=254 time=0.590 ms

--- 10.10.10.2 ping statistics ---
4 packets transmitted, 4 received, 0% packet loss, time 3001ms
rtt min/avg/max/mdev = 0.566/0.612/0.688/0.052 ms
MDS-9509-2#
```

Best Practice It is critical to check the connectivity between the two gigabit Ethernet ports on the MSM and /or SSN-16 modules on both the switches before proceeding further. A ping test is sufficient to check connectivity.

Step 4 Measure the round trip time (RTT) between the two gigabit Ethernet interfaces. The RTT value is required for configuring the FCIP profile in the next step.

```
MDS-9513-1# ips measure-rtt 10.10.11.2 interface gigabitethernet 7/1
Round trip time is 425 micro seconds (0.42 milli seconds)
MDS-9513-1#

MDS-9509-2# ips measure-rtt 10.10.10.2 interface gigabitethernet 7/1
Round trip time is 425 micro seconds (0.42 milli seconds)
MDS-9509-2#
```

Note FCIP by default uses TCP port 3225. If there is a firewall between the two switches that are participating in the FCIP tunnel, then the port 3225 needs to opened up in both directions in the firewall for FCIP tunnel to come up.

Step 5   Configure FCIP profiles on both switches.

An FCIP profile must be created on both the switches for each FCIP tunnel. The fcip profile defines the characteristics of the FCIP tunnel. The profile typically specifies the max tunnel bandwidth, the min bandwidth and the round trip time between the two switches gigabit Ethernet interfaces.

The IP address assigned to the gigabit Ethernet interfaces on the switch is used in the profile configuration.

The round trip time measured in the previous step is needed for profile configuration. In this case, the time was 425 microseconds.

$\cdot\|\cdot\|\cdot\|\cdot$

Best Practice   It is strongly recommend to use the **same profile numbers (unique to a tunnel) for the FCIP profiles** configured on both switches for a given FCIP tunnel.

```
MDS-9513-1# conf t
Enter configuration commands, one per line.  End with CNTL/Z.
MDS-9513-1(config)# fcip profile 1 <-- use the same fcip profile ID on both switches
MDS-9513-1(config-profile)# ip address 10.10.10.2
MDS-9513-1(config-profile)# tcp max-bandwidth-mbps 1000 min-available-bandwidth-mbps 500
round-trip-time-us 425
MDS-9513-1(config-profile)# end
MDS-9513-1#

MDS-9509-2# conf t
Enter configuration commands, one per line.  End with CNTL/Z.
MDS-9509-2(config)# fcip profile 1 <-- use the same fcip profile ID on both switches
MDS-9509-2(config-profile)# ip address 10.10.11.2
MDS-9509-2(config-profile)# tcp max-bandwidth-mbps 1000 min-available-bandwidth-mbps 500
round-trip-time-us 425
MDS-9509-2(config-profile)# end
MDS-9509-2#
```

The FCIP profile 1 has now been configured on switches MDS-9513-1 and MDS-9509-2.

Step 6   Configure the FCIP interface on both switches.

In the FCIP interface configuration, the profile to be used and the peer information (remote gigabit Ethernet IP address) are specified. Additionally, compression and write acceleration can be configured on the FCIP interface.

```
MDS-9513-1# conf t
Enter configuration commands, one per line.  End with CNTL/Z.
MDS-9513-1(config)# interface fcip 1
MDS-9513-1(config-if)# peer-info ipaddr 10.10.11.2
MDS-9513-1(config-if)# use-profile 1
MDS-9513-1(config-if)# no shutdown
MDS-9513-1(config-if)# end
MDS-9513-1#

MDS-9509-2# conf t
Enter configuration commands, one per line.  End with CNTL/Z.
MDS-9509-2(config)# int fcip 1
MDS-9509-2(config-if)# use-profile 1
MDS-9509-2(config-if)# peer-info ipaddr 10.10.10.2
MDS-9509-2(config-if)# no shut
MDS-9509-2(config-if)# end
MDS-9509-2#
```

Step 7   The FCIP tunnel should be up and running. Use the **show fcip summary** command to see the status of the FCIP link between the two switches.

```
MDS-9513-1# show fcip summary
-------------------------------------------------------------------------
Tun prof   Eth-if   peer-ip       Status T W T Enc Comp  Bandwidth   rtt
                                         E A A           max/min     (us)
-------------------------------------------------------------------------
1   1      GE7/1    10.10.11.2    TRNK   Y N N  N    N   1000M/500M  425

MDS-9513-1#

MDS-9509-2# show fcip summary

-------------------------------------------------------------------------
Tun prof   Eth-if   peer-ip       Status T W T Enc Comp  Bandwidth   rtt
                                         E A A           max/min     (us)
-------------------------------------------------------------------------
1   1      GE7/1    10.10.10.2    TRNK   Y N N  N    N   1000M/500M  425

MDS-9509-2#
```

The above output shows the first FCIP tunnel fcip1 between the switches MDS-9513-1 and MDS-9509-2 using the standard TCP port 3235 as up and running.

The configuration steps below is for the tunnel fcip2 between switches MDS-9513-1 and MDS-9509-3 using TCP port 3500.

Step 8   Configure the gigabit Ethernet interface on the MDS switch MDS-9509-3.

The gigabit Ethernet interface on the MDS switch MDS-9509-3 is given an IP address and a subnetmask. This allows the gigabit Ethernet interface to communicate with the network.

```
MDS-9509-3# conf t
Enter configuration commands, one per line.  End with CNTL/Z.
MDS-9509-3(config)# interface gigabitethernet 1/1
MDS-9509-3(config-if)# ip address 10.10.12.2 255.255.255.0
MDS-9509-3(config-if)# no shut
MDS-9509-3(config-if)# end
MDS-9509-3#
```

Step 9   Configure an IP route so the two gigabit Ethernet interfaces 7/1 on MDS-9513-1 and 1/1 on MDS0switch-3 can communicate with each other.

An IP route needs to be configured to allow the two gigabit Ethernet interfaces on switches MDS-9513-1 and MDS-9509-3 to communicate with each other. In this recipe, the gigabit Ethernet ports are in two different subnets, so an explicit route needs to be configures on them for this communication to occur.

Best Practice   It is recommended to create a host route to each of the two gigabit Ethernet interface with a subnet mask of 255.255.255.255. This allows just the two gigabit Ethernet interfaces to communicate with each other for the purpose of creating the FCIP tunnel.

The syntax for configuring a route is shown below. For the gigabit Ethernet port 7/1 on the switch MDS-9513-1 to communicate with the gigabit Ethernet 1/1 on switch MDS-9509-3, perform the following route configuration on switch MDS-9513-1.

```
MDS-9513-1# conf t
Enter configuration commands, one per line.  End with CNTL/Z.
MDS-9513-1(config)# ip route 10.10.12.2 255.255.255.255 10.10.10.1 interface
gigabitethernet 7/1
MDS-9513-1(config)# end
MDS-9513-1#
```

The preceding configuration provides this information: to reach 10.10.12.2, use the gateway 10.10.10.1 and use interface gigabit Ethernet 7/1 on switch MDS-9513-1.

Similarly, for the gigabit Ethernet interface 1/1 on switch MDS-9509-3 to communicate with gigabit Ethernet interface 7/1 on switch MDS-9513-1, apply the following route configuration on switch MDS-9509-3.

```
MDS-9509-3# conf t
Enter configuration commands, one per line.  End with CNTL/Z.
MDS-9509-3(config)# ip route 10.10.10.2 255.255.255.255 10.10.12.1 interface
gigabitethernet 1/1
MDS-9509-3(config)# end
MDS-9509-3#
```

Step 10 Ping the gigabit Ethernet interfaces to ensure that they can communicate with each other.

From the switch MDS-9513-1, ping the IP address of the gigabit Ethernet interface 1/1 on switch MDS-9509-3. Similarly, ping the IP address of the gigabit Ethernet interface 7/1 on switch MDS-9513-1 from switch MDS-9509-3. This can be done from the switch prompt.

```
MDS-9513-1# ping 10.10.12.2 interface gigabitethernet 7/1
PING 10.10.12.2 (10.10.12.2) from 10.10.10.2 gige7-1: 56(84) bytes of data.
64 bytes from 10.10.12.2: icmp_seq=1 ttl=254 time=0.637 ms
64 bytes from 10.10.12.2: icmp_seq=2 ttl=254 time=0.610 ms
64 bytes from 10.10.12.2: icmp_seq=3 ttl=254 time=0.596 ms
64 bytes from 10.10.12.2: icmp_seq=4 ttl=254 time=0.611 ms
--- 10.10.12.2 ping statistics ---
4 packets transmitted, 4 received, 0% packet loss, time 3016ms
rtt min/avg/max/mdev = 0.596/0.613/0.637/0.028 ms
MDS-9513-1#
```

```
MDS-9509-3# ping 10.10.10.2 interface gigabitethernet 7/1
PING 10.10.10.2 (10.10.10.2) from 10.10.12.2 gige7-1: 56(84) bytes of data.
64 bytes from 10.10.10.2: icmp_seq=1 ttl=254 time=0.688 ms
64 bytes from 10.10.10.2: icmp_seq=2 ttl=254 time=0.606 ms
64 bytes from 10.10.10.2: icmp_seq=3 ttl=254 time=0.566 ms
64 bytes from 10.10.10.2: icmp_seq=4 ttl=254 time=0.590 ms
--- 10.10.10.2 ping statistics ---
4 packets transmitted, 4 received, 0% packet loss, time 3001ms
rtt min/avg/max/mdev = 0.566/0.612/0.688/0.052 ms
MDS-9509-2#
```

Step 11 Measure the RTT between the two gigabit Ethernet interfaces.

Measure the RTT between the two gigabit Ethernet interfaces. The RTT value is required for configuring the FCIP profile in the next step.

```
MDS-9513-1# ips measure-rtt 10.10.12.2 interface gigabitethernet 7/1
Round trip time is 424 micro seconds (0.42 milli seconds)
MDS-9513-1#
```

```
MDS-9509-3# ips measure-rtt 110.10.10.2 interface gigabitethernet 1/1
Round trip time is 424 micro seconds (0.42 milli seconds)
MDS-9509-3#
```

Note   FCIP uses TCP port 3225 by default. Since the FCIP tunnel (fcip1) between MDS-9513-1 and switch MDS-9509-2 is already up and using TCP port 3225, this FCIP tunnel (fcip2) needs to use another TCP port. In this configuration TCP port 3500 is used to configure FCIP tunnel fcip2.

Step 12   Configure the FCIP profile on both the switches.

In the FCIP interface configuration, the profile to be used and the peer information (remote gigabit Ethernet ip address) are configured. Additionally, compression and write acceleration can be configured on the FCIP interface.

Best Practice   It is strongly recommend to use the same profile numbers (unique to a tunnel) for the FCIP profiles configured on both switches for a given FCIP tunnel.

Since the gigabit Ethernet interface in MDS-9513-1 is shared between two FCIP tunnels fcip1 and fcip2 the WAN bandwidth needs to be shared between the two tunnels.

In this recipe the WAN bandwidth is assumed to ne 1 gigabit. The bandwidth in this recipe will be split 50:50 between the two FCIP tunnels. Each tunnel will have a max bandwidth of 500 mb/s and a min bandwidth of 400 mb/s.

```
MDS-9513-1# conf t
Enter configuration commands, one per line.  End with CNTL/Z.
MDS-9513-1(config)# fcip profile 2
MDS-9513-1(config-profile)# port 3500 <-- TCP port configuration
MDS-9513-1(config-profile)# ip address 10.10.10.2
MDS-9513-1(config-profile)# tcp max-bandwidth-mbps 500 min-available-bandwidth-mbps 400
round-trip-time-us 425
MDS-9513-1(config-profile)# end
MDS-9513-1#


MDS-9509-3# conf t
Enter configuration commands, one per line.  End with CNTL/Z.
MDS-9509-3(config)# fcip profile 2
MDS-9509-3(config-profile)# port 3500 <-- TCP port configuration
MDS-9509-3(config-profile)# ip address 10.10.12.2
MDS-9509-3(config-profile)# tcp max-bandwidth-mbps 500 min-available-bandwidth-mbps 400
round-trip-time-us 425
MDS-9509-3(config-profile)# end
MDS-9509-3#
```

The FCIP profile 2 is now configured on switches MDS-9513-1 and MDS-9509-3 using TCP port 3500.

Step 13   Configure the FCIP interface on both switches.

In the FCIP interface configuration, the profile to be used and the peer information (remote gigabit Ethernet IP address) are specified. Additionally, compression and write acceleration can be configured on the FCIP interface.

```
MDS-9513-1# conf t
Enter configuration commands, one per line.  End with CNTL/Z.
MDS-9513-1(config)# interface fcip 2
MDS-9513-1(config-if)# peer-info ipaddr 110.10.12.2 port 3500 <-- TCP port Config
MDS-9513-1(config-if)# use-profile 2
MDS-9513-1(config-if)# no shut
MDS-9513-1(config-if)# end
MDS-9513-1#
```

```
MDS-9509-3# conf t
Enter configuration commands, one per line.  End with CNTL/Z.
MDS-9509-3(config)# interface fcip 2
MDS-9509-3(config-if)# peer-info ipaddr 10.10.10.2 port 3500 <-- TCP port Config
MDS-9509-3(config-if)# use-profile 2
MDS-9509-3(config-if)# no shut
MDS-9509-3(config-if)# end
MDS-9509-3#
```

Step 14   The FCIP tunnel fcip 2 should be up and running. Use the **show fcip summary** command to see the status of the FCIP link between the two switches.

```
MDS-9513-1# show fcip summary
```

Tun	prof	Eth-if	peer-ip	Status	T E	W A	T A	Enc	Comp	Bandwidth max/min	rtt (us)
1	1	GE7/1	10.10.11.2	**TRNK**	**Y**	N	N	N	N	**500M/400M**	425
2	2	GE7/1	10.10.12.2	**TRNK**	**Y**	N	N	N	N	**500M/400M**	425

```
MDS-9513-1#

MDS-9509-3# show fcip summary
```

Tun	prof	Eth-if	peer-ip	Status	T E	W A	T A	Enc	Comp	Bandwidth max/min	rtt (us)
2	2	GE1/1	10.10.10.2	**TRNK**	**Y**	N	N	N	N	**500M/400M**	425

```
MDS-9509-3#
```

The above output shows the status of the two tunnels IDs 1 and 2 are trunking on switch MDS-9513-1 and one tunnel with the ID 2 is trunking on switch MDS-9509-3.

Configuring FCIP Using DCNM SAN

Data Center Network Manager (DCNM) SAN (formerly called Cisco Fabric Manager) can also be used to configure FCIP tunnel. The following recipe demonstrates how FCIP is configured using DCNM SAN. For this recipe, the gigabit Ethernet interface 1/1 on MDS-9513-1 and gigabit Ethernet interface 7/1 on MDS-9509-2 are used. The topology used in this recipe is shown in Figure 11-4.

Figure 11-4   FCIP topology for DCNM SAN

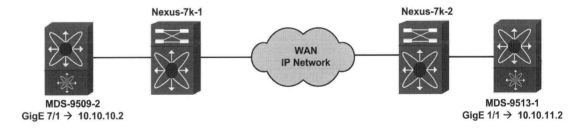

To configure FCIP tunnel between the switches MDS-9509-2 and MDS-9513-1 the required steps are detailed below:

Note   For DCNM SAN FCIP wizard to work, the fabrics that need to be connected using FCIP must be discovered in DCNM SAN prior to using the FCIP wizard.

Step 1   Launch DCNM SAN Client and log on.

Step 2   Select ISLs --> FCIP in the Physical Attributes Pane. This selection is highlighted with a blue rectangle in Figure 11-5. Once FCIP is selected, the right pane is populated with a list of switches seen by DCNM SAN, including the state of the FCIP in each switch.

Step 3   Select the required switch present in the right-hand side pane. In this case, it is MDS-9509-2.

Step 4   Expand the drop-down box in the **command column** and select the **enable** option. This is highlighted using a red rectangle in Figure 11-5.

Figure 11-5   Enable FCIP Through DCNM SAN

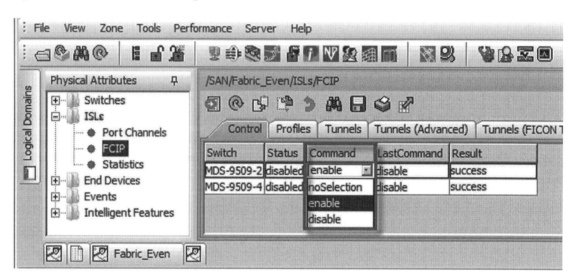

Step 5   Apply the changes to the switch MDS-9509-2 to enable FCIP on it. Click the green **Apply Changes** icon heliolatry in blue (see Figure 11-6) to apply the changes and enable FCIP on the switch MDS-9509-2.

Figure 11-6   Apply Changes to Switches Through DCNM SAN

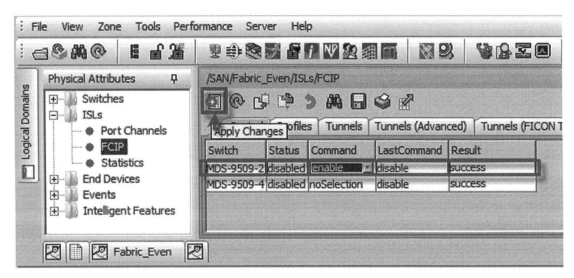

Once the changes are applied, the result of the changes can be seen in the **Last Command** and **Result** column as shown in Figure 11-6.

Figure 11-7   FCIP Enable Results

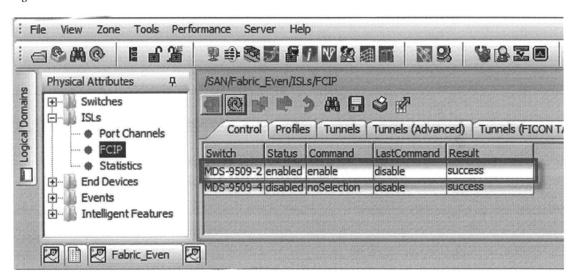

Step 6   Perform steps 1 through 4on switch MDS-9513-1 to enable FCIP on it.

Step 7   Configure IP addresses for the gigabit Ethernet interfaces on switches MDS-9509-2 and MDS-9513-1.

   a. From Physical Attributes pane, expand **Switches**, expand **Ethernet Interfaces** then select **IPS** (see Figure 11-8).

   b. In the **General** tab select the switch MDS-9509-2 and gigabit Ethernet interface 7/1. In the **Status Admin** (highlighted in red) column pull-down menu, change the port state to **up**.(Figure 11-8)

Figure 11-8   *Enabling the gigabit Ethernet Interface 7/1 on Switch MDS-9509-2*

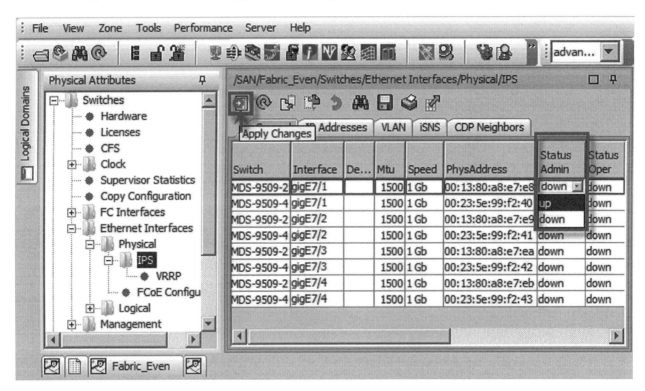

c. Click the green **Apply Changes** button highlighted in blue in Figure 11-8. This enables the interface gigabit Ethernet7/1 on MDS-9509-2.

d. Ensure that the Status Admin and Status Oper columns are both up as seen in Figure 11-9 and is highlighted in red.

Figure 11-9   *gigabit Ethernet Ports Operational on MDS-9509-2*

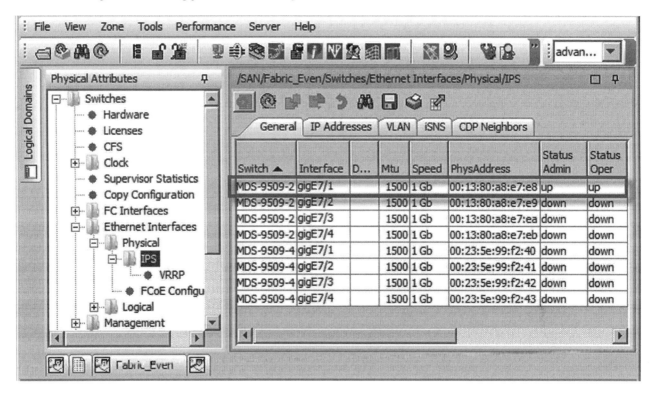

e.   Select the **IP Addresses** tab on the right-hand pane. It is highlighted in blue in Figure 11-9.

f.   Then select the **create row** button highlighted in red in Figure 11-10. This results in a popup dialog box, select the switch MDS-9509-2 and add the interface, that is, gigabit Ethernet port 7/1 and its IP address and net mask. The gigabit Ethernet port 7/1 on MDS-9509-2 in this recipe is assigned an IP address of 10.10.10.2 and a mask of 255.255.255.0 (/24).

Figure 11-10   Assign IP Address to the gigabit Ethernet Ports on MDS-9509-2

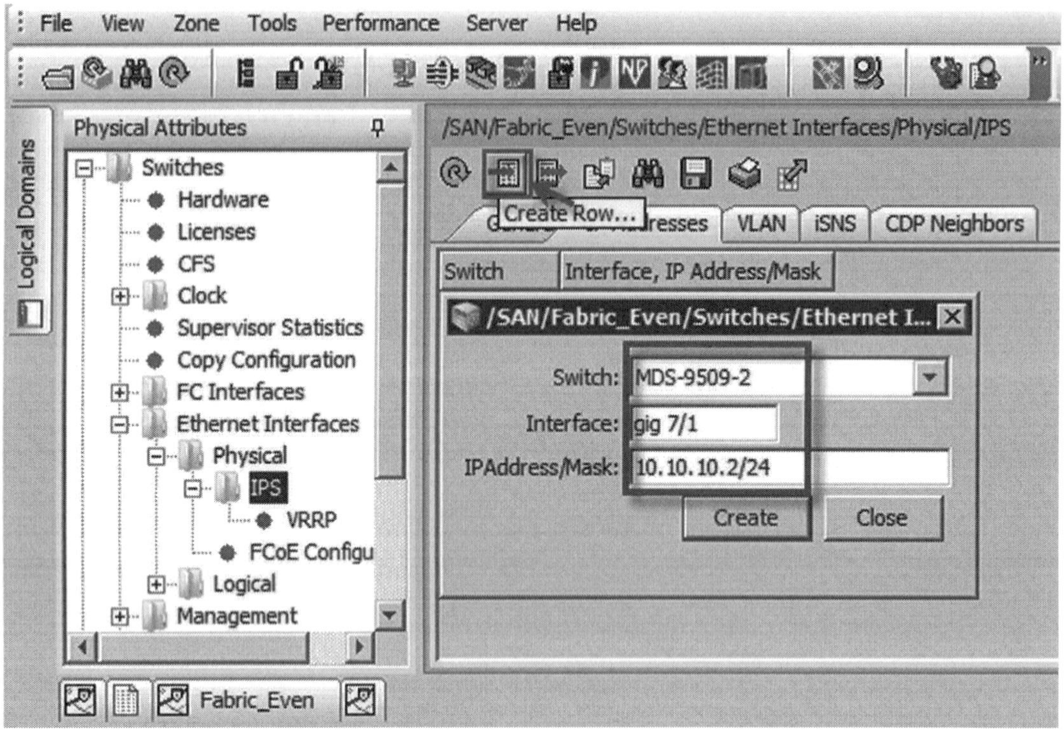

g. Click **create** to assign gigabit Ethernet 7/1 the IP address. After the IP address is assigned to the interface, the IP address is displayed on the right-hand side pane highlighted in blue in Figure 11-11.

Caution   The IP address for the ports on the MSM 18+4 / SNN-16 modules must be in a different subnet than the management interface. This is critical for FCIP to work on a switch.

Figure 11-11   *Assigned IP Address for the Interface gigabit Ethernet1/1 on MDS-9509-2*

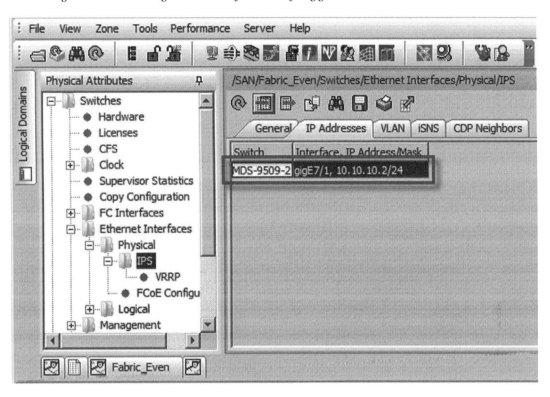

Figure 11-11   *Assigned IP Address for the Interface gigabit Ethernet1/1 on MDS-9509-2*

Step 8   Repeat step 6 on the switch MDS-9513-1, which is the other switch involved in the FCIP configuration. This process enables gigabit Ethernet 1/1 and assigns it the IP address 10.10.11.2 and net mask of 255.255.255.0 (/24). The end results are shown in Figure 11-12 and Figure 11-13.

Figure 11-12   *Gigabit Ethernet Ports Operational on MDS-9513-1*

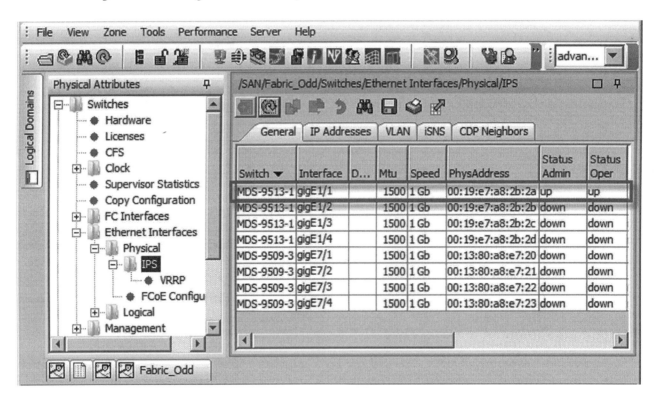

The Status Admin and the Status Oper of interface gigabit Ethernet 1/1 on switch MDS-9513-1 should both be up. Figure 11-12 shows the status of the gigabit Ethernet port 1/1 and is indicated in a red box.

Figure 11-13 Shows the ipaddress assigned to the interface. In this recipe gigabit Ethernet 1/1 in switch MDS-9513-1 is assigned an ip address 10.10.11.2 with a subnet mask of 255.255.255.0 (/24) It is indicated by a red box.

Figure 11-13   Assigned IP Address for the Interface gigabit Ethernet1/1 on MDS-Switch-3

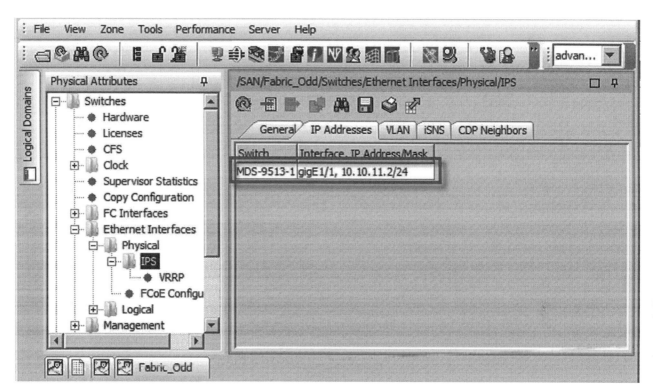

Best Practice   It is recommended to create a host route to each of the two gigabit Ethernet interfaces with a subnet mask of 255.255.255.255. This allows only the two gigabit Ethernet interfaces to communicate.

Step 9   Create the FCIP tunnel between the two gigabit Ethernet interfaces. Select the **FCIP Tunnel** icon highlighted in red in Figure 11-14. This then launches the FCIP wizard which can be used to configure the FCIP tunnel between MDS-9509-2 and MDS-9513-1.

Best Practice   The wizard is ideal for configuring point-to-point FCIP tunnels, but we recommend using the CLI to configure complex multi-way tunnels.

Figure 11-14   *Starting FCIP Tunnel Wizard in DCNM SAN*

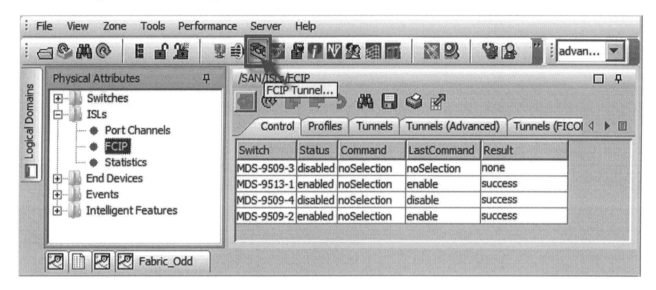

The FCIP Tunnel Wizard launches as shown in Figure 11-15.

a.   In the wizard, enter the two switches between which the FCIP tunnel needs to be configured. In this recipe, the tunnel is between MDS-9509-2 and MDS-9513-1. Select the **Next** button.

Figure 11-15   *. FCIP Configuration Wizard*

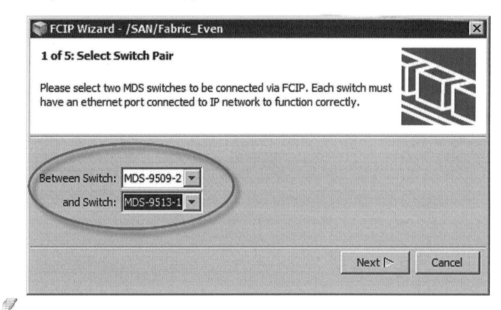

Note   If DNS is configured for the MDS switches, the DNS names of the switches can be used. If DNS is not configured, then logical switch name or IP addresses will be used instead.

b.   In the next screen, select the gigabit Ethernet interfaces that have been configured. It is gigabit Ethernet 7/1 on MDS-9509-2 and gigabit Ethernet 1/1 on MDS-9513-1. (See Figure 11-16)

Figure 11-16   Configured and Available gigabit Ethernet Ports

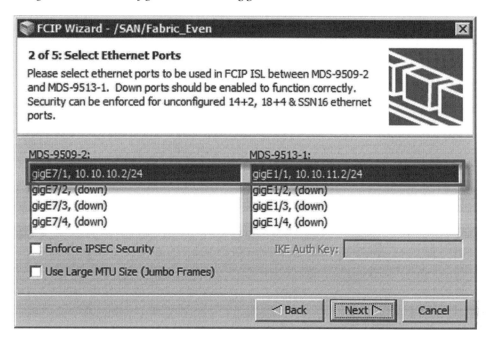

c. To protect the FCIP tunnel using IPSec, check the **Enforce IPSEC Security** check box. This is shown in Figure 11-17.

Figure 11-17   Configuration of IPsec for the FCIP Tunnel

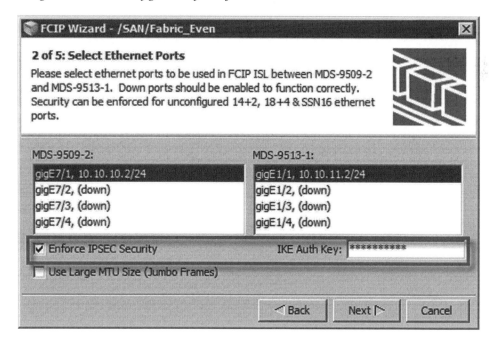

d. The IPsec configuration requires an Internet Key Exchange (IKE) authentication key. Input an IKE authentication key (a pass phrase or key) as shown in Figure 11-17.

Best Practice   For the IKE authentication key, it is recommended to use a strong key or pass phrase. The length should at least be 8 characters or longer with a combination of case, numbers.

e.   Click **Next**. This will bring up the route configuration required to make the gigabit Ethernet interfaces on the switches MDS-9509-2 and MDS-9513-1 communicated with each other to create a FCIP tunnel.

This route configuration can be done in this wizard for both switches or individually on each switches CLI prompt. Both methods are explained below. The Figure 11-18 shows the filed that need to be populated to configure routing.

Figure 11-18   Configure Routing on both switches

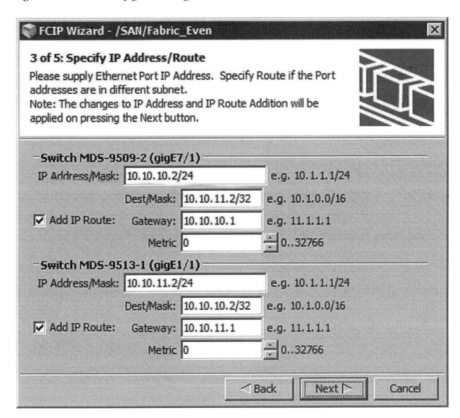

The route needs to be configured for both the switches. In Figure 11-18 the route configuration on switch MDS-9509-2, for interface gigabit Ethernet 7/1 has the destination ip address as 10.10.11.2 with a subnet mask of 255.255.255.255 (/32) as seen above. The default gateway is 10.10.10.1.

Similarly on switch MDS-9513-1, for interface gigabit Ethernet 1/1 has the destination ip address as 10.10.10.2 with a subnet mask of 255.255.255.255 (/32) as seen above. The default gateway is 10.10.11.1.

Best Practice   When configuring the FCIP required routes, the destination ip address requested is the ip address of the gigabit Ethernet interface on the remote FCIP peer switch.

The route can also be configured from CLI. The CLI commands to configure the same are shown below.

For the gigabit Ethernet port 7/1 on the switch MDS-9509-2 to communicate with the port gigabit Ethernet 1/1 on switch MDS-9513-1 using gigabit Ethernet 7/1, the following route configuration must be done on switch MDS-9509-2.

```
MDS-9509-2# conf t
Enter configuration commands, one per line.  End with CNTL/Z.
MDS-9509-2(config)# ip route 10.10.11.2 255.255.255.255 10.10.10.1 interface
gigabitethernet 7/1
MDS-9509-2(config)# end
MDS-9509-2#
```

The above configuration provides the following information: To reach 110.10.11.2, use the gateway 10.10.10.1 and use interface gigabit Ethernet 7/1 on switch MDS-9509-2.

Similarly, for the gigabit Ethernet port 1/1 on switch MDS-9513-1 to communicate with gigabit Ethernet port 7/1 on switch MDS-9509-2 using gigabit Ethernet 1/1, the following route configuration must be done on switch MDS-9513-1.

```
MDS-9513-1# conf t
Enter configuration commands, one per line.  End with CNTL/Z.
MDS-9513-1(config)# ip route 10.10.10.2 255.255.255.255 10.10.11.1 interface
gigabitethernet 1/1
MDS-9513-1(config)# end
MDS-9513-1#
```

The preceding configuration provides the following information: To reach 10.10.10.2, use the gateway 10.10.11.1 and interface gigabit Ethernet 1/1 on switch MDS-9513-1.

Step 10   Ping the gigabit Ethernet interfaces to ensure that the gigabit Ethernet ports can communicate.

From the switch MDS-9509-2, ping the IP address of the gigabit Ethernet interface 1/1 on switch MDS-9513-1. Similarly, ping the IP address of the gigabit Ethernet interface 7/1 on switch MDS-9509-2 from switch MDS-9513-1. This can be done from the switch prompt.

```
MDS-9509-2# ping 10.10.11.2 interface gigabitethernet 7/1
PING 10.10.11.2 (10.10.11.2) from 10.10.10.2 gige7-1: 56(84) bytes of data.
64 bytes from 10.10.11.2: icmp_seq=1 ttl=254 time=0.627 ms
64 bytes from 10.10.11.2: icmp_seq=2 ttl=254 time=0.609 ms
64 bytes from 10.10.11.2: icmp_seq=3 ttl=254 time=0.595 ms
64 bytes from 10.10.11.2: icmp_seq=4 ttl=254 time=0.650 ms

--- 10.10.11.2 ping statistics ---
4 packets transmitted, 4 received, 0% packet loss, time 3001ms
rtt min/avg/max/mdev = 0.595/0.620/0.650/0.027 ms
MDS-9509-2#

MDS-9513-1# ping 10.10.10.2 interface gigabitethernet 1/1
PING 10.10.10.2 (10.10.10.2) from 10.10.11.2 gige1-1: 56(84) bytes of data.
64 bytes from 10.10.10.2: icmp_seq=1 ttl=254 time=0.636 ms
64 bytes from 10.10.10.2: icmp_seq=2 ttl=254 time=0.575 ms
64 bytes from 10.10.10.2: icmp_seq=3 ttl=254 time=0.603 ms
64 bytes from 10.10.10.2: icmp_seq=4 ttl=254 time=0.620 ms

--- 10.10.10.2 ping statistics ---
4 packets transmitted, 4 received, 0% packet loss, time 3003ms
rtt min/avg/max/mdev = 0.575/0.608/0.636/0.033 ms
MDS-9513-1#
```

f. Click **Next**. This will apply the routes on both the switches. This also brings up the FCIP tunnel properties and the round trip time (rtt) measurement utility seen in Figure 11-19.

g. As shown in Figure 11-19 the FCIP tunnel properties are specified. These properties include maximum and minimum bandwidth for the tunnel, estimated RTT, write acceleration and compression. The maximum bandwidth, minimum bandwidth and the round trip time values are mandatory, the last two mentioned, compression and write acceleration are optional.

Figure 11-19   Define Tunnel Properties

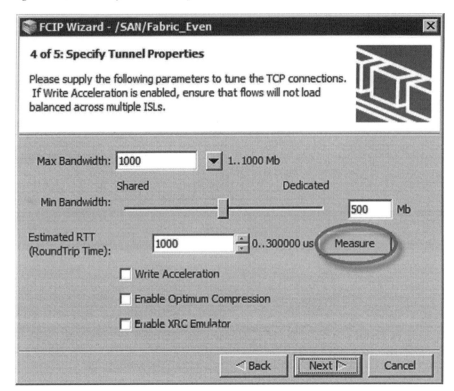

h. Set the maximum bandwidth for the link (see Figure 11-19). Max Bandwidth is the maximum value the FCIP tunnel is allowed to use. If the IP link is dedicated for FCIP, then set Max Bandwidth to maximum available bandwidth of the IP link. For this recipe the maximum bandwidth is set to 1000-Mb/s (1-Gb/s).

i. The minimum bandwidth value is based on whether the link is shared or dedicated to FCIP. If the IP link is shared by multiple applications, then it is recommend that the this value is set to a reasonably low value, say half of the maximum bandwidth value.

j. Click **Measure** to estimate the RTT circled in red.(see Figure 11-19). The RTT displayed in microseconds should be entered into the estimated RTT dialog box in the **Specify Tunnel** properties screen. In this topology, the RTT measured was 88 microseconds (see Figure 11-20).

k. In this recipe compression and write acceleration features are required. To turn on these features check the write Acceleration and compression options as shown in Figure 11-19.

Best Practice If multiple tunnels are setup for the same physical gigabit Ethernet interface on a switch, ensure that the total bandwidth for all the tunnels configured on that interface is not greater than the total bandwidth available or equal to 1000Mb which ever is smaller.

Note Cisco SAN-OS Release 2.1.x and higher strictly enforce bandwidth set by the maximum bandwidth property. Traffic shaper enforces the bandwidth allocated strictly.

Figure 11-20   Measure RTT output screen.

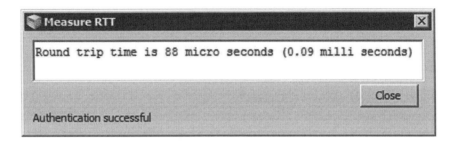

l.   Turn on write acceleration and compression by checking the corresponding check boxes. This is shown in Figure 11-21 highlighted in red. The discovered estimated RTT that was 88 microseconds ia entered into the "Estimated RTT" field as shown in Figure 11-21 highlighted in green.

Figure 11-21   FCIP Tunnel Properties Configuration wizard

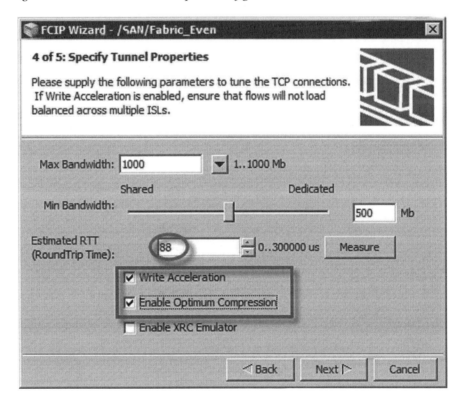

m.   Click **Next**. This will bring up the create FCIP ISL dialog box shown in Figure 11-22.

Figure 11-22   Create FCIP ISL

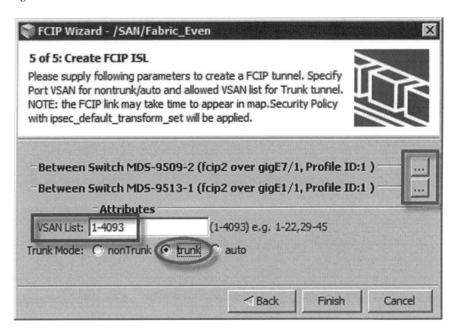

Step 11 Verify the switches and the interfaces being connected.

Step 12 Select the buttons for each switch interface, highlighted in red to configure the profile ID for the FCIP tunnel.

Best Practice It is recommended that the tunnel id be same on both sides of the FCIP interface. This makes trouble shooting a lot simpler if need arises. The tunnel id is set to 2 in this recipe as seen in Figure 11-23 and Figure 11-24 below.

Figure 11-23   FCIP Tunnel ID Config for MDS-9509-2

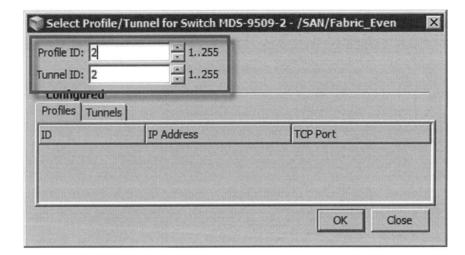

Figure 11-24   FCIP Tunnel ID config for MDS-9513-1

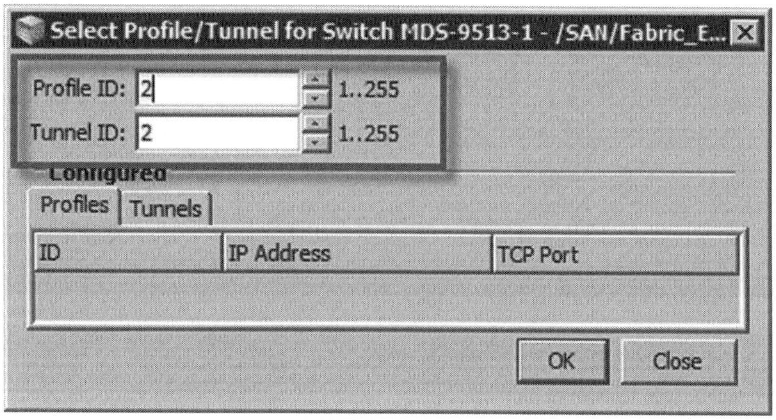

Step 13   Select trunk to turn on trunk mode (see green circle in Figure 11-22). This mode allows multiple VSANs through the link.

Step 14   In this screen, the VSANs allowed through the FCIP link can be changed in the VSAN list dialog box. In the recipe, all VSANs (1 - 4093) are allowed through the FCIP tunnel. This is highlighted in blue in Figure 11-22.

Step 15   If IPSec is configured, the **Finish** button brings up the prompt to enable IPsec on switches MDS 9509-2 and MDS-9513-1 if it is not already enabled on the switches. Select **Yes** to complete the tunnel creation (see Figure 11-25).

Figure 11-25   IPSCE Enable Prompt on the Switches

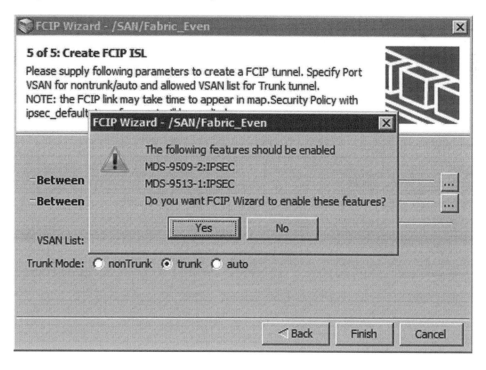

Step 16   Check the tunnel status by selecting the ISL from the Physical Attributes on the left-hand pane. Then check for the FCIP status on the right-hand side pane (see Figure 11-26). The tunnel status is highlighted in red.

Figure 11-26   FCIP ISL Status

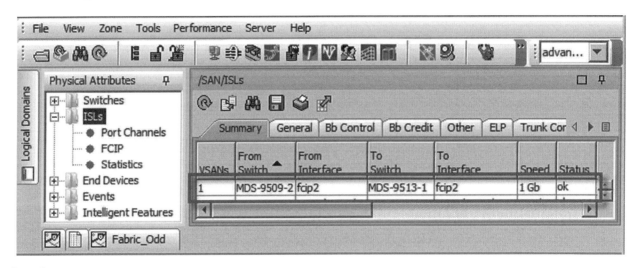

Best Practice

The default compression mode select by the wizard is the Auto.

Step 17   From the properties of the FCIP tunnel, select **ISL** --> **FCIP** --> **Tunnels (Advanced)** as shown in Figure 11-27.

Figure 11-27   FCIP Tunnel with IPSec, Write Acceleration and Compression enabled

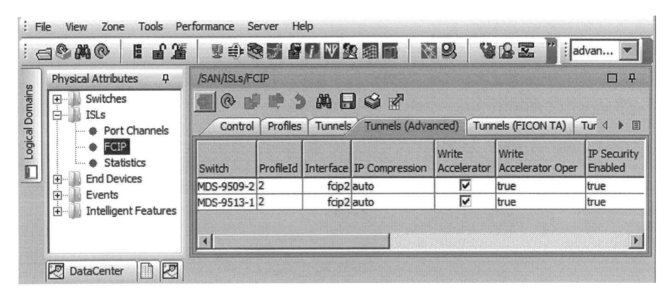

Tunnel creation is complete. The FCIP link secured by IPSec is configured and up.

Enabling Tape Acceleration using DCNM SAN

To enable tape acceleration from DCNM SAN, follow these steps:

Step 1 From the Physical Attributes pane, expand ISLs and select FCIP (see Figure 11-28).

Step 2 In the right pane, choose the **Tunnels** (**Advanced**) tab.

Step 3 Check the **Tape Accelerator** check boxes on both switches (see the blue box in Figure 11-28).

Step 4 Click the green **Apply Changes** icon to apply the config to the switches (see the red box in Figure 11-28).

Figure 11-28   Activating Tape Acceleration in DCNM SAN

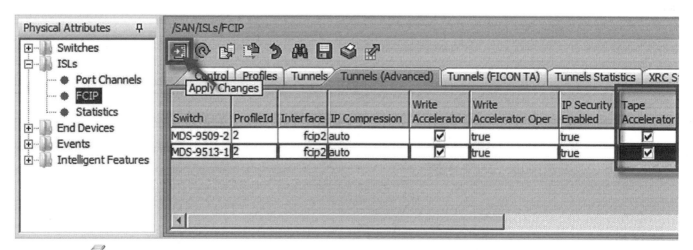

Note For Tape Acceleration to work, write acceleration on the FCIP tunnel must be enabled. Also, tape acceleration will not function if multiple, equal cost paths or a port-channel exists between the two switches.

Figure 11-29   Tape Acceleration Enable status

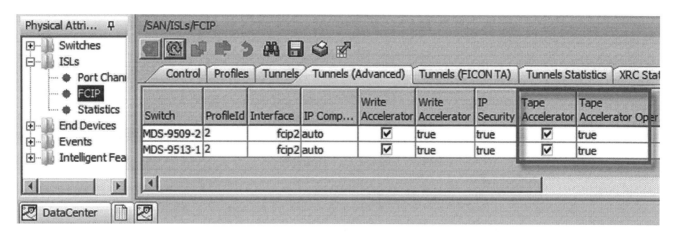

Step 5   From the properties of the FCIP tunnel select **ISL** --> **FCIP** --> **Tunnels (Advanced)** as shown in Figure 11-29. The Tape Accelerator is true for the fcip2 tunnel, is highlighted in Figure 11-29 using a red box.

Testing and Tuning the FCIP Link with SET

SAN Extension Tuner (SET) is used to test and tune the performance for the FCIP link. SET generates SCSI I/O commands and directs them to virtual targets. SET allows for variation of the I/O type (read/writes) transfer size and the number of concurrent I/Os generated.

SET lets the user determine I/Os and throughput (MB) per second, as well as I/O latency. This helps in the fine tuning of FCIP throughput. The data generated can be used to validate characteristics of the WAN circuit, as well as determining the potential throughput of the FCIP tunnel without involving a host or disk subsystem.

SET is used to create consistent traffic flows, and enable such features as write acceleration, tape acceleration, compression, and encryption to determine their effect on the throughput of the tunnel. Also, SET is used to tune modifications to the FCIP tunnel's round trip time, and view maximum and minimum bandwidth.

SET can also be used to model an array to see if the array is performing up to specifications (number of outstanding I/Os and the size of transfers).

Best Practice   SET requires the **SAN_EXTN_OVER_IP** license to work.

SET also requires the following resources:

- Two IPS modules.
- An FCIP link between the switches.
- One unused gigabit Ethernet port per switch to act as a initiator or target.
- The physical layer of the second gigabit Ethernet port should be up.
- iSCSI enabled on both the switches.
- SAN-EXT-TUNER enabled.

SET works by creating virtual initiators and targets behind two gigabit Ethernet ports. These virtual devices are created in a VSAN, they have port world-wide names (pWWNs), and they obtain FC IDs just like real end devices do. They are required to be zoned together to communicate, and they send standard Fibre Channel Protocol commands to each other which are handled by the Fibre Channel infrastructure as is normal Fibre Channel traffic. The frames are routed via FSPF to their destinations and can travel on E and TE ports through MDS and non MDS switches. If the minimum requirements are met, SET can be used to test optical networks not just FCIP links.

While the same gigabit Ethernet port that is configured for FCIP can be used as a target or initiator, we do not recommend it because this may interfere with the ability to generate sufficient bandwidth. Always use an unused gigabit Ethernet port for the initiator and target.

Note   This SET recipe assumes that the FCIP link is already up and functional. For directions, see Configuring FCIP with the CLI, page 11-2

For this recipe, the following resources are used:

- Switch: MDS-9509-2:

    Additional gigabit Ethernet port: gigE7/1

    VSAN 1000

    Virtual nWWN: 10:00:00:00:00:00:00:00

    Virtual pWWN: 20:00:00:00:00:00:00:01

- Switch: MDS-9513-1

    Additional gigabit Ethernet port: gigE1/1:

    VSAN 1000

    Virtual nWWN 11:00:00:00:00:00:00:00

    Virtual pWWN: 30:00:00:00:00:00:00:01

To tune a link, follow these steps:

Step 1   Enable the second gigabit Ethernet port on both the switches. In this recipe Gigabit ethernet port 7/2 in MDS09509-2 and Gigabit ethernet port 1/2 on MDS -9513-1 is used for SET.

Best Practice   This additional gigabit Ethernet port does not require an IP address to be assigned. Only the physical layer is required to be up.

```
MDS-9509-2# conf t
Enter configuration commands, one per line.  End with CNTL/Z.
MDS-9509-2(config-if)# interface gigabitethernet 7/2
MDS-9509-2(config-if)# no shut
MDS-9509-2(config-if)# end
MDS-9509-2#

MDS-9509-3# conf t
Enter configuration commands, one per line.  End with CNTL/Z.
MDS-9513-1(config-if)# interface gigabitethernet 1/2
MDS-9513-1(config-if)# no shut
MDS-9513-1(config-if)# end
MDS-9513-1#
```

Check to ensure that the physical layer of the gigabit Ethernet port is up and running.

```
MDS-9509-2# show interface gigabitethernet 7/2 brief
--------------------------------------------------------------------------------
Interface          Status    IP Address     Speed    MTU    Port
                                                            Channel
--------------------------------------------------------------------------------
GigabitEthernet7/2     up        --             1 Gbps   1500   --

MDS-9513-1# show interface gigabitethernet 1/2 brief
--------------------------------------------------------------------------------
Interface          Status    IP Address     Speed    MTU    Port
                                                            Channel
--------------------------------------------------------------------------------
GigabitEthernet1/2     up        --             1 Gbps   1500   --
```

Step 2   Enable iSCSI on both the switches MDS-9509-2 and MDS-9513-1 if it is not already enabled.

```
MDS-9509-2# conf t
Enter configuration commands, one per line.  End with CNTL/Z.
MDS-9509-2(config)# feature iscsi
MDS-9509-2(config)# enable iscsi module 7
MDS-9509-2(config)# end
MDS-9509-2#

MDS-9513-1# conf t
Enter configuration commands, one per line.  End with CNTL/Z.
MDS-9513-1(config)# feature iscsi
MDS-9513-1(config)# iscsi enable module 1
MDS-9513-1(config)# end
MDS-9513-1#
```

Step 3   Enable the iSCSI on the second gigabit Ethernet interface of both switches.

```
MDS-9509-2# conf t
Enter configuration commands, one per line.  End with CNTL/Z.
MDS-9509-2(config)# interface iscsi 7/2
MDS-9509-2(config-if)# no shut
MDS-9509-2(config-if)# end
MDS-9509-2#

MDS-9513-1# conf t
Enter configuration commands, one per line.  End with CNTL/Z.
MDS-9513-1(config)# interface iscsi 1/2
MDS-9513-1(config-if)# no shut
MDS-9513-1(config-if)# end
MDS-9513-1#
```

Verify that the iSCSI interface is up and running.
```
MDS-9509-2# sh interface iscsi 7/2 brief
-----------------------------------------------------------------------------
Interface        Status        Oper Mode        Oper Speed
                                                (Gbps)
-----------------------------------------------------------------------------
iscsi7/2         up            ISCSI            1
MDS-9509-2#

MDS-9513-1# sh interface iscsi 1/2 brief
-----------------------------------------------------------------------------
Interface        Status        Oper Mode        Oper Speed
                                                (Gbps)
-----------------------------------------------------------------------------
iscsi1/2         up            ISCSI            1
MDS-9513-1#
```

Step 4   Enable SET on both switches.

```
MDS-9509-2# conf t
Enter configuration commands, one per line.  End with CNTL/Z.
MDS-9509-2(config)# feature san-ext-tuner
MDS-9509-2(config)# end
MDS-9509-2#

MDS-9513-1# conf t
Enter configuration commands, one per line.  End with CNTL/Z.
MDS-9513-1(config)# feature san-ext-tuner
MDS-9513-1(config)# end
MDS-9513-1#
```

Best Practice   Using a **separate VSAN** for SET ensures that devices in other VSANs are not impacted by the SET traffic.

Step 5   Create a separate VSAN for SET N ports.

```
MDS-9509-2# conf t
Enter configuration commands, one per line.  End with CNTL/Z.
MDS-9509-2(config)# vsan database
MDS-9509-2(config-vsan-db)# vsan 1000 name SETVSAN
MDS-9509-2(config-vsan-db)# end
MDS-9509-2#

MDS-9513-1# conf t
Enter configuration commands, one per line.  End with CNTL/Z.
MDS-9513-1(config)# vsan database
MDS-9513-1(config-vsan-db)# vsan 1000 name SETVSAN
MDS-9513-1(config-vsan-db)# end
MDS-9513-1#
```

Step 6   Configure nWWN and N port on both switches.

The N port pWWN on switch MDS-9509-2 is configured as 20:00:00:00:00:00:00:01with a nWWN of 10:00:00:00:00:00:00:00. Similarly, on switch MDS-9513-1, the N port pWWN is configured as 30:00:00:00:00:00:00:01 and nWWN of 11:00:00:00:00:00:00:00. Both the N ports are made a part of VSAN 1000 which is created just for SET.

```
MDS-9509-2# san-ext-tuner
MDS-9509-2(san-ext)# nwwN 10:00:00:00:00:00:00:00
MDS-9509-2(san-ext)# nport pWWN 20:00:00:00:00:00:00:01 vsan 1000 interface
gigabitethernet 7/2
MDS-9509-2(san-ext-nport)#end
MDS-9509-2#

MDS-9513-1# san-ext-tuner
MDS-9513-1(san-ext)# nwwN 11:00:00:00:00:00:00:00
MDS-9513-1(san-ext)# nport pWWN 30:00:00:00:00:00:00:01 vsan 1000 interface
gigabitethernet 1/2
MDS-9513-1(san-ext-nport)#end
MDS-9513-1#
```

Verify that the created VSAN has logged on to the fabric.

```
MDS-9509-2# sh flogi database
-------------------------------------------------------------------------------
INTERFACE   VSAN    FCID        PORT NAME               NODE NAME
-------------------------------------------------------------------------------
iscsi7/2    1000    0x410002    20:00:00:00:00:00:00:01  11:00:00:00:00:00:00:00
Total number of flogi = 1.
MDS-9509-2#

MDS-9513-1# sh flogi database v 1000
-------------------------------------------------------------------------------
INTERFACE   VSAN    FCID        PORT NAME               NODE NAME
-------------------------------------------------------------------------------
iscsi1/2    1000    0x0c0003    30:00:00:00:00:00:00:01  11:00:00:00:00:00:00:00
Total number of flogi = 1.
MDS-9513-1#
```

Step 7   The **show fcns database vsan 1000** command should display both the pWWNs in VSAN 1000.

```
MDS-9509-2# show fcns database vsan 1000
VSAN 1000:
--------------------------------------------------------------------------
FCID         TYPE  PWWN                     (VENDOR)      FC4-TYPE:FEATURE
--------------------------------------------------------------------------
0x0c0003     N     30:00:00:00:00:00:00:01                scsi-fcp
0x410002     N     20:00:00:00:00:00:00:01                scsi-fcp
Total number of entries = 2
MDS-9509-2#
```

```
MDS-9513-1# show fcns database vsan 1000
VSAN 1000:
--------------------------------------------------------------------------
FCID         TYPE  PWWN                     (VENDOR)      FC4-TYPE:FEATURE
--------------------------------------------------------------------------
0x0c0003     N     30:00:00:00:00:00:00:01                scsi-fcp
0x410002     N     20:00:00:00:00:00:00:01                scsi-fcp
Total number of entries = 2
MDS-9513-1#
```

Step 8   Create a zone set and a zone in VSAN 1000 so the SET N ports can communicate. Zone these devices from DCNM SAN with the CLI as shown.

```
MDS-9509-2# conf t
Enter configuration commands, one per line.  End with CNTL/Z.
MDS-9509-2(config)# zoneset name ZS_santune_vsan1000 vsan 1000
MDS-9509-2(config-zoneset)# zone name Z_SET_VSAN100
MDS-9509-2(config-zoneset-zone)# member pwwn 20:00:00:00:00:00:00:01
MDS-9509-2(config-zoneset-zone)# member pwwn 30:00:00:00:00:00:00:01
MDS-9509-2(config-zoneset-zone)# exit
MDS-9509-2(config-zoneset)# exit
```

Step 9   Activate the zone set. If enhanced zoning is enabled for this VSAN, then commit the zone changes.

```
MDS-9509-2(config)# zoneset activate name ZS_santune_vsan1000 vsan 1000
Zoneset activation initiated. check zone status
MDS-9509-2(config)# end
MDS-9509-2#
```

Step 10   Verify that the zone set is active and the two N ports are able to communicate.

```
MDS-9509-2# show zoneset active vsan 1000
zoneset name santune vsan 1000
  zone name Z_SET_VSAN100 vsan 1000
  * fcid 0x410002 [pwwn 20:00:00:00:00:00:00:01]
  * fcid 0x0c0003 [pwwn 30:00:00:00:00:00:00:01]
MDS-9509-2#
```

Step 11   Create tasks that either read or write from one N port to another. Two tasks, one to read and one to write, are created as examples. In the examples, the N port on switch MDS-9509-2 acts as initiator and the N port on switch MDS-9513-1 acts as a target.

Note   By default, an all-zero pattern is used as the pattern for data generated by the virtual N ports. Optionally specify a file as the data pattern to be generated by selecting a data pattern file.

```
MDS-9509-2# san-ext-tuner
MDS-9509-2(san-ext)# nport pWWN 20:00:00:00:00:00:00:01 vsan 1000 interface
gigabitethernet 7/2
MDS-9509-2(san-ext-nport)# read command-id 1 target 30:00:00:00:00:00:00:01 transfer-size
1024000 outstanding-ios 5 continuous <-- read command
MDS-9509-2(san-ext-nport)# write  command-id 2 target 30:00:00:00:00:00:00:01
transfer-size 1024000 outstanding-ios 5 continuous <-- write command
MDS-9509-2(san-ext-nport)#
```

Best Practice   The **transfer size should be a multiple of 512.** The test can be continuous or can be limited to a certain number of transactions.

Step 12   Gather throughput and performance data on the switch.

```
MDS-9509-2# show san-ext-tuner interface gigabitethernet 7/2 nport pWWN
20:00:00:00:00:00:00:01 vsan 1000 counters
Statistics for nport
Node name 10:00:00:00:00:00:00:00 Port name 20:00:00:00:00:00:00:01
        I/Os per sec              :  18
            Reads                 :  50%
            Writes                :  50%
        Egress throughput         :  9.06 MBs/sec (Max - 9.12 MBs/sec)
        Ingress throughput        :  8.62 MBs/sec (Max - 10.45 MBs/sec)
        Average response time     :  Read - 572450 us, Write - 568564 us
        Minimum response time     :  Read - 343728 us, Write - 331788 us
        Maximum response time     :  Read - 1350666 us, Write - 990794 us
        Errors                    :  0
MDS-9509-2
```

```
MDS-9513-1# show san-ext-tuner interface gigabitethernet 1/2 nport pWWN
30:00:00:00:00:00:00:01 vsan 1000 counters
Statistics for nport
Node name 11:00:00:00:00:00:00:00 Port name 30:00:00:00:00:00:00:01
        I/Os per sec              :  17
            Reads                 :  58%
            Writes                :  41%
        Egress throughput         :  8.84 MBs/sec (Max - 10.47 MBs/sec)
        Ingress throughput        :  9.02 MBs/sec (Max - 9.42 MBs/sec)
        Average response time     :  Read - 447611 us, Write - 424872 us
        Minimum response time     :  Read - 36986 us, Write - 124183 us
        Maximum response time     :  Read - 1165843 us, Write - 1386055 us
        Errors                    :  0
MDS-9513-1#
```

Collecting the data over the specific period of time will help calibrate the link and further tune the link for optimal throughput and performance.

Step 13   Stop the data gathering tests.

```
MDS-9509-2(san-ext-nport)# stop command-id 1
MDS-9509-2(san-ext-nport)# stop command-id 2
MDS-9509-2(san-ext-nport)#end
MDS-9509-2#
```

IO Acceleration

IO Acceleration (IOA) provides a clustered, highly available and transport agnostic method of providing write acceleration to end devices. It has the advantage over FCIP with Write Acceleration in that it does not require FCIP tunnels to be created, as is the case with native Fibre Channel over optical networks or in those cases where the requirement for multiple tape drives to be accelerated exists.

It is supported on both the multi protocol Services Module and the Storage Services Node. When IOA is being deployed on these line cards, the engine to be configured is dedicated to IOA and cannot run other applications at the same time. However, in the case of the Storage Services Node, the other engines on the line card can be configured for other applications.

Prior to configuring IOA the following conditions should be met and verified:

- IOA licenses should be installed on all switches that will have IOA configured on them with a count equal to the number of engines to be used.
- WAN links should be tested and verified
- FCIP tunnels should already be created
- Port-Channels should already be created
- Zones should already be created for the end devices to be accelerated
- IO between hosts and storage should be tested to validate that the above configurations are working. The throughput will be slow, but this will provide a baseline to judge the IOA performance increase.

For this example the following topology is used:

Figure 11-30   IOA Topology

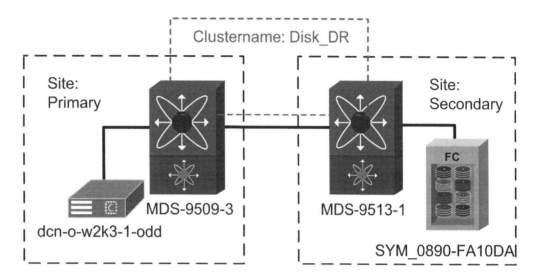

To configure IOA perform the following steps which uses both the CLI and DCNM:

Step 1   On both switches enable the **cluster** and **IOA** features via the command line.

```
MDS-9513-1# conf t
Enter configuration commands, one per line.  End with CNTL/Z.
MDS-9513-1(config)# feature cluster
MDS-9513-1(config)# feature ioa

MDS-9509-3# conf t
Enter configuration commands, one per line.  End with CNTL/Z.
MDS-9509-3(config)# feature cluster
MDS-9509-3(config)# feature ioa
```

Step 2   On both switches, create the IOA interfaces via the command line.

```
MDS-9509-3# conf t
Enter configuration commands, one per line.  End with CNTL/Z.
MDS-9509-3(config)# int ioa 7/1
MDS-9509-3(config-if)# no shut
MDS-9509-3(config-if)#

MDS-9513-1# conf t
Enter configuration commands, one per line.  End with CNTL/Z.
MDS-9513-1(config)# int ioa 1/1
MDS-9513-1(config-if)# no shut
MDS-9513-1(config-if)#
```

Step 3   Assign each MDS to a site

```
MDS-9509-3(config)# ioa site-local primary

MDS-9513-1(config)# ioa site-local secondary
```

Step 4   Switch over to DCNM, and select the **Tools** pull down menu.

Step 5 Select **I/O Acceleration** to launch to IOA Manager and the two sites are displayed.

Figure 11-31   IOA Manager

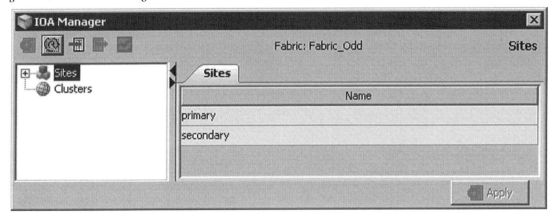

Step 6 Click on **Clusters**.

Step 7 Click on the blue arrow button to **Add** a cluster.

Step 8 Provide a cluster name.

Step 9 Specify where the cluster should be stored. The name of the site will be listed next to the switch name. A popup will inform you that the cluster is being created. See Figure 11-32

Figure 11-32   IOA Cluster Created

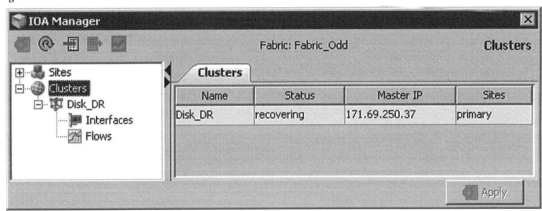

Step 10 Expand the site name.

Step 11 Select **Interfaces**. See Figure 11-33

Figure 11-33   IOA Add Interfaces

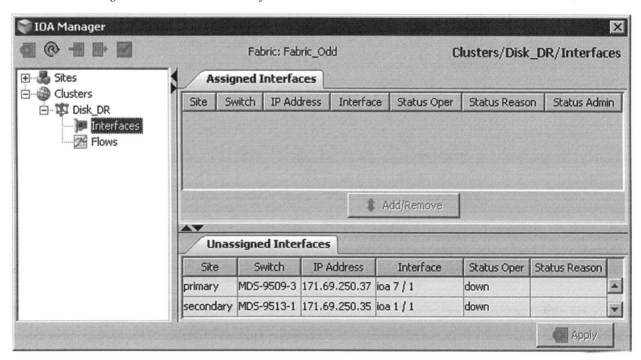

Step 12   Select the two Interfaces and click **Add/Remove**, to move them into the Assigned Interfaces pane.

Step 13   Click **Apply**. If IOA is running on a Grace Period license, a popup message providing this information will appear. See Figure 11-34.

Figure 11-34   IOA Add Interfaces Complete

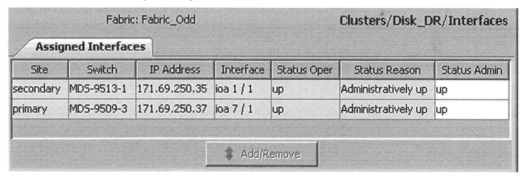

Step 14   In the left hand pane, select **Flows.**

Step 15   In the **Unassigned Flows** pane, select the flow(s) to be accelerated.

Step 16   Click the Add/Remove button to add them to the **Assigned Flows** pane.

Step 17   In the resulting pop-up dialog, click **Add Flow.**

Best Practice   It is recommended to perform compression as part of an FCIP tunnel and not as part of the IOA flow as the FCIP based compression can compress the entire Fibre Channel frame.

Step 18   Enter a **Flow Group name**. A flow group is a grouping of flows with common attributes (Write Acceleration, Tape Acceleration or Compression).

Step 19   Click **Apply**. See Figure 11-35

Figure 11-35   *IOA Flow Creation Complete*

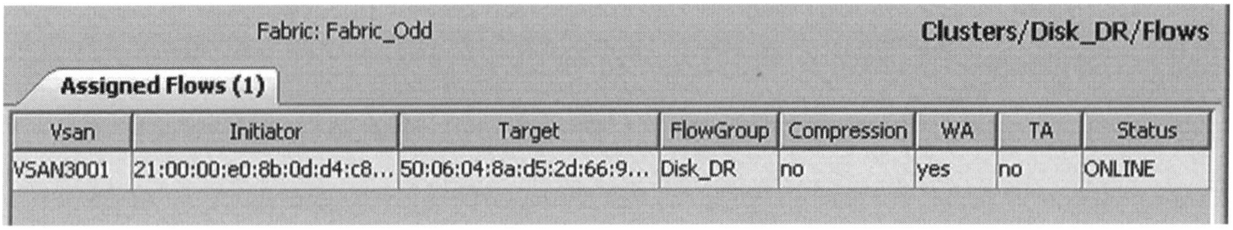

Fabric: Fabric_Odd						Clusters/Disk_DR/Flows		
Assigned Flows (1)								
Vsan	Initiator	Target	FlowGroup	Compression	WA	TA	Status	
VSAN3001	21:00:00:e0:8b:0d:d4:c8...	50:06:04:8a:d5:2d:66:9...	Disk_DR	no	yes	no	ONLINE	

At this point, IO Acceleration has been configured.

## CHAPTER 12

FICON

On the MDS family of switches, a VSAN is able to be configured to carry FICON traffic. FICON is the protocol that is used by IBM zSeries mainframes to communicate with their associated storage devices. It leverages the same infrastructure as fibre channel with some exceptions. Namely that it does not require zoning, the fibre channel name server and there can be no more than two fibre channel switches between the initiator (called a Channel) and the storage port (called a Control Unit). FICON uses the term *Cascaded Mode* to refer to a topology where there is more than one switch participating in the FICON VSAN.

It does require additional methods to be implemented such as Fabric Binding which do not allow switches to join the VSAN unless explicitly configured on the existing switches as well as in order delivery which guarantees the in order delivery of packets even when there are topology changes. Also, it requires static domain IDs and that the configuration is saved whenever changes are made.

The ability of the MDS to configure VSANs to carry FICON traffic enables the MDS to provide storage connectivity for both open systems traffic, such as UNIX or Windows and mainframe traffic at the same time but logically isolated from each other. Further protections can be configured such as VSAN based role based access control (RBAC) such that open systems SAN administrators cannot modify the FICON VSANs and the FICON administrators cannot modify the open systems VSANs.

The Mainframe package license is required on all switches that will be carrying FICON traffic.

Best Practice   Leverage the ability of Device Manager to see all the FICON Port Numbers on a switch. See Device Manager with FICON Port Numbers which is Figure 12-4 on page 12-10

Configuring New FICON VSANs

The following recipes provide procedures on how to create either standalone or cascaded mode FICON VSANs.

Cisco Storage Networking Cookbook for NX-OS release 5.2

Configuring a FICON VSAN via CLI

To configure a FICON VSAN perform the following procedure:

The following assumptions are being made:

- VSAN ID: 100
- Domain ID: 10
- Cascaded Mode: No

Step 1 Run the **setup ficon** command. This script similar to the one used to perform initial switch configuration will provide all the necessary options to configure a FICON VSAN.

```
MDS-9513-1# setup ficon
              --- Ficon Configuration Dialog ---

This setup utility will guide you through basic Ficon Configuraton
on the system.

Press Enter if you want to skip any dialog. Use ctrl-c at anytime
to skip all remaining dialogs.


Would you like to enter the basic configuration dialog (yes/no)[yes]:yes

Enter vsan [1-4093]   :100

vsan 100 does not exist, create it? (yes/no)[yes]:yes

Enable ficon on this vsan? (yes/no)[yes]:yes

The following options required for ficon will be enabled:
        In-order-delivery
        Fabric binding

    Configure domain-id for this ficon vsan (1-239)   :10

    Would you like to configure ficon in cascaded mode: (yes/no)[no]: no

    Enable SNMP to modify port connectivity parameters? (yes/no)[yes]:yes

    Disable Host from modifying port connectivity parameters? (yes/no)[no]:no

    Enable active=saved? (yes/no)[yes]:yes

Would you like to configure additional ficon vsans (yes/no)[yes]:no

The following configuration will be applied:

vsan database
vsan 100
do sleep 1
in-order-guarantee vsan 100
fcdomain domain 10 static vsan 100
do sleep 1
fabric-binding enable
fabric-binding activate vsan 100 force
zone default-zone permit vsan 100
ficon vsan 100
```

```
Would you like to edit the configuration? (yes/no)[no]:no

Use this configuration and apply it? (yes/no)[yes]:yes
MDS-9513-1#
```

.ı|ı.ı|ı.

Best Practice   If multiple VSANs are required to be created, the above configuration, can be modified and pasted into the CLI instead of re-running the ficon setup script.

Step 2   Display the FICON VSAN:

```
MDS-9513-1# show ficon vsan 100

Ficon information for VSAN 100
  Ficon is online
  VSAN is active
  Host port control is Enabled
  Host offline control is Enabled
  User alert mode is Disabled
  SNMP port control is Enabled
  Host set director timestamp is Enabled
  Active=Saved is Enabled
  Loadbalance is srcid-dstid
  Number of implemented ports are 250
  Key Counter is 2
  FCID last byte is 0(0)
  Serial number is 06.000DEC6D5044
  Date/Time is same as system time (Mon Sep 26 10:48:47.588486 2011)
  Device Allegiance not locked
  Codepage is us-canada
  Saved configuration files
    IPL

MDS-9513-1#
```

Configuring a FICON VSANs via DCNM

This recipe will provide the procedure to configure a single FICON VSAN via DCNM.

The following assumptions are being made:

- VSAN ID: 200
- Domain ID: 20
- Cascaded Mode: No

Step 1   Select the **Create VSAN...** icon at the top of the DCNM window. This is the same icon used to create a VSAN for open systems traffic.

Step 2   First, check the FICON checkbox, this will alter the dialog box so that it displays the FICON specific options.

Step 3   Select the switch to configure the FICON VSAN

Step 4 Specify the VSAN ID,

Step 5 Specify the domain ID from the available list by entering it in the cell next to the switch to be configured for FICON.

Step 6 Check the box **Enable Fabric Binding for Selected Switches**. See Figure 12-1 on page 12-4

Figure 12-1   *Create FICON VSAN dialog*

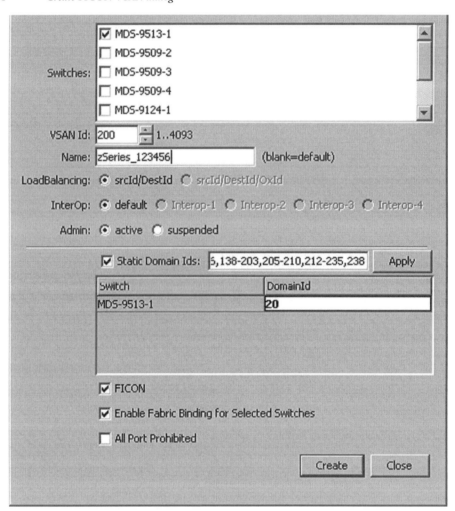

Step 7 Click **Create**.

At this point the FICON VSAN is created and ports can be moved into it using DCNM, Device Manager or the CLI.

Configuring a Cascaded Mode FICON VSAN

This recipe will provide the procedure to configure a single FICON VSAN via DCNM.

The following assumptions are being made:

- VSAN ID: 300
- Domain ID: 23, 24
- Cascaded Mode: Yes
- Port-Channel ID: 1
- FICON Port Number to assign to Port-Channel 1: 0xf9

Step 1   Create any Port-Channels that will carry the FICON traffic between the switches and make sure that the trunk allowed list will allow the FICON VSAN to traverse once it is created.

Step 2   Select the **Create VSAN...** icon at the top of the DCNM window. This is the same icon used to create a VSAN for open systems traffic.

Step 3   First, check the FICON check box, this will alter the dialog box so that it displays the FICON specific options.

Step 4   Select the switches to configure the FICON VSAN

Step 5   Specify the VSAN ID,

Step 6   Specify the domain IDs from the available list by entering it in the cell next to each the switch to be configured for FICON.

Step 7   Check the box **Enable Fabric Binding for Selected Switches**. See Figure 12-2 on page 12-6

Figure 12-2   Create a Cascaded FICON VSAN dialog

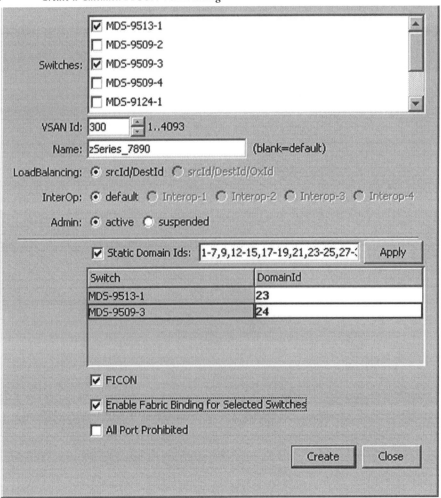

Step 8   Click **Create**.

Step 9   Open up **Device Manager** for both switches

Step 10   Select the **Interface** pull-down menu then **Port-Channels**

Step 11   In the FICON Address box, click and select one of the available FICON port numbers. See Figure 12-3 on page 12-7

Note   A FICON port number, or address needs to be assigned to the port-channel on each MDS. Otherwise an error will be displayed such as 2011 Sep 18 10:37:20 MDS-9509-3 %PORT-5-IF_TRUNK_DOWN: %$VSAN 300%$ Interface port-channel 1, vsan 300 is down (Error disabled - ficon not enabled)

Figure 12-3   Assigning a FICON Address to a Port-Channel

Step 12   Click Apply.

Adding a New Switch to an Existing FICON VSAN

Adding a new switch to an existing VSAN is very similar to the process of creating a cascaded mode FICON VSAN. When designing the topology for the FICON VSAN, remember that FICON traffic cannot travel across more than two switches between the Channel (hba) and the Control Unit (storage port).

The assumptions for this recipe are the following:

- Existing FICON VSAN: 200
- Existing domain ID: 20
- Existing swwn (show wwn switch): 20:00:00:05:30:00:18:a2
- New domain ID: 21
- New swwn (show wwn switch): 20:00:00:0d:ec:6d:50:40
- Port-Channel has already been created and is configured to allow VSAN 200 to trunk across it.
- FICON Address for Port-Channel: 0xf9

To create the VSAN on the second switch and add it to the existing FICON VSAN perform the following:

Step 1   On the existing switch, configure Fabric Binding to allow the second switch to participate in the FICON VSAN:

```
MDS-9509-3# conf t
Enter configuration commands, one per line.  End with CNTL/Z.
MDS-9509-3(config)# fabric-binding database vsan 200
MDS-9509-3(config-fabric-binding)# swwn  20:00:00:0d:ec:6d:50:40 domain 21
MDS-9509-3(config-fabric-binding)# swwn 20:00:00:05:30:00:18:a2 domain 20
MDS-9509-3(config-fabric-binding)# fabric-binding activate vsan 200 force
MDS-9509-3(config)#
```

Step 2   Run the setup ficon script on the new switch

```
MDS-9513-1# setup ficon
                --- Ficon Configuration Dialog ---

This setup utility will guide you through basic Ficon Configuraton
on the system.

Press Enter if you want to skip any dialog. Use ctrl-c at anytime
to skip all remaining dialogs.


Would you like to enter the basic configuration dialog (yes/no)[yes]:

Enter vsan [1-4093]   :200

vsan 201 does not exist, create it? (yes/no)[yes]:yes

Enable ficon on this vsan? (yes/no)[yes]:yes

The following options required for ficon will be enabled:
        In-order-delivery

    Configure domain-id for this ficon vsan (1-239)   :20

    Would you like to configure ficon in cascaded mode: (yes/no)[no]:yes

        Configure peer wwn (hh:hh:hh:hh:hh:hh:hh:hh): 20:00:00:0d:ec:6d:50:40

        Configure peer domain (1-239)   :21

        Would you like to configure additional peers: (yes/no)[no]:yes

        Configure peer wwn (hh:hh:hh:hh:hh:hh:hh:hh): 20:00:00:05:30:00:18:a2

        Configure peer domain (1-239)   :20

        Would you like to configure additional peers: (yes/no)[no]:no

    Enable SNMP to modify port connectivity parameters? (yes/no)[yes]:yes

    Disable Host from modifying port connectivity parameters? (yes/no)[no]:no

    Enable active=saved? (yes/no)[yes]:yes

Would you like to configure additional ficon vsans (yes/no)[yes]:no

The following configuration will be applied:

vsan database
vsan 201
do sleep 1
in-order-guarantee vsan 201
fcdomain domain 20 static vsan 201
fabric-binding database vsan 201
swwn 20:00:00:0d:ec:6d:50:40 domain 21
swwn 20:00:00:05:30:00:18:a2 domain 20
fabric-binding activate vsan 201
zone default-zone permit vsan 201
ficon vsan 201

Would you like to edit the configuration? (yes/no)[no]:no

Use this configuration and apply it? (yes/no)[yes]:yes
```

Note   In a single switch topology, the Fabric Binding database is empty, however, in a Cascaded Mode configuration, the Fabric Binding database contains both switch's entries.

Step 3   On both switches, determine an available FICON port number to assign to the port-channel

```
MDS-9509-3# show ficon port-numbers assign logical-port
ficon logical-port assign port-numbers 224-249

MDS-9513-1# show ficon port-numbers assign logical-port
ficon logical-port assign port-numbers 224-249
```

Step 4   Configure the FICON port address for the port-channel on both switches

```
MDS-9509-3# conf t
Enter configuration commands, one per line.  End with CNTL/Z.
MDS-9509-3(config)# interface port-channel 1
MDS-9509-3(config-if)# ficon portnumber 0xf9

MDS-9513-1# conf t
Enter configuration commands, one per line.  End with CNTL/Z.
MDS-9513-1(config)# interface port-channel 1
MDS-9513-1(config-if)# ficon portnumber 0xf9
```

At this point the cascaded FICON VSAN should be up and it should be trunked across the port-channel.

How to Block/Unblock FICON Ports

In FICON environments, there may be a requirement to block or prohibit a Channel from accessing a specific Control Unit by having the enforce the requirement. To perform this ability using Device Manager perform the following procedure:

In Device Manager, selecting the

Step 1   Launch Device Manager for the FICON enabled switch to be managed.

Step 2   For ease of viewing in Device Manager, select the **Toggle FICON/Interface Port Labels** button, Figure 12-4.

Figure 12-4   Device Manager with FICON Port Numbers

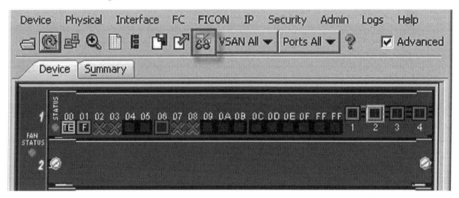

Step 3   Under the FICON pull down menu, select **VSANs**.

Step 4   Select the VSAN to be configured by clicking on the VSAN number in the first column.

Step 5   Select Port-Configuration

Step 6   Click the boxes in the grid corresponding to the ports to be blocked or prohibited. See Figure 12-5.

Figure 12-5   FICON Port Block and Prohibit Dialog box

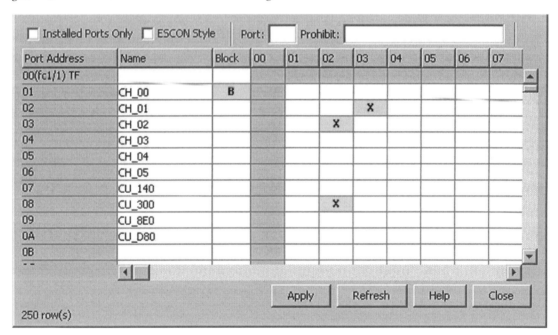

Step 7   Click **Apply**.

CHAPTER 13

iSCSI

Internet SCSI (iSCSI) is a standards-based transport protocol used to transport SCSI packets over TCP/IP. This protocol is used to carry SCSI commands and the SCSI response. iSCSI uses the existing TCP/IP infrastructure to provide block storage to servers. The protocol allows hosts to connect and to access storage over a a TCP/IP network using a network interface card. iSCSI, like the Fibre Channel Protocol (FCP), provides servers with access to Storage Area Network (SAN) attached storage arrays or to a network (TCP/IP) attached native iSCSI storage array.

The servers require iSCSI driver to be installed on them to act as a bridge between the SCSI and the TCP/IP layers. The iSCSI driver translates the SCSI command and responses from the server to the storage devices into an iSCSI payload that is carried over traditional TCP/IP networks. It also translates the incoming iSCSI payload from the storage to the server into the SCSI command or response on the servers.

Gigabit Ethernet NICs are widely used as a standard connectivity interface for iSCSI on servers. This can provide up to 1-Gb/s speed connectivity between host and storage.

With the advent of 10 Gigabit Ethernet in the Data Centers iSCSI can be used as a viable (speed) transport mechanism for servers to access block based storage without having the need to connect to a SAN.

There are two types of iSCSI storage devices:

1. Native iSCSI devices that connect to the TCP/IP network and are either initiators, such as servers or targets such as disk arrays.

2. iSCSI gateways that provides a bridge between a FC SAN and LAN infrastructures, enabling iSCSI enabled servers to access block storage that is connected to the Storage Area Network (SAN). Such devices include the MDS's Multiprotocol Services Module (18+4) or the Storage Services Node (SSN-16) module.

An iSCSI initiator is available for all major Operating Systems in use. The iSCSI driver can use existing NICs to provide iSCSI storage connectivity. In an I/O intensive environment it is recommended that a pair of NICs be dedicated for block storage access using iSCSI, both for performance and redundancy. It is also recommended to deploy TCP off-load Engines (TOE) for greater performance requirements. TOE cards are NICs which can offload TCP processing and some even have the ability to off-load iSCSI processing as well.

In order for the MDS 9200 and 9500 series switches support iSCSI, they require one of the Storage Services modules, or in the case of the 9222i, can support it natively. Both the Multi protocol Services Module (MSM 18+4) or the Storage Services Node (SSN-16) Module support iSCSI. The MDS switches support multiple configuration methods for iSCSI. The different configuration modes are iSLB (iSCSI server load-balancing), transparent mode, and proxy mode. These different modes of configuration are described in the following sections.

Note   Though the IPS-4, IPS-8 and the 14+2 modules can be use for iSCSI they are not supported in NX-OS 5.x and above.

iSLB Configuration Mode

The iSLB configuration mode is ideal, for all but the smallest iSCSI deployments. iSLB allows the incoming iSCSI sessions from various servers to be load-balanced over a group of Gigabit Ethernet interfaces either across the same or multiple switches. This also allows for fail over of an iSCSI session to other Gigabit Ethernet interfaces in the group of switches used for load-balancing, if one or more of the interfaces fail.

The iSLB configuration uses Virtual Router Redundancy Protocol (VRRP) for fail over and load balancing among the various Gigabit Ethernet interfaces used in the configuration. The load balancing on the switch is based on the load on each of the Gigabit Ethernet interface, and is automatically calculated and enforced on the switches. If the Gigabit Ethernet interfaces using VRRP are located on multiple switches, the switches on which the Gigabit Ethernet interfaces reside have to be interconnected using a port-channel for fail over and load balancing to work. The interconnected iSLB enabled switches use CFS to distribute the iSLB configuration between them. The iSLB mode can perform automatic zones and zone set activation, if so configured. The recipes below use explicit zones.

Best Practice   Cisco recommends iSLB based iSCSI configuration for all forms of iSCSI deployments using the MDS 9000 SAN switches.

Configuring iSLB on an MDS Switch

The topology used for this recipe has two MDS switches connected together using a port-channel. The switches used are MDS-9509-2 and MDS-9509-4. The MDS-9509-2 has two Gigabit Ethernet interfaces and the switch MDS-9509-4 has one Gigabit Ethernet interface enabled for iSCSI. A total of three servers are used as the iSCSI client that connects to the target port (see Figure 13-1).

Figure 13-1   *iSLB Topology*

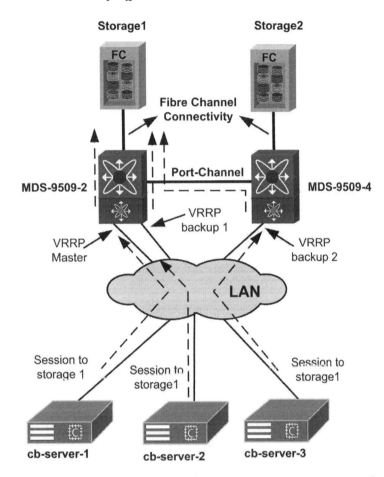

The topology has two storage ports one from storage array storage1 and another from storage array storage 2, connected to MDS-9509-2 and MDS-9509-4 switches using Fibre Channel ports. Both the switches have one MSM 18+4 module in each. The Gigabit Ethernet port 1/1 and 1/2 on MDS-9509-2 and Gigabit Ethernet port 2/1 on MDS-9509-4 are used in this recipe. All three iSCSI clients in this configuration use the same storage port storage1 to access their LUNs.

iSLB requires the two switches MDS-9509-2 and MDS-9509-4 involved in this example to be interconnected through a port-channel to ensure proper load balancing and fail over functionality. Refer to Port-channels, page 5-1 on creating and managing port-channel.

Note   If multiple switches are involved in the fail over configuration as seen in Figure 13-1 the switches need to be interconnected using a port-channel for the iSLB load balancing and fail over to work correctly.

To configure an iSLB based iSCSI configuration, follow these steps:

Step 1   Enable iSCSI in the switches involved in the iSCSI topology. Do this before attempting to configure iSCSI on the switches involved in this configuration.

The iSCSI feature needs to be enabled on the switch and on a line card before iSCSI related commands can be run on the switch. The commands **feature iSCSI** and **iSCSI enable module <x>** commands enable iSCSI on the switch and the selected module.

```
MDS-9509-2# conf t
Enter configuration commands, one per line.  End with CNTL/Z.
MDS-9509-2(config)# feature iscsi
MDS-9509-2(config)# iscsi enable module 1
MDS-9509-2(config)# end
MDS-9509-2#

MDS-9509-4# conf t
Enter configuration commands, one per line.  End with CNTL/Z.
MDS-9509-4(config)# feature iscsi
MDS-9509-2(config)# iscsi enable module 2
MDS-9509-4(config)# end
MDS-9509-4#
```

Step 2   Configure the IP address on the Gigabit Ethernet interfaces in all the switches involved.

```
MDS-9509-2# conf t
Enter configuration commands, one per line.  End with CNTL/Z.
MDS-9509-2(config)# interface gigabitethernet 1/1
MDS-9509-2(config-if)# ip address 172.22.38.140 255.255.254.0
MDS-9509-2(config-if)# no shut
MDS-9509-2(config-if)# interface gigabitethernet 1/2
MDS-9509-2(config-if)# ip address 172.22.38.144  255.255.254.0
MDS-9509-2(config-if)# no shut
MDS-9509-2(config-if)# end
MDS-9509-2#

MDS-9509-4# conf t
Enter configuration commands, one per line.  End with CNTL/Z.
MDS-9509-4(config)# interface gigabitethernet 2/1
MDS-9509-4(config-if)# ip address 172.22.38.145 255.255.254.0
MDS-9509-4(config-if)# no shut
```

Step 3   Enable the respective iSCSI interfaces in all the switches involved.

```
MDS-9509-2# conf t
Enter configuration commands, one per line.  End with CNTL/Z.
MDS-9509-2(config)# interface iscsi 1/1-2
MDS-9509-2(config-if)# no shut

MDS-9509-4# conf t
Enter configuration commands, one per line.  End with CNTL/Z.
MDS-9509-4(config)# interface iscsi 2/1
MDS-9509-4(config-if)# no shut
```

Step 4   Enable CFS distribution for iSLB on all the switches in the topology.

```
MDS-9509-2# conf t
Enter configuration commands, one per line.   End with CNTL/Z.
MDS-9509-2(config)# islb distribute

MDS-9509-4# conf t
Enter configuration commands, one per line.   End with CNTL/Z.
MDS-9509-4(config)# islb distribute
```

Step 5   Configure the VRRP group to include all the Gigabit Ethernet interfaces that are part of the configuration. The VRRP group ID 50 is used in this example.

```
MDS-9509-2# conf t
Enter configuration commands, one per line.   End with CNTL/Z.
MDS-9509-2(config)# interface gigabitethernet 1/1
MDS-9509-2(config-if)# vrrp 50
MDS-9509-2(config-if-vrrp)# address 172.22.38.146 <-- Virtual Router for VRRP group 50
MDS-9509-2(config-if-vrrp)# no shut
MDS-9509-2(config-if-vrrp)# exit
MDS-9509-2(config-if)# exit
MDS-9509-2(config)# interface gigabitethernet 1/2
MDS-9509-2(config-if)# vrrp 50
MDS-9509-2(config-if-vrrp)# address 172.22.38.146 <-- Virtual Router for VRRP group 50
MDS-9509-2(config-if-vrrp)# no shut
MDS-9509-2(config-if-vrrp)# end
MDS-9509-2#

MDS-9509-4# conf t
Enter configuration commands, one per line.   End with CNTL/Z.
MDS-9509-4(config)# interface gigabitethernet 2/1
MDS-9509-4(config-if)# vrrp 50
MDS-9509-4(config-if-vrrp)# address 172.22.38.146 <-- Virtual router for VRRP group 50
MDS-9509-4(config-if-vrrp)# no shut
MDS-9509-4(config-if-vrrp)# end
MDS-9509-4#
```

Step 6   Configure VRRP iSLB load balancing. First enable iSLB load balancing for the VRRP group configured in the preceding step in all the switches where the VRRP group resides. In this example, that includes switches MDS-9509-2 and MDS-9509-4.

```
MDS-9509-2# conf t
Enter configuration commands, one per line.   End with CNTL/Z.
MDS-9509-2(config)# islb vrrp 50 load-balance

MDS-9509-4# conf t
Enter configuration commands, one per line.   End with CNTL/Z.
MDS-9509-4(config)# islb vrrp 50 load-balance
```

Step 7   Enable the iSCSI initiator in dynamic iSLB mode so that the new iSCSI initiators are initialized as iSLB clients and not iSCSI clients.

Note   The iSCSI initiators cannot be converted into iSLB initiators automatically. The initiators have to be removed and re-configured.

```
MDS-9509-2# conf t
Enter configuration commands, one per line.  End with CNTL/Z.
MDS-9509-2(config)# iscsi dynamic initiator islb

MDS-9509-4# conf t
Enter configuration commands, one per line.  End with CNTL/Z.
MDS-9509-4(config)# iscsi dynamic initiator islb
```

Step 8   Configure iSLB initiators for all the iSCSI clients statically. This is a requirement for load balancing. Assign the iSLB initiator to a VSAN. The system dynamically assigns a pWWN for the initiators configured.

```
MDS-9509-2# conf t
Enter configuration commands, one per line.  End with CNTL/Z.
MDS-9509-4(config)# islb initiator name iqn.1991-05.com.microsoft:cb-server-1
MDS-9509-4(config-islb-init)# static pWWN system-assign
MDS-9509-4(config-islb-init)# vsan 1000
MDS-9509-4(config-islb-init)# exit
MDS-9509-4(config)# islb initiator name iqn.1991-05.com.microsoftcb-server-2
MDS-9509-4(config-islb-init)# static pWWN system-assign
MDS-9509-4(config-islb-init)# vsan 1000
MDS-9509-4(config-islb-init)# exit
MDS-9509-4(config)# islb initiator name iqn.1991-05.com.microsoft:cb-server-3
MDS-9509-4(config-islb-init)# static pWWN system-assign
MDS-9509-4(config-islb-init)# vsan 1000
MDS-9509-4(config-islb-init)# end
MDS-9509-4#
```

Step 9   Configure iSLB virtual targets that will be zoned to the previously created iSLB initiators. Allow the configured initiators to access this target. The virtual target will be assigned its own pWWN, which can be seen using a **show fcns database** command.

Note   The initiators have to be authorized to access the virtual targets. There are two ways to accomplish this. The first method uses the **all-initiator-permit** option for each virtual target configured. The second method is to individually allow each individual initiator to access the virtual target. This recipe uses the first method.

Best Practice   If *all-initiator-permit* method of access is configured for any target, it is strongly recommended that array based LUN Masking be deployed to prevent unauthorized LUN access.

```
MDS-9509-4# conf t
Enter configuration commands, one per line. End with CNTL/Z.
MDS-9509-4(config)# islb virtual-target name iqn.storage1-CL3D
MDS-9509-4(config-islb-tgt)# pWWN 50:06:0e:80:03:4e:95:23
MDS-9509-4(config-islb-tgt)# all-initiator-permit
MDS-9509-4(config-islb-tgt)# end
MDS-9509-4#
```

Step 10 Configure the iSCSI initiators on the servers such that the virtual target address is that of the virtual router interface address. In this recipe, configure the iSCSI initiator on the hosts / servers with the Virtual Router interface address of the VRRP group 50 configured previously. In this recipe it is 172.22.38.146.

Step 11 Configure the required zones and add them to the zone set by creating the required zones and zoneset to permit the initiators to access the virtual target configured. In the recipe, VSAN 1000 uses enhanced zoning. The zone database has to be committed before activation. Then add the zones to a zoneset if one exists or else create a new zoneset and add the zones as members to it. Finally activate the zoneset for the zone changes to take effect.

Note   While using enhanced zoning, the zone database has to be committed before activating the zoneset.

```
MDS-9509-4# conf t
Enter configuration commands, one per line.  End with CNTL/Z.
MDS-9509-4(config)# zone name Z_islb_pc1 vsan 1000
MDS-9509-4(config-zone)# member symbolic-nodename iqn.1991-05.com.microsoft:cb-server-1
MDS-9509-4(config-zone)# member device-alias storage-CL3D
MDS-9509-4(config-zone)# zone name Z_islb_pc2 vsan 1000
MDS-9509-4(config-zone)# member symbolic-nodename iqn.1991-05.com.microsoft:cb-server-2
MDS-9509-4(config-zone)# member device-alias storage-CL3D
MDS-9509-4(config-zone)# zone name Z_islb_pc14 vsan 1000
MDS-9509-4(config-zone)# member symbolic-nodename iqn.1991-05.com.microsoft:cb-server-3
MDS-9509-4(config-zone)# member device-alias storage-CL3D
MDS-9509-4(config-zone)# zoneset name ZS_islib vsan 1000
MDS-9509-4(config-zoneset)# member Z_islb_cb-server-1
MDS-9509-4(config-zoneset)# member Z_lslb_cb-server-2
MDS-9509-4(config-zoneset)# member Z_islb_cb-server-3
MDS-9509-4(config-zoneset)# exit
MDS-9509-4(config)# zone commit vsan 1000
Commit operation initiated. Check zone status
MDS-9509-4(config)# zoneset activate name ZS_islb vsan 1000
Zoneset activation initiated. check zone status
MDS-9509-4(config)#
```

Step 12 Run the **show zoneset active vsan 1000** command to see the status of the zone set.

```
MDS-9509-4# show zoneset active vsan 1000
zoneset name ZS_islb vsan 1000
  zone name Z_islb_cb-server-1 vsan 1000
  * fcid 0xea0001 [symbolic-nodename iqn.1991-05.com.microsoft:cb-server-1]
  * fcid 0x8b0100 [pwwn 50:06:0e:80:03:4e:95:23] [storage-CL3D]

  zone name Z_islb_cb-server-2 vsan 1000
  * fcid 0x8b0100 [pwwn 50:06:0e:80:03:4e:95:23] [storage-CL3D]
  * fcid 0xea0004 [symbolic-nodename iqn.1991-05.com.microsoft:cb-server-2]

  zone name Z_islb_cb-server-3 vsan 1000
  * fcid 0x8b0102 [symbolic-nodename iqn.1991-05.com.microsoft:cb-server-3]
  * fcid 0x8b0100 [pwwn 50:06:0e:80:03:4e:95:23] [storage-CL3D]
MDS-9509-4#
```

Step 13   Run the **show islb vrrp summary** command to see the load-balance status.

```
MDS-9509-4# show islb vrrp summary

                          -- Groups For Load Balance --
-----------------------------------------------------------------------------
              VR Id                VRRP Address Type          Configured Status
-----------------------------------------------------------------------------
                50                      IPv4                        Enabled

                       -- Interfaces For Load Balance --
-----------------------------------------------------------------------------
                                                         Initiator  Redirect
    VR Id      VRRP IP            Switch WWN      Interface    Load    Enabled
-----------------------------------------------------------------------------
       50  172.22.38.146 20:00:00:0d:ec:24:5e:80    GigE1/1     1000      Yes
       50  172.22.38.146 20:00:00:0d:ec:24:5e:80    GigE1/2     1000      Yes
M      50  172.22.38.146 20:00:00:0d:ec:24:5b:c0    GigE2/1     1000      Yes

                    -- Initiator To Interface Assignment --
-----------------------------------------------------------------------------
Initiator  VR Id         VRRP IP            Switch WWN              Interface
-----------------------------------------------------------------------------
iqn.1991-05.com.microsoft:cb-server-1
           50    172.22.38.146 20:00:00:0d:ec:24:5e:80    GigabitEthernet1/1
iqn.1991-05.com.microsoft:cb-server-3
           50    172.22.38.146 20:00:00:0d:ec:24:5b:c0    GigabitEthernet2/1
iqn.1991-05.com.microsoft:cb-server-2
           50    172.22.38.146 20:00:00:0d:ec:24:5e:80    GigabitEthernet1/2
MDS-9509-4#
```

The **Interfaces For Load Balance** section in the output displays the VRRP group members in the configuration. This section also identifies the interface that is the designated master for the configuration. The Master is identified by a M against it. In the above configuration the interface on cb-server-3 is the designated master.

The **Initiator To Interface Assignment** section shows how the initiators are distributed to the various Gigabit Ethernet interfaces for load balancing.

In a multiple switch topology, the commands "**cfs commit**" and "**cfs distribute**" are recommended to distribute the iSLB configurations to all the switches involved in the topology.

Step 14   Activate the zoneset with the iSLB zones.

Step 15   Then on the servers scan for new LUNs to discover the iSCSI LUNs.

Configuring iSCSI initiator in Transparent Mode

In the following recipe the configuration of iSCSI in transparent mode on an MDS switch is described in detail. In transparent initiator mode, every iSCSI initiaor is made available as Fibre Channel (virtual) initiator. This allows for the iSCSI hosts to be treated as a regular fibre channel host for all practical purposes. This in turn allows for the same level of control similar to that of a Fibre Channel initiator, like each iSCSI initiator having separate zoning and lun masking to storage devices it needs to access. This mode is great if very granular control like lun masking is required for each iSCSI initiator. This also means that every iSCSI initiator will have to configure and presented as a fibre channel (virtual) initiator which could be lot of a configurations if a large number of iSCSI initiators are required.

Best Practice For large installations, it is recommended that iSCSI should be configured using the proxy initiator mode, see Configuring iSCSI initiators in Proxy Initiator Mode, page 13-14.

The topology for transparent mode iSCSI recipe is shown in Figure 13-2. Transparent mode is only recommended when very granular ACL requirements (individual zoning and lun masking) or for very small iSCSI deployments.

Figure 13-2   *iSCSI Transparent Mode Topology]*

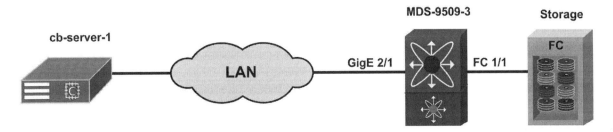

The iSCSI topology consists of a Windows 2008 server using a Gigabit Ethernet NIC for iSCSI storage access. It is connected to the Local Area Network. IN this configuration the NIC is dedicated for iSCSI. The NIC dedicated for iSCSI on the host is assigned the IP address 172.22.38.45. On the switch MDS-9509-3 the MSM (18+4) module is in slot 2. The Gigabit Ethernet port 2/1 on the MSM module is connected to the Local Area Network and has been assigned the IP address 172.22.34.83. The storage port from the array is connected to the Fibre Channel port 1/1 on MDS-9509-3. This recipe uses IQN (iSCSI qualified name) to configure the iSCSI initiator.

Caution The IP address for the Gigabit Ethernet ports on the MSM module should be in a different subnet than the management interface of the MDS switch. This is a requirement for iSCSI to work properly.

The steps to configure iSCSI initiator in transparent mode on the MDS switch are as follows:

Step 1 Configure the Gigabit Ethernet interface on the MDS switch.

The Gigabit Ethernet interface on the MDS switch is given an IP address and a subnet mask. This allows the Gigabit Ethernet interface to communicate with the network.

```
MDS-9509-3# conf t
Enter configuration commands, one per line.  End with CNTL/Z.
MDS-9509-3(config)# interface gigabitethernet 2/1
MDS-9509-3(config-if)# ip address 172.22.34.83 255.255.254.0
MDS-9509-3(config-if)# end
MDS-9509-3#
```

Step 2   Configure IP routes as required. In the recipe, the initiator on cb-server-1 is in the 172.22.38.0 subnet, the Gigabit Ethernet interface on the MSM module is in the 172.22.34.0 subnet. To allow the initiator and the Gigabit Ethernet port to communicate, an IP route has to be configured on the switch.

```
MDS-9509-3# conf t
Enter configuration commands, one per line.  End with CNTL/Z.
MDS-9509-3(config)#ip route 172.22.38.45 255.255.255.255 172.22.34.1 interface
gigabitethernet 2/1
MDS-9509-3(config)# end
MDS-9509-3#
```

Note   It is critical to check the connectivity between the host NIC card and the Gigabit Ethernet port on the MSM module on the switch before proceeding further. A ping test is sufficient. Ping the Gigabit Ethernet interface from the host. Similarly ping the host from the switch.

..|....|..

Best Practice   It is recommended to use host based routes when configuring routes rather than network based routes.

```
MDS-9509-3#ping 172.22.38.45 interface gigabit ethernet 2/1
PING 172.22.38.45 (172.22.38.45) 56(84) bytes of data.
64 bytes from 172.22.38.45: icmp_seq=1 ttl=127 time=1.18 ms
64 bytes from 172.22.38.45: icmp_seq=2 ttl=127 time=0.483 ms
64 bytes from 172.22.38.45: icmp_seq=3 ttl=127 time=0.479 ms
--- 172.22.38.45 ping statistics ---
3 packets transmitted, 3 received, 0% packet loss, time 2006ms
rtt min/avg/max/mdev = 0.479/0.716/1.186/0.332 ms
MDS-9509-3#
```

Step 3   Enable the iSCSI interface 2/1 on the switch MDS-9509-3. Along with enabling the iSCSI interface, additional iSCSI-related TCP tuning can be performed. In this recipe the default values are used.

```
MDS-9509-3# conf t
Enter configuration commands, one per line.  End with CNTL/Z.
MDS-9509-3(config)# interface iscsi 2/1
MDS-9509-3(config-if)# no shut
MDS-9509-3(config-if)# end
MDS-9509-3#
```

Step 4   Configure the iSCSI initiator on the switch MDS-9509-3. This configuration can be done in multiple ways. It can be done using the IP address of the initiator or using an IQN (iSCSI Qualified Name). This example uses an IQN name. Most iSCSI drivers or clients can automatically assign an IQN name on the host. The IQN name has to be at least 16 characters long. The IQN name can also be manually assigned. If it has to be manually assigned the IQN name has to be unique through out the network.

The Windows 2008 server comes with iSCSI stack pre-loaded. The iSCSI initiator properties pre-configures the IQN name. The initiator properties allows the lookup of the IQN name and to change it if necessary (not recommended). In the iSCSI Initiator Properties utility, select **Configuration** tab to see the system assigned IQN name for the server. The system assigned iSCSI Qualified name is iqn.1991-05.com.microsoft:cb-server-1 (see Figure 13-3).

Figure 13-3   *iSCSI Initiator Properties*

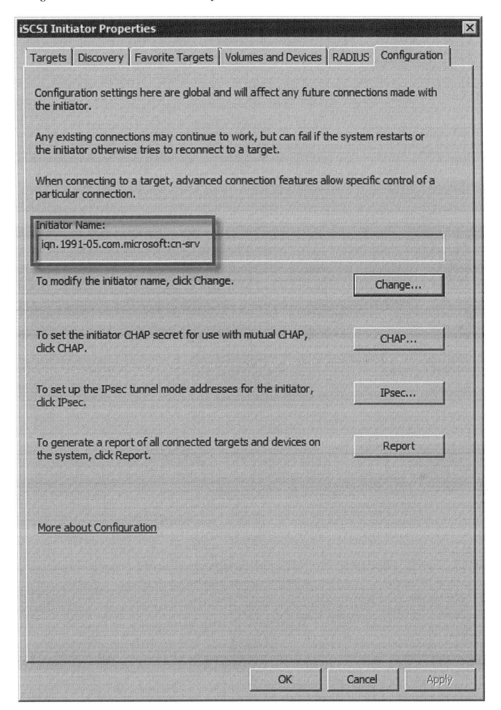

Figure 13-3 shows the screen capture output of the IQN name in the iSCSI initiator properties interface highlighted in red. For the Linux OS, this information is found in the /etc/initiatorname.iscsi file. This information is required to configure the iSCSI initiator on the switch.

```
MDS-9509-3# conf t
Enter configuration commands, one per line.  End with CNTL/Z.
MDS-9509-3(config)# iscsi initiator name iqn.1991-05.com.microsoft:cb-server-1
MDS-9509-3(config-(iscsi-init))# static pWWN system-assign 1 <-- system assigned
MDS-9509-3(config-(iscsi-init))# vsan 1 <-- Must be a member in the Targets VSAN
MDS-9509-3(config-(iscsi-init))# end
MDS-9509-3#
```

In this recipe, the IQN assigned by the system is used. If it needs to be changed, ensure that the new name is unique and is at least 16 characters long.

Optionally, a pWWN can be assigned to the initiator. The system can automatically assign a pWWN to the initiator as shown in the configuration above.

Alternatively the pWWN can be statically assigned by the administrator as shown in the tip below.

Best Practice   If an iSCSI initiator needs to have the same pWWN previously used by a host, such as when converting a host from Fibre Channel to iSCSI, assign the pWWN manually with the commands shown. This alleviates the need to modify the LUN masking database on the array.

```
MDS-9509-3# conf t
Enter configuration commands, one per line.  End with CNTL/Z.
MDS-9509-3(config)# iscsi initiator name iqn.1991-05.com.microsoft.cb-server-1
MDS-9509-3(config-iscsi-init)# static pWWN 21:05:00:0d:ec:02:2d:82 <-- manually assigned
MDS-9509-3(config-iscsi-init)# vsan 1000 <-- Must be a member of the Target's VSAN
MDS-9509-3(config-iscsi-init)# end
MDS-9509-3#
```

Best Practice   The best practice recommendation is to allow the system to automatically assign the pWWN as the system can maintain unique pWWN. If pWWNs are assigned manually then it needs to be unique in the SAN.

The iSCSI initiator can participate in multiple VSANs. To talk to a target, the initiator has to be a member of the VSAN in which the target resides. In the preceding example, the target belongs to VSAN 1000.

Note   Alternatively, the IP address of the iSCSI initiator can be used for the configuration. Assigning a static pWWN is also an option. While zoning an iSCSI interface, IP address can be used in place of its pWWN or IQN name.

An example of configuring iSCSI initiator using IP address is shown below.

```
MDS-9509-3# conf t
Enter configuration commands, one per line.  End with CNTL/Z.
MDS-9509-3(config)# iscsi initiator ipaddress 172.22.38.45
MDS-9509-3(config-(iscsi-init))# static pWWN system-assign 1 <-- system assigned
MDS-9509-3(config-(iscsi-init))# vsan 1000 <-- Must be a member in the Targets VSAN
MDS-9509-3(config-(iscsi-init))# end
MDS-9509-3#
```

Step 5 Configure the virtual target on the switch MDS-9509-3.

```
MDS-9509-3# config t
Enter configuration commands, one per line.  End with CNTL/Z.
MDS-9509-3(config)# iscsi virtual-target name iscsi-jbod-1
MDS-9509-3(config-iscsi-tgt)# pWWN 22:00:00:20:37:5a:40:26
MDS-9509-3(config-iscsi-tgt)# end
MDS-9509-3#
```

Each storage port is assigned a virtual target name. This name has to be 16 characters long. Then the pWWN of the storage port is assigned to the virtual target. This completes the configuration of a virtual target.

Step 6 Permit the initiator to communicate with the virtual target already configured.

```
MDS-9509-3# conf t
Enter configuration commands, one per line.  End with CNTL/Z.
MDS-9509-3(config)# iscsi virtual-target name iscsi-jbod-1
MDS-9509-3(config-iscsi-tgt)# initiator iqn.1991-05.com.microsoft.cb-server-1 permit
MDS-9509-3(config-iscsi-tgt)# end
MDS-9509-3#
```

The virtual target can be configured to allow all initiators to communicate with it. In this example, the virtual target is only configured to communicate with one initiator, iqn.1991-05.com.microsoft.cb-server-1.

Step 7 Create a zone with the iSCSI initiator and the virtual target as its members. Add this zone to the zone set and activate the zone set. This enables the iSCSI initiator and the virtual target to communicate with each other. The zone can be created either with the IQN name or with the IP address or with the pWWN that was assigned to the initiator. In this recipe, it is created using the pWWN.

The following example shows zoning with the pWWN of the virtual target and initiator:

```
MDS-9509-3# conf t
Enter configuration commands, one per line.  End with CNTL/Z.
MDS-9509-3(config)# zone name Z_iscsi_tst vsan 1000
MDS-9509-3(config-zone)# mem pwwn 22:00:00:20:37:39:9c:1f
MDS-9509-3(config-zone)# mem pwwn 21:05:00:0d:ec:02:2d:82
MDS-9509-3(config-zone)#end
MDS-9509-3#
```

```
MDS-9509-3# conf t
Enter configuration commands, one per line.  End with CNTL/Z.
MDS-9509-3(config)# zoneset name ZS_ISCSI vsan 1000
MDS-9509-3(config-zoneset)#member Z_iscsi_tst
MDS-9509-3(config-zoneset)end
MDS-9509-3#
```

The example below shows zoning with the pWWN of the virtual target and the IQN of the iSCSI initiator:

```
MDS-9509-3# conf t
Enter configuration commands, one per line.  End with CNTL/Z.
MDS-9509-3(config)# zone name Z_iscsi_tst vsan 1000
MDS-9509-3(config-zone)# member pwwn 22:00:00:20:37:39:9c:1f
MDS-9509-3(config-zone)# member symbolic-nodename iqn.1991-05.com.microsoft:cb-server-1
MDS-9509-3(config-zone)# end
MDS-9509-3#
```

Step 8 Activate the zone set to allow the zone members to communicate.

```
MDS-9509-3# conf t
Enter configuration commands, one per line.  End with CNTL/Z.
MDS-9509-3(config)# zoneset activate name ZS_ISCSI vsan 1000
Zoneset activation initiated. check zone status
MDS-9509-3#
```

Configuring iSCSI initiators in Proxy Initiator Mode

This recipe details the proxy mode configuration for iSCSI on a MDS switch. In proxy initiator mode, one Fibre Channel initiator is used for all iSCSI clients that access the switch using the same iSCSI interface (iscsi1/1 for example). The initiators use the pWWN assigned to the iSCSI interface. The iSCSI interface to which an iSCSI client will log in is configured in the client and must be permitted by the virtual target configured for that initiator.

Proxy mode is advantageous over transparent mode when the configuration requires multiple iSCSI initiators to access the same Fibre Channel target. For example, if 20 iSCSI initiators need to communicate with a Fibre Channel target, in transparent mode, 20 iSCSI initiators and 20 zones need to be created, and array based LUN masking has to be updated for all 20 initiator instances.

On the other hand, proxy initiator mode is easier to manage than transparent mode as it allows for centralized management of the iSCSI configuration, as all iSCSI clients accessing the same switch interface use the same iSCSI initiator.

First, a pWWN is assigned to iSCSI interface. Then this pWWN is zoned with the Fibre Channel target so that the proxy initiator can see the LUNs presented by the virtual target. All the LUN masking and zoning are performed only with the proxy initiator. As new hosts (iSCSI clients) are added, they are exposed to only the LUNs they need to see as no new zones are needed and no modifications to the array's LUN masking need to be done.

Best Practice   The best practice is to create a virtual target for each host and configure the virtual target to only expose the required LUNs to that particular iSCSI initiator.

The proxy initiator is not restricted to a single VSAN. As iSCSI clients are configured and given access to storage ports in different VSANs, a proxy initiator is created dynamically in the new VSANs. The maximum number of initiators that need to be zoned would be the number of proxy initiators that have iSCSI clients in a particular VSAN. This is far fewer than under transparent mode, where a Fibre Channel initiator is created for every iSCSI client.

The topology used in the iSCSI proxy initiator recipe is shown in Figure 13-4. It has two Windows servers cb-server-1 and cb-server-2 both on the same subnet. Both servers's iSCSI interfaces are on the 172.22.38.0 network.

Caution   The IP address for the Gigabit Ethernet ports on the MSM module should be in a different subnet than the management interface of the MDS switch. This is a requirement for iSCSI to work properly.

Figure 13-4   iSCSI Proxy Topology

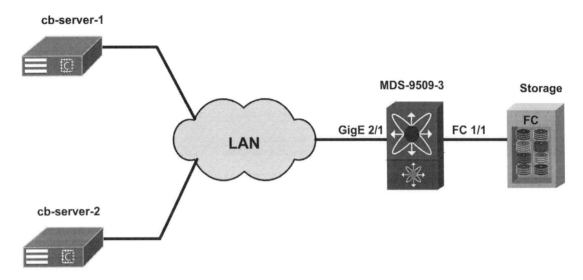

To configure iSCSI initiators in proxy mode on an MDS switch, the steps are as follows:

Step 1   Configure the Gigabit Ethernet interface on the MSM module in the MDS switch. The Gigabit Ethernet interface on the MSM module on the switch is given an IP address and a subnet mask. This allows the Gigabit Ethernet interface to communicate with the network.

```
MDS-9509-3# conf t
Enter configuration commands, one per line.  End with CNTL/Z.
MDS-9509-3(config)# interface gigabitethernet 2/1
MDS-9509-3(config-if)# ip address 172.22.34.83 255.255.254.0
MDS-9509-3(config-if)# end
MDS-9509-3#
```

Step 2   Configure IP routes if required. In the recipe, the initiators cb-server-1 and cb-server-2 are in the 172.22.38.0 subnet, while the Gigabit Ethernet interface is in the 172.22.34.0 subnet. To allow the initiator and the Gigabit Ethernet port to communicate, an IP route has to be configured on the switch. A host-based route is configured to allow the Gigabit Ethernet port to communicate with cb-server-1 and cb-server-2 hosts.

.ı|ıı.ı|ıı

Best Practice   It is recommended to use host based routes when configuring routes.

```
MDS-9509-3# conf t
Enter configuration commands, one per line.  End with CNTL/Z.
MDS-9509-3(config)# ip route 172.22.38.45 255.255.255.255 172.22.34.1 interface
gigabitethernet 2/1
MDS-9509-3(config)# ip route 172.22.38.46 255.255.255.255 172.22.34.1 interface
gigabitethernet 2/1
MDS-9509-3(config)# end
MDS-9509-3#
```

Configuring iSCSI initiators in Proxy Initiator Mode

Note   It is critical to check the connectivity between the host NIC card and the Gigabit Ethernet port on the MSM module on the switch before proceeding further. A ping test is sufficient. Ping the Gigabit Ethernet interface from the host. Similarly ping the host from the switch.

Step 3   Ping the Gigabit Ethernet interface from the hosts. Similarly ping the host from the switch.

```
MDS-9509-3# ping 172.22.38.45 interface gigabit ethernet 2/1
PING 172.22.38.45 (172.22.38.45) 56(84) bytes of data.
64 bytes from 172.22.38.45: icmp_seq=1 ttl=127 time=1.18 ms
64 bytes from 172.22.38.45: icmp_seq=2 ttl=127 time=0.483 ms
64 bytes from 172.22.38.45: icmp_seq=3 ttl=127 time=0.479 ms
--- 172.22.38.45 ping statistics ---
3 packets transmitted, 3 received, 0% packet loss, time 2006ms
rtt min/avg/max/mdev = 0.479/0.716/1.186/0.332 ms
MDS-9509-3#

MDS-9509-3# ping 172.22.38.46 interface gigabit ethernet 2/1
PING 172.22.38.45 (172.22.38.45) 56(84) bytes of data.
64 bytes from 172.22.38.46: icmp_seq=1 ttl=127 time=1.18 ms
64 bytes from 172.22.38.46: icmp_seq=2 ttl=127 time=0.483 ms
64 bytes from 172.22.38.46: icmp_seq=3 ttl=127 time=0.479 ms
--- 172.22.38.46 ping statistics ---
3 packets transmitted, 3 received, 0% packet loss, time 2006ms
rtt min/avg/max/mdev = 0.479/0.716/1.186/0.332 ms
MDS-9509-3#
```

Step 4   Enable the iSCSI interface on the switch MDS-9509-3. The iSCSI interface 2/1 (which is the same port as the Gigabit Ethernet interface) needs to be enabled. Additional iSCSI-related TCP tuning is available. In this recipe default values are used. The **switchport** command is used to enable proxy initiator mode for the iSCSI interface 2/1. It is also used to assign a pWWN to the iSCSI interface.

```
MDS-9509-3# conf t
Enter configuration commands, one per line.  End with CNTL/Z.
MDS-9509-3(config)# interface iscsi 2/1
MDS-9509-3(config-if)# switchport proxy-initiator nWWN 21:05:00:0d:ec:02:2d:82 pwwn
21:05:00:0d:ec:02:2d:82
MDS-9509-3(config-if)# no shut
MDS-9509-3(config-if)# end
MDS-9509-3#
```

Step 5   Add the iSCSI interface to the required VSANs. Do this to allow the iSCSI interface to communicate with the virtual target to see the LUNs in different VSANs. The commands below add the iSCSI interface 2/1 to the VSAN 1000. This is the VSAN to which the Fibre Channel target is connected. Once this is complete, the interface iSCSI 2/1 will be able to log on to the fabric.

```
MDS-9509-3# conf t
Enter configuration commands, one per line.  End with CNTL/Z.
MDS-9509-3(config)# iscsi interface vsan-membership
MDS-9509-3(config)# vsan database
MDS-9509-3(config-vsan-db)# vsan 1000 interface iscsi 2/1
MDS-9509-3(config-vsan-db)# end
MDS-9509-3#
```

Note   The **iscsi interface vsan-membership** command is required to make the iSCSI interface part of multiple VSANs.

Step 6 Configure a virtual target on the switch MDS-9509-4.

```
MDS-9509-4# config t
Enter configuration commands, one per line.  End with CNTL/Z.
MDS-9509-4(config)# iscsi virtual-target name iscsi-jbod-1
MDS-9509-4(config-iscsi-tgt)# pWWN 22:00:00:20:37:39:9c:1f
MDS-9509-4(config-iscsi-tgt)# end
MDS-9509-4#
```

The virtual target is a name assigned to the storage device. This name has to be 16 characters long. Then the pWWN of the storage port is assigned to the virtual target as shown previously. This completes the configuration of a virtual target.

Step 7 Create a zone with the iSCSI initiator and virtual target as members. This enables the initiator and the target to communicate with each other. The zone can be created either with the IQN name, IP address, or pWWN assigned to the initiator. In this recipe, it is created using the pWWN. Add the zone to the zone set.

```
MDS-9509-3# conf t
Enter configuration commands, one per line.  End with CNTL/Z.
MDS-9509-3(config)# zone name Z_iscsi_tst vsan 1000
MDS-9509-3(config-zone)# mem pwwn 22:00:00:20:37:39:9c:1f
MDS-9509-3(config-zone)# mem pwwn 21:05:00:0d:ec:02:2d:82
MDS-9509-3(config-zone)# end
MDS-9509-3#
```

```
MDS-9509-3# conf t
Enter configuration commands, one per line.  End with CNTL/Z.
MDS-9509-3(config)# zoneset name ZS_ISCSI vsan 1000
MDS-9509-3(config-zoneset)# member Z_iscsi_tst
MDS-9509-3(config-zoneset)# end
MDS-9509-3#
```

Activate the zone set to allow the zone members to communicate with each other.

```
MDS-9509-3# conf t
Enter configuration commands, one per line.  End with CNTL/Z.
MDS-9509-3(config)# zoneset activate name ZS_ISCSI vsan 1000
Zoneset activation initiated. check zone status
MDS-9509-3#
MDS-9509-3# show zoneset active vsan 1000
zoneset name ZS_iscsi vsan 1000
  zone name Z_iscsi_tst vsan 1000
  * fcid 0xd90002 [pwwn 21:05:00:0d:ec:02:2d:82]
  * fcid 0xd90000 [pwwn 22:00:00:20:37:39:9c:1f]
MDS-9509-3#
```

.ılı.ılı.

Best Practice To achieve LUN security, create a virtual target with access to specific LUNs for each initiator.

Step 8 Configure a virtual target for each initiator and configure LUN masking for the initiator. When the zone is successfully activated, the LUNs available on the storage port are visible to the iSCSI interface. As this interface could be a proxy iSCSI interface for many iSCSI initiators, some form of LUN security must be enabled. This recipe creates a virtual target with access to specific LUNs for each initiator. The iSCSI interface can see 10 LUNs (LUN 11 to LUN 20 in decimal). The configuration allows the server cb-server-1 to see LUNs 11 - 14 (decimal) on the array.

```
MDS-9509-3# config t
Enter configuration commands, one per line.  End with CNTL/Z.
MDS-9509-3(config)# iscsi virtual-target name iscsi-jbod-1
MDS-9509-3(config-(iscsi-tgt))# pwwN 22:00:00:20:37:39:9c:1f fc-lun b iscsi-lun1
MDS-9509-3(config-(iscsi-tgt))# pwwN 22:00:00:20:37:39:9c:1f fc-lun b iscsi-lun2
MDS-9509-3(config-(iscsi-tgt))# pwwN 22:00:00:20:37:39:9c:1f fc-lun d iscsi-lun3
MDS-9509-3(config-(iscsi-tgt))# pwwN 22:00:00:20:37:39:9c:1f fc-lun e iscsi-lun4
MDS-9509-3(config-(iscsi-tgt))# initiator ip address 172.22.38.45 permit
MDS-9509-3(config-(iscsi-tgt))# end
MDS-9509-3#
```

Allow the server cb-server-2 to see LUNs 16 - 20 (decimal).

```
MDS-9509-3# config t
Enter configuration commands, one per line.  End with CNTL/Z.
MDS-9509-3(config)# iscsi virtual-target name iscsi-jbod-1
MDS-9509-3(config-(iscsi-tgt))# pwwN 22:00:00:20:37:39:9c:1f fc-lun 10 iscsi-lun1
MDS-9509-3(config-(iscsi-tgt))# pwwN 22:00:00:20:37:39:9c:1f fc-lun 11 iscsi-lun2
MDS-9509-3(config-(iscsi-tgt))# pwwN 22:00:00:20:37:39:9c:1f fc-lun 12 iscsi-lun3
MDS-9509-3(config-(iscsi-tgt))# pwwN 22:00:00:20:37:39:9c:1f fc-lun 13 iscsi-lun4
MDS-9509-3(config-(iscsi-tgt))# pwwN 22:00:00:20:37:39:9c:1f fc-lun 14 iscsi-lun5
MDS-9509-3(config-(iscsi-tgt))# initiator ip address 172.22.38.46 permit
MDS-9509-3(config-(iscsi-tgt))# end
MDS-9509-3#
```

After these changes, both servers should see the LUNs allocated to them through the virtual target created for each. There is no need to create additional zones when new iSCSI clients are added. If the iSCSI clients need access, zone additional targets to the iSCSI interfaces as shown in Step 7 of Configuring iSCSI initiators in Proxy Initiator Mode, page 13-14.

5627200R10173

Made in the USA
San Bernardino, CA
14 November 2013